VOICELESS INDIA

This is the truth.
As from a blazing fire, sparks,
being like unto fire, fly forth a thousandfold,
thus are various beings brought forth
from the Imperishable, my friend,
and return thither also.—

MUNDAKA—UPANISHAD.

VOICELESS INDIA

Gertrude Emerson Sen

(GERTRUDE EMERSON SEN)

Revised Edition
With Introductions by

PEARL S. BUCK
RABINDRANATH TAGORE

ILLUSTRATED

The John Day Company · New York

CONTENTS

ACKNOWLEDGMENT

WITHOUT help of various kinds from various persons, this book could never have been written. To Louis D. Froelick, former editor of *Asia*, always an enthusiastic supporter of my plans of travel even when they took me far away from my editorial desk, thanks are due first, together with the other members of the *Asia* staff and organization. Some of the material incorporated in this book has already appeared in a slightly different form in the pages of the *Asia* magazine. To Sir Richard Burn, who directed my steps toward Oudh, I am also indebted. The Maharaja of Balrampur, who extended every courtesy to me during the year I lived in his estate, Kanwar Jasbir Singh, special manager of Balrampur Estate, whose unfailing support and practical assistance made the whole of my work possible, and all the estate officials, for their many friendly services, have left me under a debt of gratitude that can never be canceled. My friend Miss Elsie Weil has also helped in the preparation of the book manuscript in more ways than I can say.

found them.

INTRODUCTION TO THE REVISED
AMERICAN EDITION

THIS BOOK, now appearing in a new and revised edition, is
as fresh and as true to India's life as the day it was written.
There are two reasons for this. The first reason is that the
life of India has not changed, especially the life of India's
villages. They remain today as they have been for the last
centuries, poor, struggling clusters of people, ignored by all.
The second reason is that Gertrude Emerson in this book
wrote of eternal humanity, of men and women and children.

I suppose that life in the average Indian village is more
essential in its bareness than in any other place in the world.
I had thought that some of the villages of North China were
surely among the barest in the world. But I found that I did
not know what poverty was until I had visited the villages
of India. There indeed are the people poor, living by the
earth and on the earth, their houses of earth, their few utensils of earth, sometimes the only furnishings of the house
beds of clay and little pedestals of clay for seats and tables.

In the face of such preposterous and outrageous poverty,
in the face of deeper misery and ignorance than can, I verily
believe, be found in any other part of the world, certainly
any part that I have seen, a sensitive and intelligent woman
might have written a diatribe of anger and accusation. Instead she has chosen to do the far more telling thing—she
has written of life exactly as she saw it and experienced it
in a single Indian village.

It may be asked how, being a western woman, she could
have shared in this life to the extent that she did. The answer
is that she went to that village empty. She took no western
conveniences with her, she ate what the village offered, she
lived in a simple village-built house. She took no prejudices

with her, either, and no preconceived notions, not even the cold scientific spirit of research. She simply went to the Village of Five Trees and lived there, as she might have gone to a village in her own country, taking the people as she found them.

Of course few persons could have done this as effectively as she did. For this woman has peculiar gifts. Her greatest gift is that of being able to share in the life of others, forgetting herself. Even in India she was able to do this. But she also has another gift and it is the ability to tell of what she sees in fine, clear, pure language, so that the reader sees what she sees and understands what she feels.

And indeed, the time has come for Americans to understand the people of India. There are nearly four hundred million of them, most of them living in villages such as this Village of Five Trees. A huge country, a great and ancient people, clinging still to the vestiges of a high civilization but in the midst of a country which is the second richest in the world in many of its natural resources, a people destined for freedom and self-government, a people who look to democracy as their one hope: America cannot relegate India.

For such understanding no better book than this one has been written. Without blame, without rancor, with nothing but profound human wisdom, it reveals India's people, through the clear window of reality.

PEARL S. BUCK.

INTRODUCTION TO THE BRITISH EDITION

In her *Voiceless India*, Miss Emerson has amply proved that she has her own natural right of a sensitive mind to come to a people who happen to be foreign to her and in judging whom she has done herself justice. The bond of kinship that prevails within a community not only protects it from wanton cruelty and injustice from inside but is the natural nerve channel through which we directly feel our own race in its entirety. But the stranger from outside can easily be unjust, owing to the fact that he has not to pay for his conduct in his own feeling and be checked by that deeper sensibility which goes directly beyond the miscellany of facts into the heart of a living unity. And for the sake of his own benefit and others' safety he must bring with him his inner light of imagination, so that he may feel truth and not merely know facts. It is fully evident that Miss Emerson is gifted with this rare faculty, that she has realized a complete vision of an alien life by making it her own.

It is a very hard trial for a Western woman to have to spend long lonely months in an environment where most things conspire to hurt the modern taste and standard of living. The author of this book did not choose the comfortable method of picking up information from behind a lavish bureaucratic hospitality, under a revolving electric fan, and in an atmosphere of ready-made official opinions. For the materials of the present book she did not move about among the upper circle of the modern sophisticated India where communication was through her own language and tendencies of mind were not wholly unfamiliar to her. She boldly took it upon herself unaided to enter a region of our life, all but unexplored by the Western tourists, which had the one great advantage, in spite of its difficulties, that it offered no other path open to the writer but that of sharing the life of the people. In fact, in this adventure of hers she followed the examples of the true born travelers of that golden age of traveling when the pilgrims across the seas and mountains did not carry with them their own mental and physical habits —the barricading aloofness of their own race and culture.

And I can easily imagine what the author had to pay for her experience, not in money but in a part of her life itself. The constant toll that a pitiless climate exacts from our vitality for the barest privilege of living, the mean tyrannies of the tropics that often cause desperate discomforts and, what is worse, a perpetual state of subconscious irritation in our mind, are enough provocation for a foreigner to make him unreasonably vengeful in his judgment and language. There is no sign of that in Miss Emerson's writings, not even of a temptation to be superciliously funny at any awkwardness of the simple village folk among whom she lived. These villages had no allurements of the romantic India, incomprehensibly mystic in her ritualism, or ineffably grand in her relics and ruins. The background of life they had was dull and drab, with no lurid fascination of vice so important for making its detailed descriptions gratifying to some readers in their search for a vicarious enjoyment under the cover of moral indignation. All this has given an opportunity to disclose the personality of the writer herself, not only through the intellectual sanity displayed in this book, but, what is more precious, in her depth of human sympathy.

She never idealized, not even for the sake of literary flourishes, any aspects of the village life to which she was so intimately close. She never minimized the primitive crudities of its features, things that were stupid, ungainly, superstitious, or even evil in their moral ugliness, but her narration, in spite of its unmitigated truth, never hurts, because all through it runs the gracious touch of the woman, the pure instinct of sympathy which, while it bares and handles the sores, is yet tender to them. And these unfortunate Indian villages, deserted by their own capable men, neglected with scant notice by their politicians, cruelly ignored by their government, dumbly suffering unspeakable miseries, putting all the blame upon their inexorable fate, bent down to the dust by the load of indignities, deprived of education, sanitary or medical help, living upon a pitifully meager ration of food that has hardly any nutrition, and a scant supply of water full of microbic menace—they need a true woman's heart to give them voice, for they are like children in their utter helplessness disowned by their parents.

What Miss Emerson has discovered concerning the poverty of the Indian village, causing it to sink down under the weight of a land tax too heavy to be borne, has been openly acknowledged, to their credit, by a small band of Indian civilians who have been obliged to administer the system which they saw actually crushing the poor. Sir William Hunter said many years ago: "The Government assessment does not leave enough food to the cultivator to support himself and his family throughout the year." Sir Henry Cotton and Sir William Wedderburn, both high officials, have confessed the same unpalatable truth. More recently still, Mr. C. J. O'Donnell, who held in his own day one of the chief administrative positions in the Government of India, has declared: "It makes little difference to three hundred million Indian peasants what the Simon Commission may recommend, but I fear that the *ryot* will remain 'the most pathetic figure in the British Empire'; for 'his masters have ever been unjust to him, and Christendom will have one more failure to its discredit.'"

I feel personally grateful to Miss Emerson for the masterly picture she has drawn of our pathetic village life, so vivid and yet sober in its color—the honest color of truth; for I myself have spent some part of my youth in its neighborhood and have made it my mission with all my inadequate individual resources to befriend them who are friendless, who are eternal tenants in an extortionate world having nothing of their own.

RABINDRANATH TAGORE.

FOREWORD

No ALIEN can hope to catch more than a fragmentary vision of what India is, much less become the voice of the voiceless millions. The following pages merely record the day-to-day life of one little northern Indian village as it unfolded before my eyes over a period of many months. Nothing bearing on Indian village life has been withheld for the purpose of creating a particular impression or advancing any political thesis. Nothing fictitious has been added.

I have chosen the title *Voiceless India*, in spite of the restricted field of study, because the life of one village cannot be isolated from the common life of India. Agriculture is the chief occupation for three quarters of the population. Nine tenths of the people are villagers. It is these villagers, poor, simple and illiterate, who cherish the traditions of centuries and keep alive the essentially Indian spirit.

Looked at from without, India presents a picture of bewildering diversity—geographical variety, many ethnic and racial groups, different levels of culture, different languages, caste segregation, peculiar local customs, antagonistic religious beliefs. All these suggest the impossibility of any underlying unity. Yet the bird's-eye view, as Tagore has said, is not necessarily truer than the human one. The million Hindu pilgrims from every corner of India who annually visit Benares melt into the scene and become one with it. They *are* Benares. Mussulmans answering the call to prayer at Aurangzeb's great mosque are equally at home in Benares. Only the Europeans and Americans who hire boats and have themselves rowed on the Ganges past the crowded *ghats* remain incongruously apart. Anyone who penetrates even a little beneath the surface of Indian life must be astonished at the remarkable likeness of the ideals, social and spiritual, binding the people together.

FOREWORD

In making a book out of the circumscribed world of a single village, I have necessarily to exclude most of what is glamorous about India. The magnificent palaces and forts which lure tourists from the other side of the earth do not come within this limited horizon. Here are no gold-domed temples; only shrines of cracked mud. "The wealth of Ind," which tempted Columbus to sail west when the eastern route was temporarily closed to Spain, and so brought about the accidental discovery of the Americas, is not to be found in the stricken villages. India has never lacked genius, and men with capacity for leadership and great saints continue to emerge from time to time out of village obscurity. But the impoverished soil scarcely offers them fit nourishment. India's educated men, like educated men everywhere in the modern age, gravitate to the cities. Where else can they earn a living?

The village suffers. To-day it lacks vital energy to adapt itself to economic and administrative changes imposed from without—some of these the costly result of selfish or mistaken policy on the part of alien rulers, some inevitable with changing times. One can always hope present ills will become to-morrow's benefits and blessings. Under foreign tutelage, India has grown self-conscious, and national sentiment has been roused through the length and breadth of the land. When reconstruction is set in motion from the village upward, instead of from the city downward, India will once again be great.

Meanwhile the village holds fast to all that is left of its heritage. The Village of Five Trees, too small to be marked on any map, was my narrow door. It taught me more of the deep-rooted Indian view of life, Indian ways of thought and Indian ideals than all the cities of India put together. Clogged with superstition and dark with ignorance the village life may be, but through it and beyond a light shines.

BOOK ONE

HERE AND THERE *a microscopic atom of humanity was sil-houetted against a lonely world of water, sky, and shining mud. It moved slowly forward, scattering seed from a basket*

THE AUTHOR *made her formal entry into the Village of Five Trees on a baby elephant, and thereafter she soon became well acquainted with elephants and their ways*

WHEN THE GOLDEN THATCH *was in place over the* Happy House, *built by a thousand people more or less, the poor of Pachperwa came to share in a distribution of grain, held in accordance with the Indian tradition that an act of charity should accompany every celebration*

RAM LAKHAN, *who became assistant punkah-puller at the Happy House, could sing and sew and make bridegrooms' crowns out of dyed newspapers, or scale a termite nest*

A VILLAGE CHILD *explained that two little clay horses and a chariot of colored threads set out in the fields in cholera time betokened an offering to a local goddess*

"CRICKET," *the Mohammedan bird catcher of Pachperwa,*
laid his trap at the edge of one of the village tanks and then
worked it from a distance by means of a long bamboo rope

A HINDU CLERK *of the tahsil customarily took a tenant's*
thumb-print whenever a legal signature was required. Only
one out of forty-four in the district could read and write

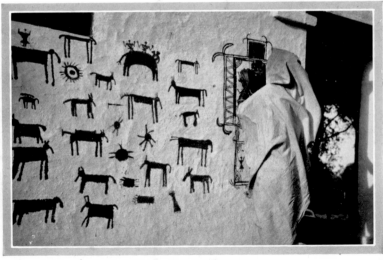

THIS TAHSIL MESSENGER *entertained his fellows by reading to them stories of the gods and heroes of ancient India. The woman is decorating the kitchen of the Happy House*

CHAPTER I

The Village of Five Trees

At the end of a month of camping I said good-bye to my new Indian friends, the Jasbir Singhs, and turned my face toward Pachperwa, Village of Five Trees. An official of the estate of the Maharaja of Balrampur met me at the station with fifteen or twenty men to carry my bedding roll and three bags. He apologized because the local elephants had been lent to English officials for holiday shoots in the neighboring jungle and only a baby, which did not count, remained for me. This was Champa, aged seven years.

A baby elephant is not much bigger than a horse, though considerably broader. With some difficulty the driver made the little thing go down on its knees. I stepped first on the cushion of one of its hind feet, next on the tail, which somebody held looped like a stout rope, and scrambled awkwardly up on the pad. As the train whistled and rumbled away, Champa shied and set off at a run. Behind us, across the dried fields, marched the *Tahsildar* and burden bearers. Clinging to the pad ropes and trying desperately not to fall off, I made my triumphal entry into the Village of Five Trees.

Everything had been carefully arranged for my comfort through the courtesy of Kanwar Jasbir Singh, manager of the Balrampur Estate to which the village belonged. Four tents from the Maharaja's supply department were set up under the canopy of a huge tree close to the divisional headquarters. One for me, two for the servants, and the fourth, a cook tent. The cook himself, in a new white turban and long olive coat, stood salaaming respectfully. The Tahsildar escorted me formally to the tent door.

Jawahir, whose name meant "jewel," announced that breakfast was ready. I was hungry, since I was not yet used to the Indian custom of telescoping breakfast and luncheon into one meal, served anywhere between ten and noon, with only a cup of tea to start the day off, at six. Bringing dishes he had been preparing since his arrival the day before, Jawahir proudly served the first breakfast in my own tent-hold at Pachperwa.

On his eager petition and the boast that he could cook in Hindustani, Mussulmani, and European styles, I had taken Jawahir with approval of the estate authorities from a humble position in the kitchen of the Maharaja's European guest house at Balrampur. This first effort was obviously a demonstration of what he considered his European style, specializing in potatoes. He served potatoes in four different ways, Julienne, French fried, mashed, and boiled. He also produced goat meat, heavily spiced and made into patties, and rice curry. A very rigid cornstach pudding, set in a ring of cold mashed potato, came on as finale. Mentally I drew a heavy line through "European style." We should do better, I felt, with native methods of cooking.

I had reached the end of a journey of several thousand miles. We unstrapped the bedding roll, and Jawahir's mother-in-law, an independent little grandmother of forty-five who was to serve as *ayah*, made the bed. I hung my clothes over the cord conveniently stretched along the interior of the tent at the point where the walls met the sloping roof, set out my few toilet necessities, and arranged books, papers, and typewriter on the table. My home was officially in order.

Camping is understood as a fine art in India, where its tradition goes back to Mogul days. The tent was divided into three compartments—a space in front, like a covered veranda or sun parlor, with transparent curtains of split bamboo, a main room, twelve feet square, and a bathroom at the back. The inner walls and ceiling were of yellow cloth, printed with gay flowers, the outside was khaki-colored. Over a thick layer of straw were blue and orange striped *daris*, the familiar cotton rugs of India, generally of prison manufacture. Padded curtains, which could be rolled up or dropped at will, served as front and back doors. The tent was furnished with a comfortable tape bed, tables, chairs, a dressing table with a mirror, a washstand with white enamel pitcher and bowl, an old-fashioned commode, and a zinc bathtub. The dishes and cooking utensils, bought in Lucknow, the nearest large city, Jawahir had arranged in the cook tent. Two screened food boxes, four lanterns, a table lamp, a charcoal brazier, and a large quantity of soap completed my housekeeping equipment.

I experienced a pleasurable feeling. On a previous visit to India I had traveled through all the main provinces of British India and a number of the Indian States. I had listened patiently to what hundreds of people had to say about India and Indians—in English—from the Viceroy and Mahatma Gandhi down to Abdul Aziz, my Mohammedan bearer. But India had eluded me. Some day I would come back and pick out a village to live in as the logical starting point, since nine tenths of the people of India are villagers. And here I was.

This particular village I had stumbled upon more or less by accident. India has something like three quarters of a million villages. As far as I was concerned, one would do quite as well as another.

I had no sooner landed in Bombay than I was offered villages with prompt and generous enthusiasm on every side. An Indian woman doctor said she knew just the right spot in the Punjab. A Madrasi pointed out that only in a Dravidian village of the South could one hope to see the "real India." "After all," he insisted, "the Aryans are merely foreign immigrants of a few thousand years ago." A Calcutta friend urged Bengal because in that province village conditions were at their worst! Gandhi, whom I visited at his *ashrama* near Ahmadabad, was afraid that I might become ill

in an ordinary Indian village, with its uncertain water
supply and insanitary conditions. I must have a clean,
healthy village, which he would find for me in Gujarat
—or, if I insisted on going elsewhere, one of his Congress
workers in Bihar would take me under his wing.

In spite of all these friendly offers of assistance, I managed to reach Allahabad in the United Provinces still un-
committed, cherishing the thought that I would pick my
own village. Unexpectedly everything was settled for me
by a letter from an unknown English official in the provincial
administration. On the basis of a casual letter of question and
the recommendation of a friend in London, this gentleman
had gratuitously taken upon himself the task of finding me
a village. I confess my breath was taken away. The letter
read:

I have made arrangements for you to live in the
north of the Gonda District, in Oudh, close to the Nepal
border. The village is called Mansurwa and it is in
the Tulsipur *tahsil*, about three miles from Jarwa railway station. The village belongs to the Maharaja of
Balrampur, a boy of about thirteen, whose estate is
now being managed by the Court of Wards which
corresponds to some extent to Chancery in England.
The manager of the estate is Kanwar Jasbir Singh.
He is a grandson of the Maharaja of an Indian State in
the Punjab and is a Christian. He was educated in
England. On November 25 I expect he will be in Allahabad, and it may be possible to arrange a meeting with
him then. I have just written to ask him to start out to
build your house, but he says it will be about six weeks
before it will be fit for you to live in, owing to damp. I
suggest therefore that while it is being constructed you
should live in tents, which I think he will be able to
arrange for. He can also let you have simple furniture.
You will find the nights at this place, especially in a
tent or in a mud house, much colder than at Allahabad,
especially from the middle of December to the end of
January, and you will need plenty of bedding. I think

you had also better discuss with Indians at Allahabad the question of food. In a village like Mansurwa you will be able to get very little but rice, maize, possibly coarse wheat flour and coarse salt and a few condiments. Butter will not be available unless you make it yourself by shaking a bottle. I am doubtful whether you will get any vegetables except potatoes and perhaps something like a small pumpkin. Bread of the Western variety will have to be obtained from Balrampur or Gonda. You will of course boil all water or milk that you use, and I presume you will have a small collection of medicines.

To get to Mansurwa, your best way is through Lucknow. You change at Gonda for Balrampur. You had better stay there for the night and go on in the early morning to Gainsari where you change again for the Jarwa branch. Kanwar Jasbir Singh will probably arrange for an elephant to get you out to the village.

I hope this village will suit you. I have had the District Magistrate and the Police Officer of the district informed of your coming. You will of course realize that there is always a danger of burglary, and I would advise you to take nothing of any appreciable value and keep as little money with you as possible. There is probably a post office at Jarwa to which you could have money sent in small amounts as you needed it.

For the first time my village jumped out of the realm of speculation and took on the stark outlines of reality. A day or two later, I had my first interview with Kanwar Jasbir Singh, a distinguished-looking man with marked racial qualities of feature, whose Oxford English was extraordinarily perfect. He advised me to come on to Balrampur at once and discuss the details of my venture before he went out on a cold-month camping tour of the estate.

Pachperwa, in the northeastern part of the United Provinces, and not Mansurwa, eventually became my home. While the question of a suitable cook was awaiting solution, it was suggested that I join the young Maharaja on his morning rides out into the country. Pateshwari Prasad Singh, Maharaja of Balrampur, I learned, was the richest boy in the United Provinces, which boasted a population of roughly fifty millions. He owned an estate the size of Rhode Island, giving him an income of a million and a half dollars a year. As I stood waiting on the guest house steps at seven o'clock the morning after my arrival in his little capital, the Maharaja himself, a shy, solemn, overgrown boy, came riding up, touched his helmet with his riding crop in formal salute, and said "How do you do?" in slow, careful English.

Through narrow lanes and out again into open fields yellow with mustard and *arhar* clattered our little cavalcade, the Maharaja and his Rajput aide, the English riding master and I, and four outriders, two in front and two behind, bearing lances with fluttering red and white pennants. I had a few glimpses of thatched huts clustered here and there and tenants running to the doorways to greet their Maharaja with folded hands, Hindu style, or a curious bob and salute, Mohammedan style. But it was not my privilege to see many villages from horseback. The second morning my horse stumbled and went down on both fore knees, and I had the unpleasant surprise of picking myself up from the ground with a broken right wrist. One of the outriders galloped off to fetch a carriage, and I was driven back to the guest house in crestfallen mood. The Maharaja renamed the road where I had my spill "Emerson Road."

The wrist was soon set by the local Indian doctor. Kanwar Jasbir Singh and the Kanwarani Sahiba, as his wife was called, insisted that I could not go off at once to Mansurwa. Why not go camping with them? There would be shooting parties in the jungle. There would be plenty of villages to inspect, and I could listen to the many problems coming up for settlement by the manager and his staff of Indian assistants. I could begin studying Hindustani with the camp clerk, who was also tutor to the manager's two boys. "Do come," begged the Kanwarani, who had spent three years at college in the United States. "You do not know how much we shall enjoy having you with us."

Three weeks later, in the course of our camping, we reached Tulsipur, the closest point in the itinerary to Mansurwa. I borrowed a car, and accompanied by the two boys and Anand Sarup, familiarly referred to as the Deputy Sahib—then assistant manager in charge of the eastern division of the Balrampur Estate—set out to inspect my village.

We drove for an hour or more through open country and light forest, at one point plowing across sand and fording a shallow river. We passed a few small villages—flies, bony cattle, mongrel dogs covered with sores, timid children with uncombed hair, incredibly thin old men. Then more forest, said to be a haunt of tigers and leopards, and at last a tiny clearing with exactly seventeen houses surrounded by fields in which the recently cut paddy was stacked in great golden mounds. This was Mansurwa. Near the faint tracks of the road some neat piles of sun-dried bricks caught and held my eye. Yes, explained the Deputy Sahib, these had been carted all the way from Tulsipur, forty thousand of them, for my house. I gazed upon my forty thousand bricks and contemplated the prospect of becoming, for the first time in my life, a householder, in that lonely spot at the edge of the Indian jungle.

The seventeen families of Mansurwa led too restricted an existence to give any conception of normal living conditions in India. When I found that no food except rice could be obtained in this tiny settlement, and that I should have to send three miles away to Jarwa, a small trading post on the Nepalese border, for all my supplies, I turned my back on Mansurwa. In recommending it, the English official, I later came to know, had not intentionally tried to dispose of a troublesome investigator. He knew I wanted "a small village, preferably off the railway," and an Indian subordinate had dutifully recommended the smallest and most remote one he could find.

Thinking over all the villages I had seen, I now decided to settle in the one where we had camped the first week of December, since this appeared to offer the best possibilities.

Pachperwa (pronounced *Putch-pair-wah*) means simply "five trees," but no one in the village could ever point out the particular five trees for which it was named. Several *shisham* trees, which look a little like poplars, grow about the station, and for some distance the station road is bordered with them. Where the road swings to the southeast and, just before you enter the village, crosses the one coming from Utraula—on cold days Dowdhe the tailor sits here outside his shop plying the treadle of a Singer sewing machine with bare toes and warming himself in the sun—four tall trees stand up. If there was ever a fifth, no sign of it remains. The nearest I came to solving the mystery of the name was the clue offered by an old man who once waved his hand vaguely to the south and said the five trees were somewhere in that direction, *bahut dur*, a long way off.

The village itself, in its humble garb of mud and thatch, is no different in appearance from countless villages scattered over the plains of northern India, though as Indian villages go it is considered large and prosperous. From even a little distance you would not notice it at all. The brown dwellings have a way of sinking down into the earth of which they are made. The wide sky dwarfs them to nothingness. In the time before the rains, fields and shadeless village are dead, uniform brown. At the end of June, when the whole flat country suddenly becomes inundated, and in place of fields there is a vast sheet of water casting back the intolerable glare of sky, the village is a point lost in endless space. Later, when the fields are green with waving rice or yellow with mustard or blue with linseed, the houses, too, sprout broad notched leaves on their weathered thatches, where moon-faced pumpkins grow. Then you would certainly think it was a pumpkin patch, not a village, you had strayed into.

Restless for anchorage, the eye lights upon the mountains

to the north. Fourteen miles away above the level fields rise
the foothills of the Himalaya. That is where British India
ends and Nepal begins. But beyond the first two ranges,
halfway up the sky, shine out the far distant snow peaks.
That is where time ends and eternity begins. In Hindu
thought, the Abode of Snows has been the home of Shiva,
the Great God, from before the beginning. Incredibly high,
white, and beautiful are those peaks. In the early morning
and at sunset the gigantic slopes glow with warm rose and
orange lights, cut across by cold blue shadows. In winter,
when I first saw them, the mountains seemed to stand right
up over Pachperwa; then slowly they began to withdraw.
But even when March dust or May heat or summer rains
had blotted them from sight, they used to come back from
time to time, pale fair ghosts with spring-white clouds about
their heads. I never tired of looking out from the village
through this mountain window.

During my first weeks in Pachperwa I knew that I should
be on probation with the villagers. Would they be friendly?
One Englishwoman who had spent thirty years in India
had assured me that no villagers would have any respect for
me. I was too footloose and unattached. Even Gandhi was
doubtful whether they would accept me as a friend, unless
some Indian whom they trusted acted as go-between. I
decided not to evince too much personal interest in their
affairs, but simply to make my friendliness felt as opportunity presented itself. I stayed about the tent most of the
time. If I went for a walk I took the Ayah with me, as
proof of my respectability, or Asgar Ali, the village boy
who was added to the ménage at Jawahir's request for an
assistant. It was two weeks before I slipped off alone to the
bazar one day, only to discover some time later that the
Tahsildar had delegated one of his men to follow me wherever
I went, to render assistance in case of need.

Meanwhile there was much speculation in the village about
why I had come. Not only all the villagers of Pachperwa
but all those who came to the tahsil on business made it a

point to pass the tent and inspect me. Sometimes I would look up and see a little row of women standing far off by the road, gazing fixedly at me. A hundred times a day I heard the servants being questioned. Who was I? Where had I come from? What was I going to do in Pachperwa? Since they did not know much more about me than the villagers they made up what answers they pleased, taking pains, of course, to explain that I was somebody very important.

Through the Tahsildar and the Assistant Tahsildar I learned of all sorts of wild rumors afloat. It was said that I was a spy of the government; that the king of my country had sent me to investigate the condition of the country around Pachperwa, and, if I made a favorable report, no doubt he would go to war with the British king and take Pachperwa. One man announced that a certain holy Mussulman in a town fifty miles away had given out that though he knew the real reason I had come, he could not divulge it. Perhaps the curiosity of the people of Pachperwa served as the bridge between them and me. It was not long before I was getting smiles in exchange for smiles.

Attached to the village and officially classed as part of it are three hamlets. These lie strung along the station road. The first is Jagdishpur, "City of the Lord of the World." It has forty-five houses but no well. The inhabitants have to cross several fields to fetch their water from the next hamlet, Bargadwa, "Place of a Banian Tree." The third hamlet, known as the Nai Bazar, or "New Bazar," is really the grain market of Pachperwa. From here the road, a palimpsest written over with bare footprints and hoofmarks, runs straight south for a short distance, overshadowed by fine old mango trees. On one side lie open fields, the ugly chimneys of Haweli Singh's brick kiln, and the new schoolhouse. On the other are the ramshackle buildings of the tahsil headquarters, with a large mango grove, like an orchard, to the east; then a little dispensary that is also the post office, and another mango grove where a market is held every Wednesday. At the southeastern corner of the second grove is the police station.

The real village lies just beyond. Possibly it has two hundred houses—the official figure was 336 houses for Pachperwa and its hamlets together—but five or six minutes' walk in any direction brings you through the village and out again into the fields. Isolated farmhouses do not exist in this part of India. Cultivators herd together in small villages, going out to work in the adjoining fields. Every scrap of available land is needed for cultivation. The population of the villages is therefore almost as dense as that of the cities.

The houses of Pachperwa are very small, with sloping roofs of thatch or occasionally small tiles. None of them is more than one story high, and few are more than ten or twelve feet wide. They huddle compactly together in solid, irregular rows, fronting directly on the dirty little lanes and alleys. Open spaces here and there mark the position of wells, and on the outskirts of the village are two large *jhils*, or tanks with artificially constructed embankments, and some good-sized threshing floors. Many of the houses have some sort of shop in front, with commodities placed on benches under a projecting roof. Instead of gardens—villagers cannot afford gardens—a small court is to be found at the back of the house, enclosed by walls high enough to keep out the prying gaze of neighbors. There is generally, too, a flat space of ground a few feet square near the front door, where the earth has been pounded down hard for drying grain or peppers. All the floors are of earth, and you never see a window, since windows are viewed with dislike as something through which strangers would be able to look in upon the sanctity of home. Light filters into the dark little interiors from doorways opening on street or court.

The Village of Five Trees does not know telephones, gas, electricity, ice, running water, plumbing. Not a single Indian conveyance, such as an *ekka*, is for hire, even at the station. Mine was the only newspaper. But something is left in spite of the deficiencies, something that flows imperturbably on, through all manner of adversity. Life, it seems, can exist even where all modern conveniences are absent.

If the mud and grass houses are dissolved in the rains or destroyed by fire, as they often are, the villagers at once replace them with the patience of ants reërecting their dome of sand crushed by a careless foot. Fresh mud is scraped together out of the road, leaving a hollow that fills with water in the next rainy season and soon becomes the breeding place of malarial mosquitoes. After a troubled week or two, life resumes its trammeled course with a kind of obstinate orderliness.

Outcastes have always lived apart in India. So, here in the village, the despised groups, leather workers, weavers and scavengers, live by themselves at the southwest side of Pachperwa. Though a few of the leather-working caste find a traditional employment in skinning the dead cattle of the village, this occupation cannot support many families, and most of them now hire themselves out as plowmen or field workers. In spite of a change of work the "untouchables" still bear the stigma of the ancestral association with dead or unclean things. Their houses are the poorest in the village, some of them little more than tumble-down huts consisting of a single room two or three yards square.

No fixed rule prescribes where other people are to live. They tend to group themselves according to the caste occupations they practise in addition to cultivating a little land as tenants of the Maharaja of Balrampur. The Mohammedan butchers occupy one quarter, the wood-turners another. Most of the Hindu goldsmiths have their shops in a rough circle at the west side of the village. The small tradesmen, confectioners and tobacco sellers cluster at the entrance in the part known as the Old Bazar, in distinction to the New Bazar on the way to the station.

In the New Bazar live all the big traders, those who buy up the grain of the cultivators and then get their money back by selling them cloth and acting as wholesale dealers to the *Banias*, or little traders. They are all *Marwaris*, coming originally from Marwar, a small section of western Rajputana, but now scattered broadcast over India. Even though a Marwari starts life with nothing, he is sure to accumulate a fortune before he dies, according to popular belief.

Though the Marwaris came to Pachperwa only twenty-five years ago, when the branch railway line was extended connecting the village with the outside world, their shops in the New Bazar are two or three times bigger than any of the other shops. It is to the New Bazar that most of the bullock carts come creaking after the fall and spring harvests, and it is from the New Bazar that they start for the station, loaded with heavy brown bags. The records entered in mysterious Marwari script in the long, flexible, red cloth account books of Jokhi Lal, owner of a score of shops in different parts of India and the richest dealer of Pachperwa, mount up into thousands of *rupees* every year.

I can see Jokhi Lal yet as I first saw him, coming up the path that led past the tent under the big *pakar* tree to the tahsil. In those days he was much concerned with his re-election as headman of the village council. Short, fat legs stuck out from under his white draperies, and his pointed slippers turned up and out. The index of his opulence was the straining of the buttons on his white coat. Outside of business, Jokhi Lal was very pious. His dark face was always marked with broad bands and splashes of sandal paste, put there before his morning worship. Passing my tent, he would invariably stop, raise his folded hands and beam at me from under a tiny turban of canary yellow, wound in countless strands of finger thickness.

Only gradually does the village reveal unguessed riches, the inheritance of better days. The old carts—not the new ones—are often elaborately carved. Even the great heavy wheels that go bumping through the mud have borders which must have taken patient hours to chisel. A few of the houses have beautifully carved door frames. Once I watched two women sitting in their courtyard grinding maize. The round stone they turned was delicately chased. At the shop of Kalu, a tobacco seller and maker of hookah stems, the tobacco was stored in large gayly painted jars of his own decoration. Gaudy cloths for quilts, freshly stamped by Rajab, the village dyer, hung in front of his shop on a rope of grass. A few doors away the twisted little Mohammedan potter, my special friend, scratched designs on many of his clay pots, which he filled in with white, yellow, or black.

For a crowning example of sheer extravagance there was Mahadeo's new door. Mahadeo, whose name means "Great God," was a confectioner who lived beside a shrine marked by a lone clay elephant with a broken trunk, under a tree from which a parrot screamed all day as he perched upside down in an iron cage. Rebuilding his house, Mahadeo ordered a master carpenter from Utraula to make him a new door, carved with rosettes from top to bottom, and this door cost a hundred rupees, the whole of thirty-five dollars. I imagined every time Mahadeo went in or out of his door, he thought to himself, "This is the finest door in the whole village, and I paid a hundred rupees for it!"

Stopping to admire the door was the way I first got acquainted with Mahadeo and his family. Afterward I often stopped to watch him making his sugar-and-milk concoctions. A big iron cauldron rested over a charcoal fire in the covered space which was in reality the front room of the house. Mahadeo or his brother was usually stirring the liquid. When it was done it turned the color of straw, and Mahadeo ladled it into a bowl with a wide mouth. Now came the crucial moment. Stirring all the time, he deftly spilled fat drops over the rim of the bowl on to a dusty piece of gunnysack spread on the dirt floor. He made long rows of drops up and down the gunnysack. In a few seconds, these hardened into the familiar candy that sold in enormous quantities in the village. He and his brother made other sweets also, for weddings and special celebrations, and these were often decorated with thin coats of silver-leaf. The shop was a great rendezvous for red and yellow hornets with dangling legs, not to mention innumerable flies.

A little farther down the same street were some Bania houses I was especially fond of. The whole front walls, under the projecting roofs, were decorated as gaudily as Rajab's cotton cloths. Strange birds and fantastic animals, roosters with curled tail feathers, square-shaped buffaloes, elephants with oddly abbreviated trunks, dolichocephalic horses with ears like mules', marched along between borders of brilliant flowers. The startling effect was produced with white, yellow, and green paints, but principally vermilion. The white was lime, the yellow was turmeric, the green was a cheap importation from Germany, and the red was red lead.

From centuries of making *chauks*, sacred squares for Hindu religious ceremonies drawn with colored powder on the ground, Hindu women have acquired skill as artists of a limited kind. It is they who twist a bit of cotton around the end of a stick, dip it in color, and draw patterns, without previous tracing, on the walls of the village houses. But the art is dying. Most villagers do not paint their houses nowadays and look with a sort of tolerant contempt on those who do.

I must not forget, either, the house of Yasin Khan the Pathan. Yasin oiled his black beard and smiled a trifle unctuously. His father still cultivated tobacco, and in all probability Yasin would be following his humble calling had not fortune lifted him to dazzling heights. It was rumored in the village that Yasin's riches came from a pot of rupees plowed up in his fields, but Yasin himself gave a more prosaic explanation. For some years he had held the leather contract for Pachperwa, paying a fixed sum to the Balrampur Estate for all the skins of the village cattle dying during the year. When the World War came and leather sold for soldiers' shoes at fabulous prices, he made a fortune. Yasin felt aggrieved when the price of leather dropped, but he took care not to let his fortune dwindle away. He lent it out to the villagers at 96 per cent interest.

Yasin, by virtue of being Mohammedan, did not suffer social ostracism on account of his leather business, and his house at the northwest corner of Pachperwa was a striking testimony to his palmy days. It was not much larger, to be sure, than an ordinary house, but on two sides it had ornamental arches with delicate plaster tracery. What gave it real distinction, however, was its coat of whitewash. No other house in Pachperwa, not even Jokhi Lal's in the New Bazar, was so pretentious.

Asylums of space and cleanliness, occupying a place apart in the life of the village, are the mosque and the temple. The mosque, standing in the very center of Pachperwa, is easily recognized by two little false minarets. The old man who sings out the call to prayer five times a day cannot climb up these minarets, since they are of solid brick, but stands on the ground below. A high gate with a wooden door shuts off the sacred enclosure from the street. Over it is an arabesque and an inscription in Urdu. This proclaims: "Let everything be sacrificed in God's name. The Kaaba is in the heart where God dwells." Inside is a clean open court of cracked cement, where the faithful kneel in serried rows on strips of cloth or matting at one o'clock every Friday. The service is conducted by the Maulvi Sahib from the proper place within the mosque, a shallow whitewashed edifice with three arches, over which are plaster incrustations. Humble as the village mosque is, there is something spacious about it, something not unworthy. Centuries have shaped the fashion of its scalloped arches, its rounded domes, its court open to the sky.

The Hindu temple is in a large garden behind a wavy wall in the New Bazar. Its gate leads directly into the rest house, where Hindu strangers are welcome to pass the night. Such rest houses, attached to temples or put up by the charity of individuals, are common all over India. They correspond to Mohammedan *sarais* and European hotels, except that there is no charge and, on account of caste restrictions, no food is served.

The temple garden is green with fruit trees, papaya, custard apple, guava, bitter oranges. There is also a *bel* tree, because bel leaves are an offering especially pleasing to Shiva. In one corner of the garden, near the well, is a Shiva shrine. Beneath the tall conical roof are the stone symbol of the god and a marble effigy of Nandi, his sacred bull. Near by are a few flower beds. From the back of an elephant you can just look over the wall from the road and see the temple gardener watering his marigolds, asters, poppies, roses, and white *bela* flowers, sweet as jasmine. The heads of the marigolds are commonly offered to Shiva—though white is his favorite color—but Rama and Sita and Lakshman, the white-faced dolls in stiff brocade standing in a row inside the little white temple in the heart of the garden, welcome any kind of flowers from their devotees. Sometimes the gardener strings flower necklaces to adorn them. Rama, legendary King of Ayodya, or Oudh, as it is called to-day, was long ago transmuted into a god and now sits enthroned in every Hindu heart.

A Hindu does not require any temple for worship, though he is fond of temples and little open-air shrines, and will often make a gesture of reverence simply in passing them. As the Mussulman finds his real place of prayer, not in the mosque, but by the roadside or in the field, wherever the daily hours for prayer overtake him, so the orthodox Hindu reserves a special corner of his house for worship, and every member of the family will go there at his own fixed time to recite a prayer, repeat a few holy words, make an offering of water or flowers before some favorite image, or perhaps to sit in quiet meditation.

No one in the village except the priest, whose duty it was, felt called upon to attend the morning and evening *puja* at the temple of Ram Chandra in the New Bazar, though one of the eighteen boys who attended the temple Sanskrit school usually rang the bell, while the priest blew for a long minute or two on his conch. But the bell and the conch told the village of Pachperwa that the temple ritual was being observed in the ancient way, as the sun rose above the mango grove to the east or sank in yellow haze behind the two tall chimneys of Haweli Singh's brick factory.

CHAPTER II

The Happy House

M Y FIRST responsibility, once the selection of the village was made, was to find a suitable site for a house. It would not be possible to live under canvas as soon as the hot weather set in, and anyway I wanted to feel that I belonged to the village. All the land everywhere about was owned by the Maharaja of Balrampur, who had given permission for me to build my house wherever I wanted. It only remained to pick the spot.

A day or two after my arrival the Deputy Sahib appeared on the scene to help settle the matter. He was a man of fifty or more, with a kind, sensitive face. What I liked best about him was a manner of grave and attentive politeness, which did not change whether he was talking to me or listening to the petition of the humblest tenant.

Accompanied by the Tahsildar and an appropriate body-guard carrying long bamboo sticks, we set out to investigate the village real estate possibilities. The Deputy Sahib and I walked side by side, but the Tahsildar lagged an awkward step behind. Later I noticed that the Assistant Tahsildar always walked a step or two behind the Tahsildar, and other members of the staff some distance behind him, and I perceived a punctilious observance of recognized social distinctions. Personally, I never grew used to seeing a man jump up from the ground as I passed, or get off his little country pony to stand politely as I walked by. But these are time-honored courteous ways of people to whom modern ideas of equality and democracy have yet to penetrate. Officials, both

English and Indian, make much of their superior position.

The whole of Pachperwa turned out, agog with speculation, as we walked through the village. There was not a
single vacant spot, apparently, for a new house to be built.
On the north the land was said to be under water during the
rainy season. The fields came right up on the west, and
on the east the proximity of the police station was undesirable from my point of view. I thought the villagers might
associate me too closely with the police officer. The treeless
tract to the south, which seemed all that was left, did not
meet with the approval of either the Deputy Sahib or the
Tahsildar, who considered it a little too lonely to be safe.

Early next morning I had a sudden inspiration. Somewhere between the tahsil buildings and the dispensary I
vaguely remembered having seen, on my first visit early in
December, a small shrine half hidden among trees. A search
soon revealed the crumbling mud platform with a row of
quaint clay elephants, like children's toys. Just beyond rose
a low, flat-topped hill overgrown with weeds and bushes. A
little gray-brown owl sitting on one of the trees above the
shrine stared down in obvious disapproval; then gave a hoot
and flew away. A *nilkant* would have meant good luck, but
no "blue-throat" happened to flash past on lapis lazuli and
turquoise-banded wings. In any case, my choice was made.

The hill had an artificial look. It was almost square, with
curious mounds at the four corners, and it was surrounded
by a grassy moat. The only practical approach seemed
to be by way of the shrine, where the ground was high. As I
stood on top I was twenty feet above the tree-bordered road
and a hundred feet back from it. An altitude of twenty feet
in Pachperwa gives a radius of vision equal to that from the
bridge of a ship. Below me unrolled the life of the road, but
the clouds of heavy white dust raised by the bullock carts
had a chance to settle on the slope of the hill. The mango
trees did not quite hide the iron chimneys of Haweli Singh's
brick factory across the way but softened the incongruity.
Some arhar fields—Indian peas, but more like lentils—the

yellow dispensary, and the village school lay to the south. In the opposite direction were the shrine and tahsil buildings with a glimpse of the Himalaya between. Trees grew at the back and around the edge, and one very old shisham was in just the right spot to promise shade against the burning sun of April and May. Though hidden from sight by the grove, the village itself was not two minutes away.

The Tahsildar could think of only two objections. The hill was rather far from the tahsil well, from which my water would have to be drawn, and it was said to be a popular resort for snakes in the rainy season. The first difficulty could be met by the addition of a water carrier to my household. As for the second, if the worse came to the worst, I was ready to add herpetology to my study of village life. That same afternoon the Deputy Sahib laid down a cat's cradle of strings, marking off the foundations of my house.

The Tahsildar, a Brahmin by caste, happened to mention that Hindus observe certain prescribed customs in preparing to build a new house. A pundit, or learned Brahmin, is consulted about an auspicious day to begin the work. Then the ground is duly consecrated, and finally the pundit is again consulted about an auspicious day to move in. He offered to see that my house, too, was properly started, and fortunately the very next day was a favorable one. Our Sub-Inspector of Police had verified this point in connection with a ceremony he was holding for the piercing of the ears of his seven-year-old son. We might, said the Tahsildar thriftily, take advantage of the Sub-Inspector's musicians, as well as of the presence of a "big pundit" he had summoned to the village. The hour for my puja, or religious ceremony, was accordingly set for eight the following morning, and messengers were sent out to invite all the important members of the community.

The invited guests, Jokhi Lal and the Marwaris of the New Bazar, the Doctor, the Sub-Inspector of Police, the Schoolmaster, the *Patwari*, or village accountant, his cousin, a member of the District Board, and the whole of the tahsil staff of ten or fifteen persons had already assembled the next morning when I arrived on the scene. In the background were the uninvited guests, fifty or more in number, with my three servants. The Ayah in her green shawl had the distinction of being the only woman present besides myself. Next to her stood Asgar Ali and Jawahir. As Mussulmans, I wondered what they were going to think of my Hindu puja. Later the Ayah expressed her views. One could get rid of devils in a much simpler way. "All you have to do," she explained, "is to have someone read the Koran."

A spot about a yard square near one end of the cat's cradle had been scraped bare of grass. To make it ceremonially pure, it had received a fresh coat of mud and cow dung, and the pundit was engaged in marking out a design with flour and a magenta powder. Four banana shoots stood upright at the four corners, and in the center was an ordinary red clay water jar, adorned with a marigold necklace. On top of the jar a saucer of grain had been placed, and on top of that another saucer with oil and a lighted wick. Two or three large brass plates filled with marigolds, some marigold necklaces neatly wrapped in squares of banana leaves, water, milk, *ghi*, or boiled butter, a small pile of copper coins, some loose mango leaves, and a sticky mixture of turmeric and rice were on hand, constituting the essentials for a small but respectable puja.

The pundit spread a white goat's-hair rug on the ground near the sacred square and sat down cross-legged, facing north. He looked mysterious and impressive, with a big white turban on his head and a fine red line, indicating that he was a worshiper of the goddess Kali, painted vertically between his eyebrows. Some lesser pundits fell into two rows behind him, and then I was told to sit on a rug placed at right angles. I should have felt rather nervous if the Deputy Sahib had not sat down beside me, promising to tell me everything I was expected to do. Standing under a tree on one of the guard mounds, the musicians were piping, tootling, drumming, and clashing cymbals for all they were worth, announcing to the village at large that something important was about to happen.

Our puja was addressed to Ganesh. This fat-bellied little Indian god—elephant's trunk coiled about his neck and shoulders, four hands clasping conch, discus, mace, and water-lily—guards the niche above the door in millions of houses. Every Hindu child knows how Ganesh got his elephant's head. Created by Parvati one day out of a lump of mud and imbued with life, he was set to guard the doorway of her house while her husband Shiva was gathering flowers on Mount Kailash. When Shiva returned, the strange little boy refused to let him pass, and Shiva angrily struck off his head. Then, to appease Parvati, he sent messengers in every direction with the instruction that the head of the first living creature encountered was to be brought to him. One of the messengers returned with the head of an elephant, which Shiva clapped on the shoulders of Ganesh, restoring him to life.

For his dutiful obedience to Parvati, Ganesh is worshiped by Hindu mothers, who hope thereby to obtain for their own sons some of the qualities of this favorite son of the gods. He it was, legend says, who took down the dictation of the *Mahabharata* from the sage Vyasa, and his name is invoked in the formula *Sri Ganesaya namah*, "I bow to Ganesh," at the beginning of every Sanskrit book. As the remover of all obstacles and impediments and the bringer of success, he is particularly worshipped on the eve of any new undertaking. He is indeed a friendly little god, made so by all the prayers that have gone his way from countless hearts through countless centuries. He is a childlike image of man's eternal hope that he is going to get the better of fate.

To Ganesh, then, the adventure of the Happy House, as I heedlessly called it in those first days, was consigned with appropriate Sanskrit texts from the pundit and his ragged assistants, who chimed in on the refrains. Ganesh was not present in visible form but was considered to have taken up temporary residence in the water jar. Hindus understand that symbols are symbols. They create these according to their need and destroy them again—the need fulfilled— with unselfconscious simplicity.

The pundit commenced by sprinkling me with Ganges water and shaking a few drops of ghi over the flame burning in the saucer on top of the jar. Then he handed me two marigolds, instructing me through the Deputy Sahib to toss them at the base of the jar. The remainder of the ceremony consisted in our alternate offerings to the water jar of turmeric and rice, leaves, *areca* nuts, coins, and marigolds. Finally the pundit lighted some camphor chips and sandalwood on a brass plate. As he waved this in all directions, symbolically driving away evil, everybody stood up and passed his hands through the purifying smoke of the consecrated fire. The Deputy Sahib slipped me a rupee to hand the pundit, who also rescued the puja coppers by putting in his thumb and pulling them out of the rice and marigold pie. A garlanding of guests and general offering of sweets ended the puja. Immediately workmen came forward with spades to start digging, and at the same instant the crows, watching operations from the big shisham overhead, flew down and began picking up the grains of rice from under Ganesh's water jar.

That evening the Tahsildar sent me over a slip of paper on which he had written out a neatly itemized account— pundit, sweets, musicians, and charity to a lame man. The total came to two *rupees*, twelve *annas*, six *pies*. Roughly, one dollar, to insure the protection of Ganesh, remover of all untoward impediments and bestower of success, for a whole year! What insurance company would have done it so cheaply? A by-product of the puja was that the news of it spread through the village and bazar, and the villagers were said to be highly pleased.

One of the guests, the Doctor, had suddenly been reminded by my puja of a long-forgotten incident. When he is not being a doctor, he is the postmaster of Pachperwa, and, as his white beard attests, he is also a purveyor of history. He is indeed an old inhabitant, having moved to the village thirty-eight years ago. He had once seen two old men sitting on my hill, looking very disconsolate. When he asked them what the trouble was, they shed copious tears. They had been servants of a Tharu headman who once lived there. Now he was gone, and the house was gone, and nothing but grass and weeds were left. Lowering their voices, they confided that at a certain spot, over which the house formerly stood, treasure was buried. If the Tahsildar would divide it with them they were willing to point out the place. Some digging did indeed bring to light the silver base of a hookah and a silver cup, but nothing more.

The Doctor was quite sure that before the Mutiny of 1857 a Tharu headman had collected rents at Pachperwa for the Raja of Tulsipur who then owned the land. At the time of the Mutiny, the Raja of Tulsipur resisted the British annexation of Oudh. Subsequently his whole estate was confiscated and given over to the Raja of Balrampur, who supported the British.

Tradition had it that the Tulsipur Raja one day summoned the Tharu headman. A summons generally meant a demand for money. The headman sent a bag of rupees to Tulsipur and stayed at home. A second time the Raja sent for him, and a second time he despatched coin. When a third summons came he decided he had better go in person to Tulsipur, but he was met at the next village by soldiers sent out by the angry Raja and hacked to pieces for his insolent delay. His whole household, fearing further vengeance, fled to the mountains that very night.

Even though the secret hoard, supposedly left behind, was not unearthed in the process of laying the new foundations, the story wove a bit of legend about my hill. It also explained the grassy moat and the four guard mounds.

A stranger arriving in an Indian village and believing that with mere money he could build himself a house would soon realize his mistake. Without the invisible backing of the manager of the Balrampur Estate, I should have got nowhere. To begin with, carpenters are a village institution. They inherit the privilege of making and repairing the village plows, carts, oil mills, and other necessities of life, in return for which they receive a fixed allotment of grain from each cultivator. Naturally their work for the cultivators comes first, and no transient outside employment can compete with it. Then, there are no casual laborers in an Indian village. Practically all who have land are cultivating their own fields. Everybody else in the village is busy with his own particular caste work, and money cannot bribe him to undertake any other kind.

If the Tahsildar, who managed everything for me in feudal style, had not ordered the various rent contractors of the surrounding villages—there were at least fifty within a radius of five miles—to supply the necessary labor, no labor would have been forthcoming. As it was he simply sent out an order for so many carpenters, so many men to carry bricks, so many children to fetch water and mud, so many villagers of any sort to dig sods for the lawn. Fifty or a hundred came one day from one village and fifty or a hundred the next day from another. The only workmen hired by the month were a head carpenter from the town of Utraula, eighteen miles away, and two competent masons from Balrampur.

More than a thousand people, by this system, contributed to the building of my three-room house in the nine weeks it took to complete it. Sometimes I used to wish for a dozen trained workers instead, but I realized, on these occasions, that I was merely being American.

We began at the beginning. One day I watched the arrival of several bullock carts with big roughly hewn logs from the estate forest to the north, three logs to the load. The next day some of the logs were imbedded in the ground, one end slanting upward. Thereafter men squatted, one on top of a log and one on the ground, pulling a saw back and forth between them, while fresh green sawdust piled up below. Meanwhile an honorable company of eight carpenters assembled under some trees back of the Tahsildar's house. As the thick planks were turned over to them, they began chipping away, making frames for the eleven doors and thirteen windows specified in the rough plan of the house.

Upon these carpenters I began practising my first timid Hindustani. As soon as I appeared, armed with a little red phrase book, one of them would drag out from some mysterious spot a string bedstead for me to sit on. My monologue ran something like this: "Is that steel?" "Is this iron?" "This is a hammer." "That is a saw." The carpenters politely said, "*Hai.*" Sometimes they repeated the words with the proper accent.

It was one of the carpenters who had the distinction of being my first patient. One day when I was sitting as usual on the bed, a little fellow with a squint eye stood up and opened his mouth cavernously before me. His gestures and expression unmistakably announced that he was suffering from toothache. Not having any remedy to offer him, I promised to send for one. An appeal to the doctor at Balrampur soon brought a bottle labeled "tooth paint." On the morning of its arrival the original sufferer did not happen to be present, but another carpenter insisted that he, too, had a toothache. If free medicine was to be distributed, somebody ought to take advantage of it. He indicated an almost inaccessible back tooth of the upper jaw, and with cotton and a broom straw I applied the "paint." He allowed me to finish. Then he politely informed me I had painted the wrong tooth—the bad one was in the lower jaw.

The carpenters worked in a cheerful, easy way. They were supposed to come at seven and stay until five, with an hour or two off at noon, but they generally arrived at ten and melted away at four. They took long pulls at a bubbling hookah, passing the pipe fraternally from one to another. Their tools were few and extremely simple: an adz, the back end of which served as a hammer, an iron T square, a tiny plane with a wooden handle worked by two men at a time, a short saw, a clay bowl of brick dust mixed with water, a marking string. They gripped heavy timbers in the vise of their toes.

Once, wanting some flat boards for shelves laid across the lower part of two tables, I carefully measured the desired length and breadth in inches and asked the Tahsildar to convey the information to one of the carpenters. This man had a less complicated technique. He arrived with four thin reeds, broke these off to the required sizes, and cut his boards accordingly.

Presently I discovered that five different sizes of window frames were being made. Everybody was astonished that I thought this mattered. The variation, it was explained, was due to natural differences in the length of the lumber. When it came to the doors, some of which were of fine teak and some of poor mango wood, I assumed that my front door would be teak. After the doors were in place, I discovered the worst mango boards disgracing the front of the house while teak adorned the bathroom at the back.

Even the *mistri* carpenter from Utraula, a tall, thin, black-bearded Mussulman with a mouth overflowing with teeth—he seemed to have more than his share—had to wrestle with such foreign eccentricities as screened windows and doors. Stretching wire netting was a difficult task. But hinging the doors was even worse. The hinges had to be taken off and put on several times before a single door could be closed. European steel hinges are coming into use, even in villages, but a doorpost that swivels on a hollowed-out stone is more familiar. The house was to be glassless, since glass is a luxury unknown to the Indian countryside, as it was to Europe three centuries ago. My suggestion that the clumsy wooden shutters should be made to fold back in halves, involving the use of more hinges, cost many hours of worry to the carpenters' guild. But the mistri redeemed his honor by carving designs on the brackets for the thirteen windows of the Happy House. This he did out of sheer love, because it was the work he could do best. All the handles of his tools were carved.

Under the singing supervision of the two masons from Balrampur, the brickwork progressed at encouraging speed. Cartloads of sun-dried bricks hauled over from Haweli Singh's factory were dumped near the little shrine. Mud bricks are not stored in quantity. They are baked by four days of Indian sun and delivered to order. The cement for the house came from a hole in the front yard. The clay, with a little cow dung and water, was trampled to the right consistency by a woman with a *sari* tucked well up above her bare knees. She kept scooping the sticky mixture into flat bowls, which children bore off on their heads and delivered to the masons.

A man named Dukhi was much in evidence as the house-building went on. His beard, parted in the middle and combed sidewise, was dyed bright red, but through the holes in his cotton cap the hair showed gray. I was told that he was a Mohammedan barber, temporarily serving as foreman. At first I thought him a bad-tempered old man. I often caught him brandishing a long switch at the children, and I never came near the house that I did not hear him shouting, "*Jaldi, jaldi, kam karo!*" "Hurry up, hurry up, do your work!" When I resented this slave-driving, Dukhi insisted that the lazy fellows would do no work at all unless he kept after them. Only gradually did it dawn on me that Dukhi's energy was confined to windy shouting for my sole benefit. If I came around unexpectedly I generally found him propped up against some boards, peacefully sleeping. The urchins laughingly skipped out of reach of his switch.

Just the same, these child workers troubled me. In the early days of the Indian winter their few rags were pitifully inadequate. The mud spilled down over their faces and dried in white splashes, giving them the look of little ghosts. I asked the Tahsildar whether we could not do without them.

"But the children are very happy to work," he said. "I am paying them an anna and a half a day. More come than we can use."

The half starved little things were indeed "very happy" to earn their three cents. What could I do? Asgar Ali began taking over a big tray of candy, purchased in the bazar, every afternoon. At first four boys and one girl were working on the house. After the candy distribution began children appeared and begged to be employed. Presently it developed that, in addition, all the schoolchildren in Pachperwa were trailing up the hill to join the candy line. Then the grown children put in a plea not to be left out, and Dukhi, speaking for himself, supported their cause. The supply was increased to meet the demand, and in the end Dukhi, from the top of a pile of bricks, distributed a daily ration of brown sugar-candy to every person working on the Happy House.

One morning, when the house was still in its early stages, I happened to be standing with the Tahsildar watching the window frames go into place. A messenger came over from the tahsil to say that a pundit from the New Bazar had arrived. As we walked back the Tahsildar mentioned he had sent for him to learn the auspicious day for his family to start living in the new wing of their house at Balrampur. The wing had been ready for five months, but the stars had not yet permitted the family to move. For the third time, a pundit was to be consulted.

It occurred to me that I, too, had better inquire about an appropriate moving day, and the Tahsildar invited me to come along with him. The three of us sat down at a table, and the Tahsildar produced a long scroll, which proved to be his horoscope. I had no horoscope, but the pundit said he would try to manage without one. While he consulted a fat tome and reckoned the position of the stars influencing our lives, we waited anxiously. At last he shut his book. The Tahsildar was to move on February 6th, after 8 A. M., and I was to move on February 24th, at precisely 7:57 A. M.

The day and the hour may have been auspicious, but, when they arrived, the house was barely ready for thatching. Not for another three weeks, as a matter of fact, did I transfer my abode from the tent to the Happy House.

Had it not been for the clouds of dust that by March began to blow up every afternoon, life in the tent under the big tree would have been wholly delightful. I bought a cow and learned to make butter, not by shaking a bottle, as I had been instructed to do, but by beating cream in a bowl with an egg-beater, and then, when it was too stiff to beat any more, pressing it with a fork and rinsing it with water until the butter came, a fresh white pat. I began studying Hindustani with the village Schoolmaster. He did not know a word of English, and after a fortnight I came to the conclusion he also did not know how to teach. For the most part he sat mutely silent. I made better progress talking to his pupils, some of whom paid daily visits to my tent.

Life seemed extraordinarily full of things to do and to learn. Each morning I set my watch by a pocket sundial, steadying the needle toward the Himalaya. Except for the station clock and one at the tahsil, Pachperwa, to all appearances, had no mechanical means of knowing the time. But time made little difference in the village. At the end of the first month I discovered that all my sundial calculations had been based on an error of ten degrees in latitude and were quite inaccurate, but this mistake did not affect my scheme of life in any way. A villager, when he wants to gauge time, squints at the sun and sees that it is early morning or past noon or late afternoon. Time matters not at all in relation to minutes and very little as to days. It is only recurring seasons, with specified work to be done in the fields, which compel notice. Like the villagers, I almost forgot the passing days. Then one morning, sitting inside my tent, I saw silhouettes of a dozen men with towering loads of grass moving across the flowered cloth wall of the tent. They were Tharus, carrying my future roof on their heads.

Until dispossessed some centuries ago by the Rajput clans of Tulsipur and Balrampur, the Tharus—one of those innumerable primitive tribes in India whose history is unwritten—occupied the whole of the Oudh tract lying along the base of the Himalaya. Their Mongolian features and distinctive customs proclaim their non-Aryan origin. Nowadays half Hinduized, they live in settlements of their own at the edge of forest land on both sides of the Nepalese border, maintaining a precarious existence by hunting and cultivating strips of fields. Although looked down upon by Hindus and Mussulmans, they have a reputation for being brave, hard-working, and of independent spirit. I have heard Englishmen who have had dealings with them maintain that they do not know how to tell a lie.

At the request of the Tahsildar, a Tharu headman from a village fourteen miles from Pachperwa undertook to make my roof. Tharus do better thatching than anybody else in the *Tarai*, as the sub-Himalayan tract is called. The headman was really a little king. Unless he himself had ordered his Tharus to work for us, they would not have done so. Fifty of them came, bringing bundles of two kinds of grass, coarse *khar* and soft *bankas*. One boy wore a fine red sash and a string of red seeds around his neck. The others were plainly dressed in short white jackets open over bare chests and scant *dhotis*, drawn back between the legs and tucked in behind. Like Hindus, they kept uncut a single strand of hair, but instead of twisting these sacred hairs into a tiny inconspicuous knot on top of the head, the Tharus wore a long bushy lock falling to their shoulders.

Two Tharus sat on the ground and made rope of the fine grass. They held lengths of grass firmly with their toes and twirled the strands in their hands, feeding in grass lengths as needed. Bundles of this twine were tossed to the men on the roof. A number of bamboos, previously soaked in water to make them resistant to rain, had been split into narrow strips. These the Tharus tied down horizontally across the rafters. Then they took bunches of coarse grass and tied them firmly to the bamboos, with the loose ends streaming down like hair. They worked in one long line, beginning at the bottom and progressing upward. When they had finished, the thatch stretched over the Happy House like a field of cloth of gold, eight inches thick.

The Tharus took five days to make the roof, and they were paid in wine, their own immoral but happy coin. Except when they serve as beaters in the jungle, Tharus never work for money and would scarcely know what to do with it if they had any. But occasionally they can be bribed to do a little work for wine. They have a great reputation for wine-bibbing, distilling their spirits from rice, if no better variety of country liquor is available. As the price of my roof, the headman asked for his fifty men a bottle apiece of the village wine made from *mahuwa* flowers, but the Tahsildar thought this exorbitant and cut the amount in two.

My *bangla*—the Indian word is familiar as bungalow in English—was now all but ready. It really looked very comfortable and attractive. The middle room was fourteen feet square; the two smaller ones were fourteen by eight. I chose the north room as a bedroom because it promised to be cooler in the hot months ahead, and opening off this was the bathroom. A wide veranda surrounded the whole house. Out of deference to snakes, the plinth was eighteen inches above the ground level. The floors were made of burnt brick. Another house of three rooms for the servants, and a small building for a kitchen, completed my establishment.

The mud bricks of house, servants' quarters, and kitchen were plastered over inside and out with a layer of mud mixed with cow dung and water. This cow-dung plaster is in universal use in India. Without the dung to give adhesion, the mud soon disintegrates. As soon as the preparation dries, there is no odor, and the effect is like adobe. A final coat of whitewash made everything clean and satisfactory.

For finishing touches Kalu the tobacconist painted the woodwork, Dowdhe the tailor prepared a robin's-egg blue ceiling cloth dyed by Rajab, and other villagers deftly wove reed curtains for the veranda. The ceiling cloth was a protection against snakes, scorpions, and similar creatures fond of making their home in a thatched roof. The cloth followed the slant of the roof in the big room, twenty-five feet high in the center, but was stretched flat in the two smaller rooms. I always had a pleasant feeling, when I looked at it, as of blue sky over my head.

In his rank as chief artist of the village, rather than as tobacconist and maker of hookah stems, Kalu was prevailed upon to set to work with his banana-stalk brushes. Since village woodwork is seldom painted, brushes are not used in country districts. Stripping a stalk, Kalu chopped it into six-inch lengths. Each length, mashed at one end, made a rough brush, but these banana brushes, I noticed, soon wore out. I took pity on him and sent to Lucknow for an imported horsehair brush. As for the paint, that was a never-ending source of trouble. The paint itself came from Balrampur in the form of a green powder, but this had to be mixed with a paste previously made by rubbing a hard yellow mineral on a wet stone. As Kalu never twice mixed paint and paste in the same proportions, the green changed color with startling rapidity. One door would be just the right shade of soft bluish green, the next would verge on grass, the next would be as dark and somber as a tropical forest. No two doors or windows turned out alike.

Paths of red brick dust and a lawn for the top of the hill, carried up in chunks on the heads of some fifty persons from the grass moat at the bottom, finished the nine weeks' labor. The Happy House was ready for occupancy.

It cost, according to the Tahsildar's account—a huge sheaf of papers scribbled over in Urdu and Hindi and frequently thumb-printed by way of receipt—746 rupees, equal to about two hundred and fifty dollars! The wood had been a present from the estate. Items of expense included the sawyers' bill of $35.00, Kalu's bill of $5.00 for painting, the salary of the mistri, equivalent to $8.00 a month, wages of lesser carpenters at twelve cents and sixteen cents a day, of masons at twenty-four cents a day; cost of bricks, $55.00; of nails, bolts, and hinges, which had to be imported, $22.00. The dyer was paid $1.50 for dyeing the ceiling cloth, and the tailor sixty-five cents for sewing and hanging it. Dukhi was awarded $6.00 as foreman. These prices represented, more or less accurately, the current rates for work around Pachperwa. But many people, as I found out afterward, were never paid at all. The Tahsildar simply ordered them to work, and they had no choice but to obey.

On the day I moved in, the Tahsildar and his staff of clerks were compelled to go to Balrampur for the quarterly account day, leaving behind only the Assistant Tahsildar, down with fever. I went over to the house early to direct the arrangement of my things as half a dozen men and boys brought them along. The Ayah and the cook stayed at the tent, and Asgar Ali, my boy, ran back and forth between the tent and hill. A fearful dust storm was blowing, and everything arrived covered with coats of gray powder.

At the close of the afternoon the Assistant Tahsildar, called the *Peshkar*—literally one who submits papers—came over, feeling very weak. A trail of people came up the hill, first the stout little Doctor, then Haweli Singh, then the effusive Sub-Inspector of Police, then the polite and un-officious Inspector of Roads and member of the District Board, then the autocratic old *Jamadar*—whose office at the tahsil was somewhat like that of a quartermaster—then the Mohammedan Station Master, and finally a wandering ascetic. Asgar Ali had to bring out all my nine chairs. The road inspector's small boy folded his hands in salaam and lisped a gracious speech of welcome, for which he had been carefully rehearsed. The Sub-Inspector's little girl came forward and shyly thrust a bouquet of marigolds at me. All expressed pleasure that I had come to live in Pachperwa. Several of the villagers also appeared, bearing offerings of sweets, nuts, raisins, and fruits, arranged on round trays. I felt that I had been given a very fine housewarming.

When the Tahsildar came back from Balrampur, I fulfilled my social responsibilities in taking up formal residence
in the village. Word was sent out that there would be a
distribution of grain for poor people. A hundred and fifty of
them arrived at the specified hour and waited patiently for
members of the tahsil staff to make the distributions of rice
and pulse from the brown bags stacked near the shrine. The
women and children who had worked most faithfully on the
house also received gifts of clothes.

Originally I intended to confine my entertainment to those
in need, but in the end I weakened and gave a dinner party
for the tahsil staff, the chief tradesmen, the Doctor, the
police officials, the Schoolmaster, the pundits, the village
postman, the Station Master, and all those who had performed any special services in connection with the building
of the house—about forty persons in all. One of the big
Marwaris from the New Bazar did the cooking and supplied
the leaf plates, neatly sewn together with stems. The Tahsildar undertook to seat the guests. Large cloths were spread
on the bare ground in front of the house, just beyond the
fringe of grass. All the Mussulmans were seated at one of
these "tables," Hindus of three castes at another, the
orthodox Brahmin postman all alone, the Marwaris by
themselves, and the Tharu headman by himself. The servants
were permitted to carry off a share of the feast after the
others had been served.

In order not to cast embarrassment on the party, I ate
my own dinner beforehand and merely looked on from a
distance. Only fried food, milk preparations and sweets
were served, because caste laws prohibit promiscuous eating
of rice or anything boiled. Since neither I nor my Mohammedan servants had had anything to do with the feast, my
Hindu guests could partake of it without breaking any of
their rules. Afterward we had a display of fireworks, made
in the village. It was nearly midnight before all the guests
had departed, and the village sank once more into its accustomed quiet.

CHAPTER III

The People of the House

THE people of the Happy House, how endlessly amusing, puzzling, absurd, tragic, human they were! Servants only, perhaps, from an outsider's point of view; from a more intimate perspective, unconscious actors in a drama of village life all too human and real. In the West servants are paid to do their work and obliterate themselves. Work and pay are considered to cancel each other. In the East, both are secondary to the human relationship established through a service rendered and accepted. Servants become an integral part of a household, and all their little and big problems are the concern of the wage payer, as much as those of any member of the family. There were quarrels for me to settle, wounds to bind, fevers and stomach aches to mend. Marriage, divorce, birth, and death entered into our midst. And there were strange, shining moments, when resistant margins were pushed back in selfless devotion and loyalty.

Finding a cook had been my first and most serious problem. Not being able to do better, I had borrowed an assistant to the chief cook at the Maharaja's European guest house in Balrampur. Jawahir was a cadaverous man with a black beard who knew not a word of English, but he insisted that he was an expert cook. He was a Mussulman, of course, since Hindus do not serve a European in the capacity of cook. An important asset was a mother-in-law who expressed a willingness to come along as ayah. Jawahir's wages were fixed at fifteen rupees a month, roughly five dollars, an increase of two dollars over the salary he was then receiving. According to Indian custom I also outfitted him with new clothes—a warm woollen coat, two white suits, and a turban. The Ayah was to receive the same salary, and in addition two saris, a coat, and a green woollen shawl.

The additional servants who subsequently became attached to my household staff as water carrier, dish washer, sweeper, washerman, *punka* puller, general utility man, and substitute cook (when Jawahir left at the end of three months) were all recruited locally. India to some extent solves the problem of support for all by restricting the work of each. Of the impressive retinue, six were Mussulmans and three were Hindus. Not one of them knew a single word of English. Most of them lived at their own houses, and all of them provided their own food. I paid wages much higher than any of them had ever received before, but the trifling sum of twenty-five dollars a month covered the total cost.

The main problem of housekeeping centered in the question of food. I wished to live as much as possible on the village diet, but from Lucknow I procured a few luxuries: tea, coffee, cocoa, white sugar, Quaker Oats, biscuits, prunes, and apricots. Occasionally I even indulged in cheese and chocolates. At first Pachperwa offered more variety than I had been led to hope for. Goat meat and mutton were to be had, but I decided not to eat meat, partly because I felt my standing might be higher with the Hindu community if I refrained and partly because the insanitary conditions of the butcher shops made me prefer vegetarianism. From the Mussulmans and Tharus chickens could generally be bought, for from eight to ten cents apiece. Eggs were also procurable, and the tanks of the vicinity provided fish. But when the hot weather came, the chickens shrank to such pitiful size I could not bear to eat them. The fish arrived done up in straw, stiff with age and too muddy in flavor to be palatable. The hens ceased to lay.

Fruit was equally uncertain. In January the Tharus used to come along with baskets of tangerines from Nepal to exchange for cloth or wine, and occasionally the market offered custard apples, stringy little bananas, or guavas. Then came papayas for a brief space, and flat tasteless watermelons the size of grapefruit. Great misshapen jackfruit, mangoes, and litchis also appeared in season. Many were the days, however, when I had to fall back on prunes and apricots, apricots and prunes.

As for vegetables, potatoes and pumpkins, as I had been warned, appeared indeed to constitute the chief ones. One desperate day I searched the dictionary for the name of every vegetable I could think of and recited the list to the startled Jawahir. Then I made the happy discovery that greens and eggplants were commonly on the market, and cauliflower, carrots, and beans, occasionally. In addition to these, there were two or three Indian vegetables, unfamiliar but agreeable in flavor. After Jawahir had learned to cook vegetables in water instead of frying them in ghi and to serve them hot instead of preparing them at four for dinner at eight, I considered the food problem solved. Having only two meals a day, plus tea in the early morning and afternoon, simplified matters materially.

Jawahir was a born pessimist. In all the time he was with me I never once saw him smile, and the only optimistic utterance he ever gave vent to was his boast that he was familiar with Hindustani, Mussulmani, and European styles of cuisine. If, as a rare treat, I had cheese or chocolates for dinner, Jawahir saw no reason why chocolates or cheese would not be equally welcome for breakfast. Why not, indeed, except for the mere matter of custom? When I suggested that we try Hindustani cooking, I discovered that ghi was an essential ingredient. Ghi is a perfectly good substitute for butter or lard, but too much fried food is hard on the digestion, and I soon had to banish it from my table. Mohammedan cooking is built up on preparations of spiced meat, but meat, also, was off my list. In spite of this taboo, Jawahir's first weekly expense account, translated into English by a tahsil clerk, recorded "four heads of goats, ten annas." The goat heads, it seemed, had been used for soup-stock. Even soup became a difficult proposition after I forbade the purchase of any more heads. Poor Jawahir found all his styles badly cramped.

Whether my refusal to eat goat-head soup, spiced meat, and fried vegetables was the cause, or whether it was homesickness for his family at Balrampur, I cannot say, but Jawahir grew gloomier and gloomier as the weeks passed. Toward the other servants he maintained a manner of haughty superiority. He even ordered the tahsil people about, borrowing luster from his connection with me.

On Fridays he dressed in clean clothes—he did not care how dirty he was on other days—and went to mosque, and on Wednesdays he betook himself to the bazar with a large cloth in which to bring back a week's supply of vegetables. These were his two diversions. When Ramazan came round, the month in which good Mussulmans do not touch food or smoke or even take a drink of water between sunrise and sunset, he added a third form of entertainment. At night I could hear him reading aloud in sepulchral tones to his mother-in-law and Asgar Ali. He read the Koran, from a paper edition printed in the stiff Nagri characters, which are easier than the flowing Persian script usually associated with Mohammedan writings in India. But his chief solace against all the ills of life was his water pipe. After the dishes were cleared away and the servants had eaten their dinner, prepared by the Ayah while Jawahir was serving mine, I would fall asleep to the comfortable sound of his hookah, like a purring cat.

Trouble arose when Jawahir's weekly accounts showed signs of unmistakable padding. For three successive weeks, for example, his statement recorded that I had eaten eight cents' worth of potatoes. Finally my appetite registered three dozen eggs in one week. In Pachperwa eight cents bought sixteen pounds of potatoes. Was it possible, I asked Jawahir, for a single person to eat so much in one week? With a disdainful gesture, he showed how he always threw out the small potatoes. As for the eggs, had he not made what he was pleased to call a cake? And so with various other items. I did not wish to press the point, but I mildly suggested that a daily, instead of a weekly, accounting might be desirable.

"That," said Jawahir with imperturbable composure, "I will not do. I will write the account only once a week."

A week passed. Jawahir continued to do the cooking, and nothing more was said about a daily account. Everything might have passed off smoothly if Jawahir had not taken this inopportune moment to ask for an increase in wages. As I left the breakfast table one morning, I noticed a sheet of paper ostentatiously spread out on my desk. It read:

SIR,
    Most humbly and respectfully I beg to lay a few lines for your kind consideration that since 4 months I am working with hard labour with this hope that some consideration will be made in my present pay but still no regard has been made in my present pay. At this low pay, I cannot pull on. I, therefore, request that your honour would be good enough to accept my resignation within a fortnight. In this act of kindness I shall be very thankful.

        Your most obedient servant,
              JAWAHIR.

The letter, drafted for him by a clerk of the tahsil, was presumably intended as a basis for negotiations, but I accepted it as final, and Jawahir took a dignified departure. The vacancy was immediately filled by Din Mohammed, one of the tahsil peons, or messengers, recommended by the Tahsildar, and though Din Mohammed had had even less experience as a cook than Jawahir, he had a contented and happy disposition, and in the nine months he remained with me he was never guilty of stealing as much as an anna.

The Ayah seemed relieved when she heard her son-in-law was to leave us. She made a face and said, "Let him go!" On the morning of his departure, which chanced to be the first day of the month, when salaries were due, she secretively begged me to withhold all but four rupees of her fifteen. Was it possible that Jawahir was in the habit of extorting money from his mother-in-law? I remembered that once, as she was tucking in the mosquito curtain of my bed, she told me how happy she was to be independent.

"If you have money, come! If you have no money, go!" she said dramatically. "It is always like that."

Of my staff of villagers, Miriam, the Ayah, was certainly the most respectable, and she was also the most devoted to me, with the possible exception of Din Mohammed. I can see her yet as we finally parted at Lucknow, one hand thrust through the window of the car to smooth my cheek with a fluttering gesture of affection, her face drenched with tears!

Before the death of her husband she was well off, as villagers go. They had a hundred *bighas* of fields, she used to boast, and fifty cows and fifty goats. Sometimes it was twenty-five cows and fifty goats, and sometimes fifty cows and twenty-five goats, but the twenty acres of land did not vary. Then the husband died, and her own brother, she said bitterly, became her *dushman*, her enemy, and robbed her of everything. At this point she invariably remembered her children. "Ten children, and eight dead!" she would say, dropping her hands with a gesture such as Job might have used. "Ten children, and only two left!" The corners of her mouth worked strangely, her chin quivered and tears welled.

In an effort to comfort her I fell back uncertainly on her own fatalistic philosophy. Immediately a tone of resignation came into her voice, and she dried her eyes on the edge of her sari. "Yes, all is the will of Allah. He gives and he takes."

Her chief duties were the care of my bed and the sweeping of the house, perhaps an hour and a half of work a day. As soon as I was up she removed the bedclothes, including the two-inch purple mattress of local manufacture, and carried everything out to hang across a bamboo pole in the sun. An admiring crowd on the sidelines made audible comments on my "fine cloths." Shuffling back again in her heelless slippers, she fetched a bundle of straws tied with a string, which she called a broom, and gave a few cursory scratches to the cotton rugs. It took me some time to persuade her to sweep first and dust afterward. India does not know the use of house brooms, since these are impractical for earthen floors, but a good housewife will give her threshold and the place where she cooks, at least, a fresh coating of mud and cow-dung plaster each morning. After making the bed and smearing some "Cobra Polish" on my dusty shoes, which she rubbed with a cloth tightly wrapped round one finger, the Ayah's work was done, until it was time to open the bed again and let down the mosquito curtain.

As time went on, I discovered many other things the Ayah could do. She could fish and fly kites, successfully cutting the string of her enemy's kite. She was not afraid to take a lantern and stalk watchfully around the house on dark nights. After her husband's death, she had guarded her own fields at night, while crops were ripening. Sometimes she had encountered snakes or big lizards in the fields. These she had stoned to death, selling the lizard skins for shoes.

Her abilities as an actress were of the first rank. She would tell me how our Jamadar had been beating a peon with shoes that morning, and she would give herself swinging cracks about the head and back to show how he did it. Beating with shoes is a great indignity in India, especially on the head, since that is the most honorable part of the body. Shoebeating is a more humiliating punishment than beating with a stick. Once, when we were discussing drugs, she sat down on the floor, pretended to smoke *ganja* until she grew drowsy and finally fell over, as if unconscious. Then she indicated how the head "dances" after drinking *bhang*. Her enemy brother in Balrampur was addicted to drugs, and she had seen their effect at close range.

Her eyesight was not good, but she could sew very neatly, an unusual accomplishment among village women. They have little need to sew. Their saris come woven in finished

lengths of six or seven yards, requiring nothing but drap-
ing to make them the most beautiful, the most modest, and
at the same time the simplest costume for women in the
world. Made of cotton and costing a dollar, or of exquisite
gold-brocaded Benares silk, worth fifty dollars, the sari is
always the same. But the Ayah thriftily took all my scraps
and made them into caps for Jawahir's little boy or jackets
for herself. She also sewed a quilt for cold little Asgar Ali,
justifying the name of Mother, by which the other servants
addressed her.

In the mornings, she would greet me with a little salute
and dip from the waist and a "Salaam, *huzur*," to which I
replied "Salaam, Ayah." Huzur, variously translated as
"your excellency," "sir," "your highness," or "presence," is
the common form of address to a person of superior position. The Ayah salaamed all my visitors in the same respectful manner, but if they did not immediately respond, she repeated her salaam in a loud tone, impossible to ignore.

Soon after I moved into the bungalow, I asked a village
woman to paint one of the outer walls of the kitchen in
approved village style. Tempted by the white surface of
the long back wall of the servants' house, close to mine, I
then embarked on some decoration myself, copying at nearly
life size a spirited elephant fight from a Mogul miniature
reproduced in Manucci's *Storia do Mogor.* This innocent
pastime created fervent interest in the community. People
came even from long distances to watch me work. Presently
the Ayah and Asgar began decorating the pillars and front
wall of their house, and the morose Jawahir went so far
as to paint a flower on one pillar. But the Ayah was not
content with this limited expression of her talent. She
emerged one day from mysterious seclusion, bearing a small
elephant modeled from potter's clay. She had painted it
very cleverly, but its crowning glory was a saddlecloth made
from the gilt papers of an empty chocolate box.

Her great interest in jewelry I took to be one of her
little vanities. Each month, after pay day, she blossomed

out in some new ornament. Lifting her sari to show a pair of clinking anklets, which seemed far too heavy for her thin little legs, she would remark, "Thirteen rupees, four annas, but twenty rupees of silver in weight!" Then, invariably she would add:

"I am spreading the name of my Miss Sahiba all over the countryside. My Miss Sahiba gives me food and clothes. She has given me this, and this, and this"—and she touched her bracelets, her anklets, her silver collar, her earrings.

"But I did not give them to you. You bought them with your own money!"

All such specious argument fell on deaf ears. Wages she never considered as anything but a gift.

One day I teased her a little. Here she was a grandmother, and certainly she was not beautiful. "I have the face of a jackal," she often remarked of herself. Even her jewelry failed to hide her plainness. The sobering truth came out. All this jewelry was merely to pay for her funeral. She had nearly enough now—only one more pair of bracelets, for eight rupees! Jewelry, in her eyes, was an investment to buy her admission to the *durbar* of God.

Her gratitude and loyalty were touchingly manifested on more than one occasion. Once a violent quarrel with Jumai, the water carrier, disturbed the peace of a quiet afternoon. When angry she would scream at the top of her lungs, and nothing could stop her until her stream of abuse ran out from sheer exhaustion. It seemed that she had caught Jumai, the thief, the robber, the ingrate, eater of my salt that he was, pulling straws out of my thatch to use for lighting his hookah. Did not this bring bad luck to the owner of the house, as everyone knew? Now, at the very least, I should have news of a death by the next mail.

Another memory I cherish more. It was the very worst of the hot season with the thermometer registering close to 130 degrees in the sun—105 inside the house—and I was lying sick with mango poisoning. The Ayah sat on the floor beside the bed fanning me, her eyes full of tears. With motherly satisfaction she watched me take some soup, my first nourishment in two days. As I finished she remarked, "Now Din Mohammed and I will eat something, too." I learned that neither of them had touched a mouthful for two days. "How could we eat, when you were ill?" the Ayah asked simply.

Lowest in the social scale of those who served me was the Hindu sweeper, an "untouchable," responsible for disposing of the house waste. He also brushed up leaves and swept the veranda and the paths around the Happy House. Sometimes his daughter-in-law, a large, well built woman, tattooed on arms, hands, and face, took his place. They were *Doms*, but were called *Mehtar* and *Mehtarani*, sweepers. The sweeper was a poor wretch with sticks of legs and a protruding lower jaw that gave him an astonishingly ape-like appearance. He was as aboriginal looking as if he had just stepped down from the ancestral tree. At the beginning he used to squat a little distance away and stare at me by the hour. I literally felt the painful struggle of thoughts trying to break through the thick cloud in which his mental faculties seemed to hang suspended.

When I asked about his family, he replied that his son was dead and he had neither children nor grandchildren. More questioning brought out that Pachperwa had only two families of scavengers. Villagers do not ordinarily require the services of a sweeper; they simply go out into the fields, or to some waste bit of land, usually designated as "jungle." Only where women are kept in seclusion or when a household steps up in the social and economic scale is a sweeper essential. My sweeper and his daughter-in-law took care of eight or nine houses in the village, for which they received pitiful sums varying from four to twelve annas a month. For the work at the tahsil, requiring three daily visits, they received two rupees a month. Presents of food also came their way on occasion. "I have grown old as a sweeper," the Mehtar concluded abruptly. I thought he was stressing his age, but presently it dawned on me this was a way of saying he did his work well.

He wore a very short dhoti—so short that, when his black cotton jacket was fastened, he looked as if he had only the jacket on. It was impossible not to see the thinness of his legs—they were nothing but skin taut over bone— and I could count every one of his ribs. I told Jawahir to make enough rice and curry and *chapatis* for breakfast every morning to provide the sweeper with a good meal. The sweeper sent back word that he would not be able to accept. Although he took scraps from anybody else, as a Hindu, he said, he could not touch cooked food from the household of one belonging to the "Christian caste." This was something of a blow, especially when I found him willing to eat Mohammedan food. The real reason, I think, was my utter strangeness to him.

The washerman was a low-caste Hindu, but there was nothing degraded or menial in his bearing. He was tall, dignified, and courteous, and he adapted himself intelligently to my requirements. His own way of washing the village clothes was to rub them with a mixture of fuller's earth and ashes, soak them overnight, and then pound them on a washboard set up at the edge of a swamp in the fields. Afterward he spread them out on the ground, and the sun did the rest. Though soap is known in the village, it is expensive, and the familiar saying, "When *Dhobis* compete, then only does soap reach the clothes," certainly held good for Pachperwa.

Feeling that my clothes would fare better if washed at home, I made arrangements with the Dhobi to come to the house every Monday. I provided a zinc tub and introduced him to hot water and Lux. In the end we abandoned hot water as a troublesome innovation, and he even had his way of spreading things on the ground instead of hanging them on the bamboo clothesline, from which they always blew off. Quite regularly, as the Dhobi blew up the charcoal fire inside his brass iron, a curious audience gathered. He had to invent his own answers as to the uses of my peculiar garments. Sometimes it seemed to me that his technique was devised to press wrinkles in rather than smooth them out. Village dhotis and saris do not need any ironing. "Foreign clothes are very difficult," he used to confess. After all, what did it matter how one's things looked in Pachperwa?

Foreseeing the "hard labor" of preparing two meals a day for one person—also as a matter of dignity—Jawahir had informed me, immediately upon his arrival in Pachperwa, that he would need an assistant. Asgar Ali, on the recommendation of the Tahsildar, thereupon presented himself, very self-conscious and anxious to be taken. Asgar was named for the grandson of Ali, son-in-law of the Prophet. He said he was thirteen; his mother later told me he was twelve; and I guessed him to be nearer fourteen. He was slim, wore his hair parted on one side, and smiled engagingly. Born and bred in the Pachperwa briar patch, he had no knowledge of the larger world beyond that derived from a five-mile journey once made to the next point on the railway line.

Asgar at once became slave to everybody. He fetched water from the well, washed the dishes, scrubbed the kettles with ashes and straw, ground the curry powder, tended the lamps, heated water for my bath and cleaned the tub, ran to the bazar for anything Jawahir forgot, boiled the milk, and brought a charcoal brazier to the tent when the sun went down. What other menial tasks he performed under Jawahir's thumb, I do not know. There was also talk of having Asgar learn to milk my cow, as a safety precaution against infections or watering. I presented him with a cake of soap and a tin soap box purchased in the bazar and supplied him with a special towel for his exclusive use as milkman. Asgar was willing to try anything, but the cow was not. She kicked him several feet away, while her calf butted him, and the regular milkman from the New Bazar continued to come morning and evening and do the milking. The soap box was converted into a pocketbook.

The evening of the day on which Asgar Ali had his mis-adventure with the cow I attended my first social function in Pachperwa, the puja of the Sub-Inspector of Police, held in honor of the ear-piercing of Dhuni, his seven-year-old son. The ceremony took place at the Sub-Inspector's house at five in the afternoon, a goldsmith, a barber, and the big pundit who afterward conducted my house puja offici-ating. Fireworks and a feast followed the ceremony, and then we sat shivering under an awning until nearly twelve, watching a play presented by local actors. The men stalked about the stage, chanting their lines with many promptings, to the accompaniment of drum and cymbals and a droning harmonium.

Presently two dancing-girls entered. It took me five minutes to discover that the prettiest of the two *ranis* in the play, the one dressed in a rainbow sari with a ruby ring through her nose and tinkling anklets strung with bells, was no other than my own Asgar Ali. He sang his lines in a loud boyish voice, and his gestures were monotonous, but in appearance he made a very pretty little princess.

One day I asked Asgar to take me to see his mother. The house, surrounded by a fruit garden, was on the outskirts of the village near one of the large tanks, or ponds, in which cattle were watered. Some pigs were wallowing in it as we passed, and Asgar expressed proper Mohammedan con-tempt for the low-caste Hindus willing to keep swine. His white-haired, white-bearded father greeted me with great dignity and no apparent surprise. One would have thought that foreign ladies called at his house frequently. The mother, Asgar's married sister, and two younger children also appeared to welcome me, and I was invited to sit on a bedstead, over which a cloth had first been spread, under the trees, and the older sister brought a handful of small round fruits, like thorn apples. Afterward I was taken on a tour of the garden and allowed a peep inside the house. Both house and garden had come into the possession of the family many years back, I was told. As far as I could gather,

Asgar's father did nothing for a living except sell his fruit and beg. For some unknown reason, he received regular allotments of grain every harvest from certain families in the vicinity, and with great solemnity he was constantly making his rounds to collect what was "due" him. The mother, tall and well built, had a strikingly independent manner, and it was from her, I concluded, that Asgar and his brothers and sisters inherited both their looks and their intelligence. The handsomest of the children was little eight-year-old Akbar Ali, whose lustrous black eyes and long lashes gave him peculiar charm.

When Asgar first came to me he owned one shirt and one dhoti and a strip of faded red cotton cloth. This last he wore over his head and shoulders like a shawl during the day and wrapped himself in it when he curled up in a corner of the Ayah's tent at night. New dhotis were procured from the bazar, and the tailor came to measure him for shirts and a blue cloth jacket. Asgar was soon peacocking about in his new outfit. At the end of the first month he invested half his salary of three dollars in a pair of shoes, made to order in the village, and black socks, held up by round green garters. He also bought himself a bone ring dyed black and set with imitation pearls, at a cost of six cents.

With each passing month, Asgar added new items to his wardrobe. He acquired two pink undershirts with Japanese cherry blossoms painted on the satin strips in front, and a red vest with brass buttons. He conceived a sudden ambition to wear trousers instead of a dhoti, and had the tailor make him a pair in the conventional fashion, very full in the seat and tight fitting below the knee, of white cotton cloth. The day he first put on trousers he went home for luncheon by a roundabout way, in order to escape the teasing of his village friends. His black locks, at first uncovered, were soon crowned with a magnificent red velvet cap with gold braid.

Asgar's interest in animals was another side of his char-

acter. He was responsible for all our household pets. The
first arrival was a baby partridge. Its wings had been
clipped, and it had a hurt foot, which he wanted me to doctor. He had bought the partridge, expecting to train it for
fighting, but the partridge did not live to fulfill his hopes.
He next procured a young monkey and took it with him on
a string wherever he went. As a sign of ownership, he
fastened a brass ring with a dangling bit of red glass into
one of its ears. Asgar soon tired of walking about with his
monkey and left it tied to a pillar outside his room. One
day out of boredom it bit its string in two and made for
the jungle, brass earring and all. Still another of his ven-
tures in pets was a baby mongoose, caught in his own garden. Rikki Tikki, as we named him, was soon answering to
his name and running about everywhere, perfectly at home,
though he spent most of his time in the kitchen. If Din
Mohammed took ten steps in any direction, Rikki Tikki
scampered after him.

Asgar's most promising trait was a quick intelligence.
When the village ironsmith succumbed before the task of
cutting out two round pieces of tin with holes in the center,
to serve as protectors for my candlesticks, Asgar promptly
manufactured what was needed out of a tin biscuit box with
a pair of scissors. He had never been to school and knew
nothing of the mysteries of reading and writing, but two
weeks after I started giving him English lessons he knew
the English alphabet, could count up to twenty, and had
mastered the art of telling time. As a reward for the last
accomplishment I gave him a cheap wrist-watch, ordered
from Lucknow, which became his most treasured possession.

He had learned how to cook by watching Jawahir, and it
was he who helped Din Mohammed over his first difficult
days. Just before Moharram, the Mohammedan month of
mourning, he was very busy making *tazias*, bamboo and
paper tombs to be carried in the mourning procession. He
procured the bamboo from his garden, bought stamped
papers from the dyer, and begged his string from me. The

tazias cost him four annas apiece, and he sold them for a rupee each. The Peshkar told him he ought not to commercialize his religion like this, but I praised him for his commendable industry.

In the early spring, I left Pachperwa for a brief pilgrimage to some of the famous Buddhist holy places. Realizing that Asgar would probably have few such opportunities in his life for travel, I told him to pack his bundle and come along. Though he had never heard of Buddha, he enjoyed intensely the excitement of trains and strange places. The climax of the adventure was having a glimpse of Calcutta, with its miracles of electric lights and fans, plumbing, lifts, motor cars, motion pictures, and stuffed birds and animals in the Indian Museum.

When we were returning from Calcutta our adventure threatened to turn into a tragedy. Asgar had been riding in the third-class compartment provided for servants of first- and second-class passengers. It was his habit to hop out at stations and come and look in at my carriage window. It suddenly dawned on me that I had not seen him for two or three hours, and at the next station I went to look for him. There was his bundle in the rack, but an occupant of the compartment said Asgar had not returned when the train left Moghal Sarai Junction. I had his ticket, and all the money he had was the change from his luncheon rupee, rattling round in the tin soap box. At Lucknow, I appealed to the police, who telegraphed his description to various railway centers, and I also wired to Balrampur and Pachperwa. How on earth could I ever return to the village and face Asgar's mother, having lost her son! After two days of complete silence, a brief message from Kanwar Jasbir Singh reported Asgar safe in Balrampur. By the salty tear dropped into my already too salty porridge at the Carlton Hotel, I realized the strain of anxiety I had been under.

Asgar's adventures almost duplicated Kim's. While I was journeying to Lucknow, he had journeyed to Allahabad, having jumped on the wrong section of our train at Moghal

Sarai. He spent the night at the station and next morning, without a ticket, climbed aboard another train, this time having assured himself it would take him in the right direction. When a ticket inspector came along, Asgar told of belonging to a somewhat fabulous Miss Sahiba, for whom he had never heard any other name. The inspector was to be put off with no tall tales. First he tried to take Asgar's precious wrist-watch as the price of his ticket, and when Asgar resisted he haled him to the police station at Fyzabad, where the boy received a sound drubbing for stealing train rides. Thereafter, grown wise, he ducked all railway officials, jumped off moving trains to bide his time in the long grass near stations, and warily approached humble folk like himself to ask about the train he should take next. His knocks in the hard world became decorations of honor in village perspective, and Asgar Ali, a hero in Pachperwa, thoroughly enjoyed telling the story of his dinnerless, frightened days in the wide world.

April came, with the wheat and pulses reaped, the mango blossoms fallen, old leaves dropping off and new ones unfurling within the same week, bulbuls and cuckoos doing their best to announce that these hot, lusterless days were spring. By the end of the month all vegetation had withered, and the starved bullocks and water buffaloes roamed the countryside vainly searching for a few mouthfuls of something green. All day and night they kept coming to the top of my hill, where something of a lawn still survived through careful watering. Asgar chased them by day, and I arose from my bed on the lawn and chased them by night, since the servants slept far too soundly to wake, even when they were called. The Tahsildar suggested that Fakire (pronounced Fakiray), an older brother of Asgar's employed as a peon at the tahsil, had better sleep near my house and help guard it.

In addition to chasing cattle, Fakire was soon promoted to be my evening newspaper. Fakire's work as peon took him all over Pachperwa tahsil, and, thanks to his fearlessness and independence, he was not in the least afraid to serve as local gazette. Every evening after dinner he came in, squatted on the floor, and for ten or fifteen minutes narrated the chief events or hearsay of the day.

Fakire, like a true villager, had not a good word for the police. "See what happened to Baghwan!" he said one evening. "What happened?" I asked. Baghwan was a Mohammedan gardener, then serving as water carrier, and a story about him certainly promised first-column interest.

Baghwan, it seemed, had a wife too sick to do the housework any more; so she and Baghwan agreed that he had better take a second wife. As a Mussulman, Baghwan was entitled to four wives, if he chose. He had no difficulty in finding one, in spite of the fact that he was cross-eyed, but four days later a man turned up who claimed that the woman was already married to him.

"She is my wife," said the man.

"No, she is my wife," said Baghwan.

"I tell you she is my wife!" said the man.

Baghwan's rival did not waste more words, but rushed off to the police station, where he was promptly locked up and told to pay ten rupees if he wanted to get out. He sent for the money and then Baghwan and the disputed wife were summoned. Baghwan was taken aside and asked how much he was willing to pay. "Nothing," said Baghwan. He could get another wife without any trouble and at no cost to himself. The woman was packed off with husband number one.

It did not occur to me until the next day to ask what was the matter with Baghwan's first wife. "Leprosy," the Ayah answered quite casually. "Her fingers are gone so she cannot cook any more." Though Baghwan was apparently free of infection, I thought it wiser to find another water carrier.

If I was somewhat startled at Baghwan's easy way of taking wives unto himself—Asgar told me that he had tried several—I was also startled to have Fakire ask me a few weeks later whether he should not get a divorce. Fakire was about twenty-five. He had a very pretty wife who lived at his parents' house, but she had been running away frequently in the past six years to an uncle in Nepal, just across the border. Her complaint was that she did not like living with Fakire's family. Now she had gone again, and Fakire asked earnestly whether he should fetch her back or refuse to have anything more to do with her and take another wife.

"What do your parents say?"

"Father says nothing, and Mother says, 'What can you do if the girl keeps on running away all the time?'"

I concluded to stay on the conservative side and advised Fakire to bring her back and give her at least one more chance.

Din Mohammed, when he took Jawahir's place in May, made up in cheerfulness, willingness, and honesty for all that he did not know and never learned about cooking. He, too, was married, but his wife lived in Tulsipur with her father, since he had no home to bring her to. His own parents had both died while he was a child. His wife was expecting a baby, he confided. He would be greatly pleased if it was a boy.

"Not if it is a girl?" I asked.

"No. A girl goes away to her husband's home and never comes back unless her husband beats her or does not give her food or clothes. There is much weeping when she goes and much weeping if she comes back. Also, a girl costs money. Her clothes and jewelry cost many rupees, and you have to pay many rupees to get her married. She earns nothing. But a son never leaves his father's house, and he is an asset and a comfort to the heart."

Some weeks later Din Mohammed, red-eyed, announced the birth of a daughter. "Everything comes from Allah," he said resignedly, and invited me to name her. I named her Raziya Begum, a good Mohammedan name signifying "patience."

Not long since, came a letter from Din Mohammed, disseminating the perfumed eloquence of the professional let-

ter writer, but behind the words I detect the friendly remembrance of his own simple heart.

MY GREAT HELPER DEAR MISS SAHIBA,

I am weaping why God departed me from you. My
whole family is grievously sad on account of your sweet
talking and kind action. Nothing but the photo of your
kindness and yourself comes to our mind. We all pray
to God about your long life and prosperity. We pray
to God to grant you success in every work and intention
of your life.

I salaam you with my folded hands. Tell my salaam
to your brothers, to your sister, to your father and
mother, and to the rest of your family. My wife
salaams you very eagerly and she says salaam to all
the members of your family. My daughter Raziya
Begum, whom you named, tells you a very loving
salaam. All my family make salaam to you and all your
family. We pray to God for your health and welfare.

Your well-wisher & faithful servant,

DIN MOHAMMED.

When Baghwan left, his place as water carrier was taken
by Jumai—whose name in translation means "Friday"—a
lean, concave man with pointed beard turning gray. Jumai
petitioned to combine the work of water carrier with that of
pulling the punka I had just installed and to draw double
salary. The punka, a heavy beam eight feet long with a
yard-deep green cloth flounce, hung from the center of the
living room. When pulled from outside by a leather cord
running through a hole over the door, it fanned the languid
air above my head as I sat at my table. I was afraid the
double work would be too much for Jumai, but the Ayah
pleaded for him, saying he had earned nothing for months
and was very poor, and he himself protested an insatiable
passion for work. I need not have feared. Jumai proved to
be the laziest man in Pachperwa.

He regularly went to sleep as he squatted on his little
mat on the veranda, knees hooked up to his chin. Every

twenty minutes the punka stopped swinging and I had to shout to wake him up. He did not keep the water tins clean. He was caught drawing the household water from a well known to have bad water, because it was a few steps nearer than the Tahsildar's good well. He left at noon for his food and did not come back until three, instead of two, while I suffocated during the hottest hours of the day. He was thriftless, greedy and dishonest. But there was something about the way he blinked his eyes as if to ward off the verbal blows of a scolding, about his disarming smile and his eager childlike expression, that made me forgive him for his many sins ten times a day. In the end I think I kept him just to see how bad a servant he could be.

Where he managed to put away all he confessed to eating I never could figure out. He was almost as thin as the sweeper. One morning after breakfast Din Mohammed and I fell to discussing the high cost of living. Din Mohammed said he himself ate a pound of rice a day, with curry, at a cost of five rupees a month. Half his salary went to his wife, and he had two and a half rupees left for spending money. The Ayah, he added, spent only three rupees a month; she was old and did not have to eat much. Jumai called from the veranda, "I eat more than eight rupees a month—two pounds of rice every day, a half pound of *dal* and sweets!" I suspected that this greediness—spending three dollars a month for food is extreme greediness in Pachperwa—was mere empty boasting, but I was not sure.

Jumai came from thriftless stock. His father, a dyer by caste, had given up his traditional work to become a tobacco dealer. When I told Jumai that he, too, was well acquainted with the tobacco business, he gave one of his joyous laughs. He was forever smoking a *chillum* filled with the rank weed cultivated in some of the village fields. Jumai's wife was dead, but he lived with a married brother who worked for the Sub-Inspector of Police. The brother, inappropriately named Godly, was equally thriftless, and the two of them together first ate up all their possessions and then ate up the house over their heads. Another villager was persuaded to let them share his house, but because they never paid any of the rent they had promised to pay he was always on the point of turning them out.

Jumai was the only one of the servants who repeatedly asked for an advance on his wages. When he put his hands together like a pleading child and told me he had not an anna for food, I could not resist him. In addition to what I gave him, he borrowed from Din Mohammed and the Ayah, and sometimes tradespeople came to collect from me the sums he had long been owing them but had not the slightest intention of paying.

Yet I came to believe he was not without some virtue. The Ayah told me that Khudai, the brother, often beat his wife and refused to feed her and her child. For eleven months, she said, Jumai had helped take care of her. I felt a spasm of guilt for having thought him worthless.

One afternoon Jumai came streaking down the road. He appeared at the door and breathlessly asked permission to go to the station and get his brother's wife. When Asgar told me a few minutes later that she was running away and Jumai wanted to catch her, I regretted having given the permission. It seemed to me I ought to support the woman's movement in Pachperwa. Back came Jumai, driving the woman in front of him with a little switch. She was carrying a three-year-old child in her arms. Tearfully she told me that Khudai had been beating her again and pulled up her short jacket to show some marks. Pointing to certain blemishes on Jumai's stretched skin, she said the brother beat him, too. She begged me to let her spend the night at my house to avoid another beating. Before long Khudai arrived on the scene, and I became vaguely aware of trouble flowing out from the servants' house. When the quarreling threatened to arouse the neighborhood, I summoned all three of them into my stern presence.

She ate too much, said the brother, and talked bad language besides. She ate a rupee's worth of food every day!

When pressed, he acknowledged that his monthly salary at the police station was seven rupees. His salary and Jumai's together did not equal the amount he said his wife consumed. Jumai here put in that Khudai gave her nothing whatever. I looked at Khudai as severely as I could, and, properly cowed, he fell at my feet imploring me to say nothing of his marital differences to the Sub-Inspector. He promised never to beat his wife again, and she on her part promised to refrain from abusive language. The trio departed in amicable accord.

Then a bomb dropped out of the sky. The Peshkar, to whom I described the incident, said the real reason of the friction was known to the entire village. Jumai and his brother simply shared one wife between them. "Jumai's case is especially bad," added Din Mohammed, "because Jumai is the elder brother." Jumai's excuse was that his own wife had died years before and he was too poor to provide himself with another. His poverty, however, did not excuse him in the eyes of the village. Both Hindu and Mohammedan custom forbids polyandry.

A few days later, as Jumai was pulling the punka cord, I noticed that he was crying mildly. He murmured something about "No money to buy clothes," but I pretended not to hear. He had a way of making remarks in a low contemplative tone, as if thinking aloud to himself. The remarks followed a fixed pattern: "Hungry. No food to-day. Not one anna in the house. Not a Bania willing to give me credit. If the *sirkar* would only give me eight annas!"

Din Mohammed, clearing the breakfast table, volunteered the news that the wife's baby had died the preceding night. I felt distinctly shocked. When I had seen it only three or four days before, it had appeared quite well.

"Why did you not tell me the baby was sick?" I asked Jumai.

"We didn't know it was," he replied simply.

The sniffs resolved themselves into a bleak statement that there was no money for clothes—funeral clothes for the baby. "They will cost twelve annas, but where are we to get twelve annas?" I gave him a rupee and told him to go home for the day.

"Whose baby was it?" I asked Din Mohammed. "Khudai's or Jumai's?"

"Not Jumai's and not Khudai's. She used to be married to a man in Balrampur. It was his baby," Din Mohammed replied.

Jumai came back while I was having tea, looking thinner than ever, if such a thing were possible. He had obviously been crying. To give him the relief of talking, I asked him if the funeral was over and if everything had gone off properly. "The tailor charged one rupee, eight annas," he burst out indignantly. "He refused to make the clothes for less." He had given one rupee, all he had, promising to pay the extra eight annas later. There were other expenses, too. Charity had to be dispensed at the grave, and twenty *fakirs* had been fed. "Four annas' worth of rice, four annas of wheat, two of dal, four of sweets," he enumerated, "and four annas to the Hindu who dug the grave."

The family thought of raising the funeral money by begging an anna here, an anna there, after the village fashion in time of distress, but Jumai stood firm. "No," he said, "the sirkar gave one rupee. Nobody else shall give anything. I myself will pay the rest from my own wages." And the Banias, relenting in this moment of affliction, advanced the necessaries on credit. Of course I gave Jumai enough to cover the deficit, but knowing his weakness I suggested he had better hurry back to the village and settle with his creditors at once.

Jumai took pains to tell me the next day that the Sub-Inspector had not given Khudai anything to help toward the funeral. As it happened, the Sub-Inspector called that same evening, and in the course of conversation the death of our respective servants' wife's baby was mentioned. "Oh, yes, I gave Khudai two rupees for funeral expenses," said the police officer casually. The wife herself came to the house two days later. When I told her how sorry I was about the baby, she cried a little and then mentioned that she had had to sell a sari for one rupee to raise the money required besides the rupee Jumai had contributed through me. Some questioning soon brought out the fact that Jumai had given only the first rupee; the brother, nothing. Each of them, it appeared, had invested two rupees in a private gorging of sweets. Thus does life wind its tortuous course where stomachs are empty.

One other portrait remains to be drawn, that of Ram Lakhan. One night I was stretched out in a long wicker chair while the Ayah sat beside me, telling me with pride how her grandmother had been foster nurse to an illegitimate son of the Maharaja's grandfather, by a Mohammedan concubine. Suddenly we heard a boy's loud caroling on the road. I suggested that she go fetch the singer. Off she went and plucked Ram Lakhan out of the dark into the lamplight of the Happy House. He had on a dirty dhoti and ragged jacket, but a pair of silver bracelets, two little gold earrings and a talisman necklace gave him social respectability. His face was distinctly his own. He had a well formed little nose, full curved lips in the classical tradition of the Ajanta frescoes, and slightly protuberant, large brown eyes. He was eleven, but a vague, childish roundness still lingered in his face.

Another boy was with him, also a singer, but the second boy's voice was ordinary, where Ram's set the heartstrings vibrating. The two of them sat on my floor and in turn sang me their repertoire, Ram accompanying his friend by slapping his bare leg and making a peculiar clicking sound in imitation of a drum. One of Ram's songs was of Sita, the heroine of the *Ramayana* close to the Hindu heart, though Rama reigned at Ayodya some three thousand years ago. "Why do you banish me from your presence without fault? If fault unknowingly I have committed, let me be forgiven. Let your light not be withdrawn from me, O my Lord," Sita's cry rang forth on Ram Lakhan's lips.

Then again the wailing refrain, "Why do you banish me without fault?"

Rama's namesake said he was the son of the temple gardener in the New Bazar. He also informed me that he could read a little Hindi, having once gone to school for a few weeks, but that his father objected to his attending school, tore up his books, and broke his ink bottle.

I knew the gardener well. Two gold studs hammered into his upper front teeth indicated that he had unusual foresight. They were to pay his passage across the river of death. A bit of gold for this purpose, purifying *tulsi* leaves, and holy Ganges water are customarily placed in the mouth of a dead Hindu just before his cremation. At first I had felt flattered by the necklaces of fragrant bela flowers and rosebuds the temple *Mali* brought me every day. When I perceived that they were merely an excuse for extracting annas, I told him he need not trouble to bring any more necklaces. After this he did not come oftener than twice a week.

Feeling that I might effectively bring my now ponderable influence to bear in the matter of getting Ram back to school, I sent a message requesting the Mali to come to see me the following evening. Garland in hand, he arrived promptly. The Jamadar, also present, remarked that Ram was born in the island of Trinidad. Had the Mali been in Trinidad, I asked in surprise. No, said the Jamadar, he was not his father's son. "He means," explained the Peshkar, "that Ram's mother was a corrupted lady."

The Mali's objection about letting Ram go to school was that the teachers made the boys do personal work for them. In addition, Ram was bad. He ran away from home and had fights with other boys. It seemed to me that most of his crimes could probably be traced to lack of outlet for an active spirit, but I looked appropriately grave. Mollified, the Mali said Ram could go to school if he wished. So it was settled. Ram was to go to school. Outside of school hours, to keep him out of mischief, he was to become assistant punka puller to Jumai. Ram on his side promised to stay at home nights and not run away any more.

At six o'clock the very next morning, I myself took Ram Lakhan across the road and duly entered him in the Pachperwa elementary school on payment of a fee of one anna. Three more annas outfitted him with the cap requisite for school attendance, a reed pen, chalk for making white ink to write on his black school-board and a new ink bottle. From this time on, Ram stopped every morning on his way to school to present me with a loose handful of flowers from the temple garden. When school was over at eleven, he relieved Jumai at punka pulling or ran errands. He was happy as the days were long.

The buttonless jacket—nothing but holes loosely tied together with bits of frayed cloth—in which he had first appeared, was rolled up and tossed down the side of my hill with a magnificent gesture. He now wore one of the white shirts Dowdhe the tailor had made for him and a clean new dhoti. His first earnings, like Asgar's, went to the purchase of a pair of shoes. Shoes, in the eyes of villagers, are a mark of social distinction. Nine tenths of the villagers go barefoot, too poor to dream of shoes. Ram Lakhan's widetoed, untrammeled feet had never yet been imprisoned in leather. At the end of the first day he began to limp; at the second two big blisters appeared on his heels and he could scarcely hobble. Still he could not bear to part with his precious shoes, pride outweighing agony of the flesh. It was only my temporary confiscation of the shoes that gave his feet a chance to get well.

One morning Ram unexpectedly appeared at my screened door accompanied by a woman dressed in a yellow sari. "Huzur, this is my mother," he announced. I had not met Ram's mother before. She looked about thirty. Her mouth was red with *pan* juice. Yes, Ram was born in Trinidad, she said in a composed voice, but he was only two months old when she had brought him to India. Without any particular embarrassment, she added that his father lived in

Itiathok, a village some distance away in another tahsil of the Balrampur Estate. Her own husband lived in Pipra. Just who the Mali was in whose house she and Ram resided in Pachperwa was not altogether clear. In any case, she complained that on many days the Mali provided no food. Insincere tears began to flow as she insisted that often she had to beg food for herself and Ram. Since she was wearing a gold nose ring, several heavy bracelets of silver, and a much finer sari than the average village woman, her case did not seem as desperate as she made out.

The real purpose of her visit presently came to light. She had heard in the village that I was intending to take Ram Lakhan back to America with me. She had come to ask me not to do so, because he was married! The ceremony had taken place three years before, when Ram was eight. The child wife was still in her parents' house in Nepal, and, according to custom, would not join her husband for some years. When I asked Ram how old she was, he answered, "Little! So big!" He held his hand out about three and a half feet from the ground. It was hard for me to contemplate Ram as a married man.

Punka pulling very soon ceased to be the enthralling business of the first few days. Jumai fell asleep at the end of twenty minutes; Ram ran off to get a drink and several times forgot to come back. He asked if he could not come inside the house and fan me instead with a long-handled bazar fan. Inside were many things that fascinated him, chief among them my Pixie phonograph, or "fornograph," as he called it. Though foreign music was strange, Ram liked it, particularly the loud records of Caruso. After watching me once or twice, he learned to crank and start the machine and could be trusted to run it by himself.

Then he had countless things he was bursting to tell— how, for instance, he was a master hand at making *moras*. Moras are crowns worn by bridegrooms, often made of flowers. Ram made his of paper. It is the flower-gardening caste which has the exclusive privilege of making moras, and this would be his occupation, Ram said, when he grew up. Casting his eyes on some old Allahabad *Leaders*, he asked if he might have them for his crowns. In a few days he produced his latest masterpiece, a glory of scarlet and green paper flowers in festoons a yard long.

A thoughtful friend at home, convinced that necessaries as well as luxuries must be lacking in my Indian village, had tucked several packets of needles into a letter. Though needles could be bought in Pachperwa, these were much finer than any in the bazar. I distributed packets as *bakshish* to the intimate household—one to the Ayah, one to the Mehtarani, one to Asgar Ali's mother, and one to his sister. Presently I heard a small voice coming through the window. "Huzur, *sui?*"—"Great One, a needle?" begged Ram, nose pressed flat against the screen.

"But what do you want with needles? You cannot sew."

"Oh, yes," he replied eagerly, "I can! I can sew buttons, and I can also sew on the tailor's foreign machine. Come and see!" So Ram the button sewer also received a packet of American needles.

"When you go away, huzur, I shall cry for four months," he remarked pensively by way of thanks.

One of Ram's tasks was to stand by, while I was making my elephant mural decoration, and hold the bowl of water for the brushes. After finishing the elephants and giving them a carpet of red flowers to trample, I saw that the three windows in the wall were in need of Mogul borders. I began with Din Mohammed's window at the north end of the house. Ram was standing beside me one morning as usual. His face was turned inward against the whitewashed surface of the wall. He remained strangely silent. At last I asked him what the trouble was. "Everybody calls me *chor*," he said, ungluing his face from the wall. Two big tears balanced on the ends of his eyelashes and rolled down his cheeks.

I knew well enough why he was being called a thief. A tobacco seller of the village, a member of Asgar's theatrical troupe, had given into Asgar's custody a broken silver watch on the chance that somebody of my household, going to Balrampur, would take it along to be mended. Asgar had had the watch in his keeping for ten days. Suddenly it vanished. Ram Lakhan was known to have gazed admiringly upon it twice, and Ram Lakhan, who had also learned to tell time, was known to envy Asgar the possession of a watch above all other things. Asgar openly accused him of the theft.

"Did you take the watch?" I asked, intent on a green leaf I was painting.

He assured me he had not, had never taken anything from me or mine, never in his life taken anything from anybody! Tears fell thick and fast. I called the other servants. Unless guilt could be proved, I announced, no one in my house was to call another a thief. Asgar, unshaken in his belief that Ram was the culprit, flayed him alive with his eyes. The next day Ram Lakhan did not come to pull the punka or hold the bowl or run any errands. Three days passed, and still Ram did not turn up. I thought it was the heat that made time drag. Then I realized that I was missing his morning gift of bela flowers, his piping, his contagious enthusiasm, his comments on life, men, and events in Pachperwa. I sent the Ayah to fetch him back.

Very dirty, hands rose-red from dyeing *Leaders* to make bridegrooms' crowns, he came. There was a wistful break in his voice as he explained his absence. Asgar was thinking all the time that he was a thief. He could not stay in a place where such unjust thoughts of him were held. The Ayah had also brought with her a material witness, a boy whom Asgar quoted as saying he had met Ram Lakhan with the watch. No, said the small boy, he had not seen Ram Lakhan with the watch. He had heard that Ram Lakhan had stolen a watch. Who in Pachperwa had not heard the news, broadcast by Asgar? But if Asgar said he had seen Ram with the watch, then Asgar was lying. Asgar's eyes were fixed on infinite space, and somehow he had the look of having lied. In the opinion of the *panchayat*, consisting of the Ayah, the barber Dukhi, and me, proof of Ram's guilt was not established, and the case was dismissed. Five minutes later Ram was sitting contentedly on his little mat, making currents of hot air blow all the papers off my desk. The mystery of the watch remained unsolved.

One trouble was no sooner settled than Ram Lakhan's complex fate dealt him another blow. A week later, as he was pulling the punka in the afternoon and singing lustily, he stopped abruptly, having just remembered something. "There was no food at my house to-day," he remarked. The temple Mali saw no reason to supply Ram with food when Ram was earning money of his own, and he had also refused Ram's mother anything. "He cooks his own food by himself and eats it alone at the temple," Ram concluded. Then he went off with the annas I gave him to the bazar.

The next day he seemed less gay than usual. He announced that his mother was going away to Pipra tahsil, where her husband was. The Mali had told Ram if he came near his house any more he would beat him. "I keep thinking," said Ram, "who is going to give me any food? This it is that I keep thinking."

I knew, but a Hindu could not eat with my Mohammedan servants. I felt certain the Peshkar would board Ram for me, but I had to ask him. Meanwhile I reminded Ram of his gift of song. "You can sing sweetly. When things are not right, try not to cry. Sing!"

The clouds were still low the following morning. Ram set himself to cleaning up brick chips beside the new channel for distributing the bath water to the parched lawn. With a gulp, he unburdened his heart. His mother was about to depart. His Pipra father had said he would tear off his necklace and bracelets and choke him if he ever came back there. His Mali father said the only food he would get at his house would be a good beating. His Itiathok father did not care what happened to him. Life looked very black at that moment to Ram Lakhan. "I can't sing now. I am hungry," he wailed. But when I told him the Peshkar had agreed to give him two good meals every day, and that it must be time now for one of them, a little of his old buoyancy came back.

All went smoothly for a brief space. A bed was procured for Ram and placed between the Ayah's and Asgar's, in the veranda of the servants' house. He ate with the Peshkar's cook, a kindly old man who took an interest in him. Even for Ram's future, I thought, a solution had presented itself. Dr. Saxena, the Indian district health officer who made periodic visits to Pachperwa, told me he would take Ram and train him for medical work if Ram wanted to come to Gonda after I left. "I can learn English if I go to Gonda!" said Ram enthusiastically, calculating the advantages of the medical profession against those of making flower crowns for bridegrooms. Then once more unexpected forces were brought to bear in the swift small drama of his life. During morning prayers at school something queer happened to his legs. He fell down. As soon as he got up he fell down again, and the teacher sent him to me with a temperature of 103 degrees.

All day Ram lay on his bed, sleeping heavily. Now was Asgar's moment of triumph. He perched on the edge of Ram's bed, and whenever Ram tossed and opened his eyes, Asgar leaned forward and whispered that a *shaitan*, an evil spirit, had surely clutched him. He was to be punished at last for having stolen the watch. The evil spirit did not loosen its hold, and for five days Ram burned with fever.

Fakire returned from Pipra, where tahsil business chanced to take him, reporting that Ram Lakhan's mother, too, was ill. She wanted to see him because she thought she was going to die and before her death she wished to give him her jewelry. Ram dragged himself from his bed, begging me to send him to his mother. I suggested that we send a messenger instead, to find out exactly how she was, but Ram was not satisfied. "Look in your books and see how my mother is," he kept urging. "The books must tell." Surely I knew as much as the pundits, and I ought to be

able to cast the stars and trace the secret course of events!
The Tahsildar advised me to let him go, and with a peon
from the tahsil he started out at four the next morning,
ill as he was, to walk the sixteen miles to Pipra.

Six weeks passed. From time to time I heard that, though
his mother had recovered, Ram was still ill, that he lay all
day on his bed, too weak to get up. In Pipra there was no
doctor and no possibility of getting any medical aid. Twice
I sent word to his mother that if she would bring Ram back
to Pachperwa, I would gladly pay for a palanquin to fetch
him. At last one day came the news that she and Ram had
arrived in the bazar. She was telling people she had consulted a Tharu witch woman, and the witch woman had
found out the cause of Ram's sickness. I had put a curse on
him. How else explain a lingering fever—which might
possibly have been called typhoid in English? I had no
children of my own. Everybody knew my fondness for Ram.
The evidence was conclusive.

Ram's mother came to collect the four rupees for the
palanquin bearers, and Ram, too, paid me a call, very thin,
his cheeks still hot to the touch. After the verdict of the
witch doctor I felt I was walking on precarious ground. If
anything happened to Ram I knew I should be held responsible. Perhaps it would be better for him to stay at the
house of the Mali with his mother. "But there is no bed in
the Mali's house," his mother remarked insinuatingly. So
Ram's bed was duly sent after him.

Gradually Ram Lakhan grew better, but he never again
returned to pull the punka at the Happy House. He was
just well enough to come to the station to say good-bye on
the day I left the village forever. "Don't forget about Dr.
Saxena in Gonda," I called out to him. "No," said Ram
listlessly. But I knew that Ram Lakhan would not go to
Gonda.

CHAPTER IV

Doctoring without a License

Nobody can live in an Indian village and escape seeing the terrible misery to which the flesh of the villager has fallen heir. Sanitation and medical science, as developed in the past century by Western genius, are unknown here. Armed only with credulity, the villager wages constant and heartrending battle against diseases which are chiefly the result of conditions he cannot control, such as climate, or cannot change by himself, such as poverty and ignorance.

Before I had been a week in Pachperwa, I had to answer, however inadequately, a call for help. Without previous training or qualification I became a "doctor" overnight, ministering as best I could to sick villagers, along with the white-haired *Babuji* of the dispensary, with barbers who are traditionally the rural surgeons of India, herdsmen who act as bone setters, itinerant quacks who offer cure-alls of dried leaves and powdered roots, pundits who recite Sanskrit texts, beggars, calling themselves holy, who profess to heal by laying on of hands, and sorcerers who chant mystical spells and proffer charms. I was something new and might as well be tried as any of these. My services cost nothing. Most important, I stood for that vague but powerful force known as Western civilization.

The climate is particularly bad in the Tarai, along the base of the Himalaya, where the plain lies less than four hundred feet above sea level. During half the year, the tropical heat causes the rapid growth of many kinds of bacteria and at the same time reduces physical energy. The slope of the land is so slight that the heavy rainfall of the mountains turns the whole region into a lake for three months. As the water subsides innumerable swamps and jhils are left behind. In the Gonda district these cover a sixth of the total area. At all times of the year water is everywhere close to the surface. Conditions like these inevitably spell malaria. In the region immediately touching the forests no one but the apparently feverproof Tharus can survive at all. The whole Tarai population are chronic sufferers from malaria, contributing a high quota toward the 1,300,000 deaths conservatively estimated as the annual malarial toll for India.

The unparalleled poverty means undernourishment for millions upon millions. Between thirty and forty of these millions are said to be perpetually on the verge of starvation. Taking the population as a whole, food consumption proportionately equals in quantity only one third that of the people of the United States. But the quality, too, is infinitely poorer, lacking in both variety and in nutrition. Rice is the chief product of the Tarai, but even this is a luxury. Many who cannot afford rice live entirely on pulses. Milk is beyond the means of most. In the district where I lived, 526 people to the square mile, 750 if uninhabited forest was excluded, were trying to subsist on agriculture or the occupations immediately connected with it. Lack of resistance to disease and no recuperative reserve were inevitable. Poverty explains why the people cannot have mosquito nets and why, to a very great degree, they live under unspeakably insanitary conditions in rural India.

Ignorance is another chief cause of sickness. The villagers do not know that dust and flies carry disease. They do not know the connection between stagnant water and mosquitoes and malaria. They do not understand that trachoma is infectious. They have no idea that a leper is of any danger to the community. They do not associate polluted wells or streams with cholera or typhoid. They are ignorant that their way of disposing of human waste spreads the hookworm from which 80 per cent of them are suffering. They find no connection between the number of infant deaths and the time-honored methods of their mid-wives. Knowledge of this sort is comparatively new, even in the West. How are poor Indian villagers to be expected to possess it unless those who know pass it on to them?

In the many decades that Oudh has now been under Eng-lish administration, since its annexation by the East India Company, many improvements have naturally been carried out. Yet it is apparently easier to build roads and construct railways and telegraphs and put down lawlessness and carry out land surveys and legislate for improvement in the posi-tion of tenant farmers than to protect the health of people, raise their standard of living, or educate them. From the medical point of view, the outstanding accomplishment has been the handling of epidemics. But epidemics are the excep-tion, and under normal times and conditions, the health problem remains unsolved. The reason is not far to seek. The sums available for rural medical work are pitifully inadequate. For general sanitation in our area, the district health officer said there was an expenditure amounting to a sixth of a cent a year per head of the rural population, and this figure, as I understood it, included the salaries of sanitation officers. By way of contrast, out of the total funds available to the government, normal expenditure for military purposes is more than ten times that for medical relief and public health.

When the Indian villagers first began coming to me with infected fingers or sore eyes I acted on the assumption that disinfectants and cleanliness at least could do no harm. I washed clean cuts with iodine and dirty ones with lysol or permanganate of potassium solution and bound the wounds with clean gauze. When mothers brought babies whose eyes were infected, I put a few drops of boric water in the eyes and told the mothers to keep washing them with warm water and the cotton I gave them, and to bring the babies back for more drops until their eyes were well. But matters did not rest here.

Villagers believe in miracles. They immediately transformed me into a miracle worker, and my reputation spread over the tahsil and east through the surrounding countryside into Basti and Gorakhpur districts and north into Nepal. More and more people came, bringing more and more serious illnesses for me to cure. When I told them I was not a doctor and that they must go to the Babuji at the free dispensary, they stubbornly insisted, "The Babuji does not give good medicine to poor people like us." When I tried to persuade someone in need of expert attention to make the short journey to the hospital at Balrampur or at Gonda, the answer was: "How can I go to Balrampur? Who will prepare my husband's food or take care of my children while I am gone?" Or, "There is much work to be done in the fields, sirkar." The final argument to every assertion of incapacity to help on my part was always the same. "But we have heard your name. We have been told that you will give us good medicine. Six *kos* have we walked to come to you. *Bahut garib admi.* We are very poor, sirkar."

The appeal of human suffering and helplessness had to be met somehow. My medical library was contained in one small volume, *A Medical Guide for Non-Medical Missionaries,* presented to me in Allahabad by the author, Dr. Douglas N. Forman of Ewing Christian College and the Naini Agricultural Institute. I laid in a stock of simple medicines and dressings from Lucknow and gratefully accepted others donated by Dr. Saxena. One of the three rooms of the Happy House was converted into a supply room. The east veranda became my "office," where from half-past six until half-past ten or eleven every morning men, women, and children presented themselves for treatment.

As the sky reddened behind the black trees, I would be waked by low voices. From my bed on the lawn I could make out a group of women standing a little way off, watching me intently. One flicker of the eyelids, and they would press forward murmuring, "Great suffering!" while one held out an ulcerated arm or leg for me to see through the mosquito net. They were not supposed to come so early, and they were not supposed to come around to the north side of the house so long as I was in bed. Shuffling to my rescue the Ayah would shout angrily: "Is Miss Sahiba your father's servant? Go and wait on the east side of the house!"

When I appeared on the veranda, fifty or even a hundred people would be squatting about there and on the lawn. Mingled with the sick were ordinary beggars. All would crowd up at once. "My stomach aches very much." "I see very little, as if smoke came in front of my eyes." "Huzur, look at my sore leg." "I have a very bad cough, huzur." It did not take long for me to acquire a comprehensive medical vocabulary.

With the aid of Asgar Ali and the Ayah I first set about clearing the veranda and sorting out obvious cases for which I knew I could do nothing. These I directed to go elsewhere. Then I administered pills, castor oil, argyrol, ointments, bandages, or advice. In the pitiful procession filing across my veranda day after day, I was brought face to face with fevers of every kind, goiter, dropsy, rheumatism, tuberculosis, anemia, smallpox, leprosy, dysentery, jaundice, endless stomach complaints, broken bones, syphilis, epilepsy, insanity, cuts and abrasions, boils and abscesses, skin diseases, blood poisoning, worms of every variety, rickets, scorpion and dog bites, trachoma and every other known eye trouble.

The most difficult thing to face was the childish faith of nearly everybody that I could, if only I would, cure anything—with one pill or a single dose of something. A thousand times did I point out that I was not a doctor, that I was very ignorant about their sicknesses. Oh, no, I was merely displeased for some reason! Patiently the victim would tell me all over again that he was very poor, that he had come far, that he suffered much. I think every blind person for a hundred miles around came and looked up at me with straining blank eyes, asking hopefully to be made to see. "I have medicine for red eyes," I would say as gently as I could, "but not white eyes. I can do nothing for white eyes." There was not much change of expression. The old man or woman, led by a son or daughter, or the young mother with her blind baby, would go on sitting there under the tree for a minute or two, giving me a chance to relent and change my decision. Then the Ayah or someone else near by would repeat like an echo, "No medicine for white eyes!" and finally add, "*Jao!*"—"Go!" In the silence that followed I could feel the pain of somebody's disappointment, as if I had betrayed a precious trust.

Many cases of cataract presented themselves. With an air of perfect confidence I assured scores of old people that if they would only go to the hospital at Balrampur or Gonda, the doctor there, who was very clever, would make a little cut without hurting them at all, take out the "curtain" inside their eyes, and restore their sight within a week. The dread of the villager for any sort of operation was too strong to permit his seeking the only method of possible relief. I recall only a single exception.

I was sitting alone late one evening, in the open space in front of my house commonly called the *maidan*. A gentle murmuring under the trees beside the shrine attracted my attention. When I asked who was speaking a voice answered: "We have come from our village of Gainsari because of the child's eyes, but we are late. We are spending the night here under the trees. In the morning we shall ask if medicine can be given." I invited the owner of the voice to approach, and an elderly peasant stepped out of the shadows followed by a young woman and a boy. While the grandfather, who said he belonged to the herdsman caste, was telling how the boy, now eight, had been blind from birth, the little fellow put out his hands and began to feel the canvas steamer chair in which I was sitting.

"What is this, *Dada?*" he asked.

"It is the chair of the sirkar, child," answered the grandfather.

"I want a chair like this," the child insisted softly.

"But who can make you such a chair?"

"You can make it for me, Dada!"

I drew him to the lantern light without hope. There, unexpectedly, I saw the two opaque white spots in the eye centers, signifying cataract. I explained to the grandfather that the "big doctor" at Gonda might be able to cure the boy. I promised him a personal letter to the Doctor Sahib and three rupees for train fare and food. To my great delight, he said they would take the early morning train. The son was dead and this little grandson was all he had left. The Ayah offered to share her bed with the Hindu mother and child. Rolling himself up in his sheet, the grandfather lay down beside them on the hard ground.

Some days later I heard from Dr. Jaensch, civil surgeon at Gonda. It was a case of congenital cataract, he wrote, but he had been able, by a needling process, to bring partial vision to one eye. If the grandfather would be patient and would bring the boy back to Gonda again after the first eye had healed, he hoped to operate with equal success on the second eye.

Most of the blindness, if it is not syphilitic in origin, is the result of infection and might easily be prevented. My preaching on the necessity for immediate care in all cases of eye infection soon began to bear fruit. Occasionally even late at night loud groans drew me to the veranda, to find someone there clutching a filthy rag to a flaming eyeball. The eye cases were especially prevalent during the hot weather, when the dust blows constantly, but after five days or a week of argyrol or silver nitrate, with several daily washings of boric or salt solution, most of them cleared up satisfactorily. But old cases of trachoma were much too difficult and stubborn to yield to my inexperienced treatment.

One day I received a note in English from a Mohammedan tutor in a wealthy family of East Bargadwa, two miles beyond Pachperwa. "The bearer who is my friend is carrying his only son before your honor for the eye inspection, which has been caused by the smallpox a week ago," I read. "Kindly administer the medicine if you can or advise for treatment." (Smallpox is another very common source of blindness.) I put a drop of weak argyrol in each of the baby's eyes and told the father to bring him back the following day. The next morning the man was there, squatting in front of the veranda with the child in his arms. When I looked at its eyes I saw that they were dead, like gray stones! I felt so weak I could not speak or move. The baby's eyes had only been watering a little the day before, and the terrible thought flashed into my mind that in some way I had blinded him. While I was still standing over the child, speechless, I heard the father saying, "He has not seen for fourteen months." What a sense of heavenly relief flowed from those otherwise painful words! Of course I had mistaken another father and baby for the pair of the day before.

Two groups of patients I found particularly difficult— those who returned day after day with old incurable ills for which I had already told them I could do nothing, and those who, when told to let me see them again, said they had a long way to come and it was much trouble. If I said I was unable to treat stomach aches of five years' standing or coughs of long duration, members of the first group immediately insisted they had had the ache only five months or five days, the cough only since Wednesday. If it was a case of "white eyes" that could not be cured, they asked for medicine for pain in the back instead. The other class seemed utterly unconscious of the seriousness of a given condition. Many a baby with running ears I saw once and never again. Infected fingers swollen to three times their natural size and needing most careful attention received but a single dressing. Another supreme difficulty was the matter of diet. Directions about swallowing pills and powders were easy to give, easy to understand and easy to follow. But when a mother brought a baby wasted with diarrhea or dysentery and I tried to explain that for twenty-four hours it must have nothing but water and afterwards milk at half strength for several days, she would reply that, if she did not feed it when it was hungry, the baby would cry. To her, the idea of being a good mother simply meant giving her child plenty to eat and, to the best of her limited ability, trying to make it happy.

One of my irritatingly amusing problems had to do with bottles. It was impossible to keep enough bottles on hand for dispensing washes and liniments. Also, though I wrote to Lucknow, I was unable to secure any wax paper for ointments. The ointment difficulty was solved by using leaves from a neighboring banian tree, picked fresh by Asgar Ali every morning. But the bottles caused trouble to the end. Like the Doctor, I finally insisted that a patient must supply his own bottle. He always began by protesting that he did not know where to find a bottle. He knew very well that he could get a dirty one in the bazar for a quarter of a cent and a clean one for from two to four cents, but naturally he did not want to part with a precious pie. When I remained obdurate, he would depart reluctantly to fetch a bottle. The one he brought was invariably too small or too big, and always black inside. I would ask him to clean it. Three times he would return with it dirty, and each time I would instruct him to put sand and water in and shake until the bottle was clean. Finally, in despair, I would accept it and rinse it with boiling water from the kettle I kept heated on the veranda.

In the first weeks of my medical practice, a great many Hindus objected on caste principles to using my spoons, glasses, or water. I used to say at once: "Are you Hindu? Then bring your own cup and water." Later I learned that in the case of medicine an exception to caste rules has now been generally recognized. Anybody who goes to a hospital is required to use the hospital appliances. Much time was lost waiting for a man to go off and get his own spoon or *lota* of water, or borrow one from somebody of his own caste. So I just appeared with my kitchen tablespoon of castor oil and poured it down the man's throat before he had time to think about it. Objections soon died down. In one point I had to give in. Although I was very careful to produce a bottle of alcohol and wash my thermometer after use in the presence of everybody, Hindus frequently resisted having it put in their mouths. Even Ram Lakhan used to spit energetically each time I thrust the mercury bulb under his tongue.

On account of their caste prejudices, Hindus on the whole were more difficult to deal with than Mussulmans. But during the month of Ramazan, the Mussulmans suddenly presented a new front. Very few would let anything pass their lips until after sunset. It was a novel thought that a religious fast had to include quinine or salts, and that, for this reason, fever or severe colic must be endured without relief until the sun went down.

By the time I had cleaned up my medicine shelves and washed my hands for the twentieth time, I felt as if I had done a strenuous day's work, though it was only eleven. I was quite ready to go inside and have breakfast, cooling off a little under Jumai's manipulation of the punka. But in spite of an effort on my part to keep the rest of the day free, people continued coming for help at all hours. Often there were urgent cases, not to be postponed.

It was quite usual for me to hear the servants, who were not particularly enthusiastic about my clinic, driving late comers away. The Ayah's shrill tones echoed vociferously and then unexpectedly died down one May evening. She called out that I had better look at this case. A man had brought a small daughter in a terrible condition. She had fallen and cut her hand, completely severing the third finger and very nearly severing the second as well. The poor little hand held up for my inspection was so mangled that I urged the father to take her quickly to the dispensary, assuring him that the Babuji would know how to dress it much better than I. "We have just come from the dispensary, but Babuji only said: 'The dispensary is closed now. Come back in the morning!'" was his answer. I sent for a bowl of hot water, fetched the alcohol bottle and some cotton, steeled my nerves, and by lantern light set to work. Never in my life, I think, have I seen bravery equal to that nameless Indian child's! She did not cry out once nor even wince. She kept her eyes fixed on her severed fingers with a mournful, drawn look and even tried to help by spreading them apart. When I had to cut away the torn flesh, I begged her not to look. The father quickly threw her sari over her face and pressed her little head tight against his breast. Still no sound came from her. Who teaches such courage? God—or generations of self-immolating mothers? Of such stuff were the Indian *satis* of old.

The father had saved the fragment of finger and now produced it out of a dirty cloth. I had not the faintest idea whether it could be made to grow back in place. Quite suddenly, with a wave of anger, I recalled the Doctor, whom I had been too busy to think about for twenty minutes. "We are now going straight to the dispensary," I announced. The father picked up the little girl, and Asgar, carrying a lantern, led the procession down the hill.

The Doctor was sitting on the well curb with the inspector of roads and the four school teachers, singing college songs or Vedic hymns—I did not care which just then. Would he trouble himself to come and look at a serious accident case? I inquired. Affably enough, he unlocked the dispensary room, brought out his cleansing apparatus, washed the child's hand very thoroughly, threw away the useless soft little finger tip I had been cherishing, and made a neat bandage. When my ire cooled I remembered that the Doctor was not at all hard-hearted, very far from it. But in thirty-eight years of village practice he had seen so much suffering he had grown used to it. There was always pain, always distress to be alleviated, and he was entitled to some hours of rest. Probably in this instance he simply had not looked at the child's hand at all, or he would have cared for it on his own account—not merely because of my asking.

I could not see that Indian parents were any less concerned over a sick girl than a sick boy. Many times a particularly touching devotion to little daughters was revealed to me. Once agonized screams abruptly terminated the performance of a stray juggler who had stopped at the house. Another child was deposited on the veranda. This time the father and mother by turns, starting at four o'clock in the morning from their village in Basti district, had carried their nine-year-old daughter the whole twenty-four dusty miles. For eight days, they said, at intervals of three or four hours, she had been having attacks of violent pain. Nothing they could do gave her any relief. Finally a peon of our tahsil happened to visit their village and went to their house to get a drink. It was he who had suggested bringing her to me.

I administered a dose of salts, while the poor little thing struggled and screamed, bit her father's fingers when he forced her mouth open, and held her breath until I was afraid she would strangle. Then, worn out, she unexpectedly fell asleep. The mother sat down under the trees and drew the slender little body across her knees, pillowing the head upon her lap. While we waited for the salts to take effect I asked if there were other children.

"There were two more, but they are dead. Only this daughter is left," said the mother.

"But this daughter is worth more to us than seven sons to another," said the father quickly. Oh, the anxiety not to fail those who had placed the life of a daughter worth more than seven sons in my ignorant hands!

Luckily the trouble passed, or seemed to, and at the end of three days the herdsman and his wife and their precious daughter returned to their village. I never knew, on occasions of this sort, whether the assistance I gave had any permanent value. I did not see these people again.

Besides the hundreds of ailing folk who came to my house, I saw numbers of others in their own homes. Whenever I walked about the village a dozen people beckoned me to come inside and see somebody who was sick. Occasionally I was requested to go to another village, for some *purdah* woman unable to come to me. When I urged these women to go to the *zenana* hospital at Balrampur, where they could be properly treated by a woman doctor and nurses, I soon learned I was wasting breath. There they continued to lie, pallid and suffering, in their dark airless rooms. And two or three months later I would hear that the wife of Ram the goldsmith or of the rich rent contractor of Baidmao or of the Brahmin constable of Pachperwa or the Mohammedan clerk at the police station had died, or, worse still, that the wife of one of the Marwaris of the bazar had gone insane as a result of septic poisoning.

My first "out patient" was the wife of Nagesher Singh, a neighboring Rajput. He collected the Maharaja's rents at Baidmao, a village three or four miles from Pachperwa. He also cultivated four hundred acres of land for himself, and was the owner of Ram Piari—Beloved of Rama—an elephant I often rode. When Nagesher Singh first told me his wife was suffering from stomach trouble and wanted medicine, I answered that I could offer nothing without seeing her. Though his wife observed seclusion, he brought her to me in a covered bullock cart. The cart driver and an old servant held up a cloth between them, and the Peshkar, standing at a discreet distance on the far side, translated what Nagesher Singh's wife had to say. She was a woman of perhaps fifty. Her face was sallow, and its lines showed her sufferings. I felt then that she needed the very best care medical science could provide.

Some weeks later Nagesher Singh's wife sent a messenger, asking me to visit her. Though I knew I could do nothing for her, I went as a matter of courtesy. The elephant, which was to convey me to Baidmao, was on hand at six o'clock with a Tharu *mahout*. I put my "kit," in the form of some soda and cascara, into the loose pocket of its capacious saddlecloth. After a pleasant ride of an hour across the fields, we reached the tiny village, in which the tiled roof of the *Thekedar's* dwelling stood out from the common thatch.

A crowd lined both sides of the road, watching me in absorbed silence as I slid off the elephant. I was ceremoniously ushered inside the house, invited to sit on a square wooden bench spread with a rug, and offered a plate of nuts and raisins.

Astonished, I looked about me. I knew that Nagesher Singh was one of the so-called rich men of the tahsil. His wife was weighted down with gold ornaments. Yet I found the usual unpainted, windowless mud walls, a floor of pounded earth without covering, no furniture except the bench on which I was sitting and a string bed or two. A little painted tin trunk stood in a corner, and some saris and dhotis hung across a rope at one side of the room. Somewhere in the ground of the inner court, presumably, was a deep hole, skillfully hidden, containing Nagesher Singh's hoard of silver rupees. But of comforts, as we know them, or even the things we look on as absolute necessaries, nothing! Except for its size, Nagesher Singh's house was essentially no different from the house of the meanest tenant from whom he collected rent.

Again I implored Nagesher Singh to send his sick wife to Balrampur. It was not Nagesher Singh who stood in the way, but the wife herself who refused to go. A high-caste purdah woman finds traveling very inconvenient. How will she observe caste rules about her food in a strange place like a hospital? Who will direct her household while she is gone? She would die of homesickness away from these mud walls which have been her little world ever since she came to them as a bride. And not very long after my visit, Nagesher Singh's wife quietly turned her face to the mud wall and did not look away again.

A house I often visited in Pachperwa was that of Sheobalak, a Hindu confectioner and leading actor in Asgar's company. His frail four-year-old daughter was much on my mind during the heat of April and May. About the nature of her ailment there had been no question. After obtaining careful directions from the district health officer, I gave her the necessary vermifuge. But the child did not get well. Whenever I passed her father's shop, I would find her sitting forlornly on a low stool in the midst of the iron plates of sweets, a thin little bag of bones with dark circles under her eyes.

A few days passed without my seeing her. When I met Sheobalak on the road and asked after her, he answered, "*Achchhi hai*."—"She is all right." But one morning a relative came to the house, carrying little Dampati—Queen of the House—on her back. Her legs were as thin as match sticks, and she could no longer stand. Her lips were alarmingly white. She had ceased to take any food, even milk. It seemed that her tiny candle of life was flickering out.

Without proper nourishment, she had not the vitality to recover, but these days the bazar offered nothing suitable for a sick child to eat. Nor did Sheobalak's house provide any comforts or quiet. I had a sudden vision of it: the shop, noisy, dirty, crowded, hot; the back room, dark, full of acrid smoke from the cooking fire, cluttered with pots; the court, airless and sun-beaten, walls plastered with cow-dung fuel cakes, a baby wailing on a string bed under a protecting thatch. The parents were good people, very fond of their children, but how was goodness alone to help in this extremity? That night I hurriedly wrote to the English chemist at Lucknow, asking for the best preparation of children's food he could recommend, to be speeded by return mail.

It was the scientifically prepared food, I am sure, which really saved the child's life. Her appetite returned, color flowed back into the pale little face, her cheeks began to round out. Her father brought her around, not because she was still sick, but because she said she wanted to see me. I would take her by the hand and say: "Will you come to America with me? Let us go!" It was always a great joke, that going away to America together. Dampati and I became very fast friends.

While Dampati was at her worst, I had suddenly been faced with another and even greater cause of anxiety. As I was leaving Sheobalak's house one day, some people begged me to come into a neighboring house and see a sick Bania. He was lying on a bed, groaning miserably, in a room overflowing with women, children, and babies. He had been sick only a few hours. With a shock, I perceived that he had all the symptoms Dr. Saxena had carefully described to me as those of cholera.

There was no time to speculate or wait for developments. I hurried back for the cholera medicine I had been supplied with some weeks before, a mixture of essential oils. As soon as I could return to the house I began by dosing all the members of the family with pills of potassium permanganate, setting an example by taking one myself. The household consisted of seven women and children and no other men—bad for the enforcement of any regulations. I gave orders that one cup should be devoted to the exclusive use of the sick man. As no lime was to be had in the village, ashes had to be substituted for sanitary purposes. A teaspoon of medicine was to be administered every half hour. The teaspoon I had brought along, but how were these women to know the time? A neighbor in the crowd filling the door space, more intelligent than the rest, volunteered to come and tell them. Then I cleared the place of the crying babies and directed that everyone except the old mother should stay out of the room.

It was then two o'clock. At six I started back to see how the sick Bania was getting on. Before I reached the village, I met a young man, sent to tell me the patient was better. According to him, the Bania was now "all right." I sent instructions to the mother to stop giving any more medicine. I knew how powerful the mixture must be. Only the thought that the Bania, if he really had cholera, would probably be dead in a few hours unless I did something, had given me the reckless courage to administer it.

The mother herself arrived at the bungalow shortly after. She, too, said her son was "all right." Before I could stop her, she "took the dust" of my feet, the Hindu way of expressing veneration. But the son was now hungry. She asked what she should give him to eat. Common sense told me—little or nothing. Knowing the probable response to such a suggestion, I advised milk or curds.

The next morning when I went again to the house, I was badly frightened by the appearance of the patient. I hurried to the dispensary to consult the Doctor. The old Babuji, who never made house visits except with the prospect of a lucrative return, gave me a placid little discourse about the danger of going out in the heat of the day. But when I insisted, he sent with me his new compounder, as the dispensary assistant was called. The compounder took the sick man's pulse and temperature. Looking at me across the prostrate body, he remarked quietly in English: "He is dying. He will be dead by six o'clock." A violent attack of hiccoughs had come on, usually an indication in cholera of the approaching end. He had nothing to advise but a salt purge. On the way back he stated that in his opinion the Bania showed a very clear case of cholera. I was immensely relieved, I must confess, to hear him say so. Up till then I had been asking myself many searching questions.

I sent off a letter to the district health officer at Gonda, giving every detail of the case and asking for more specific directions in the event of future need. As I was looking for a letter on the second morning, in walked Dr. Saxena himself. It was his duty to come, he explained. He or an assistant is expected to investigate in person and at once every case of cholera reported in the district. My letter had been the equivalent of such a report. Meanwhile, the Bania, in spite of the prophecy of imminent death, was still alive. We went to the house, and this time found him a little better, though terribly weak.

A patient recovering from cholera should take nothing but water for twenty-four hours after the acute symptoms are gone, and, following that, only diluted milk for another twenty-four or thirty-eight hours. Though I had nearly killed him, in the first place by administering the extremely powerful remedy at full strength instead of mixed with water, and then by stopping the medicine abruptly, and finally by letting him have anything at all to eat, I had the satisfaction of hearing that nevertheless I had probably saved his life.

One very important thing had been neglected. Potassium permanganate should have been put in every one of the thirty or more wells of Pachperwa and its adjoining hamlets. It is really the duty of a patwari, the village accountant particularly charged with field records, to report cholera cases to the district authorities and immediately disinfect all wells. Our Patwari, when asked to explain his negligence, answered that he had only heard of the case that morning. He hurried off to perform his belated service, however, and for the next few days our villagers, rather unwillingly, were all drinking brilliant purple water. No more cases developed, and we congratulated ourselves that in Pachperwa, at least, a possible epidemic had been avoided.

But the surrounding countryside did not escape so lightly. Cholera was now raging in Basti. A woman who lived not far from Pachperwa, taken sick in Basti, returned to her own village and died the same day. Within two weeks there were thirty cases in that village, and fourteen deaths. Then a man from Bishenpur, only two miles from Pachperwa, attended the funeral of a victim in the first village. Two days later he was down. Still another man went to Bishenpur with a load of wood, spent the night, and took a drink. He died in his cart just as he reached his own village late the next afternoon. So the infection was carried from one village to another.

Though villagers do not object to leprosy in their midst and have very little fear of smallpox, they have a great dread of cholera, from the swiftness with which death so often follows an attack. Many began to flee from the infected villages, spreading disease as they went. By the third week of June seven villages within a radius of six miles of Pachperwa were declared to have cholera in epidemic form. Of these, Bishenpur suffered most. During the month the epidemic ran its course here, 105 persons out of the 400 inhabitants were attacked and 33 of these died. Altogether 51 villages in the Gonda district were affected. Cholera epidemics vary in intensity from year to year, but they are always one of the chief scourges of India, where the mortality from cholera often rises to a half million in a single year.

As soon as we were found to be in the middle of an infected area, one of the district sanitary inspectors arrived to take charge. This was Saiyid Karrar Husein, a Persian gentleman who emphatically refused to call himself Indian, though his family had lived in India for a long time. Making Pachperwa his headquarters, he went every day to the villages, distributed cholera mixture, saw that wells were properly disinfected, and ordered fly-breeding places and general dumps to be cleaned up. Dr. Saxena was excessively busy these days, flying about the whole district. I had great respect for both these men. They displayed energy, courage, efficiency, and tact in handling a difficult situation.

All three of us, mounted on two elephants, started out one afternoon for Bishenpur, the chief center of trouble. At the entrance to the village a slender bamboo pole, adorned with a green pennant, had been planted by a Mohammedan fakir as a sure means of driving the dread disease away. Not far off was a curious mound, on which thirty or forty small clay horses were ranged beside some square spider webs of colored threads fastened to sticks. The horses, I learned, were polite suggestions from the Hindus that the goddess who sent the cholera should ride away from Bishenpur and the colored spider webs were the chariots thoughtfully provided for her further convenience.

We were joined by the Patwari and the village watchman who led us to the houses of the sick. In the first house we visited, two children were lying on beds side by side. The mother sat on the floor, fanning one, and the father attended the other. Dr. Saxena asked for a cup. A small clay bowl was produced, and into this he poured his cholera mixture. "Give them a drink every hour," he ordered. Depositing two earthen pots and lime, we went on to the next house. Here two more children were sick. They were both unconscious. Obeying previous instructions to clean the house, the poor mother had just finished the work of giving the two rooms a fresh coat of mud and was then beginning to prepare the food for her third child and her husband. Two cholera victims, countless flies, and the family meal being cooked in the tiny kitchen four feet from the bed where the sick were lying! My heart sank within me. The doctor told the woman she must do the cooking outside the house, and wearily she said she would. But we all knew that she would do nothing of the sort. Caste rules make it difficult for a Hindu to cook in the open. Similar conditions prevailed in the eight other houses we visited that afternoon.

What one really wonders is, not why people die, but how they live at all under the circumstances! If a child gets cholera, the mother holds it in her lap until it is time to prepare the food, and so serves cholera to the rest of the family with their rice. If the suggestion is made that the soiled clothes of a cholera patient be burned, the answer is that in case he gets well, he will have nothing to put on. Poverty prevents such an extravagance. If nobody is stationed to watch, a water jar from a house where there is cholera carries infection to the village well. The woman who comes to the well does not realize, in spite of repeated warnings, that water is the chief source of cholera infection. Although Indians in the rural areas no longer believe that potassium in the wells is a diabolical invention of the foreigner to pollute Hindus by forcing them to drink blood, as many believed twenty years ago, they object to permanganated water on account of its slight taste and its rather terrifying color.

We encountered a very emphatic prejudice against medicine on the part of some Hindus. Though most people

offered no objection, a few stubbornly refused to let a drop
of cholera mixture pass their lips. Cholera is not, apparently,
a very old disease in India. The rapid growth of the cholera
menace in modern times is explained by increased facilities
of transportation. Yet, by a process of association, cholera
has taken on in popular imagination something of the character of smallpox, widely attributed to the anger of the
goddess Sitala.

Nearly every village has a shrine dedicated to Sitala, who
is worshiped especially by mothers. If the worship of the
goddess is neglected, she is likely to revenge herself by
taking up her abode in the body of a child. Her presence
is recognized by certain fixed signs—the signs of smallpox.
Great care must be taken to treat Sitala with profound respect, so that she will voluntarily release her victim. Any
attempt to drive her out of the body by force may only
succeed in angering her further, in which case death will
assuredly follow. But even in this event, she must still receive special consideration. The bodies of those dying of
smallpox—likewise of cholera—are buried instead of
being burned, an unfortunate reversal of the usual Hindu
practice. The campaign for vaccination in India has presented difficulties on two grounds: religious objection,
particularly on the part of high-caste Hindus, because the
vaccine comes from the sacred cow and its preparation en-
tails some discomfort to her, and the practical difficulty of
keeping the lymph fresh during the hot weather. The vaccination "season" definitely closes in March. Nevertheless,
in the light of experience, the prejudices of simple ignorance
are slowly giving way. India will follow the Western
nations in due course, effectively ridding herself of smallpox, goddess or no goddess, at no very distant time.

In certain localities a definite cholera god has been
evolved, with characteristics much like Sitala's. Around
Pachperwa, a malign goddess known as Samai, supposed by
some authorities to be a jungle goddess, bore the heavy responsibility for all our sickness. It was for her use that the

horses and chariots had been provided at the entrance to stricken Bishenpur.

The sanitary inspector offered medicine to all who could be persuaded to take it, but occasionally he met with stubborn refusal. One sick Brahmin of Bishenpur held out against all his entreaties. The Brahmin sent for a pundit *learned man* and ordered a *worship* puja for his recovery. When the sanitary inspector approached the pundit, asking if he would object to the Brahmin's taking the mixture, the pundit expressed no opposition and even urged his patron to try some of the foreign medicine. The Brahmin turned to him, demanding how he dared call himself a priest with so little faith in God! It so happened that the sick man recovered without the aid of any medicine. A few days later, in accordance with a vow, he set out with the pundit on a pilgrimage to the sacred city of Ayodya, but on the train he died of weakness.

An evidence of the myth-making tendency of villagers, as well as of their childlike faith, was a legend that sprang up after my visit to Bishenpur. On the day I was there, it was noted no one died, and all who were sick at that particular time recovered. The sanitary inspector told me that he used to strengthen his plea on behalf of his medicine by saying it was my wish that cholera victims should take it.

In Pachperwa my friend the Peshkar, very much frightened, decided the safe course would be to adopt both old and new measures at the same time. He threw handfuls of permanganate crystals into all the water used in his household during the epidemic, but he also paid a pundit to come every day for a week and recite Sanskrit texts for his personal safety at the shrine near my bungalow.

For actual protection in time of distress, Indian villagers put their real trust in Deity and not in ordinary human beings. For a catastrophe averted, it is the Deity they thank, generally in the form of some favorite god or goddess. Scarcely a day passed that prayers were not offered up at the little Devi shrine near my house. Sometimes, when matches had been forgotten, I lent mine. In return I was rewarded with brief glimpses of the superstition, faith, devotion, and spiritual insight of my neighbors, who found comfort for some of the ills of life in a larger, invisible world.

One evening I watched a man quietly lighting an oil cup and placing a new elephant among the many old broken ones on Devi's altar. When he had made his offering, I called him over. He was a Bania of Bargadwa, whom I did not know, but he told his story quite simply. Two sons, one thirteen years and the other thirteen months, had contracted smallpox. He and his wife sent for a pundit and had a puja by the bedside of the children, promising to offer an elephant and sherbet for each child at Sitala's shrine in the New Bazar and at Devi's shrine near my house, in the event of recovery. The older boy made no objection to the proposal, but the baby turned away its little head, indicating that it rejected the offer. From that moment the parents knew the baby would not live, and though it had only a very light case of smallpox, while the older son had a particularly severe one, the baby died and the boy recovered, as foreseen. "And so, according to the promise, I have brought the offerings to Mother," he concluded.

Another puja by another Bania taught me a very proper lesson in humility. I had been treating him four days for a badly infected eye. On the fifth morning I looked out of the window as I was dressing, to see my Bania there at the shrine, piously preparing to feed two Brahmins. Feeding Brahmins is a specially meritorious act, and it was evident that the Bania was having a very special puja that morning. Could it possibly have any connection with his recent eye infection, now practically cured? I asked him point-blank, and without the slightest embarrassment he acknowledged that the puja was an expression of gratitude for his recovery. Laughingly I told him he ought to give me a feast, not the Brahmins. It was not for some days that I perceived the village perspective to be a truer one than mine. To the villager, a human being may serve as an agent of God, but credit for any good he may do as a human being belongs to God, not to himself.

Although I tried to relieve a few of the immediate aches and pains of the thousands of Indians who came to me at Pachperwa, I knew that I was really accomplishing very little. It is food and education, not pills, that are needed in an Indian village. Dr. Saxena gave two talks on cholera and smallpox, one at my house for everybody who could be persuaded to come, and one at the school for the youngsters. He had a poor projection machine and a series of slides for each subject, stressing preventive measures. Between the two series, we sandwiched in Sindbad the Sailor for diversion. He also provided me with several large colored posters, graphically illustrating the danger sources for cholera, leprosy, plague, malaria, and smallpox and showing the disastrous results of insanitary care of mothers during childbirth. These posters I tacked up around the east veranda, and Asgar Ali, Ram Lakhan, and the Ayah, once they caught their meaning, never tired of explaining to wondering audiences the origin of their all too familiar ailments. With the posters came several packages of illustrated leaflets in Hindi and Urdu, published by the provincial department of health. There was a great demand for these leaflets by the schoolchildren and everybody who could read, and others begged for them, to have translated.

Other opportunities of making practical demonstrations of one sort or another presented themselves from time to time, especially within the intimate circle of my own household. On one occasion a visiting leper who had had a quarrel with Jumai appealed to me to settle the dispute. Incidentally I learned he was a *Chain,* a member of the caste which goes to the jungle and collects catechu, the gum commonly chewed with pan, and then sells it to pan dealers. After the leper had departed I asked the servants if any of them had bought gum from him. The Ayah produced a large brown lump, and Din Mohammed a small one. With an eloquent warning about the danger of putting anything handled by a leper into one's mouth, I insisted that the gum should be burned. The Ayah protested that she had paid twelve annas for her lump, which she was not intending to use for herself in any case. It was only for Jawahir to sell in Balrampur!

Yet I constantly had to remind myself, in the primitive setting of the village, that modern science is too often taken for the whole of enlightenment instead of a fragment. Without modern science, ancient Greece was able to leave the Western world an intellectual and artistic heritage it has not yet outgrown. Shakespeare did not require the schooling of modern science to fathom the depths and heights of human nature. The vision of an ideal life, preached by a Palestinian villager two thousand years ago, still dictates the highest spiritual values known to the West. So, too, without plumbing and with no conception of scientific prophylaxis, India in the past has produced great spiritual leaders out of just such insanitary little villages as Pachperwa, and may yet produce more. Health statistics are an index of an efficient concern or culpable lack of concern on the part of a government or administration for the welfare of its people, but they are not an infallible guide by which to judge the people themselves.

CHAPTER V

A Book of Beasts

HERE in the village is primary quiet—no roar of iron wheels, no factory whistle, no noise of leather eternally striking on hard pavement, no bell except the temple bell morning and evening. Four times in the twenty-four hours, if the wind is in the right direction, comes the dull thunder of the trains. Then quiet once more. Rustle of leaves, a grindstone humming like a bumblebee, the twang of a carding-bow behind some mud wall, the pleasant clinking of pewter anklets as the Jamadar's servant maid goes to the well for water.

Human voices are audible from my hill, but they do not rivet attention. The driver of a creaking bullock cart sings as he bumps along. *"Malai baraf, malai baraf!"*—"Cream-ice, cream-ice!" calls out a Hindu confectioner from the New Bazar, walking by with his iron can of pink sherbet and a stack of leaf saucers under his arm. Across the road the schoolchildren drone their lessons. Now and again the Ayah's treble rises in shrill crescendo. But above and between and around these frail notes flows the intricate orchestration of birds and beasts and insects.

Within five miles of Pachperwa are patches of virgin jungle. Not so long ago, all this part of Oudh was unbroken forest, but year by year the fields are pushing the forest farther back. Now it is only a fringe four miles deep on this side of the Nepalese border. We in the village are quite safe from tigers and leopards, and all the bears that come our way have ropes through their noses and dance to the click of little drums. But the jungle still sends forth a few bold prowlers. Every night the howls of hungry jackals, the long weird shrieks of hyenas, and the seven or eight staccato barks of little foxes echo at the edge of our village. And the sharp snarls of wolves sometimes rend the night.

To the Tharus, who live close to the foothills, the jungle is a menacing reality. When the crops are ripening in the clearings deer come down from the hills to browse. Scattered about the fields are little thatched platforms on high stilts. Men and women keep guard there all night long, shouting, singing, beating a noisy tattoo on tin cans, until day breaks, and the timid browsers go back into the forest. If the Tharus can save half their crops they think themselves lucky. But tigers and leopards stalk the deer, and now and then a tawny dynamo of energy jumps ten feet into the air and smashes down a frail platform. A human life goes out with a scream.

Or a wounded animal turns back in a sahib's shoot and mauls a beater. The limp form on such an occasion is brought on a bullock cart to the Pachperwa dispensary or sent on to Gonda, to have the ugly gashes cauterized and injections against blood poisoning administered, if it is not too late. Once I saw a man wearing a cloth mask. Half his face had been scratched off by a bear. The wood-cutters and the Tharus, coming and going, brought a jungle atmosphere into the village, reminding us of the presence of wild beasts behind the screen of forest a few miles away.

Jungle bordering on cultivation, sandy *nalas* and acres of tall tufted elephant grass make ideal tiger country. All these are characteristic of the Tarai. The Tarai jungle is fairly open woodland, cut into mile-square blocks by fire lines, like long avenues. It is frequently intersected by shallow ravines and wide, sandy river beds, which turn into raging, impassable torrents in the rainy season. Crocodiles lurk in the muddy depths of the larger rivers, and pythons and tigers haunt the green glades.

During the month I camped with the Jasbir Singhs I saw

something of Indian jungle life from the perspective of a tree platform. Most English officials and Indian rajas are addicted to sport, and the favorite method of shooting is from a *machan*. Generally several machans are tied up in a row, facing a fire line or nala. When the sportsmen have taken their places, two or three hundred beaters, starting at the far side of a forest block, drive the game out at their feet. Whenever I sat on a machan, as a spectator, I used to side with the animals and secretly hope for a lucky miss on the part of the person with whom I was sitting.

It is the potentiality of the Indian jungle that fascinates. From a tree-hung platform, it appears singularly innocent —merely a tangle of sun-flecked green. Everything is uncannily still. No one speaks after a few desultory shouts, borne faintly on the wind, give notice that the beat has begun. Gnats hover about your eyes, mosquitoes sting your ankles, flies sit on your nose, red ants attack from unexpected angles. Fifteen minutes pass and nothing happens.

Threading the undergrowth below are numberless little paths worn by the hard hoofs or soft feet of jungle creatures. Though as yet nothing unusual is to be seen or heard, you are aware that the jungle is awake. Word of danger is spreading through the green world, and many things are already on the move, fleeing from the obvious danger of men thrashing the underbrush with sticks and beating drums and shouting, toward the more sinister, unperceived danger ahead, death waiting at the point of a hidden gun.

Suddenly a lovely head, ears pricked in the direction of the growing hullabaloo, appears through an opening, and there before you, motionless, stands a white-spotted *chital* doe. After inspecting the clearing, she steps delicately forward and again stands and listens. She does not raise her eyes. The alarm is still far off. No need to hurry. She walks noiselessly across the cut and disappears among the trees. Sometimes she is followed by as many as twenty does. Jungle etiquette spares the females of the deer tribe; so these go unharmed. But should a good pair of horns come into sight, a sharp report rings out, the slender legs fold under, a head sags, and the film of death quenches the luster of big timid, beautiful eyes.

A peacock scuttles nervously out from under the brush, dragging its long train after it. Peacocks are wary. Instantly their bright little eyes spot the machan, in spite of its mask of leaves. They either run back into the brush or rise with a whir of wings and sail, tail straight out behind, toward a safe perch beyond the firing range. But they make easy targets on the wing, and roast peacock is much appreciated as a camp dinner.

The animals react differently to the alarm of the beaters. The most timid come out first, chital and *sambur*, with the females in the lead. Peacocks come at all times. Tigers and leopards are likely to appear ten minutes ahead of the beaters, though tigers have been known to wait until the very last minute, like bears and pigs. Bears are considered the most vicious of all jungle animals, and leopards more crafty and dangerous than tigers.

Wanting to see the jungle apart from the cruelty called sport, I went out twice before dawn and sat up in a machan alone. It was only four o'clock when a camp guard called me. Outside my tent loomed the huge bulk of an elephant. It knelt awkwardly, and I climbed aboard. In five minutes we had left the sleeping camp and plunged into the darkness of the jungle. Overhead, in the narrow opening above the trail, the stars glittered. It was bitterly cold. We turned into a dry river of sand, and presently the elephant was climbing a steep bank. The mahout pointed out the vague outlines of a machan in a tree overhead, and backed the elephant underneath. I pulled myself up, and the mahout and the elephant silently vanished up the nala.

I could make out nothing but a dark mass on the opposite side of the sandy waste. All consciousness was focused in listening. The last night sounds, those of the foxes, ceased. The inky blackness grew thinner, and the vague mass turned into gray trees and bushes. One chital quietly

pulling at the branches passed under the machan and out
of sight. A first bird called, loud and clear. In another quarter of an hour the air was filled with the plaintive cooing
of doves and the crowing of jungle cocks. Behind me I heard
the trumpeting call of peacocks. Day had come, and with it
the mystery of the jungle vanished.

On my last evening in camp I sat up on a machan with
Kanwar Jasbir Singh. Fresh leopard tracks had been reported in the vicinity by the Tharu hunters. This time there
were no beaters, only a black goat. It bleated piteously for
some moments after it found itself tethered in the forest,
then went down on its knees and philosophically began nibbling grass.

The forest was filled with the bedtime noise of birds. Parrots went rushing overhead in emerald flocks. A crested lark
trilled from the topmost twig of a tall tree. A peacock
crashed into a clump of bamboos a few feet away and then
flew off again. Under a sky of intense yellow the forest
seemed strangely alive. Wherever I looked I saw only tawny
stripes or black spots.

At last, at the far end of the path leading diagonally
toward the machan, something really moved. It came on
with lithe steps, swinging its head from side to side. Five
minutes of intense stillness. Then, noiselessly, majestically,
unafraid, a leopard walked in front of us in the darkening
forest, looking for the goat whose bleating it had heard.
A thrill ran through me, followed by a wave of sadness, as
a shot rang out, and the leopard dropped in the path.
Three tremors of its long tail, and its vital flame was extinguished. The goat went on nibbling grass indifferently
at the end of its tether. Yet there was rejoicing in the camp
when we returned with the big cat lying stretched between
a wheel guard and the hood of the motor. Leopards destroy
large numbers of cattle near the forest areas, and take toll
of human life as well.

In the village itself the twittering din of hundreds of
wild birds ushered in each long day. Lowing buffalo herds

returning with swollen udders from the stubbled fields as the blue smoke arose and hung like a scarf over the pumpkin patches on the roofs made the sunset hour gently audible. On nights of full moon, the pariah dogs, chased by invisible demons, raced round and round, howling like lost souls. Owls hooted and nightjars called tremulously. With a shrill whinny, some stallion broke its hobble and pounded away into the silver night.

When the grass shriveled, an insistent bellowing of hungry creatures, increasing in intensity from week to week, smote upon ears and heart. Monkeys screamed and fought incessantly in the trees, and the brain-fever bird sang its maddening refrain, over and over, louder and louder, until it almost seemed as if the vibrations from one feathered throat would shatter the world. Then came the days when everything was muted to the solo of the rain drums. Bearing no relation to any comprehensible reality, blurred figures in leaf raincoats struggled along the road, faint silhouettes in a gray world. Solitude and silence wrapped us in. Only the unmindful crows took long black stitches across the rain and cawed joyously. But the sun blazed forth every few hours. The fields began to steam, and the suppressed chorus of a million million insects broke out. Pale clouds of mosquitoes hummed in the veranda of the bungalow. Little lizards ran chattering about its walls. Crickets fiddled madly, and frogs croaked in every pool. The Peshkar came with a tale of a windy puff in his ear, as a five-foot cobra struck in the half light before dawn, missing by an inch.

The great pakar tree, which sheltered my four tents for two and a half months, was a whole forest in itself. Its trunk measured more than thirty feet, and the green vastness of its branches offered hospitality to countless birds, some of them permanent residents, others transients. Green barbets, warblers, orioles, coppersmiths, fork-tailed king crows, bulbuls, parroquets, cuckoos, woodpeckers, purple sunbirds, brown and red tree-pies, pigeons, doves, owls, big black crows, little dusty-throated house crows. and gray hornbills, all hopped or fluttered among the branches of this one great tree. Especially in May, when it was covered with tiny white berries, was it a rendezvous for all the greedy fruit-eating birds in the vicinity of the village.

On the ground under it wagtails, white-eyes, and mynas ran about, and hoopoes with zebra wings and proud cockades probed the ground with their sharp little rapiers. Out in the open, rollers, the brightest bit of color in the Indian landscape, swooped with flashes of incredible blue or watched patiently for insects, hunched up on the low branches of the acacias. In the fields, black, white, yellow vultures roosted on the low dikes, useful village scavengers; and herons and paddy birds stood motionless beside any bit of water. Occasionally, too, I caught sight of a pair of soft gray *saras* cranes with red legs, or a migratory guest in the form of a black and white stork. During moonlight nights in March and April, ducks and geese streamed overhead on their long journey across the Himalaya to Central Asia and beyond. The soft whir of wings in the air was eternally present in Pachperwa.

One morning a curly-bearded little man arrived at the door of the Happy House and offered me, presumably to eat, a black and white bird whose name I never learned. I gave him a few annas to set the bird free. As soon as he opened his hand it flew up to a branch of the shisham overhead and sang a very pretty thank-you. When he arrived the following week with two brown snipe, I had an idea that he was catching birds to have me set them free. The Peshkar, seeing me on the point of refusing this time, eagerly said he would buy the birds for his dinner, and I was forced to clinch the bargain at six cents. Like a flash, a big crow pounced upon one snipe and bore it off in its claws over the tahsil roofs.

The next time I saw the Peshkar I remarked that he might as well have had the bird for his dinner. "Oh, but I did," he said. "The crow flew to the tree by my house. I sent a man to throw something at it. The crow opened its beak, and the other bird fell down, and I ate it up. It was very good!"

The name of the enterprising Mohammedan bird catcher was Jhingar, Cricket. The next time he visited me, he came smiling with an armful of yellow melons. A bird catcher with a family of eight has a hard time of it, and Jhingar cultivated a melon patch in addition to trapping. He not only sold birds for food but he caught egrets and extracted their feathers, which eventually found their way into some raja's turban. Sometimes he was lucky enough to secure a falcon. Many a rich landlord of Oudh is glad to pay two hundred rupees for a good hawk.

Jhingar had a marvelous trick of imitating bird calls. Cutting a thin strip from a banana leaf, he rolled it between his palms to soften it and then fitted it horizontally across his tongue. From imperceptibly opened lips came the most astonishing series of cascading notes, trills, chirps, and warbles.

Jhingar took me on a trapping expedition to the jhil back of the house. Over his shoulder he carried a brown net twenty feet long and a coil of split bamboo. Perching on the coil and tied by one leg was a slender white and gray heron with pale blue feathers about the head. Two little feathers pinned its eyes shut. Jhingar explained that he had to keep his decoy bird blinded to prevent it from pecking at his eyes. After laying out the net close to the water, he carefully covered all traces of it with mud and loose sand and tied his heron by one leg over the spot. We then moved off and sat under a tree on the west bank of the jhil to await results.

Half an hour we sat. Suddenly a small dark object flew down near the tethered heron and hopped toward the water. Jhingar jerked his bamboo. Sand sprayed and the net snapped shut. Beating its wings helplessly in the meshes was a red-brown turtle dove. Jhingar carefully removed it from the net. He counted on the bird making a few mouthfuls for a Mussulman's dinner, but I held out my hand, and he graciously gave me the dove. Its whole warm body was nothing but panic heartbeats, as it watched me with frightened eyes, tiny black beads ringed with white dots. I opened my hand. It flew a little distance and then alighted, shaking itself to prove that it was free.

We also had a Hindu bird catcher in our village. This was Mangal—Tuesday—who had worked as a brick-layer on my house. Tuesday, as a good Hindu, never caught birds to eat. He dealt exclusively in cage birds—parrots, starlings, bulbuls, red munias.

He was quite as ready as Jhingar to show me his tricks. His trap was a simple affair: two small pieces of split bamboo bent in half circles and fastened together. At the margin of the tank Mangal dug up a gray cricket. Tying his little victim firmly about the waist, he suspended it by a piece of string from the intersection of the two bamboos. Then he took out a hollow tube containing sticky brown paste—juice of the jackfruit—and smeared this local bird-lime on the legs of his trap. Walking on, he dropped it with studied casualness at a promising spot under a tree. Beguiled by the cricket, birds were supposed to fly down and become entangled in the sticky bits of bamboo. To catch parrots, Mangal put some of his lime on the end of a long pole, lay on the ground under a tree, and gently poked his pole up to a branch where young parrots were sitting.

He had a still different method for trapping the tiny red munias, most popular cage birds of India, though they have only a twitter for a song. Taking four or five captive birds in a cage, he started for some unfrequented spot at the edge of the jungle. The cage was divided in the middle and had an adjustable flap on the outside. This he let down and sprinkled with grass seed. The singing of the caged birds attracted the wild ones, which soon alighted on the flap. Hidden behind a tree, Mangal pulled a string, lifted the flap and imprisoned all the birds. One day, hanging from a tree in the New Bazar, I saw a cage containing at least fifty red munias. Abdul Shah, a Mohammedan fakir of Pachperwa, said he had purchased them from Mangal for five rupees.

Though some of the village birds, particularly the parrots, do great damage to crops, they are far less destructive than monkeys, which move about in companies of a hundred or more, attacking fields of ripening grain, stripping fruit trees, stealing sweets from the bazar, making off with everything they can lay their little black hands on. More than once one of them dropped to the ground from a *jamun* tree near my kitchen, made a raid while Din Mohammed's back was turned, and carried off one of the chapatis he was about to serve for my breakfast.

In February, when the guavas were ripening, one big male, with a red face and a red seat to his trousers, discovered six guava trees close to where my tents were pitched. His band was then encamped on the other side of the road in a field of peas, engaged in stripping the stalks of the dark green pods. The monkey who discovered the guavas kept the secret to himself. Every day he used to come walking up the tahsil path, make a leap into the big pakar, and swing over into the guavas. The Ayah and Asgar Ali, who also liked guavas, vainly tried to protect the fruit. Asgar shot mud pellets from his bow, and the Ayah waved her arms and shouted. It took him just six days to clean every guava off that particular group of trees.

Our monkeys were the brown, short-tailed variety, much less handsome than the big silver-haired ones to be seen in western India or in some of the jungles. The trees around the Happy House were one of their favorite resorts. The monkeys scampered over the lawn, held conclaves at the Devi shrine, or snatched food from the servants' quarters. The mothers tended their offspring with maternal solicitude, carrying the wee babies plastered to their furry stomachs, and the older children riding on their backs. All the tribe coöperated for back-scratching and fleaing, but securing food was an individual concern. The biggest male used his position of authority to take the best of everything for himself. Occasionally a young male would challenge his right to the exclusive use of a particular branch bearing the small dark jamun berries. Screams, yells, chatterings, a tremendous shaking of the whole tree, and the big one chased the upstart away, biting him viciously if he could.

Though monkeys are vegetarians, sometimes they kill in wanton mischief. One day a monkey caught a big sand-colored owl in the grove back of the house. Asgar dashed off in pursuit. When the monkey dropped his heavy burden, he brought back what was left of the poor bird—one leg was bitten in two, one wing broken. It was bleeding and dying. "Kill it quickly," I begged Din Mohammed. The Ayah was looking eagerly at the owl. "Not take out its eyes first?" she asked. "Certainly not!" I replied, horrified at her idea. Din Mohammed piously consigned the bird's spirit to Allah, repeating the formula he always used when he dispatched a hen by slitting its throat: *"Bismillahi, allahu akbar!"*—"In the name of God; God is great!"

Asgar later explained the real motive behind the Ayah's strange suggestion. Eat the eyes of a live owl and you will see in the dark like an owl, or make an eye medicine, good for any kind of trouble, by boiling the eyes in water!

The next week the monkeys were responsible for another murder. At tea time it was the Ayah's custom to feed my big white Wyandotte rooster and his harem—purchased in Balrampur at a time when I imagined I might raise chicks for distribution among Mussulmans of the village and so improve the village poultry stock. As soon as her penetrating twitters sounded, the beautiful white rooster and his ladies ran quickly from their favorite summer resort, the spot of lawn kept damp by my bath water. On this particular afternoon one of the precious hens failed to appear. As usual, all the servants came to me to settle the dispute regarding responsibility. I suggested that instead of talking about the hen it might be wise to go and look for her.

Ten minutes of comparative calm, followed by the dénouement. Through the screened window, I see the Ayah. Silently she holds out a bunch of gory feathers, once a hen.

Behind, also speechless, Din Mohammed, Fakire, Asgar Ali, Ram Lakhan, Jumai, and a stray peon or two from the tahsil, ranged like a circle of mourners. All look at me, then at the red and white feathers, then at me again. "Monkeys," they murmur in unison.

Since anger is expected of me, I do my best to be angry, stressing the fact that this hen, so carelessly guarded by my household, cost the whole of seven rupees. Suddenly the Ayah chokes, and tears run down her withered cheeks. I distinguish words. These words have nothing to do with rupees but with the passing of the hen. Has she not fed my hens faithfully these many months? Has she not locked them up every night, safe from thieves and jackals, in the wire henhouse, and worn the key round her neck? Has she not for twenty-one days watched the hatching of their eggs, keeping the sitting hen in a box in her own room? And now, on the one afternoon when she chanced to be absent, this tragedy has occurred! All of us turn our attention to comforting the Ayah. What are seven rupees compared with love—even love for a hen?

"Cows, bullocks, buffaloes, elephants, and horses are high caste. Goats, dogs, donkeys, and pigs are low caste." It was Ayudya, a sturdy youth who sometimes worked about the tahsil, who enlightened me in respect to the social status of the village animals. Between the sacred cow and the untouchable pig the animal castes seemed to be largely regulated by matters of association or cost. A donkey, for instance, is used by washermen to carry clothes back and forth to the washing ponds and by potters for fetching wood for the firing ovens or hawking pots. Both washermen and potters are low-caste Hindus, and the animal associated with them shares their rank. The Mohammedan taboo against the pig, despised for its filthy habits, has been adopted by all save the lowest caste Hindus. Village dogs are wretched specimens of diseased skin and bones, living on chance carcasses and offal, and they occupy no place in either the affections or the economy of village life. Goats, however, are useful creatures, furnishing both milk and meat as well as an object of sacrifice, on special occasions, for Hindus and Mussulmans alike. After they have served every other end their skins are made into drums or find their way to Europe and the United States to be manufactured into glacé gloves and kid shoes. Goats are kept by the handful, two or three at most. The little *Gadariyas* have discovered a way of making goat-tending easy. They yoke three goats together, holding them by one string. This is very convenient for the goatherd but a little hard on the goats, which never want to go in the same direction at one time, and never simultaneously spy three succulent tufts of grass all in a row.

In the cities of India one sees and hears much of the sacred cow, but in rural districts the bullock dominates the scene. Indian country life would be at a standstill without bullocks. They plow the fields, draw water for irrigation from the wells, trample out the grain on the threshing floors, carry on the transport, grind sugar, press out oil, furnish fertilizer and supply fuel for cooking. Nowadays the chief use of the cow is to produce bullocks. In spite of the fact that India possesses well above three times the cattle population of the United States, actually Indian cows do not give enough milk to meet the minimum requirements of one eighth of the population. The value of milk per animal is said to average less than a cent a day.

The Hindu attitude toward the cow has always excited Western contempt or despair. For those to whom the cow, aside from her practical value, is merely a synonym for stupidity, it is difficult to understand how others can find in her an embodied goddess. True, in the dim period when the Aryan father was the sacrificer for the family, before the rise of a priestly caste, cattle were sacrificed in India, and the Vedic hymns indicate that the flesh of the sacrifice was afterward eaten. But the doctrine of non-injury received special emphasis with the development of Buddhism. Animal sacrifice fell into disrepute and finally was altogether discountenanced in 242 B. C. by an edict of the great Buddhist

Emperor, Asoka. The cow attracted to herself natural gratitude in view of the important part she and her progeny
played in the life of an agricultural people. Drinking her
milk, the Hindu affectionately called her Mother Cow, and
showered on her the homage due that exalted name. Her
quiet and gentle disposition appealed to his deepest ideals.
Cow worship took on a religious significance. For a Hindu
to-day, no sin can equal that of killing a cow. It is punish-
able with life imprisonment in several of the Indian States.
Quite recently the numerous riots between Hindus and Mussulmans over cow-killing episodes have shown that the feeling about the sanctity of the cow has not changed.

Seeing starved and sick cattle wandering about the streets
of Calcutta or Bombay, the practical-minded Westerner immediately points out the cruelty involved in Hindu superstition. "Kill off the useless cattle so that the others may
have enough to eat!" he admonishes, but he is unable to persuade India that his own slaughter houses are a happier solution from the point of view of the cattle. His advice only
stirs repugnance and horror in the Hindu. "When your
mother grows old, do you shoot her?" is the answer. If human
beings evolve through struggles and suffering, who is to
deny that the same law holds good in the animal kingdom
as well?

The charge that India is consciously cruel or indifferent
to her cattle is certainly not substantiated by anything I
saw in my village. As a rule, out of self-interest, if for no
higher reason, the villagers give the cattle the best care
they can provide. If they go half starved, so do their owners.
Straw and paddy husks for animals compare favorably with
a diet of parched grain, coarse wheat or rice for people.
Famine or a poor crop inevitably means hunger for both.

Our only grazing grounds were fields in fallow. Rice fields
are cultivated continuously, and the shortage of forage
around the village was perennial. After the fall harvesting
of rice and the spring harvesting of wheat and pulses, cultivated on higher land, the cattle were turned out to eat the

stubble. From the middle of March to the middle of June, before the rains, they roamed the barren countryside in great misery. This was the time when the buffaloes, which prefer feeding at night, made determined onslaughts upon my lawn. To help the cattle out, particularly the work cattle, the village children went forth with large baskets and scrapers and painfully dug up every tiny patch of dry grass, roots and all. Salt for cattle is a heavy tax on the slender resources of the villager. To meet this need, the cattle were taken far afield to some bit of waste land and permitted to lick the salt-impregnated clay. When the rains came at last and the country turned green overnight, the hungry bellowing of the preceding months suddenly ceased. Then, for a time, at least, the cattle were happy.

The deterioration of the cattle, with its disastrous effect on agriculture and on the health of the people, is receiving the belated attention of the government authorities. The destruction of forests, a growing population, and the taking up of grazing lands for cultivation of food crops at the cost of fodder, are largely responsible for the poor condition of the cattle. Famine, cattle diseases, and unscientific breeding are other sources of trouble. Many fine native breeds exist in different parts of India, but for the country as a whole the undersized little bullock and the cow giving less than two quarts of milk a day are the rule.

But while economists are urging the substitution of fodder crops for the poorer grain crops and agricultural experts are experimenting with pit-silos and various weeds and grasses which may be turned into suitable fodder, and while veterinaries are tackling disease and establishing scientific breeding stations in every province, and still other experts are advocating large-scale dairy enterprises, the uneconomic cattle continue to play a rôle of extraordinary value in Indian life. What India gets back for her veneration and protection of the cow is not to be measured solely in terms of money, produce, or work. Indian folklore, literature, and art have all been enriched through cow worship. Life itself, especially in the villages, acquires intangible warmth and interest because of this special attachment of human beings to the humble creatures very often sharing the same roof with them. India even expresses profound philosophic concepts through bovine figures of speech. What is this so-solid seeming world? "The puddle in the hoofprint of a cow." Krishna himself is the Divine Herdsman.

As the sun went down behind the level stretch of fields, I used to watch the herds passing in front of my house in clouds of golden haze. This is known as the hour of cow dust in India, the tranquil blending of day and night. A soft thudding of hoofs filled the air. In and out of the eddying dust shuffled the slow-moving blue-black buffaloes and the humped white cattle with slanting eyes. Astride the leader sat the small ragged herdsman, while his sister marched behind the herd. The villagers may not consciously see beauty in the home-coming herds, but they feel the mellow charm of customs and associations which have not changed in one detail for thousands of years. On occasion they garland their cows with necklaces of flowers and paint the horns of their bulls red or green.

The village herds belong to the professional herdsmen who supply most of the milk, curds, and ghi consumed in the village. Since milch buffaloes give four or five times as much milk as cows, and the milk is richer, the big herds are mainly buffaloes. But every villager who can pay the initial price of five to ten dollars keeps a cow of his own and as many bullocks as he requires or can afford for plowing. He is then assured of a supply of bullocks for the future, a little milk, and the all essential dung for fuel and plastering.

The sacredness of our village cattle was manifested only in their inviolable right to live. We had one bullock that had lost a leg when a cart overturned. For six years it had hopped about the tahsil grounds on its three legs. According to the Peshkar, the bullock led a happy life, with no more heavy carts to draw and no plowing to do.

A rich, pious Hindu, at the time of a death, is enjoined

to perform the ceremony of releasing a bull. The act of free-
ing an animal is looked on as a good deed, which may win
special favor for the deceased. Such a bull is presented to
the local temple and is never again tied up. Its practical
function is to sire the village cattle, but since it is not
selected primarily for breeding qualifications, its services in
this line are mediocre. Because of the damage it does to
the crops, the sacred bull is far from popular and as an institution is beginning to pass.

We had a sacred bull in Pachperwa, presented by Jokhi
Lal. Our bull was a malicious black and tan fellow. It used
to walk up and down the road between the two bazars, gor-
ing all the helpless cart bullocks. It entered the fields of
young grain and ate to its heart's content, unless the owner
was on hand to chase it out. It helped itself to any tooth-
some morsel in the open shops. Sometimes the sacred bull
would lie down in the exact middle of the road, and all
traffic was diverted in two streams around it until it chose
to get up. Like the three-legged bullock, it showed a predilection for my hill, and Asgar Ali often braved its snorts in
driving it off.

One might cross the whole of India and never so much
as set eyes on an elephant. But in my out of the way corner
I suddenly discovered plenty of them. The Balrampur Estate
owned fifty, and many of the rent contractors were proud
possessors of one or two. Motor cars are necessary to the
prestige of the modern maharaja, but his real magnificence
is still seen in his elephant stables. For ceremonial processions and for shooting parties, as well as for humble transport service, elephants are still in vogue.

The market price of an elephant ranges from that of a
Ford to at least as much as a Rolls-Royce, depending on
age, sex, training, gait, and general disposition. A baby is
worth approximately five hundred dollars, though the
mahout in charge of seven-year-old Champa told me she
had cost nine hundred dollars. The big tuskers used by rajas
in their shoots fetch the highest prices. One mammoth ele-

phant of the Balrampur Estate, fully as big as an African
elephant, was valued at seventeen thousand dollars. This
animal, like most of the Balrampur elephants, had been cap-
tured in an elephant drive conducted by the Maharaja's
late father in the dense jungles in the northern part of the
United Provinces. The Tharu mahout of Ram Piari, an
elephant driver for fifteen years, drew a salary of two rupees
a month, plus food and clothes. It would have taken him
some seven hundred and fifty years to earn the price of the
elephant he drove. A good elephant, according to dictates
laid down by the various mahouts I conversed with, should
be long in body. Like a ship, it rides the roads better with
fore and aft well drawn out. The neck should be small and
the forehead and upper part of the trunk well developed.
A smooth gait, speed, and a tractable disposition are other
points to consider. For ordinary purposes the female proves
more useful than the male. She has a more equable nature
and is easier to handle.

The initial price is only a part of the cost of an elephant.
To keep two or more tons of elephant satisfied, an enormous
quantity of food has to be provided. Balrampur allowed a
hundred rupees a month to feed each of its fifty elephants.
In addition, every animal had to have at least two men to
take care of it, a driver and a cook. The average elephant
received a daily ration of a thousand pounds of food. Every
night for dinner a full-grown elephant consumes about ten
pounds of rice, a half pound of salt, and ten pounds of
coarse wheat flour made into huge chapatis. The mammoth of
Balrampur required fifty pounds of grain a day. The rest
of the food consists of fodder, grass, sugar-cane, and a huge
pile of banian leaves and branches, particularly delectable
to an elephant. Since the Hindu looks on the banian as sacred
and is unwilling to cut it, Mussulmans generally monopolize
the profession of mahout. Tharus and Nepalese also become
elephant drivers along the borderland.

Back of the tahsil, close to the tank, was a grove in which
the mahouts always made camp when they stayed in Pach-

perwa overnight. Fetching their own banian leaves and branches from the jungle, some of the elephants would be coming in with towering green loads on their backs. One would be enjoying a bath in the tank. Its attendant would order it to lie down in the shallow water, first on one side and then on the other, while he scrubbed its enormous flanks with a stone. But an elephant knows how to give itself a good shower bath and will obey an order to suck up water with its trunk and spray itself thoroughly. After drinking at the tank or out of large iron scoops filled by the mahouts at the well, the elephants were all chained by their front legs to trees for the night.

Here and there, piled on the ground, lay the great saddles stuffed with straw and the thick cotton mattresses which are placed on top of these and tied in place with a harness of ropes. Little fires gleamed out where the attendants were busy cooking the elephants' dinners, each a separate affair. In big clay pots the rice was being boiled. On flat sheets of iron propped up on two bricks, the round wheat cakes, a foot and a half across, were baking. The elephants rolled their small gray or pale brown eyes in the direction of their dinner and swayed restlessly, making their ankle chains clink. The mahout stands by and helps feed his animals, tossing it sheaves of succulent leaves twisted into small bundles and neatly rolled chapatis. The elephant picks these up with the sensitive lip of its trunk, curls the trunk under, and deposits the morsel in its mouth. Sometimes the cooked meal is finished off with a baseball of brown sugar. Afterward the animals begin on the rubbery leaves and branches, and the mahouts cook their own food. Then they curl up against the saddles, wrap themselves in cotton cloths, and drop off to sleep.

The mahouts always have tales to tell of narrow escapes when a wounded leopard or tiger has sprung on an elephant in the jungle or when the animal has suddenly gone *must*. Male elephants are constantly going must, and some of them remain in this dangerous condition several months every

year. Generally certain signs give warning. A fluid begins
to drain from two microscopic holes on each side of the head.
The elephant does not know his mahout at this time and
strives to kill anybody coming within range. He has to have
all four feet fastened by heavy chains to a big tree. The
mahout stands at a safe distance to throw him his food.
Sometimes he goes on a hunger strike and has to be disciplined to eat with prods from a long sharp-pointed stick.
All the time he throws earth and leaves over himself, swings
from side to side and utters deep groans. A must elephant
occasionally succeeds in killing a mahout.

Only a week or two after I came to Pachperwa excited
shouts drew me out of my tent. I managed to understand
that a runaway must elephant had just dashed by and was
now in a field of tall arhar across the road. Here was an unexpected thrill for a mud village. I persuaded the Peshkar
to come along, and we joined a group on a bank overlooking
the field. No sign of the elephant was visible, but the children insisted they had seen it vanish into the arhar. A narrow path ran through the field. The Peshkar did not seem
very anxious to follow me when I insisted on stalking the
elephant, but he was unwilling to desert me. Tufted branches
prevented us from seeing any distance except along the
ground, where we could peer between the stalks. We moved
in cautious silence. All of a sudden I spied four gray
columns firmly planted in the green field and above, the
branches swayed slightly. That was quite near enough to
an unchained must elephant as far as I was concerned, and
we speedily withdrew. An hour later a mahout turned up in
pursuit, not of the must elephant everybody was talking
about, but merely a harmless female who had escaped in the
night from her village a few miles away—and thoroughly
enjoyed her unexpected feast in the field of ripe peas!

The elephant language, by which mahouts convey their
orders to their charges, proves how intelligent the animals
really are. *"Baith!"*—*"*Sit!*"* orders the mahout. Down goes
the great clumsy creature, back legs projecting straight out

behind. A second tidal wave, and the front legs drop, sticking out in front. *Mail* means "get up," if the elephant is sitting; "go ahead," if it is standing still. *Dale* means "drink." *Lao* orders the elephant to pick up something with its trunk and hand it to the driver. *Dhat* means "stop"; *chain,* "go to one side," *lage,* "pull" or "shove" away a tree or bush in the path. One old white-bearded mahout insisted that, south or north, all Indian elephants knew this same language, but I had no opportunity to prove his assertion.

Whenever I went any distance from the village I rode in state on a borrowed elephant. It was the only means of travel. Elephant riding for more than five hours at a stretch is body racking. Some people even experience all the sensations of being on a rough sea. On days when the dust was blowing I used to wish somebody would invent a closed elephant coupé. But in these days of swift locomotion an elephant offers one very distinct advantage. It goes slowly enough to permit one to take in the scenery by the way. Its average rate of speed is just about that of a man, slightly more than three miles an hour.

In our community we did not make use of elephant ladders. We climbed up by the rear quarters with the help of the tail. I became expert in this feat, and even when a restless elephant lurched up from its kneeling position while I was still hanging in midair, I managed to hold on to the ropes and pull myself into position. The mahout perches on the front end of the pad or on the neck and drives by pressure of his bare toes behind the big flapping ears. He also uses an *ankus.* This is a short iron goad with a large hook at one end, like an umbrella handle, which may be hung over the top of the elephant's ear. When a mahout wishes to emphasize a point of dispute with an elephant, he jabs the sharp point into the top of its head. The elephant gives out a piercing shriek, like a jamming of motor brakes, and unless very recalcitrant decides to mend its ways.

An elephant has another note, an ear-splitting trumpet,

that denotes fear. Ram Piari was carrying me across the flooded fields one July afternoon, carefully feeling the way with her trunk. Suddenly a long black water snake shot past. She gave vent to a weird shriek, so startling I nearly fell off. I could see no reason why elephants should be afraid of snakes until the mahout said they have been known to die of cobra bite.

From Champa, who shied at railway engines, to Teja Khan's ill-natured big tusker, each elephant had to be driven with careful knowledge of its personal idiosyncrasies. The mahouts, who spend their lives with their animals, know them well. They have real affection for the big gray hulks. They oil the top of their heads where a few short sparse hairs grow and they paint designs in black and white down their trunks. Sometimes the freckled ear of an elephant is decorated with a round silver earring.

The night train reached Pachperwa at half-past ten. Returning from a day in Balrampur, I would find an elephant waiting to take me the mile and a half to the village. Where else could one have an elephant meet the train? I loved the soft padding across the zigzag embankments of the fields, the swishing of the big ears, the movement of the heavy trunk swinging out to right or left, breaking off wisps of grain. And so home in the moonlight, past the little houses, all dark and still, with the white pumpkins gleaming among the dark leaves on the roofs.

About the first of June the village began to develop a snake psychology. Jumai asked me to buy him a lantern because he was afraid to go home in the dark. The Station Master cut short his evening visits so that he could see his path on the way back. Stories of last year's tragedies were exhumed and narrated for my benefit. I sent off to the Pasteur laboratory at Kasauli in the Punjab for several phials of anti-venine, ordered a syringe from Lucknow, and carefully memorized the directions of the civil surgeon at Gonda for treating a snake victim. Seven different kinds of poisonous snakes frequented our neighborhood, and it seemed wise to be ready for any emergency.

In spite of the horror aroused by the thought of deadly Indian reptiles, these creatures are actually less dangerous than American motor cars. Moreover, many deaths recorded as due to snakebite are really due to shock resulting from fright. When a snake has been seen, the person often automatically imagines he may have been bitten, and in many cases death results from heart failure. The population of the United States is roughly one third that of India. For every five Americans killed by cars only one Indian dies of snakebite. If all the people had beds and wore shoes, the fatalities would be considerably less.

Twenty inches of rain were reported as falling in thirty-six hours during our first heavy rainfall. Everything was flooded, including the snake holes on my hill. The second afternoon Asgar came to tell me he had just killed a baby cobra in the kitchen veranda. The next morning on the mat in front of the "hospital room" I noticed the ants voraciously tugging at something. It was the twin of Asgar's baby cobra, which I had quite evidently stepped on and crushed in the dark.

Then began a series of small domestic tragedies. Asgar's mongoose, Rikki Tikki, was promising to become useful. It caught two harmless, white-bellied snakes near the shrine and killed them in a flash, biting their throats. But it was not destined to greater triumphs. Jumai rushed out of the kitchen one evening shouting, "Snake—dying!" Something went cold inside of me. I thought he had been bitten. Then I learned it was the mongoose. Din Mohammed was cooking, and the mongoose was playing about his feet as usual. Suddenly, from the direction of the cement drain in the corner of the kitchen, it gave a queer cry. Jumai took down the lantern from the table, to find the little fellow writhing on the floor. I arrived just in time to see it die, its body swollen, its tiny paws crossed in front, as if the last unction had been administered. Nobody saw the snake, which must have slipped in the drain hole and out again, but Rikki Tikki's nose bore the marks of its attack.

Two of my hens also died from snake bites in the next few weeks, and a monkey curled up and expired under the trees in twenty minutes. Fakire killed a *loharin*, a small gray snake with black bands, as poisonous as a cobra, just outside the bathroom door, and I got up one morning to discover an empty cobra skin on the lawn a few feet from my bed.

Meanwhile, news came in of somebody's death from snake poisoning, first in a village here, then a hamlet there. Although I had my serum ready, I never had a chance to use it. In almost every case the person was bitten at night and was dead by morning. The first fatality of the season was that of a peon of the tahsil who lived three miles away. The next was a young girl in a neighboring village. The girl was bitten in the leg by a cobra while she was sleeping. The mother and father hurriedly summoned an *ojha*, a witch doctor. He blew on the wound, recited a charm, and assured them she would be all right in half an hour. Unfortunately his prophecy was not fulfilled. Still another victim was a woman belonging to a group of vagrant grindstone cutters encamped in the mango grove of one of our hamlets.

A young Brahmin of my acquaintance told me that his household had been plunged into mourning by the death of an uncle. The uncle was in the habit of getting up every morning at five for religious meditation. He usually went outside the house for his devotions, sitting on a low wooden platform. Arising as usual in the gray light before dawn on a certain morning, he crossed over and picked up his staff, leaning in a dark corner of the room. As he did so, he was conscious of something striking his hand. Outside he saw that one finger bore the two fatal dark red punctures of a snake's fangs. A Sanskrit verse, familiar to educated Hindus, gives the supposed antidote to cobra poison of

Charak, a famous Indian medical authority who was even quoted in European works of the Middle Ages. The Brahmin called his wife, and a servant was hurriedly dispatched to the bazar for the eight ingredients of the remedy—pepper, salt, a particular spice, two drugs, curds, honey, and butter, the whole to be mixed in equal proportions and swallowed with water. But the shops in the bazar were closed at this early hour. The Brahmin sank into a stupor and died in just one hour.

Altogether in the neighboring villages I learned of ten deaths from snake bite over the summer, and a number of extraordinarily narrow escapes. The Station Master's daughter-in-law discovered a *karait* on her bed during the night. The Peshkar had two encounters with a large cobra which invaded his quarters. The Jamadar did away with a loharin, and Fakire beat to death a large *gandais*—from his description, it must have been a Russell's viper—in the road. The Tahsildar's daughter-in-law in Balrampur was bitten by a cobra, according to his statement, but by a miracle did not die.

One hot bazar day a lean, striking-looking man with silver rings as big as napkin rings tucked round his ears, silver bracelets fashioned like snakes on his wrists, and a scarlet turban on his head came striding up the slope to my house. He was a Jogi snake charmer. I let him tootle a bit on his gourd flute, with two short bamboos inserted at the lower end. Every snake charmer has such an instrument, which was known in my district as a *bin*. The Jogi's bin was ornamented with an elaborate design of brass thumbtacks. He carried two round baskets on a pole, and out of one of them presently appeared a snake seven or eight feet long. The snake charmer said it was a young python he had caught in the jungle a month before. The python took one look around and then made straight for the dark hole in my bathroom wall. I was feeling pleased with my forethought in screening this hole on the inside, until I saw the snake give one push, lift the screen flap and vanish inside. The Jogi unwound it from my tin tub, to which it had taken a fancy.

I was more interested in talking to the man than in watching the tricks of his harmless python. He came originally from Gwalior in Rajputana, he said, and belonged to a tribe of wandering snake charmers who were all followers of the Oudh saint, Gorakhnath. They were Kanphatas, or Split-Ears, as the sect is called on account of the huge round earrings—generally of crystal or jade—worn by initiates. Two hundred of his band were now encamped in a grove of the village of Pipriha eight miles south of Pachperwa, and their stock in trade consisted of three hundred snakes. With this astonishing bit of information the Jogi begged leave to depart, since he must hasten back to his village and put his snake in water. If the snakes did not get a bath every day they would die. Then, too, they had to be fed with balls of milk and flour cooked in boiling water. Now and then they were given meat as well. He said all the Jogis slept with their snakes. He himself had two, one of which always curled up for the night on his stomach and the other on his shoulder. I suspected that my Jogi friend was something of a charlatan.

A few days later, when the Peshkar was going on tahsil business in the direction of Pipriha, I begged leave to accompany him. We set off on two elephants before five in the morning. At the end of three hours the grove with the Jogis' orange tents came into sight, but I could count only eleven of them. A ragged collection of old men, women, and children, principally dressed in necklaces of red seeds and brown *rudraksha* berries, assembled as the mahouts shouted, "Baith!" How unfortunate we had not sent word ahead, they exclaimed, when informed we had come to see their encampment. The young women were off in the fields tending the donkeys. The young men were making the rounds of the villages with the snakes. Only one defanged cobra could be mustered to puff out its hood, emit windy hisses, and stick out its purple-forked tongue with lightning flickers. The camp of two hundred snake charmers suddenly shrank to fifty and the three hundred snakes to twenty-five, by the testimony of the old man who acted as spokes-man.

He also enlightened us on a few other discrepancies in the first Jogi's tale. Though the snakes were kept on the beds at night, they were always securely tied up in their baskets. They got no daily baths. But their food, as stated, consisted of milk, flour balls, rats, and frogs. They were procured wherever they could be found, preferably young, sometimes in the jungles and sometimes in the villages. The poisonous ones were defanged with a piece of iron. I asked if Jogis ever died of snake bite. Like other mortals, they do. He pointed to several pairs of tiny white scars on his own arms and hands. The Jogis claim a knowledge of certain roots efficacious for curing snake bite, however, and these they sell in the villages.

Another old fellow, whom I singled out to photograph, proudly removed his turban and let seven feet of rusty black hair fall to the ground. Certain ascetics, ignoring the body, let their hair grow long and never cut their nails. The Jogi's hair seemed to be of two different qualities and colors, and I concluded his locks were artificially attached to give him prestige in the eyes of the villagers. "How do you fasten it all on?" I asked. With great dignity he assured me every hair was his own. These Jogis, though claiming mystic powers, were typical gypsies, not to be associated in any respect with the real religious mystics of India. The Peshkar looked on them with utter contempt. "They eat rats and jackals and foxes!" he said scornfully.

To say that a cobra "dances" is a fanciful way of saying that it does a good deal of neck-stretching. Snakes lack even the internal structure of an organ for hearing, but they must feel vibrations. They are taught to associate the bin with food, and its whine will always draw a snake out of its basket. When I asked if the snakes were trained to perform, all the Jogis laughed at the idea. The peculiar swaying movements of the cobra with lifted head and spread hood very likely indicate an instinctive preparation to strike. Snake charmers will generally be seen moving a fist back and forth in front of a cobra. Either charmed by the movement or seeking to avoid the obstacle in the path of an attack, a cobra goes through a characteristic "dance." The Indian villager is as eager to watch the performance of a professional snake charmer as a foreign tourist. The wandering Jogis, by displaying their snakes, selling their snake medicine and offering to charm snakes out of villagers' houses—generally having previously hidden there some tame ones they know will appear when they play on their gourd flutes—earn a meager livelihood.

Among the Jogis of the mango grove was a strange looking boy of fifteen or sixteen, wearing a crown of soft wavy hair. He had the pale skin of the high-born Aryan, long curling lashes and a queer expression impossible to describe. The appearance of the boy could be explained only by the inheritance of a superior strain of blood. It was he who in the absence from camp of most of the men was called upon to give us a performance of some Jogi *mantras*. He leaned over and with his finger drew a circle on the ground and quartered it. Then he began to play on his bin. A herdsman looking on was persuaded to hit the flute with a small stone. Immediately the bin was bewitched. No amount of puffing or blowing could draw a sound out of it. Finally the boy stooped, picked up some dust from the magic circle, threw it over the neck of his flute, and recited an incantation of which I understood only the words, "One, two, three and a half, Gorakhnath!" repeated several times. Thereupon the soul of the bin was freed from the spell cast upon it, and the boy finished his melody.

Again the stranger threw a stone. To my horror, I witnessed the bin slowly but surely slipping down the boy's throat. The stem of the gourd was perhaps ten inches long, and certainly eight of these went down his throat. He ran past us and threw himself flat on the ground, digging his hands into the earth in the tenseness of the struggle to prevent the bin from choking him. At last, with a terrific wrench, he jerked it out of his mouth, spattered with blood. Beads of perspiration started from his pale forehead and blood dripped from his nose as he slowly sat up. Was this acting or hypnotism? The other Jogis did not look like a sophisticated audience watching a trick. All were very serious. But then I observed that as the blood dried on the gourd it turned a peculiar pink, the color of red ink.

Though snakes ushered in the rainy season with dramatic éclat, they were by no means the most obvious of its signs and portents. In spite of my screens, a million winged things suddenly invaded the now less Happy House. It was sometimes impossible to eat because of winged termites flying into the soup or entangling themselves in the butter. Din Mohammed had to stand behind my chair and flap vigorously with a towel. There came nights when my desk was completely covered with a thin layer of transparent ecru wings. Termites, more commonly called "white ants," develop wings for the brief moment of a nuptial flight and the founding of new colonies, but their wings are so fragile they drop off at a breath.

A very characteristic feature of the Oudh landscape, wherever there are trees, is the termite skyscraper of mud and chewed vegetable fiber. Many nests are more than ten feet high. They are so hard that to be leveled they have to be chopped down like trees. One day Ram Lakhan climbed one and perched at the pinnacle, like a sailor on a mast. Some species of these destructive little insects—which eat not only dead vegetable fiber but living trees, wheat, sugar cane, groundnut, and cloth as well—make their nests underground. Burrows as deep as eleven feet have been known. A nest seven or eight feet high I once saw opened finally disclosed the royal chamber of the queen two feet below the surface of the ground, while the superstructure swarmed with millions of workers.

My night work was now chiefly confined to entomological study. The nocturnal mosquitoes that invaded the premises had a special predilection for ankles. I resorted to the old trick of sitting with my feet in a pillowcase every night, thus forestalling the worst of their depredations. Different species of mosquitoes frequented the bungalow, some brown, some black with white bands on their legs. *Anopheles*, the transmitter of malaria, I could easily recognize by its typical way of sitting on walls or screens, head and proboscis tilted down and body slanting up instead of extending in a straight line. But since mosquitoes are responsible for various fevers besides malaria, not to mention elephantiasis, I looked on all alike with aversion.

A myriad other annoying insects paid me nightly visits. I was forced to invent a trap by setting my lamp on an upturned pan placed in a larger pan filled with water. Drawn to the lamp on its tin island, many creatures hurled themselves senselessly against the hot chimney and were burned to death, caught their wings in the kerosene and were smothered, or fell into the moat below and perished. In the morning the Ayah bore off the remains. But I had two allies in my battle with insects. Sometimes an unmistakable croak in the corner of the room betrayed the presence of a toad, and little lizards ran chattering about the walls.

These visitors were of all shapes, colors, and sizes. The handsomest among them was a huge brightly colored grasshopper, yellow, blue, coral pink, and green, amazingly decked out in spots and stripes. A praying mantis came one evening and sat motionless on my desk, with hideous front claws uplifted in the air, waiting for a victim. Silvery fish-insects with forked tails ate my books. All sorts of beetles, some of them with horns and bumps or sharp prongs on their legs, paraded by. Crickets played tiddledywinks over my typewriter. Big black cockroaches scuttled about.

Horrid little stink bugs caused me genuine misery. These were smaller than shoe buttons, round and dull black, and, as their name implies, they emitted a very disagreeable smell.

Many millions of them were abroad. And I must have been visited by at least one blister beetle, as I learned to my sorrow when a red patch appeared on the back of my neck and developed into several square inches of blister which took three weeks to heal. This beetle flies by day. It excretes an acrid oil that is extremely irritating in contact with the skin. Scorpions, too, infested the house, and the Ayah was always sweeping them up from some corner, while Din Mohammed shook them out of his pans. Centipedes ran about. I took care to look in my shoes each morning before putting them on. One night the servants caught a six-inch centipede in my bedroom. It had only a few pairs of strong curved legs, like vicious claws, but they said the bite was capable of causing death, and I believed them. In endless variety, the battalions of creatures fluttered and crawled across my papers.

Still another army of invaders belonged to the order of ants. Ants were everywhere. Din Mohammed set the legs of all his tables and wire food boxes in cups of kerosene, but big black fellows always had to be picked out of the sugar. Tiny ones made their home in the cracks of the walls and in holes in the veranda floor. Sometimes I watched endless caravans of them, each bearing a cocoon, streaming up the wall and vanishing into a crack.

One sultry night I was sitting out on the maidan. A curious sawing sound I had often heard about the house of late attracted my attention. It seemed to come from the heavy horizontal beams under the thatch along the veranda. I took a lantern and found these riddled with small round holes from which dust was dropping. Borers were hard at work.

The Happy House was scarcely four months old, and yet for an instant I felt the stealthy work of destruction that had already set in. The veranda floor had sunk in several places. The wooden doors and shutters were warped. The walls had cracks in them. I was but one of its several hundred, or even several thousand, regular tenants. The discovery did not make me unhappy. I felt the house had mellowed. It was falling into place in the eternal procession of things. And I saw that nothing created is destined to survive long. The law of birth is also the law of death, and one cannot be without the other.

"They say the Lion and the Lizard . . ."

CHAPTER VI

Visitors

T HE matter-of-course way in which all kinds of people, the well along with the sick, arrived at the door of the Happy House gave me a pleasant feeling of having a part in the life of the community, alien though I was. From early morning until late at night I had scarcely a moment to call my own. Since I was not trying to live any life apart from that of the village, I had no reason to desire privacy, and all guests were welcome. Sometimes on my hill I felt a little like a goldfish in a glass bowl, but at least the element in which I was immersed was the intimate life of an Indian village.

When the bungalow was finished, thinking that in a week everybody who wanted to see the inside of it would have had a chance to do so, I let the crowds trail through. They were never-ending. After a hundred visitors had left their dusty footprints on the green rugs, I would sometimes, in desperation, refuse to admit the hundred and first. The Ayah would then plead the cause of a little group of women standing disconsolately on the lawn, telling me they had come ten or fifteen miles only to see the house. They came in, needless to say.

To me the house seemed quite Indian, but I discovered that my visitors looked on it as a wholly foreign marvel. The absence of any outer wall or inner court, the whitewashed interior, high ceilings, the number and size of the windows, wire screens, curtains, rugs, and furniture excited wonder and admiration. "It is a palace," was the general summing up. Vital concern for bedrock necessities leaves little room for rural India to think of personal comfort, much less luxury, in house-building.

Besides the simple country folk, my visitors included all the wandering beggars and musicians and religious mendicants who happened to pass through the village. Charity and hospitality are virtues preached alike by Hindu and Mussulman. The pressure of social opinion in India almost compels one to practise them. What you have, you hold in trust from God. When you are charitable, you are merely being what God intends you to be. In the belief that society ought to endow any one willing to devote his life to a search for spiritual truth, India cheerfully maintains some five million religious mendicants. It does not even ask which is a real seeker and which an impostor. It is enough that a man has adopted the outer form of a religious life. So it was not surprising that no day passed without an appeal for me to share my fabled riches.

Some of the religious wanderers announced their presence with little drums, some with miniature harmoniums, some with metal castanets, some with song, some with nothing but a crooked staff or an iron rod with rings on it. It is thus they go from village to village, making their way slowly up and down the land, visiting every important place of pilgrimage. They know countless legends, and these they recount to groups of villagers who gather under the shade of a tree to listen. Once they had no need of money, but nowadays money is required for railway tickets. They accepted a few annas from me without compunction and in return not infrequently chanted blessings upon my head. The villagers extended welcome to all these strangers, blatant hypocrites as some of them appeared, fed them and sheltered them and felt grateful for the privilege of entertaining them.

At one time we had with us for a week a Mohammedan *baba* who exuded a false odor of sanctity. He was the spiritual adviser of Yasin Khan the Pathan, and it was Yasin who first told us of his greatness, before the baba arrived in Pachperwa to gather disciples and gifts. His specialty was the swift cure of leprosy, but he also foretold the future and penetrated the inner secrets of many things. He sent the Peshkar a bit of paper on which he had written a charm, telling him that if he would wear the paper in his hat he would soon be made a tahsildar. At the same time he sent our Tahsildar a similar paper, which was to raise him to the rank of assistant manager of the estate. Then he came himself. As he sat down with us, he was careful to explain that it was really not fitting for him to go to anybody. He was the spiritual king of our district, and people should come to him. The Tahsildar was nettled. He dared to doubt that the baba had really cured twenty lepers, as he boasted. Yasin rushed off and produced the Tahsildar's own groom, who swore the baba had recently cured him of a very bad case of leprosy. "Yasin gave him two annas to say so!" the Tahsildar remarked cynically.

A gray-haired pundit of Basti, noted for his success in dealing with ghosts, was summoned by one of our Marwaris to dispossess his daughter-in-law of an evil spirit. The Tahsildar brought him to see me. I asked him how he would set about curing the girl. For four nights in succession, he explained, he would light one hundred and twenty-five small oil lamps and place them in a circle on the floor. Then he would have the girl seat herself in the middle of the circle and fix her eyes on the lights. After a time he would ask her the name of the ghost or spirit troubling her. If she could be persuaded to give the name, the ghost would immediately be driven out of her body.

"Let us test his powers," said the Tahsildar. "We will ask him who stole your thermometer day before yesterday." The disappearance of my thermometer had caused much speculation in the tahsil. First inquiring how many letters or sounds there were in the name of the stolen article, the pundit began to calculate on his fingers with an air of profound concentration. Then he announced that he would tell

the name of the thief in the morning. But he did not turn
up, and incidentally the evil spirit which made the Marwari
girl sit for hours at a time without saying a word, utterly
unconscious of her surroundings, was not induced to leave
her.

From Balrampur came another strange visitor. For three
or four days, both on his way to the Himalayan forests and
on his return, he spread his blanket under a thatched roof
near the tahsil. Long curling black hair fell to his shoulders,
framing a pale face in which the burning deep-set eyes produced an extraordinary impression on the beholder. He had
an unutterably weary look. When he said he was six hundred
years old I understood the weariness, though, had I not
been informed of his correct age, I might have mistaken him
for forty-five. What he implied was that he recalled his past
lives for a period of six hundred years. He had visited Pachperwa the last time, it seemed, two hundred years before,
when it belonged to the Tulsipur *Raj*. This *sadhu* was supposed to cure sicknesses of all kinds with bark and roots
procured from the forest.

In Pachperwa we had a man who called himself neither a
sadhu nor fakir—only a Brahmin beggar—who possessed
genuine spiritual poise. Dragging himself on a rude crutch,
he came to beg from me just as I was setting off for Balrampur one morning. To my utter amazement, the Peshkar,
who was inspecting the elephant I was to ride, angrily
ordered him to go away at once. The sight of a cripple as one
is about to start on a journey is a very bad omen, he explained. The man should have known better than to appear
at such a moment.

Fourteen years before he had been crushed by the fall
of a heavy box at the railway station. Unable to work, he
could only drag himself on begging rounds through the
village. But the village took care of him, and the old
Doctor let him sleep in a sort of outhouse of the dispensary.
Where he had originally come from, nobody knew any more.
Something other than his infirmity drew my sympathy.

He never complained about his accident. He accepted it as
the price of some sin committed in a former life. In this one,
at any rate, he surmounted tribulation with quiet mastery of
spirit. In return for an insignificant monthly contribution
he used to place his two palms together, raise them to his
forehead, and call down long Sanskrit blessings on me. The
shining responsiveness of his smile always made me feel
that in spite of his wretched body and his extreme poverty
he had something really beautiful to give our little world.

A *maulvi*, by the name of Saiyid Mohammed Niaz
Husein, remains in my memory as a religious enthusiast
of sound parts. The maulvi was an enormous old gentleman
with a bushy white beard, innumerable swathings of padded
flowered coats, and superb dignity. His friend the collector
of bazar taxes brought him to call. He began by asking
my caste, taking it for granted, when the Peshkar told him
I belonged to the Christian caste, that I had come to the
village as a missionary. Vainly I tried to explain the nature
of my interests. Well, then, he suggested, if I really wanted
to learn something about India, I had better go first to
Lucknow for two years and learn to speak Urdu properly.
"What use to learn the vulgar dialect of this insignificant
village?" I ought to follow the example of one of his ancestors, a Persian man of letters who resided at the court
of the Mogul Emperor, Shah Jahan. The Emperor ordered
him to master Pushtu as a preparation for taking up an
important administrative post on the northwest frontier.
The Persian scholar informed the Emperor with dignity that
nothing could induce him to waste his time learning the
rough language of barbarians. "There is nothing worth
while for you to learn here," the maulvi concluded bluntly.

He put me through an examination of the number of
languages I spoke and the general curriculum of my education. I did my best to impress him, but scarcely felt much
success when, peering at me intently, he broke in with,
"According to Indian custom it is not good for women to
cut their hair short in the fashion of men." Apologetically

I held out my still bandaged wrist, assuring him that until my unfortunate accident I had always worn long hair. To change the subject, I brought out three beautiful Persian manuscripts I had acquired at Isfahan, following a crooked path to India. He turned the pages slowly, translating the Persian into Urdu for the benefit of the assembled company, and pausing for the Peshkar to give an English rendering.

One of the books inspired him to a discussion of the mystic Sufi faith, of which he himself was a votary. After reading all the great scriptures of the world, including the Bible, he had ascertained that the pinnacle of religious thought was to be found in Sufism. He began to describe the delightful intimacy with God experienced by Sufis. But the Peshkar, who was getting bored, made his translations shorter and shorter and finally came to a dead stop. Just then Abdul Shah appeared on the scene, and the protracted interview was brought to an end.

Abdul Shah was of the elect of God, having personally, as he averred, attended a durbar of God in paradise. He lived in the village, but wandered about the countryside on strange errands of his own. The first time I saw him walking past the tent in a short orange dress with an orange scarf over his head, bells girdling his waist and more bells jingling about his ankles, I was startled. He was a fakir, the Ayah volunteered. "Every day he goes outside to a certain tree and sits under it. If it rains, the ground around Abdul Shah always remains perfectly dry."

Abdul Shah's thin face used to light up with a pleasant smile when I spoke to him, but the smile faded abruptly, leaving the mouth straight and peculiarly sober, the eyes hard, almost glittering. He carried a chillum, a small clay pipe bowl about the size and shape of a morning glory, and the rank odor of ganja trailed behind him as he passed. Every day he came walking along the tahsil path as if bent on urgent business, but at intervals of a hundred yards or so he would stop, raise his head, narrow his eyes, and stare

at the sun for a minute, muttering to himself. Then he
would lean backward until he nearly lost his balance, right
himself with a sudden jerk, shout, "Allah ho!" and perform
a curious pirouette, bringing his heels down hard with a
rhythmic jingle of bells. Afterward, he would look out of the
corner of his eye to see if anybody had observed him. Now
and then he sang devotional songs. On some puzzling days,
Abdul Shah thought he was a woman. Then he wore a long
skirt drawn tightly about his lean hips, and over his face,
down to his waist, hung a red cloth; for he was in purdah!
Long black cords with colored woollen balls dangled at the
back of his head, like the decorations little girls fasten in
their braids.

Though the ignorant Mussulmans of Pachperwa looked
on him as a saint, most of the Hindus said he was a harmless idiot. The Tahsildar, however, thought there was astuteness in his madness. Only when threatened with a lawsuit for
debt did Abdul abandon his wife and five children, add
"Shah" to his name, and turn holy. Before that he was
merely a confectioner, a brother of Kalu the tobacco dealer.
Once I asked Kalu whether Abdul was a good or bad fakir.
"He is my brother," Kalu answered noncommittally.

When the old Sufi saw Abdul Shah coming along that
morning, he called to him authoritatively and asked what
he, a Mussulman, meant by rigging himself up in bells like
a nautch girl. Abdul Shah smiled gently and said nothing.
The maulvi arose, bade me good-bye, and thumped away
with his staff, a ponderous figure full of ancient dignity.
Abdul Shah, in jingling bells and knee-length orange skirts,
fell in beside him. We gathered, as they walked on together,
that they were entering upon an earnest religious discourse.

Abdul Shah never bothered me in any way, though every
day he marched up the hill and circled my house with ritualistic regularity. Occasionally I had some really obstreperous
visitor on my hands. As I was finishing breakfast one
morning an erratic stranger, naked except for a loincloth,

suddenly began racing up and down outside my house. He leaped high in the air and shouted in English, "One, two, t'ree!" as he bounced. Then he turned several somersaults. When I appeared on the veranda, he came right-side-up just in front of me with a demand for clothes or five rupees. He might have been an acrobat, but he was obviously mad. I decided to ignore him and went inside again. He was not at all discouraged. He continued to loiter about for two days, all the while turning somersaults, calling on Allah, leaping in the air, shouting, "One, two, t'ree!" and reiterating a demand for money. Then I saw him astride the biggest elephant at the Devi shrine, chanting in a loud voice while he held in front of him, upside down, the torn page from some English magazine. This act of sacrilege aroused the ire of the Hindu *chaprasis* of the tahsil, who drove him off.

About this time Ram Lakhan, with all the enthusiasm of a young detective, breathlessly asked permission to come inside the house because he had something important to tell me. "That *daku*, that dangerous robber," he announced, "is not mad at all. He is only pretending. He belongs to a gang of robbers from Utraula. They want to rob your house, and they have sent this man in advance to spy out everything. The others of his band are now waiting in the bazar. He pretends to be mad, but all the time he is looking in at the windows and planning how to rob you." By a coincidence, at that very instant I glanced up and caught the queer fellow peering through a far window.

Though I did not credit Ram's story, I found a madman camping on my veranda disturbing, to say the least. I sent over to the tahsil and asked to have him escorted away. But three days later he turned up once again. The Tahsildar, the Station Master, and I happened to be sitting in front of the house in the early evening. A loud shout of "*Allah-ho akbar!*" suddenly rent the air. There he was, head thrown back and one hand cupped over his ear, like a muezzin calling the hour of prayer. The Tahsildar ordered him sternly to depart and not come near my house any more. Obediently he walked off to a safe distance. There he turned and dramatically shouted over his shoulder: "I know who you are. You are the Tahsildar of Pachperwa, and a bad reputation you have! You take bribes from all the thekedars and oppress the poor tenants. You are a wicked man." With this audacious fling he vanished.

I had spoken of Ram's conviction that the poor fellow was a dangerous robber in disguise. "Now is he mad or not?" I asked laughingly, expecting the Tahsildar to take the cue and answer that of course he was a lunatic. "I do not think he is mad," he replied drily. "He knew me very well, as you see, and he knew what he was saying." It occurred to me he would not trouble us much longer and my guess was right.

Official business brought plenty of English-speaking Indians, both Mussulmans and Hindus, on brief visits to Pachperwa, and as a matter of courtesy they nearly all came to see me. Some were estate servants. Some were government officials. If they stayed more than a day, tents were pitched in the mango grove east of the New Bazar. In this way I gradually came to know the administrative personnel of the whole region. The sanitary inspector of Persian descent, the district health officer from Gonda, a forest officer, a police inspector, a tax collector and the tahsildar and assistant tahsildar of the Utraula subdivision of Gonda district, which included Pachperwa, all dropped in at one time or another. From estate headquarters at Balrampur came the Deputy Sahib, the superintendent of the Maharaja's elephant stables, recently appointed rent contractor for Pachperwa, one of the estate engineers, the forest officer of the Balrampur estate and the superintendent of supplies.

Whenever one of these gentlemen appeared there was always a little flurry in the village. When a police inspector came, our *Thanadar* wore his khaki uniform and a pongee turban, instead of his customary loose dhoti and shirt. A magnificent red turban with a gold fringe was reserved for Mr. Eric McIntosh, District Superintendent of Police. The Tahsildar put on white flannel trousers, and the Peshkar a green cloth hat in honor of the Deputy Sahib. Minor clerks collected at a distance and salaamed ceremoniously. There were also feverish hours of catching up on records and preparing necessary reports just before the arrival of the great ones. Fortunately they never descended without due notice, so they found us ready for them, our best foot out.

So accustomed was I to informal visits from anybody and everybody that I was distinctly startled to have Asgar Ali hand me a calling card after I had been in the village some six months. It read "Wm. Massey, B. A., Assistant Master." Some English schoolteacher, I supposed, wandering about the country and accidentally stumbling into Pachperwa. But in walked an Indian. He had come to pay me his respects as a Christian, he announced, and he introduced himself as a mission high-school teacher in a large city of the province. Pachperwa was his home, however, and with his widowed mother he had just come back to it for the summer holidays. He felt much strengthened by my presence in the village! My noble Christian work was certainly going to raise the standing of his whole family with the other villagers. Might he inquire with what mission I was working?

When I told him I was not a missionary and that I had come to India only to learn, Mr. Massey looked disappointed. "So you do not do propaganda of any sort?" he asked incredulously. Still, he insisted on being cheered by the realization that my Christian life and work ought to have an uplifting influence on the ignorant and superstitious villagers.

"But you must miss your Christian friends? It must be very difficult for you to live here without any Christian companionship, and at times, no doubt, you feel very lonely?"

Again I had to disillusion him. Fortunately Mr. Massey's

own Christian optimism did not desert him. "It is indeed the Lord who supports us through thick and thin," he murmured. Then he confessed that he himself was scarcely content to live for long at a time in Pachperwa. Sometimes he felt very much discouraged. He had to keep reminding himself of the only ray of hope: "The people are beginning to grow tired of their old religion and their hideous idols. They have found out that these cannot help them in their trouble, and they are ready to see the light. They only need to be educated, and they will all come to Christ."

While I was listening to these hopeful utterances, I was wondering what it was about Mr. Massey that seemed incongruous. Suddenly I saw it was his clothes. Outside, the mercury registered 125 degrees, but there he sat suffocating in a blue serge suit, his neck choked up in a stiff white collar and bow tie, his feet encased in black socks and hot shoes. The pity of it was that William Massey was making himself uncomfortable only in deference to what he supposed to be my standards. Proof came the next time I saw him. We met accidentally in the village street. Obviously embarrassed to have me see him in ordinary dhoti and khaki shirt, he murmured apologetically: "When in Rome, do as the Romans do!"

The Masseys recalled a story I had once been told by the Doctor, in his rôle of local historian. I had asked whether any Westerner had ever lived in Pachperwa before. Yes, said the Doctor, more than thirty years ago he used occasionally to encounter a missionary named Downey walking about the village. Mr. Downey came to work among the Tharus. He established a small mission at the edge of the jungle eight miles away and made many converts. Then something unfortunate occurred. Mr. Downey vanished— "flew to the mountains" in the Doctor's phrase—together with the wife of a Hindu tailor of Pachperwa. The mission closed, and the Tharus reverted to semi-paganism as rapidly as they had been converted.

I called on Mrs. Massey at her clean little house in the

eastern part of the village a week or two after her son's visit, and as tactfully as possible brought up the subject of the mythical Mr. Downey. There was nothing mythical about him. She knew him only too well. It was to help Mr. Downey at his new mission station among the Tharus that she and her husband had originally come to Pachperwa. After the scandal, her husband had tried to carry on the work alone, but he met with little success, and eventually their funds from mission headquarters ceased. Unshaken in their faith, they stayed on, cultivating a little land.

But their religion cut them off from the rest of the community. When the elder Mr. Massey died, the widow brought up her son and two daughters in the way of good Christians. All of them received an excellent education, thanks to the encouragement and facilities of the mission. William first attended the Pachperwa elementary school, and then went on to the mission school at Gonda, the normal school at Gorakhpur, and finally to Lucknow University, where he obtained his much-coveted B. A. His mother had reason to be proud of him. Her son was the only boy in the whole history of the village ever to acquire a modern education. As a by-product, instead of earning three dollars a month like other men, he was now drawing a monthly salary of fifty dollars.

But Christianity and a Western education had apparently put a barrier between William Massey and his own people. Nowadays Indian Christians feel less constrained than formerly to adopt English names, English clothes, English habits, and to imitate foreigners in India, but the community as a whole, numbering some millions, remains peculiarly apart, in spite of exceptional individuals unselfishly devoting themselves to the general welfare.

There were many things William Massey might have done, for example, for his own village. He expressed—and for the time being sincerely felt—a wish to help. It was he who suggested that we start a coöperative society to relieve

the poor cultivators from the money-lenders' oppression.
It was a splendid idea. As a first step I begged him to draw
up a list of the money-lenders and rates of interest in
Pachperwa. He sent a few names and an apology. He would
very much like to help, as he had promised, but just now
he was extremely busy. He was writing two dramas, one on
the life of Queen Esther and the other on the life of the
Prodigal Son! The coöperative society did eventually come
into being, but not as a result of his efforts.

Like blown leaves, Indians drifted across my days, good
and bad, sophisticated and innocent, commonplace and extraordinary. Great scholars, forceful leaders, men of first
rank in the professions or in business, of spiritual insight,
these were scarcely to be looked for in Pachperwa. Broken
reflections made up the pattern of the village life. One had
need to understand the whole great Indian background,
ideals, and thoughts projected down countless centuries, to
fit the tiny fragments into place. Yet now and then, even to
the village, came one who had gathered up more than the
others, and who showed the strength of India beneath a
superficial weakness.

Back in January tent days I watched a small man coming
up the tahsil path, a white woollen blanket, boldly cross-
barred with black, flung around one shoulder like a toga,
bare feet thrust in worn shoes. His head was uncovered, and
a long lock proclaimed him a Hindu. He stopped at the tent,
greeting me in hesitant English. In the bazar he had heard
of my presence in the village. He, too, happened to be a
villager, from Nautanwa in Gorakhpur District, and he
wanted to thank me for my interest in the poor village folk
of India.

By chance, conversation turned to the subject of Buddhism. He seemed to know a great deal about it, though he
himself was a Brahmin. I learned that I was living almost
within the shadow of four places associated with "our
Lord Buddha," as the pundit deferentially called him. The

sites were constantly visited by Buddhist pilgrims from Burma and Ceylon, and occasionally small groups came all the way from China or Japan.

Lumbini Garden, the Buddha's birthplace, lay just across the Nepalese border, fourteen miles from the pundit's own Nautanwa. Kusinagara, the modern Kasia, where the Buddha passed into *Nirvana,* was in Gorakhpur district. Ten miles from Balrampur was Sravasti, site of a great monastery founded during the lifetime of the Buddha, his favorite retreat in the rainy season. To the Brotherhood and to the lay disciples at Sravasti, the Buddha addressed the greatest number of his recorded sermons. And the ruins of old Kapilavastu, the royal city of the Sakyas, where the serious-minded young Prince grew up, was supposedly only a half day's journey by elephant from the third station east of Pachperwa. Nobody had ever before mentioned these important places in the locality. In spite of the fact that Kapilavastu was within twenty-five miles of us, nobody in Pachperwa seemed ever to have heard of Gautama Buddha.

The pundit showed a fine feeling of reverence for the Buddhist teachings. He himself was doing all he could to help revive the Buddhist spirit—dead in India for more than a thousand years—and especially to create a living center of Buddhist culture at Nautanwa. A school with several students had already come into existence. It was his ambition to build up a good library, with books in English and other languages, and also to provide a rest house at Lumbini for pilgrims. To him, the deserted and lonely site of the Buddha's birthplace, marked only by a broken pillar scratched with a few lines of Pali, was an unhappy symbol of man's forgetfulness.

The first time I saw the pundit, he did not mention the strange errand which had brought him to Pachperwa, but a month later I myself made a pilgrimage to Lumbini and to the other Buddhist holy places with Asgar Ali, and the pundit acted as guide. During the long hours in bullock carts, on elephants, and in station waiting rooms, I came to know many details of his life, including the circumstances of that first visit to Pachperwa.

He came in pursuit of a runaway Hindu woman, eloping with a Mussulman. He had received secret information of the intended elopement. When the couple bought tickets to Cawnpore, the pundit also bought a ticket and boarded the same train. They tried to elude their pursuer by unexpectedly getting off at Pachperwa, but the pundit also jumped off the train. All three of them then went to the police station to settle the affair. The girl was of age and insisted she was going off with the Mussulman of her free will. Legally there was no means of stopping her. But if our Hindu Sub-Inspector of Police had not happened to be at Gonda just then, leaving a Mussulman in charge, the pundit was sure the girl might have been saved.

With my Western ideas I saw no reason why a Mussulman and a Hindu should not marry, if they loved each other. The pundit told me I did not understand the real situation. It was not a case of love but of deception. Certain Mussulmans made a regular business of seducing village women. One of these men would cautiously approach a young widow or a woman unhappily married, and presently, with a promise of marriage and a glittering tale of luxurious life in a big city, he would persuade her to run away with him. The farce at an end, she was shipped north to Peshawar and sold to a tribesman on the Afghan frontier—where women are scarce—for a few hundred rupees.

Here was a glimpse into a dark underworld such as exists in every country. But the Indian woman caught in this sort of traffic is peculiarly helpless. She has no money. She cannot write a letter. She knows, if she is Hindu, that according to caste laws she is now inexorably cut off from all help of family or friends. It was to prevent another such human tragedy, as he saw it, that the pundit had stepped down at Pachperwa on a morning of golden sunshine in late January.

Like countless other young Indians he was feeling for

his place in the movement of national self-consciousness, irresistibly sweeping India. He had given his ardent support to Mahatma Gandhi, helping carry into the villages the spinning and weaving program, which is fundamental, in Gandhi's economics, to independence. He himself was wearing *khaddar*, the handspun, hand-woven cloth of Gandhi's sermons. "I have a nice feeling when I wear this coarse cloth," he said without affectation.

The pundit was also active in the Hindu Mahasabha, an organization designed to foster various social and religious reforms in the Hindu community, primarily for the purpose of giving it greater strength in the political field. Hindu law, for instance, does not permit out-of-caste marriages, and if a Hindu woman marries a Mussulman she and her children are completely lost to the Hindu fold. The Mahasabha is trying to prevent these drains and losses and has introduced a radical program of accepting all Hindus back into the community with a proper purification ceremony, if they desire to return, and it even admits Mohammedan converts on the ground that originally they must have been Hindus who forsook Hinduism for Islam. As a local secretary of the Mahasabha, the pundit found himself involved in all sorts of semi-social, semi-political activities, but the mainspring was always a passion for service to his fellowmen and an intense love for India.

His background was one of strictest orthodoxy. The father, now dead, had been a *purohit*, one of those family priests of India who serve as spiritual teachers and perform household pujas, subsisting on gifts and on the income from a few acres of land. The mother devoted herself to her household, strictly observed all the orthodox rules, and found joy in making holy pilgrimages. After her noon bath, the pundit said, she never allowed even her own children to touch her, and rather than eat anything or swallow so much as a drop of water in the promiscuous modern railway carriage, she fasted completely whenever she was on a train. She was now seventy, and more devoted than ever to pil-

grimages. The pundit had recently taken her to Allahabad
and saw her settled in a pilgrim hostel there, for the annual
Magh Mela, attended by at least a million pilgrims. During January the old lady had taken her daily bath at the
confluence of the sacred waters of the Ganges and the
Jumna, had recited her prayers and spent her time listening to the words of holy men.

The pundit recreated for me many pictures out of his
childhood. The one I liked best was of a little boy clasping
his mother's hand in front of the Monkey Temple of Ayodya.
In Rama's city sacred monkeys swarm everywhere. Was
it not Hanuman, the monkey general, who generously
assisted Rama in the rescue of Sita when she was carried
off to Ceylon by the demon king Ravana? Pilgrims buy
sweets to offer, and the priest at the temple, after blessing
the offering, returns a part to each pilgrim to bestow on the
little Hanumans, greedily waiting.

The small Brahmin boy is very fond of sweets. Instead
of feeding the monkeys as he descends the long flight of
steps from the temple, he hides what the priest has returned.
When his mother isn't looking, he surreptitiously slips one
into his mouth. But suddenly she catches him at it. These
sweets are made of grain, and no high-caste Hindu may eat
cooked grain touched by one of a lower caste. The mother
is horrified because he has broken the ceremonial rule of his
caste. She hurries him home and washes his mouth out
vigorously many times. Then, being a mother and loving
him, she gives him some unpolluted sweets of milk and sugar
to take the place of those she threw away.

There were twelve children in the pundit's family. "But
I am the only surviving son of my mother's body." He was
sent to a priests' school at Benares. Here, in the heart of
Hindu orthodoxy, some subtle influence worked upon him.
He became inexplicably modern. Caste rules and ceremonies
had no meaning in themselves, he began to assert. They had
now degenerated into mere formulas. He did not wish to
become a priest. Fortunately his father died, unaware of the

revolutionary changes that had taken place in the spiritual outlook of his son.

For the Sanskrit, which was part of his schooling, he had continued to cherish an intense love. He spoke with glowing eyes of the beauties of Sanskrit grammar, intricate and perfect as higher mathematics. It took twelve years to learn the grammar alone, he said. Then he drew a picture of Sanskrit scholars he knew, content with poverty, forgetful of the world, sitting day after day, year after year, engrossed in their studies. Sanskrit was the one joy of his widowed sister, who lived with him and shared his own love for the jewels locked up in its treasury.

Once I asked the pundit to recite some Sanskrit for me, and immediately he chanted a Vedic hymn. At first it sounded staccato, like drum-beats, or the clippity-clop of horses' hoofs on a hard road, but slowly I became conscious of the prevailing long a's and m's. These wove a beautiful pattern of sound, producing a peculiar effect on the mind. It was while we were waiting for a train at a junction that the pundit launched into his discourse on Sanskrit. He began telling me the moving story of Sakuntala and Dushyanta, an episode in the *Mahabharata* popularized in a drama by Kalidas. Suddenly he stopped. "When I think of the beauty of those lines," he said, "it makes my hairs begin to move." In the light of the small lamp on the waiting-room table, I actually saw his hair standing stiffly out back of his ears. From the inexhaustible storehouse of Sanskrit literature, the pundit drew forth a multitude of stories of gods and heroes and sages to entertain and teach me on our Buddhist pilgrimage.

His English he had picked up entirely by himself through reading. Once an opportunity had come to him to go to the United States with a friend who offered to pay all his expenses, but he renounced it because he knew his old orthodox mother would grieve if he left Indian soil. He was averse to marriage, but for his mother's sake he had married. Should there be no descendant to carry on the rites for the ancestors,

she would look on this as an overwhelming disaster. He
spoke of his young wife with grave gentleness. She was of a
rich family. At first her thoughts were of clothes and jewelry
and material pleasure; she believed the stars were the souls
of the blessed dead. He began by teaching her to read and
write. At first she was very unhappy in his poor little home,
with the widowed sister who managed the household and
found austere joy in the pursuit of Sanskrit study and the
old mother, rapt in her religious observances and pilgrimages. But now she understood spiritual beauty, he said
simply.

His own deepest longing was to become a disciple of a
certain great *yogi* he had once met, following the ancient
path of renunciation and meditation as a means of realizing
God—the aim and end of existence to every devout Hindu.
Yet he was bound by the duties of a householder. The income from the small property was not enough to support
them, and he worked on a district paper. Lately he had
applied for the agency of the Standard Oil Company in his
locality.

There was something very gentle and sweet in the pundit's
consecration of himself to helping Buddhist pilgrims at
Lumbini—the most immediate service he could render. Just
before my visit, he had facilitated the pilgrimage of a party
of seven Japanese, and before that he had helped a Swedish
lady and a Jewish professor. These two he had carried
across the river at Lumbini on his back. I wondered what
those strangers would have thought had they known that
their Indian porter, who would accept no reward for his
help, traced his descent all the way back to a family of
learned Brahmins mentioned by Manu, and that according
to the family tradition it was Lakshman himself, Rama's
brother, who gave them their ancestral lands.

When Rama required purification for the sin of killing
Ravana, who was really a Brahmin compelled to wear the
form of a demon, the sixteen young Brahmins who dared to
perform the ceremony were driven from their homes by other

Brahmins. But Lakshman came to their assistance, ordaining that they and their descendants should possess forever those lands measured by the flight of arrows he would shoot into the north. The arrows fell far away, and in the region traced out by their flight lived the pundit, descended from one of the sixteen Brahmins of old.

BOOK TWO

CHAPTER VII

Feudal Echoes

Wɪᴛʜ the death of Aurangzeb in 1707, the Mogul Empire which had held sway in India for nearly two centuries entered upon a swift decline. The greater part of southern India broke away from the rule of Delhi. A Persian merchant, appointed Governor of Oudh in 1720, founded the dynasty of the Nawab Wazirs, as the rulers of Oudh were known until 1819, when one of them assumed the title of *shah*, or king.

The history of Oudh is inextricably bound up with the transition of the East India Company from a trading corporation to a territorial power. Warren Hastings, first Governor General over the British territorial conquests in India, cultivated the Wazir of Oudh as an ally against the eastern advance of the Marathas, a Hindu confederacy of rising power. Company troops were furnished the Wazir, in return for which he was to pay an annual subsidy of a million pounds. When the subsidy fell into arrears, the Wazir was forced, in 1801, to cede ten rich districts on the east, south, and west of his frontiers. From this time the Wazir of Oudh had to administer his territory with the advice of Company officials.

Oudh now had its back broken. When profound disorder and misrule had become the order of the day, the Company finally stepped in to reap the benefit. Acting upon instructions from the Court of Directors, the Governor General "gravely and not without solicitude, but calmly and altogether without doubt," prepared to interfere. He drew up a draft treaty. The King was to retain his title and draw a pension, but exercise sovereignty only within his own palace and parks at Lucknow. The civil and military administration of Oudh was to pass in perpetuity to the Company. In the event of the King's refusal to sign within three days, annexation was to be effected at once. What happened at the meeting in 1856, when the British Resident at Lucknow presented the draft treaty to Wajid Ali Shah, has been recorded in detail in the official papers of the day.

The Resident first communicated the import of his message to the Prime Minister, so that the King might be fully prepared to act. A few days later he went by appointment to the palace. Here the palace guards, disarmed by order of the King, saluted without presenting arms. The officials and courtiers likewise appeared without swords or weapons of any sort. The whole court wore an aspect of mourning. The King, an amiable man with a greater taste for literature than government, read the document awaiting his signature. Then, with pathetic dignity, he gave his answer, which I quote from William Knighton's book, *The Private Life of an Eastern King:*

> Treaties are necessary between equals only: who am I now that the British government should enter into treaties with? For a hundred years this dynasty has flourished in Oudh. It has ever received the favor, the support and the protection of the British government. It has ever attempted faithfully and fully to perform its duties to the British government. The kingdom is a creation of the British, who are able to make and unmake, to promote and to degrade. It has merely to issue its commands to ensure their fulfilments; not the slightest attempt will be made to oppose the views and wishes of the British government; myself and subjects are its servants.

Nothing could induce him to sign the "treaty" of abdication. Taking off his turban, he placed it in the hands of the Resident as a sign of his complete humiliation. Three days

later the annexation of Oudh was peacefully carried out.
The ex-King departed for Calcutta, intending to take ship
for England and plead his cause there, but he was not permitted to leave India. On an annual pension of 120,000
pounds he retired to a resort not far from Calcutta, where
he died in 1887.

The year following the annexation of Oudh witnessed the
famous Sepoy Mutiny, as it is known in English history—
the unsuccessful war for independence, as Indians prefer to
call it—centering in Oudh. It was put down within two
years, and the new government, transferred from Company
jurisdiction to the Crown in 1858, was faced with the
problem of bringing order into the chaos its own policies of
extortion, intrigue, and territorial aggrandizement had in a
large measure created. The stabilization of revenue was the
first reform to be put into effect.

Land has always been considered as belonging to the
State in India, and from earliest times the State has claimed
its share of the produce. Manu's Code of two thousand years
ago fixed the king's share at a twelfth to a sixth part of the
grain, or even a fourth part, under certain conditions. An
eighth part was considered a fair levy. During the Mogul
period, land revenue furnished from one third to very nearly
one half the total State revenues. In British India to-day
the land tax supplies 20 per cent of the gross income of the
government.

Two distinct methods of adjusting the land revenue have
been put into operation in British India. In the Mohammedan period the revenue collection was generally farmed out
to contractors, who received 10 per cent of the collections as
payment. Officials of the East India Company made the
mistake of looking on these contractors as landlords of the
type they were familiar with in England. At the close of
the eighteenth century under Lord Cornwallis, their
proprietary rights were recognized at the expense of the
peasant cultivators, who were now reduced to the position of
tenants. On the basis of revenue collected in the past, the

land tax to be paid by the newly created class of big land-lords, or *zamindars*, was fixed in perpetuity. This system, established in Bengal in 1793 and known as the Permanent Settlement, was also applied to limited parts of the United Provinces in 1859—including the large estate of the Maharaja of Balrampur, who allied himself with the British during the Mutiny.

Elsewhere in British India a Temporary Settlement is in force. Every thirty years officials make a fresh survey of land values and fix the tax accordingly, so that the gov-ernment may draw its share from any general enhancement of land values. Landlord ownership and peasant holdings are both recognized under this classification, and peasant proprietors, or *ryots*, hold land either individually or jointly, as a village community. Up to 50 per cent of the rental or 50 per cent of the net assets of landlord holdings is con-sidered a legitimate tax under the Temporary Settlement, though in practice the amount taken is nearer 40 per cent. For peasant holdings, the equivalent of one fifth of the gross produce has been accepted as fair in principle.

When Oudh was annexed in 1856, two classes of proprietors were found, powerful *taluqdars*, most of them representatives of princely houses, with a semi-independent status much like that of the land barons of Europe in the Middle Ages, and inferior proprietors holding their title from some particular taluqdar. The British government recognized the special position of the taluqdars. On their submission it confirmed them in their right in the land, though it did not grant them the rank of independent princes. To-day a little more than half the twenty-four thousand square miles of Oudh belongs to the taluqdars, and the actual cultivators are their tenants.

In spite of his title, therefore, the Maharaja of Balrampur ranks in the eyes of the government simply as a big land-lord. He does not enjoy the rank of a ruling prince. His estate of 1,250 square miles spreading over parts of three districts of the United Provinces, and including more than

three thousand villages with nearly a million inhabitants, is
not classed as one of the semi-independent Indian States. Of
these it may be remarked incidentally, there are some 650, of
which 108 are of major rank. One third of the total area
of India is under the ruling princes.

By government favor to Sir Drigbijai Singh, grandfather of the present Maharaja, the whole of the Balrampur
Estate, with the exception of 250 square miles or so of
purchased lands, pays a fixed tax under the Permanent
Settlement arrangement. The difference to the government
in its two systems of taxation is apparent in the amount
of tax paid on the two divisions of the estate. The bulk of
the land pays an annual tax equivalent to 166,000 dollars.
The remaining fragment of 250 square miles is assessed in
the current thirty-year period at 100,000 dollars. The gross
income of the estate amounts to 1,500,000 dollars a year.

All dry statistics! What did they mean to Pateshwari
Prasad Singh, the young Maharaja of Balrampur? As a
minor he had no responsibility in regard to his estate, which
was under the management of the Court of Wards. He was
busy with lessons, sports, the religious ceremonies in which,
as Maharaja, he had an important rôle to play. While I was
living in the Balrampur Estate, it was decided that, like any
ordinary boy, the Maharaja was to have an allowance—five
rupees a month to start with—in order to teach him the
concrete use of money. At the end of the first month he still
had his five rupees intact. He had forgotten all about them.
Everything he could want was provided for him, and he
had scarcely ever had an opportunity to know what life
is like for those who do not happen to be born maharajas.

When I was riding with him I once asked him if he did
not feel sorry for the poor villagers, shivering through the
cold months in cotton rags. "Yes," he answered, but I could
not see that he was deeply impressed. On one occasion we
were riding through a particularly fly-ridden, filthy village.

"If I were the Maharaja and if this village belonged to

me," I remarked, "I should wish to see it made clean and sanitary."

"Yes," replied the Maharaja, "the villagers are very naughty. They should keep their village clean."

His own life always seemed to me unusually lonely. His father, the late Maharaja, and his mother, the Junior Maharani, were both dead. The Senior Maharani, mother of daughters only, resided in a large red brick palace near the Armory and the Treasury, just beyond the bazars of the town. The Maharaja lived in his own palace in a quite separate quarter, near the big maidan used for polo. In this quarter were most of the officials' bungalows and the big guest house provided by the Maharaja for visiting government officials and stray Europeans. Two younger sisters also lived in the same palace with the Maharaja, but etiquette forbade him to associate with them except in a rather formal manner. They did not visit his wing, and ordinarily he did not visit theirs. In this little world, with rare visits to Lucknow, where he owns another palace, and an annual exit at the time of the hot weather to Naini Tal in the hills, the Maharaja passes his days.

From the hands of various governesses he was finally turned over to an English tutor. Outside as well as inside the schoolroom, he followed a prescribed routine. The early morning ride of two hours, certain afternoons devoted to tennis, soccer, hockey, football—the sons of estate officials made up the teams—every Friday afternoon a drive in his big white Packard car along the familiar roads, he himself taking the wheel sometimes—so days followed one another. For further diversion he watched the polo games on the maidan and listened to concerts furnished by his band. Now and then he reviewed his cavalry of forty-five men or his infantry of two hundred and fifty.

All his comings and goings were attended with formal ceremony. He drove in his carriage from his palace to his tutor's house, five minutes away. Every time he reëntered his palace, where barefoot attendants in red coats and orange turbans always stood about, a priest was at the door, ready to hold a brass tray containing rice, salt, ghi, and other articles over his head, in blessing and purification. The palace priest named the auspicious day for him to mount a new horse or put on a new garment or go into camp with his retinue or start for Naini Tal. His diet was strictly regulated, since he was overweight for his age, and all his food was carefully weighed beforehand by the Brahmin cook who prepared and served his meals. These he ate in Hindu fashion, seated on the floor and using his right hand in place of fork or spoon. In the evening he generally entertained himself playing his gramophone.

In spite of the flattering attention he received, the Maharaja was by nature unusually simple. He was noticeably timid and therefore was easily led. He showed no inclination to be vain or extravagant. His interests were centered in the little affairs of those surrounding him. He had an excellent memory. It seldom occurred to him to go against the orders others might lay down for him or to give orders himself.

His protected life was certainly very different from that of his forceful grandfather, Sir Drigbijai Singh, the tale of whose personal bravery, fearlessness, intelligence, generosity, and able administration is still frequently sung by the palace bard. Drigbijai Singh's early days were passed in a time of storm and stress, when he often had to fight for his life. After the British annexation, he readily adapted himself to the new conditions of peace. He was noted for his progressive administration, the hospitals and schools he built, the tree-lined roads he laid out and the large mango groves he had planted everywhere throughout his lands. Unfortunately he died as the result of a fall from an elephant during a tiger shoot without leaving a legitimate heir, and the succession passed by adoption to Bhagwati Prasad Singh, father of the present Maharaja.

The historical origin of the Balrampur Raj dates only from the early fifteenth century, though the family traces the line of its mythological descent to Arjuna, hero of the *Mahabharata*. The title of raja is said to have been hereditary in the family from the thirteenth century. During the reign of Jahangir, in the seventeenth century, the town of Balrampur was founded and made the seat of the raj. At the time of the Mutiny the Raja of Balrampur was recognized as the first baron of Oudh, the most powerful of all the taluqdars.

The estate administration, only temporarily under direct government supervision, naturally followed Indian formulas and customs. It is the policy of the Court of Wards not to interfere with the internal management of estates, provided the revenue is forthcoming, peace is maintained and no complaints of gross injustice or mismanagement are made. The rights of ordinary tenants are officially protected by the Oudh Rent Act of 1886 and the Amendment of 1921. A tenant is now practically assured of the right to cultivate his holding for life, and his eldest son or heir may inherit his holding for a period of five years. His rent may not be enhanced except at ten-year intervals, and a fair rate must be fixed by the officer charged with making the settlement.

For administrative purposes, the Balrampur Estate is divided into eighteen tahsils, or subdivisions. The tahsildar in charge of each subdivision is responsible for collecting the rents, not from the tenants but from the thekedars, or contractors, appointed for the villages, except in three tahsils where rents are collected directly from the tenants. The thekedars receive from 10 to 25 per cent of the rents they collect and a block of rent-free land for their own cultivation. The tahsildar also auctions off various contracts given out by the estate on a yearly basis and settles disputes among the tenants. His authority is not final, since anyone has the privilege of contesting a decision of his in the hearing of the special manager or assistant manager or even of the English deputy commissioner of the district. But in practice the tahsildar is supreme within the limits of the territory assigned to him.

The Pachperwa tahsil, roughly fifteen miles long and ten miles wide, contained some three hundred villages and was the richest tahsil of the Balrampur Estate. Its yearly income amounted to 125,000 dollars, of which a hundred thousand came from rental and the rest from contracts and special taxes.

On the theory that the land itself and everything on top of it or underneath it belongs to the Maharaja, the tenants have practically no rights except those of cultivating the actual fields for which they pay rent and occupying the houses they themselves have built or bought. For these they pay an original ground rent of eight annas for two *biswas*, one biswa measuring twenty paces, and if they sell their houses one fourth the price is claimed by the estate. The estate owns every tree. The estate owns all the wild honey, because the honeycombs are found in the trees. The estate owns the skins of all dead animals, even those of the bullocks and buffaloes that the villagers have purchased, and their bones as well, selling skins and bones separately to the highest bidders. It owns the fish in all the tanks and rivers. It owns the lizards in the fields and the mud from which bricks and tiles are made. It owns the rivers, tanks, and bridges and the ferry services. It owns the grass and wild hemp.

All these resources of the land are exploited through special contracts. The highest bidder for a village gets all the skins of the village cattle that die during the year. He hires low-caste men to skin the dead animals for him. Then he sells the skins to local shoemakers, drum makers or leather workers, or ships them off to wholesale dealers in the industrial centers. Our leather *theka* was knocked down for fifty dollars to Yasin Khan, who was also the leather contractor for four other villages. The bone contractor paid three thousand rupees for the privilege of collecting the bones of the whole estate. His representatives collected them from the dump heaps outside the village confines. The taboo against anything dead ordinarily prevents Hindus from making use of bone fertilizer, and all this valuable material was shipped away for reduction and export.

The fine grass which grows wild near the jungle is also auctioned off to a contractor. The villagers must buy their bundles of grass for making rope and string from his storehouse. Mahuwa flowers are another source of estate income. Every mango grove is rented to a contractor. In the same way jackfruit and lemon trees are given out on contract. Only the fishermen who buy the right for certain tanks and streams are permitted to fish in their waters.

One day the Tahsildar sent over word that he was about to auction three *dhup* trees growing beside the tahsil building. Benches were arranged on two sides, upon which the bidders sat. In Pachperwa an auction is never final. The three pine trees in question had already been auctioned three times. The first time they were knocked down at fifty dollars and the last time at one hundred. In competition with Haweli Singh's brother, Yasin Khan pushed the figure up to one hundred and fifty. But the Tahsildar told me he would hold the auction once more because he thought he could raise the amount at least another twenty-five dollars.

Formerly pine used to come to our area from Nepal, but later exportation was forbidden, and now it is scarce. It is looked upon as especially fine for funeral pyres, for which it is purchased by the rich at five dollars a *maund*—eighty-two pounds—and it is also used in religious ceremonies.

In the past tenants have been subjected to a host of petty taxes in the nature of manorial dues. Twenty-eight such taxes had been abolished under order of the Court of Wards just before my arrival. Among them were the local *seer* of ghi, equal to a little less than two pounds, collected for every plow in a village once a year; a tax on gardeners; taxes on oil mills and sugar mills; two annas for every *Chamar;* one rupee from every bridegroom; one rupee from every wizard; one rupee from every village or caste headman; four annas from every carpenter and from every blacksmith; *bhusa,*

husks, and arhar, to be furnished by rent contractors; taxes
on palanquin bearers and musicians, and on *kazis* officiating
at Mohammedan weddings. In most cases the thekedars were
responsible for collecting these and other small taxes from
the tenants, in money or kind.

Land rents are collected in four-anna installments, as the
saying is, that is four times a year. The rupee of sixteen
annas is a common unit in India to express measure or
proportion. The cash rent system, replacing the grain rents
of previous times, now prevails for 90 per cent of the tenants
of Oudh.

Under some of the worst Wazirs of Oudh, exploitation
was so ruthless that vast areas fell out of cultivation altogether. If a dishonest official removed from the threshing
floor the lion's share of a hard-earned harvest, what redress
had the wretched cultivator? It did not pay cultivators to
sow and raise a crop, merely to have the King's soldiers
carry it off under their eyes. The older system had one advantage, however. In lean years the rent automatically ad-
justed itself to conditions. Nowadays the tenant is responsible for his rent, just as the landlord is responsible for his
tax, whether crops fail or not, unless the situation is so desperate that a remission or postponement of taxes is decreed
by the government. Under the cash rent system, which
forces cultivators to sell grain generally at depressed harvest
prices, tenants at least know exactly what they are responsible for and can reap the benefit from better cultivation or the use of improved seed.

The main business of the Pachperwa tahsil was carried
on inside and outside the cluster of yellow buildings festooned
with black velvet mold, midway between the New Bazar
and the village. In the north wall of the principal building
was an open recess, and here the Tahsildar sat, generally
from seven to eleven, and from three to six during the cold-
weather days. In hot weather he moved out under the big
pakar tree, and his days commenced an hour earlier. His
own quarters were at one end of the same building, and at

the other was a narrow windowless room where the tahsil
money affairs were conducted. The Treasurer and his assistants squatted behind foot-high desks, writing out endless
accounts. Over their heads were shelves of clothbound books,
records of past years. Clink, clink, clink rang the silver
rupees being paid in and counted at the quarterly settlement
periods. The rupees were placed in strong mesh bags, a
thousand to each bag. Whenever the sums on hand amounted
to more than two thousand rupees, the bags of silver were
placed in a strong-box and dispatched to Balrampur by
the three o'clock morning train, under the escort of
guards.

The work of the tahsil went on in thoroughly Indian
fashion. Somewhere a clock was hidden away, but until the
Peshkar transferred it to his quarters and instituted the
custom of having a guard strike the hours on a gong suspended from a bamboo tripod, nobody ever thought of
counting time. When the Tahsildar appeared and sat down
at his table, his staff gradually assembled, and when he rose
the others melted away. There was no fixed working day, no
fixed time for doing any particular thing, no fixed time for
meals. Seven days a week, twelve months a year, were exactly
alike, except that whenever a Hindu or Mohammedan
religious festival came around or one of the multiple household ceremonies which dominate Hindu life was scheduled to
take place, a leave of absence was granted as a matter of
course. I often contrasted Indian and Western methods of
doing business, and I came to the conclusion that if the
Western method is more efficient, the Indian is more har-
monious, less of a strain on the nerves. Perhaps the subordi-
nation of business to leisurely living in India is an instinctive adaptation of the organism to environment.

Everybody made himself physically as comfortable as
possible. Any kind of costume was permissible. On cold days
colored woollen shawls or padded jackets of bed-quilt design
or tweed Norfolk coats were equally in vogue. In the hot
months bronze-skinned boys stood behind the chairs of the

Tahsildar and the Peshkar, fanning them hour after hour with long-handled fans. Some members of the staff found relaxation in chewing pan. The Peshkar's hookah rested beside him on the ground, and every few minutes he turned his head and pulled on the long stiff stem. Cows, goats and buffaloes strayed around in front of the tahsil buildings, cropping the short grass. Horses, front legs tied together, hopped about like kangaroos.

The settlement of innumerable cases involving disputes about land, infringement of rules and personal quarrels took up vastly more of the Tahsildar's time than the collection of rents. A quarter of the cases went to the Peshkar for disposal and a quarter to the eight tahsil *panches*, or advisers. The remainder the Tahsildar himself handled, with a clerk and a reader to assist him. The duty of the reader was to keep the files in order and present the written petitions for consideration. A petition writer served the tenants for a fee of three annas.

For summoning those whose presence was needed and for performing any task assigned them, the Tahsildar maintained a force of fifty men. Seven of the fifty received a regular salary of five dollars a month. The others were entitled to collect three annas every time they delivered a summons. These men, variously called chaprasis, peons, or *sipahis*—anglicized into sepoys—were officially under the Jamadar. Twenty or thirty of them were always hanging about, leaning on their stout cudgels made of solid bamboo, waiting to be sent out on messenger service to the villages. Some acted as a personal bodyguard to the Tahsildar. They also carried out his orders for administering corporal punishment to certain offenders.

Lord of our little world of Pachperwa was the Tahsildar Sahib, a Brahmin of enigmatic personality. It was a long time before I felt I understood him even a little. Under a drooping gray mustache, the chin slid away too suddenly, but a protruding lower lip supplied the determination the face might otherwise have seemed to lack. The eyes were small and light brown. Now and then he smiled faintly, but he was not demonstrative. He never raised his voice, like the Peshkar. When a petitioner presented himself in the fashion village folk deem most polite, standing on one leg and clasping his hands in supplication, he looked shrewdly at the specimen of humanity in front of him and listened in silence. Then, fixing his eyes on the far-away mountains, he pronounced judgment in a low voice—remote and dispassionate. But he was neither. He was like a man playing a game of chess. Even the movement of a pawn he watched calculatingly. He had been in charge of the tahsil three years. If he had a single personal friend among those with whom he was in daily association, no one knew it. He himself was well aware that behind the flattery with which he was surrounded were fear and dislike.

It was his ambition, the Tahsildar said, to live so simply that he could pack all his possessions and leave Pachperwa on ten minutes' notice. Though he might have made himself comfortable in his quarters at Pachperwa, he preferred to shut off the main part of the tahsil building and live in the two small rooms at one end, opening on an enclosed court. Once he invited me to inspect them. They were severely empty, immaculately clean. In one room were a chair, a strong-box, a small tin trunk used as dressing table, a bed, and over it a bamboo pole, across which, neatly folded, hung his official trousers and coats. The dining room contained only a single low wooden seat. In a shed at one side the old Brahmin cook prepared his frugal meals. He had begun his official service as a clerk at ten rupees a month, and though he was now drawing a salary of eighty rupees, he continued to live like the ten-rupee clerk. But this was not the whole story. At Balrampur, he was said to be building a house finer than that of any other official in the city.

Very astute in worldly affairs, in matters of caste, family, and religion, the Tahsildar was strictly orthodox. He did not smoke. He never touched liquor. He did not chew pan. He did not eat meat, fish, or eggs. He did not sleep during the hot time of day, like everybody else, and he observed his morning and evening worship with regularity, reciting passages from the *Vedas* in the approved manner.

I spent many hours with the Tahsildar while he was hearing cases. The Indian villager has an ingrained respect for authority and, conversely, a childlike inability to decide anything for himself. The time-honored way out of a dispute is appeal to a third party. No problem was too small or too personal to be brought to the Tahsildar.

The first case I happened to hear was that of a sturdy young man who arrived one morning sobbing loudly. His brother had beaten him. The Tahsildar sent a chaprasi to summon the brother. The two men lived in adjoining houses, and the plaintiff had pushed some logs of wood over on his brother's ground, which the brother had promptly pushed back again. This had precipitated a quarrel. Since the plaintiff was large and strong and the brother a puny little fellow, the alleged beating was absurd. "But what do you want me to do?" the Tahsildar asked finally. "Give my brother a beating," was the vindictive reply. The case was dismissed.

Many disputes over houses were examined. Since all the land is the Maharaja's, no tenant can put up even a two-foot wall without official permission from the tahsil. Here is a prolific source of trouble. The villagers are always trying to tack a few more feet on to their tiny dwellings. A wall spurts out here, an extra room grows out there, a fodder tower springs up somewhere else. In the morning the neighbors wake up to find their entrance blocked or half their path cut off. One maintains that the wall is a very old wall, not new at all, and the others insist the final coating of mud has only just dried. The decision is with the estate, and if a man cannot produce his bit of paper giving him permission to build his wall in just that place, down it comes. The fact that even the villages have no room for expansion indicates the acuteness of the land hunger in this part of India.

Sometimes a case threw sudden light on deep-rooted caste prejudices. A delegation of Hindus arrived one afternoon to enter a complaint because the contractor of their village had permitted a shoemaker to build a house in the center of the village. The Peshkar, hearing this case, decreed that the shoemaker must build himself a new house on the outskirts of the village in accordance with custom and remove to it within fifteen days. The villagers wanted him ejected at once, but the Peshkar told them their request was unreasonable. The man should have his two weeks.

One morning the voices of women in shrill altercation drew me out of my tent and over to the tahsil. The Tahsildar had some fifteen of them lined up before him, like naughty children. They had been caught secretly catching *gohs* and selling them to a local leather dealer. Gohs are big field lizards, which have furnished slippers to Indian women for centuries. But gohs are estate property. A Mussulman had paid ten rupees for the privilege of collecting the skins of all field lizards caught in Pachperwa tahsil during the year, and he did not intend to have his rights infringed. The women were pronounced guilty and made to pay a small fine.

One poor old toothless woman spent two days around the tahsil while the question of her roof hung in the balance. Her husband, now dead, had been a village watchman, and the thekedar of her village had ordered her to turn over the house where she had been living to the new watchman. The thekedar maintained that he had offered her a house in the *Kori* district, where she belonged by caste. Too possessionless to be afraid of anybody, she called the Tahsildar "Elder Brother" and monotonously reiterated that she did not want the house offered to her, but she did want the other one. Everybody, including the Tahsildar, was moved by her extreme misery and pitiful state, and the thekedar received instructions to let her have the house she wanted.

The Tahsildar was often called upon to protect tenants

against the unjust exploitation of the rent contractors. From a village a few miles to the east, four men and a woman arrived one March afternoon, at the time when the three-anna share of the rents was due. They had a curiously secretive manner, the spokesman addressing the Tahsildar in a confidential tone. They distrusted their thekedar, it seemed. If they paid him twenty rupees for their rent, he gave a receipt for sixteen. How could they know what he wrote on the paper, until they were told their receipts showed arrears in their rents? They asked permission to pay the present installment of their rent directly to the tahsil. The Tahsildar requested the treasurer to take their money, which they had brought with them, and give the receipt in his presence. Their own thumb-prints were duly registered to give the proper legal status to the transaction.

Again, villagers were constantly presenting themselves with petitions they knew in advance were illegitimate and could not possibly be granted. A police chaprasi wanted the land of his father, who had just died, entered in his son's name. By the recent Amendment to the Oudh Tenancy Act, the son of a statutory tenant may inherit the holding of his father for a period of five years. After that he has to enter into a new agreement with the estate. The chaprasi hoped to circumvent the legal restriction and have his rights recognized for a longer period. He was told, naturally, that his request was useless.

A Tharu with squinty little eyes and an open, childlike face balanced himself on one leg. His thekedar had warned him that his well, unprotected by any curb, was a danger to man and beast. He was in mortal fear that he was going to be arrested. Investigation brought out the fact that he lived in Basti district. He had come all the way to Pach-perwa, because he thought if he went near his own tahsildar he would be punished. With the assurance that he need not be afraid of arrest and the advice to make a temporary mud protection about his well soon, he went off satisfied.

A strange looking baba, with a heavy V-shaped marking

in red and yellow on his forehead and hair twisted in a grotesque knot over one eye, was another visitor to the tahsil building. Everybody except the thekedar of his village had paid the village watchman his grain dues. The tenants had appointed the baba to appeal to the Tahsildar for justice on behalf of the watchman. The thekedar himself suddenly appeared on the scene, probably having heard that a complaint was to be lodged against him. He had every intention of paying the watchman his grain, he announced with dignity, but he had not yet finished his late spring harvesting. When the work was completed, the man would receive his proper dues.

Many cases had to do with plowmen. No ordinary peasant even dreams of rising to the status of a landlord, but every villager is eager for the respectability he acquires as a tenant —of only a half acre, it may be, but still, a half acre to sow and reap as his own. The position of hired laborers is such that nothing but desperate want reduces a man to work on another's land, and plowmen are consequently recruited by the prosperous from the most wretched of the population, the Chamar and Kori castes and destitute Mussulmans. Approximately 3,500 field workers are found for every thousand farmers in England and Wales, but in the United Provinces there are only 133 laborers to every thousand tenants.

The chronic dearth of plowmen is largely due to the condition of practical slavery which is their lot. It is customary for an employer when he takes a plowman into his service to advance him a certain sum of money, called *sawak* —anything from ten or twenty to two hundred rupees. This loan is immediately swallowed up for some important event like a wedding, and the laborer practically becomes a bond slave to his master. Though not recognized by law, the debt is binding by custom. One hired laborer can cultivate six acres. His wages are customarily one fifth of the crop he produces, barely enough to feed himself and his family, who often help with the weeding. Sometimes, instead of grain payment and a cash advance, he accepts two to three dollars a month as wages. If crops fail, the ordinary plowman is compelled to draw advances of grain for subsistence, and so he sinks more and more in debt. Years pass, and there is no change in his hopeless condition of debt and starvation.

This explains why plowmen are constantly defaulting. In our district with the Nepalese border conveniently at hand, they frequently crossed over and hired themselves under more advantageous terms to new masters, or even took up land of their own. Or somebody bribed a plowman to desert, paying off the old debt as part of a new advance. To save wrangles and intrigues the Tahsildar had ruled that in his domain no plowman could leave one employer for another in the same village. If he shifted his services, he had to go entirely outside his former village.

Plowman cases came thick and fast in May, just before the heavy field work of the year was to commence. The Tahsildar used his own discretion in settling them. One man had returned after fourteen years' residence in Nepal and hired himself out to a certain thekedar. Immediately his former employer put in a claim for 140 rupees advanced twenty years before. The Tahsildar ordered him to accept 100 rupees and cancel the remainder of the debt. Another typical dispute was between a plowman, who wanted to go over to a new employer, and his old thekedar, to whom he owed ten rupees and thirty-three maunds of grain. The Tahsildar forbade him to leave until his debt was paid. The plowman would have no difficulty in getting any number of men to take him over, he said, with only this small obligation to settle. The thekedar had brought along a book containing his account with the plowman. It revealed that the plowman's one fifth share of the preceding year's harvest, which happened to be a poor one, had come to exactly nineteen maunds and eleven seers of grain—fifteen hundred pounds. He had had to borrow thirty-three additional maunds to keep himself and his small family alive.

To the Tahsildar's court also came all sorts of intimate

family affairs for adjustment. A low-caste Hindu woman
had married again, after the death of her husband. Her
former husband's parents demanded that the jewelry she
had received as a wedding present from their son be returned to them. The Tahsildar agreed, and the second husband, who represented the wife, said they were quite ready
to accede to the demand.

Another woman, a widow, had called her brother from
Tulsipur two years before to manage her eight acres, now
entered in the name of her young son. Then, having remar-
ried, she wanted her brother to leave. The Tahsildar decreed
that since she had persuaded the brother to give up his
home and move his family and his plow, he should be permitted to cultivate her fields another year, after which he
should leave. The woman was not satisfied. She left, insisting
that she would refer her case to the Deputy Sahib.

Occasionally loud voices betokened something of special
concern—sure to be a tragedy for somebody. Once I came
upon a man with a yellow turban waving his hands excitedly
and shouting at the top of his voice at the Tahsildar. Fifty
maunds of paddy had just disappeared from the mud
granary in his house. He had been away overnight. Obviously someone in the village was responsible. He had
recently had a quarrel with his Mohammedan thekedar and
was sure that some of the thekedar's men had perpetrated
the theft in revenge. The loss was ruinous; for his total
supply of food for the rest of the year and seed for the
next year's crop were gone. The Tahsildar promised to investigate, but there seemed little likelihood that the man
would actually recover his grain.

In addition to carrying on the routine work at headquarters, the Tahsildar and the Peshkar went out from
time to time to investigate particular cases on the spot. The
Peshkar took me along with him on one such occasion. We
made the usual early morning start, getting off by elephant
before six. Striking out across the dried fields, we presently

came to the village for which we were heading, a tiny
cluster of huts beside a mango grove.

The Peshkar's first task was to inspect a new well. The
well was of substantial burnt brick, with a cement curb. It
was not yet finished, but the mason working on it measured
the water and reported that it was four yards in depth. This
was satisfactory, and the villagers who had assembled were
told they could begin drawing water as soon as the ground
excavated around the well had been filled in. When I
learned that work on the well had been started sixteen
months before, the progress seemed a bit slow, especially
since the only source of drinking water for the village was
an insanitary, oily-looking pond.

Our next port of call was a good sized village with a building dispute to be settled. A Mussulman had recently erected
a fodder tower in the exact center of the road near his
house. Not only had he built a large tower, six or eight
feet high, but he had surrounded it with a square platform
of mud as a protection, so that all traffic passing this point
had to squeeze through a space barely a foot and a half wide.
The Peshkar shouted at the abashed man in his loudest and
angriest tones, took a hoe, and himself chopped the platform
away. Then he ordered the man to have the whole tower
down by night. The offender meekly promised to obey, knowing well that he did not have a leg to stand on.

We went on, led by a large group of villagers, to the
scene of another dispute. Here somebody had shifted his
silo to a position close to a well. The people were complaining that it interfered with drawing water. The Peshkar
angrily ordered the tower to be torn down. But suddenly
this man produced a permit signed by the Tahsildar and the
Peshkar was forced to withdraw his order. The next complaint was entered by a woman. Her next-door neighbor
had recently moved his fodder house two yards up her
lane in order to have room for his cart in the vacant space.
This arrangement effectively blocked her opening. A hoe

was again demanded, and the Peshkar marked a line down the middle of the mud tower. The northern half was to be chopped down by sunset.

There were two thekedars for this village, a fat Brahmin owning a twelve-anna share, and a lean Mohammedan with a four-anna share. They entertained us in an open thatched shelter. They, too, had a complaint to register. Some of the tenants were refusing to give their stipulated five days of *begar*. According to estate rules, every tenant is expected to render five days of free service a year to his thekedar and in addition as many days to the tahsildar as he may require on behalf of the estate—perhaps a week.

While the Peshkar was supporting the position of the thekedars and instructing them to send any tenants who refused to work to tahsil headquarters at once for discipline, a number of sick people mysteriously began to appear on the scene. Word of my presence was flying through the village, and out of the huts they came, mothers bringing their little babies nearly dead with dysentery, old blind women, a goiter patient, a leper with his feet tied up in dirty rags. Everywhere the same story of helpless ignorance in the face of disease, the devastating absence of care. Life seemed suddenly altogether sad. But the Mohammedan thekedar sent off for some large plates of brightly colored straw, woven by the women of his household, to present to us. The Peshkar handed one of them to our elephant driver with the remark that he might use it for the elephant's chapatis, and as we rode away it was the laughter of the village at his joke, not its groans, that echoed in our ears.

As the months passed, one aspect of the tahsil administration impressed itself on me deeply. Although the estate is for the time being under government control and could scarcely hope for an abler manager with higher personal standards than Kanwar Jasbir Singh, many of the minor officials showed a tendency mercilessly to exploit those over whom they exercised power. In this respect they merely shared a common human inheritance, but the Indian masses, illiterate and poor, are no longer protected even by the strong village organization in force until less than a century ago. Laws are not a sufficient safeguard. Unless those charged with administrative duties are stripped of the prerogatives of a sacred official class and acquire a little practical idealism, and unless the voiceless millions are properly equipped for their own self-defense, laws merely furnish new excuses for those on top indirectly to exploit and grind down the masses.

Forced labor is a feudal institution still generally practised in the Indian States and throughout rural India, though it is now under legal restriction. The law requires all government officials on district tour to pay for services exacted from villagers—eight annas a day for the use of a bullock cart, four annas in wages a day for general labor, and all supplies to be paid for according to market value. In theory, service is rendered in return for service given. The king or landlord or government assures the people of protection through an accredited representative; the grateful cultivators lend their carts for transport duty and furnish necessary supplies of wood, charcoal, milk, food and so forth. But in practice begar, as it is known, is plain extortion.

My first inkling of the extent to which the abuse can be carried was when it so happened that the Governor of the United Provinces decided that he would like to have a tiger shoot in the Balrampur forests during Christmas week. His Excellency became, naturally, the guest of the Maharaja, and the estate prepared to entertain him.

There were, I believe, eight persons in the Governor's Christmas party. At least one thousand men worked for a solid month to prepare the camp site, leveling the ground, erecting a bazar to supply food for the several hundred beaters and attendants, installing a water supply and putting up the tents. Some men were sent from Balrampur and paid nominal wages, but the rest were commandeered from surrounding villages and received nothing. Potters were rounded up and sent over to make on the spot twenty thousand pots. The number seemed extraordinary, but I was assured that pots to this number were actually produced. They included cooking vessels, water jars, drinking cups, and flower pots. At the last moment word came that His Excellency would prefer "natural surroundings," and plans for camp decoration were forthwith abandoned. The flower pots were brought back and stacked in the unused room of the tahsil, and afterward I fell heir to seventy of them, since nobody else had any use for them. Five hundred string bedsteads were requisitioned from the villages and sent to the camp. Hundreds of carts were taken to carry supplies. Forty buffaloes and twenty cows were collected from the villagers to furnish the camp milk, in addition to one or two cows especially purchased. Straw, fodder, thatching grass, and charcoal were supplied by the ton.

For all this regal entertainment of the English Governor of the United Provinces the Indian villagers had to pay. The estate voted a sum of 5,000 rupees for expenses, but part of this went to pay the beaters. At shooting parties it is customary etiquette for officials to pay their own beaters, at the rate of six cents a day with a bonus if a tiger turns up in the beat. But it was thought that His Excellency should not pay for more than three hundred of his five hundred beaters, and the estate took care of the rest. Needless to say, the Governor himself could scarcely have known the questionable background of his pleasant ten days, and as a guest of the Maharaja of Balrampur he was under no responsibility to inquire. I doubt whether even the leading estate officials were aware of the extent to which begar was exacted within the tahsil.

My own house was a case in point. When I came to the village, I did not know more than a hundred words of Hindustani and naturally I was not in a position to supervise the enterprise of house-building. The Tahsildar managed everything for me. It was not for some weeks that it began to dawn on me that forced labor was being used. I kept telling the Tahsildar I wanted everybody who worked on the house to be paid a fair wage according to local standards, but he once remarked that I would make it difficult for him to obtain free tahsil service. Hundreds of those who carried bricks and earth must have gone unpaid. As the laborers came in groups a day or two at a time from many different villages, it was impossible to check over the list. I tried to feel later on that my free "dispensary" was some slight return to the community at large for my unwitting use of its services under the traditional system of extortion.

But this open tax officially recognized as legitimate was nothing compared with the constant secret extortion practised upon luckless tenants and thekedars. Whenever an official arrived and set up camp it was the duty of the Jamadar of the tahsil to see that the ground where the tents were pitched was covered with straw, that charcoal or wood was on hand, that a supply of milk was forthcoming, that carts were waiting to move the outfit on to the next camping site. The occasion was always one for general looting. Subordinate officials had even worked out a system for turning begar into cash profits for themselves. A bullock cart was wanted. If the thekedar requested to furnish it could not secure one or needed his cart for other purposes, he paid five rupees instead. Five hundred bundles of thatching grass might be required for renovating estate buildings. If a man said he had no grass to spare, he had to hand out ten rupees in its place. A mere demand for grass was commonly recognized as a money exaction. Four seers of milk might be ordered. Four seers stood for two rupees. A jungle thekedar was told to send wood. With a sigh, he substituted seven rupees. A canister of ghi was requisitioned. The person upon whom the demand fell found it cheaper to pay four rupees. Since not one thekedar, but several, would be exploited for each and every supposed need of an official, large sums found their way into somebody's pocket, or more generally into several pockets.

The grafting system spreads from the top down. A thekedar bears much the same relation to the tenants of his village that the tahsildar bears to the thekedars. When he wants a cart or has to provide one for somebody else's use, one of his servants goes out and stands at a bridge or some convenient spot where carts must pass and holds up every driver in turn, with the unwelcome news that he must come at once and do some work for a superior. The poor man wants to take his grain to the bazar or to work in his own fields, and he offers the peon six annas to let him off. After holding up several villagers in the same fashion, finally, when the time is exhausted, he fixes on a victim, who is compelled to come along and work as ordered. Theoretically the thekedar can exact five days of free labor from every tenant, and the tahsil can take a week, but in reality there is very little check of any sort, if the man with power chooses to exploit those under him. There are too many ways in which retaliation is possible, should a tenant resist.

I could scarcely doubt that the local estate officials with whom I came in contact were culpable. The opportunities were too many, the pressure too great, the tradition too fixed. In many cases, however, custom actually approved certain forms of indirect bribery. Presents called *nazarana* and *salami* are made on certain occasions by a subordinate to his superior. I found that every thekedar was expected to make a "present" to the tahsildar with or after the payment of the fourth installment of his rent, in July or August. It was not official bribery, since it was not payment for any specific favor, but was intended rather to purchase general good will for the ensuing months. But the annual present, judging by the murmured complaints I heard, was not exactly voluntary. Since the amounts ranged from fifty rupees for a small village to two hundred or more for a large one, the summer meant a rich harvest to the tahsildar. It was commonly understood that estate tahsildars might hope to retire in ten years with a hundred thousand rupees, if all went well.

That Indian administration in many departments, gov-

ernmental and private, is corrupt, everybody knows quite
well. Europeans always assume that an Indian can and
ought to live on a few dollars a month while they themselves spend hundreds. Salaries for the lower Indian officials
are utterly inadequate. Our tahsildar, for instance, responsible for the administration of a territory with a population of eighty thousand people and handling the collection
of an annual revenue of 125,000 dollars, received a salary
of less than one dollar a day. The Peshkar drew ten dollars
a month. These men had studied up to university standard,
spoke English well, and ranked as men of superior training and position. Another main source of trouble is complete uncertainty of office. Tenure is largely dependent on
the personal equation. The inevitable conclusion is, "Make
hay while the sun shines." It is the old maxim of office
in every country of the world. The only difference I could
discover in this respect between Pachperwa and New York
or Chicago was that, while graft in the latter could be estimated in millions of dollars, in my Indian village it was in
hundreds of rupees.

CHAPTER VIII

The Village and the Government

A<small>N</small> I<small>NDIAN</small> village not belonging to a maharaja or big landlord would have closer ties with the government than we had. "Goaramint," as it was occasionally referred to, played no permanent rôle in Pachperwa consciousness, though its ghostly hand was known to hold the ultimate power. Visiting officials were treated with unctuous politeness and nervous dread by local authorities, with unstudied politeness and beguiling simplicity—masking astonishing depths of reserve—by humble nobodies. They were here to-day and gone to-morrow, symbolizing a petition to be laid at somebody's feet, a fluttering hope that it might be granted, inspiring a sense of awe that great ones like the Tahsildar and the Thanadar suddenly grew meek and stood up respectfully to take orders from the lean pale Englishmen or their subordinates. These men were respected and feared, but scarcely loved. Among the younger generation, dislike of the sahibs is to-day almost universal. How can it be otherwise? Their ways are alien to Indian ways, they themselves—with but rare exceptions—unsympathetic to everything Indian. But only one man, squint-eyed Devi Prasad, openly dared to express antagonistic political views.

Devi Prasad was a professed Non-coöperator. He was supposed to have been converted in the Balrampur bazars. He was educated, in the sense of being able to read and write, and he could talk persuasively. During the early days of the Non-coöperation movement, which had its rise after the Amritsar catastrophe in the spring of 1919, he put on khaddar and went about the villages telling the tenants not to pay their rent and not to perform begar service. India was going to get rid of the foreigners. Everybody was going to be rich. Soon all would ride in motor cars.

The villagers listened. Perhaps Devi Prasad was right. Still, if they did not pay their rent, they were certain to be turned out of their little plots of land, and then where would their food come from? Devi Prasad's *swaraj* might give luxuries, but would it supply necessities? They took up a collection for Devi Prasad, in pice and handfuls of grain, and paid their rent as usual when the installments fell due. Later, when Devi Prasad was arrested and sent to Gonda jail for a year, they were thankful they had not followed his advice. Government, whatever it was, was like caste or cholera. It was futile to fight it. Just the same, the words sank in. Devi Prasad had a timid following.

I made the acquaintance of our outstanding Non-coöperator under peculiar circumstances on the very first day I joined the Pachperwa camp of the Jasbir Singhs. At the manager's request, the Tahsildar escorted me on a walk through the village. On the way back we stopped at the dispensary. On the veranda floor lay a corpse-like figure wrapped in a gray sheet. It looked rather dreadful. I asked what the trouble was, and the Tahsildar perfunctorily translated my question to the Doctor. His apathy disappeared as he listened to the latter's reply.

"This man is a bad character," he presently announced. "His name is Devi Prasad, and he calls himself a Non-coöperator. He has given the estate much trouble. He stirs up the tenants. Eight or ten of my men fell on him as he was coming from the station last night and beat him with *lathis*. It seems his arm is broken."

When I settled at Pachperwa a month later, Devi Prasad came round to see if I could do anything for his injured arm, now hanging stiff and crooked as a fish hook at his side. He was not prepossessing, with his squint eye, but he showed a certain grotesque good humor. Beatings were evidently quite in his line. He appeared to take them, like his prison sentence, as a mark of real distinction. Non-coöperators, like adherents of any political party, are good, bad, or indifferent. When Devi Prasad wasn't non-coöperating by word of mouth he was very much an ordinary villager, worrying about his crops and making a desperate effort to raise the necessary rupees to marry his younger sister, a responsibility resting upon him since the death of his father. Presumably he also paid the Maharaja's representative the rent of his own six acres, or he certainly would not have been permitted to retain them.

Another Non-coöperator who visited Pachperwa was a lawyer who had renounced a successful practice in support of Gandhi's movement for complete nonrecognition of the government. He had not, like many others, taken it up again after the movement had died down. Instead he had joined an organization, affiliated with the National Congress, to give free legal advice to villagers. This organization was supported by voluntary contributions and had branches in every district. The purpose was to save the villagers from ruinous exploitation at the hands of unscrupulous lawyers, and to instruct them in their rights as tenants. This man, who spoke excellent English, betrayed real feeling for the wretched condition of the Oudh tenants when he called upon me. He was particularly incensed over the abuses of the begar system. His society was using most of its funds to buy supplies required by officials on tour, so that the villagers might be protected from this perennial extortion. Unfortunately funds were insufficient. I could not see that any of the burden had as yet been removed from the thin shoulders of the villagers of Pachperwa.

The strength and popularity of the Nationalist campaign in the villages, however, was not to be underestimated. When Mahatma Gandhi made a tour of the Gonda District, he received voluntary contributions amounting to considerably more than a hundred thousand rupees. Money poured in from every source, including numbers of women's associations. The Oudh villagers might profess little interest in debates of the Indian Legislative Assembly at Delhi, but they all knew the meaning of swaraj, and most of them were convinced that in some mysterious way, when self-government came, they would be less hungry. Nowadays whenever mass civil disobedience breaks out in India, the government has to face one of the most serious problems it has yet had to face—the grim program of non-payment of taxes. To judge by the nation-wide demonstrations against the salt tax, the timidity that formerly characterized the Indian villagers and made them utterly helpless is now fast disappearing. In its place is a new fearlessness, the outcome of a growing solidarity.

Formerly the Indian village was entirely self-sustaining and very largely self-governing. Fields and grazing ground were common property, furnishing all necessary food. Any surplus, instead of being exported, as it is now, was stored against times of shortage or famine. Under lawless rule the peasants suffered severely, and they were always subject to ill treatment by dishonest tax collectors. Yet, as a communal group, they were better able to resist oppression than they are as so many weak individuals. Even during the Mohammedan period there was no attempt on the part of the rulers to interfere with the traditional Hindu village organization. It was not until the advent of the British and their introduction, less than a century ago, of a centralized administration that village life began to lose its old autonomous character and to sink toward its present low level.

There is plenty of partial evidence in the reports of East India Company officials to show what the old-time village institution was like. The accounts of early travelers also contain incidental references. Living tradition is itself an important source of information; for customs and habits thousands of years old continue to persist, though they have lost their vitality under the alien influence of the present régime.

The village headman, responsible for paying to the collectors the revenue due the ruler from the village and for maintaining general order, had a more or less hereditary position. He was assisted by the village accountant, who kept a careful record of field production and saw that every family received its proper share in the harvest distribution, including the village servants. The most characteristic aspect of village life was its self-sufficiency. This was possible because the village remained an ancestral home from generation to generation. Disputes were settled by a council of influential elders, known as a panchayat, originally consisting of five members. Watchmen, paid out of the village grain, were charged with police duties. A few artisans made all the essential tools and utensils in return for a fixed share of the crop. A barber and a washerman served the village on the same basis. A goldsmith generally managed to do a thriving private business. A local money-lender acted as general financier. Local weavers produced cloth for ordinary use, commonly from yarn spun by the women of a household. A priest who performed the family religious ceremonies, and very often a teacher who gave simple instruction to the sons of the better tradesmen and well-to-do members of the community, fulfilled the remaining needs of the village. A man did not desert his home as his prosperity increased, but attained standing and honor within the community by practising the traditional virtues of a householder. He built a temple or a tank for his village. He planted trees. He dispensed charity. He contributed to the support of poor students.

The present scheme of administration in India, applicable to British India only, is based on the Government of India Act of 1919, put into actual operation in 1921. Central and provincial governments have been made distinct, with certain subjects of administration allocated to each. To the central government, for example, now fall defence, external relations, customs, salt and opium administration, the departments of post and telegraph, civil and criminal law, police, railways, currency, and coinage. The provincial governments handle such "transferred" subjects as local self-government, public health and sanitation, education, public works, and agriculture. A limited franchise has come into existence, in which the principle of communal representation has been deliberately set up, but both in the provincial legislative councils and in the Legislative Assembly, the central representative body, a certain number of seats are reserved for government appointees. In matters of finance, the elected representatives of the people are under executive control. They have no voice over military appropriations and the viceroy and the English provincial governors, through powers reserved to them of vetoing any bill or certifying the necessity for enforcement of any rejected bill can always override the Indian vote.

The so-called "reforms" were first proposed during the war of 1914-1918 at a time when a revolution in India would have been fatal to England. In judiciously vague phraseology, the new policy was proclaimed. It looked toward the "gradual development of self-governing institutions with a view to the progressive realization of responsible government in India as an integral part of the British Empire."

As a part of the program, there was to be a general examination of the working of the governmental reforms at the end of ten years, presumably as a preliminary step to a further extension of self-government in India.

In accordance with this provision the ill-starred Indian Statutory Commission—which incidentally was not Indian at all but a purely British body—began its investigation of Indian affairs under the leadership of Sir John Simon in 1928. From the start it worked under the handicap of bitter Indian opposition, which took the form of a general boycott. Its report, issued in June, 1930, proved once more the inacceptability to those concerned of foreign official investigations which, however conscientiously performed, necessarily fail to take into account the psychological factors in any demand for independence. Various recommendations were duly made—a federal union eventually to include both British India and the semi-independent Indian States, self-government to be granted the provinces in accordance with their capacity to exercise it, abolition of the clumsy scheme of "dyarchy," or divided responsibility, extension of the franchise from 2½ per cent to 10 per cent of the population, more revenue to be made available to local bodies. No mention of dominion status, however, appeared in all the 747 pages of the two-volume report. The Indian press and public sentiment almost universally rejected it, convinced that it offered nothing to satisfy Nationalist demands. Much water has since flowed under the political bridges.

The cautious proposals of the Simon Report are now outdated and superseded by more recent events. The first Indian Round Table Conference met in London without Gandhi and without the participation of any Nationalist delegates. To the surprise of India no less than of England, the Indian Princes supported the idea of an immediate federation of their States and British India, thus making possible an effective Indian constitution. Gandhi and some twenty thousand political prisoners were thereupon released from His Majesty's jails.

Relations between the village at one end and the government at the other, as they stand at present, are technically controlled through district headquarters. British India is divided into 267 districts, each district roughly averaging four thousand square miles, with a population not far short of a million. Within the various provinces the districts are grouped together into divisions under commissioners, but the deputy commissioner—also known as a magistrate or collector—in charge of a single district, stands before the people as the most important and immediate representative of government. He exercises combined administrative and judicial functions and has an ample staff of subordinates, including a few Englishmen and a number of minor Indian officials and petty clerks. The district officer, a doctor, who goes by the title of civil surgeon, a superintendent of police, a judge, possibly a forest officer and a railway man or two, with their wives, make up the little world of officialdom at district headquarters. The district itself is divided into tahsils for purposes of revenue collection. Indian tahsildars are in charge of these, and under them come the *kanungos*, who supervise the work of the village accountants. For policing and postal service, district "circles" are established. District and municipal boards are responsible for roads and education, "transferred" subjects. Such, in skeleton, is the administrative system that reaches out to lay hold upon the Indian village.

The forty thousand miles of railway lines now extending in a vast network all over India have brought many changes into the rural areas. The Pachperwa bazar was filled with small articles unknown in Oudh a quarter of a century ago —many of them worthless, it must be confessed. Others undoubtedly indicated a rise in the standard of living. I could not feel that Asgar Ali was better off for wearing socks made in Japan or a ring from Czecho-Slovakia, or even for admiring himself in a German mirror. On the other hand, the railway brought coal to Pachperwa for Haveli Singh's manufacture of bricks and hauled salt and iron and cloth and many other useful commodities at a cheap rate. It also bore away great stacks of lumber and grain with considerable profit to the contractors and merchants.

The meter-gauge railway line, a branch of the Bengal and Northwestern, swinging in a loop from Gonda to Gorakhpur, was our most tangible connection with the outside world. Four trains a day staggered along the embankment at the rate of ten to twelve miles an hour. The villagers themselves used the railway as a matter of course for going on visits and making pilgrimages. Passenger fares in India are the cheapest in the world, averaging less than two cents a mile for all classes together. The Indian people have always traveled extensively within their own country, but formerly a journey could not be lightly undertaken. Nowadays one can cross from Calcutta to Bombay, a distance of 1,350 miles, in less than two days and nights, and travel from Peshawar, on the border of Afghanistan, to Tuticorin, in the extreme south, in less than five days.

Great emphasis is usually laid on the British contribution of railways to India. The fact that railways are of this age and that India would have had them inevitably is often overlooked. The railways, moreover, have permitted the strategic control of India by a foreign power and the economic penetration of the country. There seems to be justification for the view of many economists that the development of waterways first, would have served Indian interests better. The railways have not been a philanthropic gift. British capital has always been guaranteed its interest, no matter whether the railways were made to pay or not, out of the revenues supplied by the Indian taxpayers.

The railway development, however, is responsible for the modern postal service, knitting the country closer together. Where no dispensary exists, the rural postal agent has added the sale of quinine to his functions, and larger offices accept savings accounts and issue postal life insurance policies. In Pachperwa, the Doctor, who acted as postmaster in his spare time, received as many as a hundred letters a day for distribution within the village and the surrounding area.

Sometimes contingencies arose. When a money order for fifty rupees came one day for a tahsil peon, the sum was so large the Babuji could not dream of paying it out of the postal funds on hand. He had to collect from "outside," and before the peon actually received his money three weeks elapsed. Stamps, too, presented a troublesome problem. The Babuji seemed to feel that he ought to economize on stamps. Once we ran out of stamps altogether, and for three whole days letters had to be dispatched to Gonda with cash. Yet he was methodical and careful. He spent five or six hours a day, at the minimum, sorting letters and writing out accounts in the little cubbyhole that served as an office, at the entrance to his house. Squatting on the floor, amid a clutter

of letters, perhaps bare to the waist as the village barber
shaved him, he solemnly undertook to represent the government postal department at the very inadequate salary of
four dollars a month, plus fees on postal orders and parcels.

Besides the Babuji we had two full-time village postmen,
drawing salaries of a trifle over five dollars a month. One
collected and dispatched the mail and delivered letters in
Pachperwa. The other made the rounds of some three
hundred villages and hamlets within the tahsil, served by our
branch post office. Jagganath Prasad, the young Brahmin
who went out to the villages, was my favorite. I shall never
forget the "God save you, sir!" with which he handed me
my first letter. His great brown eyes reminded me of a
frightened deer. But not long after, he announced one morning, "I feel very loves for you!" It was his naïve way of
telling me that my presence in the village brought pleasure
to the general community. The Brahmin compounder at the
dispensary, with whom he lived when not out on his round,
said that Jagganath Prasad always prayed in his morning
and evening puja, "God save the Miss Sahiba."

His work was not easy from a physical standpoint. He
walked on an average twenty miles a day, calling at all the
villages within his jurisdiction at least once a week. He was
able to lighten the work of distributing mail by planting
himself in a conspicuous spot and delivering letters in person at the Wednesday bazar, to which everybody came
crowding from the surrounding countryside. While he was
away he scarcely ever knew where the nights would overtake him. If a parcel was to be delivered for which money
had to be collected, he often waited hours while the owner
scurried around raising the required sum. He himself was
frequently called upon to read letters he brought to illiterate
persons from equally illiterate relatives or friends, who had
had recourse to professional letter writers. He also drafted
answers for an anna or two.

But wherever the nights found him, he was sure of
hospitality. There was always somebody at whose house he

could stay. He could accept uncooked rice offered by any Hindu of respectable caste, but he had to cook it himself. He always carried along his cooking pot and his own drinking vessel. As a result of the irregular meals he was beginning to experience digestive trouble and was eager to be transferred to Tulsipur, where his wife lived in an older brother's household. Much as I knew I should miss the benefits of his daily petition to God to save me, I wrote a model letter to the authorities for him to sign, and in due course the desired transfer was effected.

Since ours was a large village it boasted a government upper primary school. Like the post office, this served a radius of some miles. As a rule the Indian village school is poorly housed. The substantial brick schoolhouse of Pachperwa, opposite the dispensary, had recently been erected by the Maharaja of Balrampur. A high wall with a gate fronted the road, and behind was an enclosed court with a low open-faced building at the back. In cold weather the boys sat on long strips of cloth or matting in the court. When the sun grew hot they moved under cover.

School opened officially at eight in winter, from March on, at six, but some of the youngsters had a long way to come, and nobody was concerned with punctuality. They trailed past the Happy House at all hours, carrying their wooden slates and reed pens and little paper books wrapped in a cloth, swinging their ink bottles on a string. Although the names of two hundred boys were listed on the school register, only a quarter of that number were in daily attendance, and not more than fifteen or twenty were ever on hand for the opening morning prayer.

The straggling row which lined up outside the school wall ranged in size from a tall boy or two completing the sixth-year class to Haweli Singh's little five-year-old, who wore his hair in a pigtail hanging from beneath a purple and gold cap and had kohl around his eyes, put there by an adoring mother to make him look more beautiful. Line by line a big boy would recite the prayer, acceptable to both Hindus and Mussulmans, and the rest would repeat the words after him.

There were four teachers, a head teacher of the *Kayasth* caste—the clerical and writing caste—and three Brahmin assistants. The boys were grouped according to classes, and the four teachers were always hearing four classes recite their lessons aloud at the same time, so that all day a deafening babble arose from the vicinity of the school. The curriculum covered only simple arithmetic, some slight instruction in Indian geography, and reading and writing in Hindi and Urdu, the two vernaculars of the district.

In so far as it raised the percentage of literacy in the community, the school was a useful institution. It is a sad and shocking fact that only ten out of a hundred persons in British India can pass the simple test of literacy—ability to write a short letter in any vernacular and read an answer. With the single exception of the Northwest Frontier Province, the United Provinces rank lowest in the scale. Out of the total population of twenty years and over, eighteen males are literate for every hundred, but only two females. In backward rural areas like Oudh, the figures fall far below these averages. In our particular district of Gonda, instead of one out of ten, only one out of forty-four persons is literate, and scarcely one woman out of five hundred. It is not surprising that the tahsil did a heavy business in thumb-printing by way of registering signatures.

The inefficiency of the village school in India is well known. It does not succeed in making more than a small number literate, because only a handful of children remain in attendance for more than two years. The result is that even those who acquire the rudiments of reading and writing soon lapse into permanent illiteracy.

Part of the trouble may be attributed to mistakes in the early government educational program for India. At first the government left the problem of education to the missionaries. In 1835 it adopted as its educational policy the fostering of secondary schools and colleges for teaching

Western learning through the medium of English. The objective was primarily to train a body of men friendly to the whole foreign system who could take over minor posts at lower salaries than Englishmen were willing to accept. The scheme worked admirably until there were more Western educated Indians than there were posts to fill. Then a harvest of discontent was reaped, which has swelled with every fresh crop of B. A.'s. The policy was not suited to India's needs and is now recognized to have been a serious mistake.

Though British India maintains some fifteen universities —one of them, the University of Calcutta, with an actual enrollment of 29,000 students—the education of the masses has been almost entirely neglected. As late as 1911, when the patriot Gopal Krishna Gokhale, for the first time, tried to introduce a measure for compulsory elementary education into the old Imperial Legislative Council, it was opposed by the government on the ground that funds were not available and the time was not yet ripe for this radical step.

General educational progress in India has consequently been very slow. Since education was transferred to Indian ministers in the various provinces some years ago, a most noticeable advance in the school program has been made. More funds are now devoted to education. Primary education acts have already been passed in most of the provinces, giving district and municipal boards the right to make education compulsory for boys, and in specified areas for girls as well. It is encouraging that in the past few years compulsory education has been introduced in more than a hundred municipalities and 1,500 rural areas, but most of the rural areas are in the Punjab. English opinion as well as Indian is now tardily supporting the idea of compulsory primary education, recognizing that little improvement can be effected in the condition of rural India without a higher standard of education.

If the villagers are apathetic, it is only because they have not yet been persuaded that the government school serves any vital need in the community. The advantages of mere literacy where people are far too poor to buy books are not always apparent. The caste system has reserved to the Brahmin the performance of sacrifices and religious rituals for which a knowledge of the sacred Sanskrit texts is essential, but not even the Brahmin priest has to be literate. The tradition of oral learning has never died out in India. As for secular learning, the writing caste has always provided clerks. Where the economic scale is as low as it is in the Indian village, the labor of children is often a practical necessity and this fact, too, interferes with educational progress.

The school itself has to be remade to fill the place it should in the rural community. In the old indigenous village school system, much more widespread than is commonly supposed, the teacher belonged to the village, was supported by the village, understood the village needs. Nowadays the stagnant villages seldom produce teachers, and these are drawn from town and city populations. The wage of a village teacher until very recently averaged but three dollars a month, a sum scarcely calculated to attract the best quality of men, especially when the difficult living conditions of the village are remembered. Some improvement in the wage scale has now been realized. Our head teacher, a normal school graduate, drew a monthly salary of ten dollars; his assistants, salaries ranging from four to seven dollars.

All these men were outsiders, whose families lived elsewhere. They went home whenever they could, took little or no interest in the actual village life, ordinarily treated the villagers with marked contempt and outside of school hours kept much to themselves. Their presence was a cause of friction in the village, and the villagers neither liked nor respected them. Under the circumstances it was not surprising the school was no more popular than it was.

In Western countries women teachers have generally monopolized the field of elementary education, but in India practically all girls are married before twenty. Family and

household responsibilities ordinarily prevent them from fulfilling the rôle of the unmarried woman teacher of the West.
Hitherto only Christian Indians and Eurasians, who marry
late, and a comparatively few high-caste Hindu girls of progressive families, have been available as teachers. More
women teachers have to be found, and two proposals have
been made: to train Hindu widows and provide them with
suitable living quarters, which do not now exist in the villages, and to encourage the wives of male teachers to qualify
themselves for elementary teaching and then go with their
husbands and open girls' schools in the villages. Coeduca-
tion has even been tried out in some primary schools, with a
surprising measure of success. Within the past decade or so
there has been a 40 per cent increase in the number of girls
attending school, though there is an even greater wastage of
those who drop out at the end of the first year or two than in
the case of boys. On the other hand, a girl who is educated
has a greater potential influence. The literate mother invariably sees that her children, including her daughters, learn at
least as much as she knows. The Eurasian teacher in the
zenana school at Balrampur, which had an attendance of
more than a hundred, told me that she counted on every
one of her girls exerting a beneficial influence on at least ten
other persons in her life time.

As the ideals of Indian education change and education
becomes an integrating rather than a disintegrating factor
in the national life, the school will bring new vitality to the
people. The textbooks, many of them dull imitations of the
primers of Victorian days, need to be rewritten. The village
school curriculum should include lessons in elementary
hygiene and physical training, subjects ignored at present.
An attitude of mind receptive to ideas which will bring
greater prosperity to rural India above all must be incul-
cated.

At least since the villager generally has had no education
at all in the modern sense, he cannot be said to have been
miseducated. A golden opportunity lies ahead of Indian

THE VILLAGE AND THE GOVERNMENT 193

educators. It would seem that the radio and the motion-picture film could be effectively used as a short cut for spreading certain kinds of information quickly to the millions of illiterate villagers. At present the government still fears the radio may become a menace, because of unwelcome political propaganda emanating from centers outside India. Within India, political discussions are forbidden except in very special circumstances, and the radio programs are confined for the most part to insipid entertainment. The cost of a radio and even the annual licence fee being prohibitive for an Indian villager, there is no hope that the radio will ever reach out into the rural areas or serve any useful purpose there, unless the government takes a hand and adopts a really progressive policy. Both Russia and China have made the radio an asset in meeting the problem of illiteracy. The government, if it chose to do so, could easily put up a battery receiving set in each of the seven hundred and fifty thousand villages in India, establish sending stations in every province to take care of the local language problem, and see that daily programs were broadcast, giving useful information on the handling of epidemics and preventive hygiene, news items, monsoon estimates, weather reports, grain market prices, and helpful lectures on agriculture and other topics of universal concern. It is hard to believe that the idea would not be immediately successful, in its educational returns repaying the expenditure involved many times over.

Any modern educational policy for India has to adapt itself to a new age, but it should not be forgotten that poetic composition in India preceded writing by centuries and that culture antedated literacy. There have been long periods in the past when Indian civilization led the world. In what were called the "forest universities" of Vedic days, the search for truth and spiritual knowledge was untiringly pursued, and the results were handed down from teacher to disciple in an unbroken line. Great colleges sprang up around the Buddhist centers of a somewhat later age, still antedating the earliest Western universities by more than thirteen centuries. Archeological exploration among the ruins of Taxila in the Punjab, of Sarnath, of Nalanda in Bihar, of Sravasti, identified with Sahet Mahet—a spot only ten miles from Balrampur—have uncovered the vast halls which once accommodated thousands and tens of thousands of students. Even from far-off China men visited these places famous for learning, and they have left authentic records of the high state of civilization they found in India.

Formerly it was customary for every boy belonging to a "twice-born" caste—excluding only Sudras—to undergo a ceremony of initiation as he entered the student stage, which might last six or twelve years. During this period he commonly lived in the house of his teacher, wore simple clothes, ate simple food, observed strict laws of chastity, and otherwise submitted himself to the moral discipline believed to be indispensable to the attainment of knowledge. Though the common people did not share in this type of education, they were trained in the crafts and in caste work through a social and economic organization in many ways resembling the guild system of the Middle Ages. There were also indigenous vernacular schools.

Ideals of schooling and education are not new to India. Invasions and serious economic upheavals and foreign domination, paralyzing to any healthy national life, have held development back, but in spite of them the Indian mind continues to display traditionally brilliant qualities. Nobody need worry about India's capacity to learn, given a fair chance, as well as to make real contributions to the world.

Drugs and drink are another village problem associated with government, since the excise tax forms an important source of revenue and the excise officials are always on the job to check possible smuggling or illicit distillation. With the separation of the central and provincial administrations and their finances the excise on drugs and liquor now goes to the provincial governments, but opium remains a central government monopoly. The details of administering these departments vary in different provinces, but the main features are restricted production, storage in bonded warehouses, payment of quantitative duties on issue, retail sale under license and restriction on private possession. In Pachperwa we had one licensed drug seller and one wineshop.

The drug seller, a delicate-looking man with a drooping mustache, belonged to the Hindu confectioner's caste and was a brother of my friend Sheobalak. His tiny shop occupied a niche in the row of houses and shops leading to the New Bazar. One day Fakire took me to his shop. The proprietor hastened to produce a printed document in Urdu, which was his government license to sell drugs. He seemed to think I was an inspector. I ignored the paper, explaining that I was merely curious to see what the different kinds of drugs looked like. From behind a table spread with the usual square chunks and round drops of caramel-colored sugar making up the village confectioners' stock in trade, he brought forth a tin box containing his precious wares— opium, ganja, *charas*, and bhang. The crowd that collected at once began telling me which was which, how each was prepared, and how much it cost.

Ganja, charas, and bhang are all intoxicating products of the Indian hemp plant. The first two, mixed with tobacco, are smoked; bhang is made into a drink. Opium is constantly eaten in India, though in certain localities it is also used for smoking. The flowering tops of the cultivated female hemp plant, picked and dried, constitute ganja. Spread out on a brass plate before me, it looked like gray moss. Ganja must be rolled in the hand and crushed into a fine powder for smoking. Bhang, the dried leaves of hemp of the male or female plants, is made into a drink with water, sugar, and fruit juices. The first effect was described to me as very cooling. Later the intoxicating effects are experienced. Charas is the name given to the resin collected from the hemp plant when grown at a certain altitude. Charas comes in the form of a sticky brown lump, like opium.

The drug shop at Pachperwa paid a government fee of 110 rupees for selling eleven pounds of opium in one year; a fee of forty-five rupees, for four pounds of ganja and charas; and six rupees for twenty-eight pounds of bhang. Hemp grew wild all over the district, but under the government system the right to collect and sell the spontaneous growth under the form of bhang or to cultivate hemp for ganja, was restricted. Special contractors were allowed to bid for these privileges for a three-year period. But illicit cultivation and smuggling across the border could not be prevented, and I gathered that in Pachperwa illicit drugs were more common than the licensed kind.

The whole opium-poppy area of British India, now amounting to a trifle less than fifty thousand acres, is confined to the United Provinces. A good deal of cultivation goes on in Gonda. But ever since Warren Hastings set the policy of a government monopoly, strict control has been exercised, so that it is impossible for prepared opium to be obtained except through the government warehouse at government prices. Excise opium for use within India is issued by the provincial governments to licensed dealers in two-pound packets, costing approximately twelve dollars a pound —more than five times the price at which opium sold in Oudh when the British annexation was carried out three quarters of a century ago. It was commonly resold in Pachperwa at double its weight in silver.

The Opium Section of the League of Nations has accepted the figure of twelve pounds per ten thousand of population as legitimate annual consumption in a country with developed medical service. Studies of the Indian situation reveal uneven results. For India as a whole the figure is just double the League figure, not excessive in view of backward medical facilities, and the not uncommon use of opium as a palliative for work cattle after days of hard labor in the rain. Assam, Calcutta, and special areas elsewhere, where the consumption is far above the League standard, have been termed "black spots." The eleven pounds for Pachperwa did not indicate an overuse, since our shop served all the people from the vicinity who crowded in on Wednesday to the bazar.

Our drug users were drawn from various groups. The smell of ganja and rank tobacco often greeted me as I passed certain shops or houses. Baghwan, my one-time water carrier, was a bad offender. Mussulmans, forbidden to drink intoxicating liquors, contribute a large proportion to the numbers who take dry intoxicants. It was they who first introduced opium into India. Most Brahmins and respectable middle-class Hindus abstain from intoxicants, but the lower classes are addicted to their use. A great many mothers administer opium pills to their babies when they cry. I was informed that one pill would quiet a baby for two hours. Our drug seller rolled four pills for one *pice*, half a cent. Both Brahmins and Sikhs are forbidden to smoke, but Sikhs are notorious users of opium. Many fakirs and religious mendicants are also drug consumers. Commonly living in forests or wandering about without fixed shelter, exposed to all sorts of weather, they succumb to the temptation of drugs, partly on the accepted belief that they ward off fevers.

Once a sadhu of questionable repute who spent a week or two in Pachperwa personally assured me that ganja induced a peculiar state of mind favorable to religious meditation. "When I take ganja and concentrate my mind I see God here," he explained, touching a spot between his eyebrows. "I see him very large, as if I were looking through a *durbin*, like this." The strange "holy man" picked up a magnifying glass from my desk and held it over a typewritten sheet to show what he meant.

The whole Indian opium question has now to be reconsidered in the light of recent reforms. India, the second opium producing country in the world, ranking next to China, has long been the chief exporter. Under an agreement with

China, direct exports to that country ceased in 1913. In line with the Geneva Convention, international agreements have since been undertaken by the Indian government to ensure the total extinction of exports of opium for other than medical and scientific purposes. Under the agreement the area under poppy cultivation has been drastically reduced each year, and is now only a fraction of what it used to be. As a source of revenue, opium counts no more. In the closing decades of the past century the opium revenue reached as high as 50,000,000 dollars a year. For the government the loss is considerable. Internal consumption is now a matter under provincial control. If reforms are to be effected here, they must come from campaigns of education and through legislation. Gandhi has strongly attacked the use of both drugs and spirits, with effective results. The cutting down of toddy palms and the picketing of drug and drink shops have formed part of the recent activities of the Indian Nationalists.

The wineshop of Pachperwa was a large rambling affair at the northwestern corner of the village, just back of Yasin Khan's whitewashed mansion. The Peshkar acted as guide on the occasion of my first visit. The wine dealer belonged to the *Kalwar* caste, the wine caste, like all those who helped him. This caste ranks low in the Hindu scale because of the obloquy attaching to the occupation.

The front of the wineshop stood invitingly open, everything spotlessly clean. Inside at the back was a broad wooden counter, a bar minus the brass rail, over which customers were served. One of these I noticed squatting outside, pleasantly absorbed with a bottle labeled "English Lager"—a case of new wine in an old beer bottle! Another perched in a niche beside the entrance. With knees tucked under his chin, he sang lustily. The wine, made from mahuwa flowers, was distilled in a long wing at the side. As we entered, led by the wine dealer, the steaming atmosphere almost suffocated us. Gradually I made out a great round vat with a cover, rising from the mud floor. A fire burned in the oven beneath. The floor was punctured with many round holes, the mouths of various underground storage vats.

Country wine and spirits are made from a number of sources in India. In the south the toddy palm is a convenient source, but palms do not grow as far north as Pachperwa. Our wine was all produced from fermented mahuwa flowers. It came in three qualities—mixed with a little water, with a little more water, and with a lot of water—and cost one rupee, eight annas, or four annas a bottle, according to quality.

The mahuwa stood out sharply in the flat landscape, bony arms outspread. Large white flowers appeared on the tree in March, but immediately after, curling clusters of new leaves unfolded, a beautiful soft red, more festive than the flowers. In the Balrampur estate the flowers of each tree are auctioned in advance. Whoever bids them in collects them as they drop and afterwards sells them, principally to wine dealers. Mahuwa flowers, sun-dried, are also eaten raw, and they are made into cakes and sweets. The ripe fruit is also eaten, or the oil, pressed from the seeds, is used for soap and candles, cooking and lamps, or as an adulterant for ghi.

On economic grounds, drink was a much worse evil in Pachperwa than drugs, because many more people indulged in it. Our wine dealer had come from Lucknow five years before. He complained about the heavy tax he had to pay the government, 4,200 rupees a year, and one day not long after my visit to the shop he came around to ask if I would not write a letter to have the tax reduced. I felt compelled to decline. The tax was fixed each year, perhaps a little arbitrarily. Pachperwa, it seemed, was still classified under the outstill system, permitting combined right of manufacture and sale in return for a licensing fee. The contract distillery system has now supplanted the outstill system in most parts of India.

A little calculation showed me that, just to pay a tax of 4,200 rupees, our wineshop had to sell eleven rupees worth of wine a day—a large expenditure where a monthly wage is ordinarily only six to eight rupees. The shop, shunned by Mussulmans, was well patronized by low-caste Hindus and Tharus. On ordinary days it averaged fifty customers. On bazar day as many as two hundred dropped in for a drink and gossip. Often I heard some of them returning home late at night, singing very merrily as they passed along the road in front of my house.

The present government policy in the matter of the consumption of intoxicating drinks in India is defined as "minimum consumption, maximum revenue." A prohibition movement has the strong support not only of the block of all the Indian Mussulmans, for whom prohibition is a religious injunction, but of higher and middle class Hindus and all classes of reformers as well. Compared with Western countries, India is said to have no drink evil to speak of, except among factory workers in industrial centers. The Indian legislative bodies in some major provinces have already passed resolutions favoring abstinence or total prohibition, and an India joining the ranks of the dry countries would offer no very startling phenomenon.

The recently established village court of Pachperwa was an interesting and constructive step toward the revival of healthy village life and the development of local responsibility, introduced under the "reforms." Since an English system of law came into being for India in 1861, with high courts of appeal and lower criminal and civil courts, the disease of litigation has spread through India. The Indian's weakness is going to court. An average annual record of a civil case for every ninety persons in British India is appalling enough. Worse, 65 per cent of these cases are valued at less than one hundred rupees! To relieve the courts of this unwieldy burden of petty litigation, and to remove one of the recognized causes of the villagers' poverty, some attempt is now being made, where conditions are favorable, to reinstitute the village arbitration court of former days.

Our court in Pachperwa was being tried out experimentally. When I moved to the village, all the six panches, or judges, originally appointed on government authority, had just received their official reappointment to serve for another term of three years. They drew no pay, but their position carried prestige. The panchayat was empowered to try criminal cases involving simple assault and theft up to the value of twenty rupees, and civil cases involving property to the value of fifty rupees. Punishment was by fine, and the maximum fine allowed was twenty rupees. The jurisdiction covered six villages besides Pachperwa and its associated hamlets, but the panchayat did not attempt to interfere with any matters concerning the Balrampur Estate.

Everything was conducted with informality, and little time was lost. An effort was made to finish a civil suit in three sittings and a criminal one in two. Meetings were held twice a week. An annual average of 97 criminal complaints and 180 civil ones were effectively disposed of. The cost was next to nothing. The plaintiff paid only four annas for registering a criminal case with the village court. For bringing civil suits involving amounts up to ten, from ten to twenty-five and from twenty-five to fifty rupees, the fees were respectively, five, nine and thirteen annas. A witness received one anna.

The money from fees and fines which accumulated with the panchayat—amounting to something under two hundred rupees a year after expenses were deducted—was kept in the postal savings bank at Tulsipur and was available at the discretion of the panchayat for carrying out village improvements of one sort or another. The panchayat was empowered to undertake a certain degree of supervision in regard to village streets and general sanitation, but it contented itself with repairing two or three wells a year.

I hoped that I might be permitted to attend a meeting of the panchayat some day. The head panch, Jokhi Lal, politely assured me I should be most welcome. Nevertheless, several weeks passed before his servant came to convey a formal invitation with an announcement that he had been sent to escort me then and there to a meeting at Jokhi Lal's shop.

The three panches present besides Jokhi Lal were the Marwari cloth and grain merchants, Mahabir Prasad and Nattu Ram, and Nepal Bania of the Old Bazar. The two Mohammedan members of the panchayat, sons of the richest rent contractors of the tahsil, were not on hand. It seemed they seldom attended.

The panches were already comfortably established on Jokhi Lal's big square bench, spread with its black and white striped rug of goat's-hair. Two of Jokhi Lal's youngest children sat beside him, dressed in their gayest gold-embroidered jackets of velvet and round satin caps and the pretty nine-year-old granddaughter of Mahabir Prasad leaned affectionately against his shoulder. At the opposite end of the room and around the door, always pushing forward and always being assiduously shoved back by the panches' personal servants and the official messenger attached to the court, were the witnesses, plaintiffs and defendants, men, women, and babies, the few whose presence was required and the many who came out of curiosity.

Jokhi Lal uncorked the ink bottle beside him and opened the fat, flexible book in which he kept all the proceedings in his neat Hindi. Another book, bound in flowered calico, contained brief comments in English from the various officials, Indian and English, who from time to time inspected the panchayat records. A name was called, and a man with a white cloth about his shoulders stood out in front of the panches and began talking. He talked a long time and wept a little. Then another younger man stepped out and talked an even longer time, with fiery eloquence. He was followed by a woman, who wept copiously. I gathered that a fight had taken place. A small boy stole a stick of wood from a cart on the road, and the cartman caught him and began beating him. An older brother came to the boy's rescue, and a pitched battle ensued between the cohorts of both sides. The cohorts, now summoned as witnesses, told their story, prodded with questions from time to time by the panches. Jokhi Lal methodically wrote everything down, then read aloud what he had written and had each witness step up and approve his statement by affixing his thumb-print. It grew dark outside and darker inside. A lantern was brought and set on the table. Still the village battle went on. At last Asgar Ali arrived to light me home. A half dozen witnesses had not yet been heard. Afterward I was informed that, in the opinion of the panchayat, the cartman had been found guilty of assault and had been fined ten rupees.

Fights, petty thefts, damage to property through straying cattle, unrepaid loans, cases of "insultation"—as calling bad names was once described to me—these were the village problems patiently reviewed and judged by the panchayat. Shiva Dutt stole fifteen rupees from Govind Ram and was caught with the stolen money in his possession. He was ordered to return it and pay a fine of five rupees. Habibullah's cattle were found grazing in a field belonging to Niamat. When Niamat rounded them up and started for the pound at the police station, Habibullah appeared on the scene with a band of helpers and forcibly rescued them. He was fined five rupees. Sums ranging from fifteen to thirty-five rupees had been borrowed in three cases, and the accused had neither repaid nor "freshened" the documents. The court ordered repayment in two cases. In the third, though the accused was guilty, nothing could be done. The law stipulates that unless a case for recovery is brought within three years, it becomes void, and this case was too old.

Petty though they are, these are the disputes that loom large on the village horizon, leading the unwary into pitfalls of extravagant litigation. In a belated effort to divert the villagers away from the courts back to the local panchayat, which settles the greater proportion of its cases by amicable compromise, the government has taken a wise step. At present the movement is hampered by the difficulty of knowing the most suitable persons in the community to appoint as judges. Unless these have the real confidence of the villagers and are reasonably free of corruption, they cannot be expected to serve the village interests satisfactorily. Now the appointments are made from the top down. In time, if the village community is restored to a state of health, villagers can be trusted to choose their own panchayat. With their highly developed sense of moral values and their shrewd appreciation of character, they will not often go wrong.

CHAPTER IX

The Police Station

BY FAR the most important government servant in Pachperwa was the local police official. He had an extensive territory to supervise, actually covering 253 square miles. This took in 146 main villages, and a population of more than 53,000 souls.

In former times the villages maintained their own hereditary watchmen. These individuals did not always bear the best reputations. Yet, when a watchman turned thief, it was a matter of honor with him to commit his thieveries in another village than his own. Since remuneration came in the form of allotments of grain collected from each cultivator or from the village as a whole, watchmen who did not render reasonably good service might expect trouble when the time came for collecting dues.

The present alien system of policing, less than a century old, is patterned after the Irish Constabulary. Members of the Indian district police force above the rank of constable are recruited from the higher castes or classes, are trained in a central police school, and after six months of probation at some small post are assigned to rural police stations. As a rule they are not permitted to remain more than two or three years at one station. The salary of a sub-inspector in charge of a station and circle is about twenty-seven dollars a month. Under him are a number of constables, locally enlisted. The old pre-British village watchmen have also been incorporated into the system. They receive a red turban, a belt with a metal plate on which the word *chaukidar*—

watchman—is inscribed and a dollar a month. In return they are expected to keep a check on all matters pertaining to their villages, reporting to the police station at frequent intervals. Above the sub-inspector ranks the inspector in charge of several stations, and he in turn is subordinate to the English district superintendent of police.

In addition to district and city police there are separately organized railway police and harbor police, and as necessity arises special forces come into being to deal with particular troubles. Every province also maintains its Criminal Investigation Department, commonly known as the C. I. D., a department dealing with political and sedition cases. It supplies the authorities with intimate knowledge regarding the movements of every person in the country, foreign or native, who comes under suspicion of supporting a revolution or being a Communist or undesirable agitator of any sort. The C. I. D., unless it has ceded first place to the Ogpus, is probably the most highly and efficiently organized intelligence service in the world.

An unfortunate result of the present police system is that its officials hold themselves accountable to the government and not to the people. Police service is normally unattractive to the highest type of men. It is not surprising that the Indian police force, particularly in its lower ranks, is especially corrupt. The ordinary powers of a sub-inspector are augmented to an almost inconceivable degree by the general ignorance and helplessness of those he is supposed to protect. A low scale of pay, unlimited opportunity for extortion and graft, and the whole weight of the government ostensibly at one's back are a hard strain on the character. The feeling of the Indian villager is particularly intense against the police. The police are looked on as enemies, not only by malefactors but by the masses. Occasionally one hears of some tragic and merciless assault, when the police are surrounded and killed by a mob. Back of such incidents, forcing themselves upon public attention, is the terrible abuse to which the villagers have long submitted, without redress or protection.

Fortunately no country monopolizes either virtue or vice. Even in the prosperous United States of America, where wealth is far more evenly divided than in India and where poverty, at least, cannot often be offered as an excuse for crime, criminal tendencies manifest themselves and likewise police corruption is not altogether unknown. Thefts, including frauds and forgeries, according to the estimate of an official of the National Surety Company, are committed to the amount of two billion dollars annually. When it comes to murders, the United States outstrips India by a wide margin in the proportion of murders to population.

Our *thana*, or police station, originally established in 1880, occupied the far corner of the mango grove in which the weekly bazar was held. A walled enclosure with low buildings on three sides contained the room in which the various police registers were kept, a treasury in which sums of money or recovered stolen articles might be safely stowed away, two cells, and quarters for the constables. Close by was a pound for stray cattle. A little farther on were the Sub-Inspector's one-roomed office and his own house. The thana was a disreputable outfit of buildings with sagging roofs and discolored walls, thoroughly depressing. A year had passed since it was condemned by the authorities at Gonda and a new one recommended, but beyond the arrival of a delegation which selected a site next to the schoolhouse, nothing was accomplished during my stay in the village.

The Thanadar, as the Sub-Inspector was called, was of the second Hindu caste, the old ruling and military caste. He was the father of nine children, including grown sons. His manner, outside his family, was ordinarily overweening and rough, though like nearly all petty officials he grew extremely meek in the presence of superiors. He was above average size, and his large head had a way of looking twice as large again under a turban. He was generally to be found sitting at a table under the trees outside his office, listening to disputes and examining witnesses. At these times he dressed informally in dhoti, shirt and shoes without socks, and went with head uncovered, displaying thin curly black hair. When he went out into the villages to investigate a case, he put on shorts and a green and red sunproof coat, long yellow stockings, and a pongee turban. A heavy stick with a bulbous root for handle, polished into a formidable club, seemed also to be a part of his official equipment. Whenever Mr. McIntosh, District Superintendent of Police, came on an inspection tour the Thanadar invariably blossomed forth in a magnificent red turban with a gold fringe.

Just what part the presence in the village of a sub-inspector of police played in my own safety there, I am not sure. I have reason to believe that the Thanadar had instructions to look out for me. No doubt he and the estate Tahsildar both assumed invisible protection over me. In any case, I felt perfectly safe. I never locked my doors. During the hot season I slept outside every night with perfect equanimity, and never once did I have any unpleasant personal experience in which I had reason to feel fear. All that was ever stolen from the Happy House was a thermometer and some powdered paints I was using for my elephant wall decoration. The thermometer vanished without a trace, but after a day or two we found the thief who had stolen the paints—a little girl appointed by the Tahsildar to water the lawn. She had eaten them. Asgar produced her with grotesque blue streaks about her mouth and telltale stains on her sari.

Besides the Thanadar, the local police force consisted of a Mohammedan head constable, a clerk, and eight constables. The constables were assigned in pairs to the four divisions of the police circle, and each of them was required to circulate about his territory once a week and report to the thana. There were also seventy-one village watchmen for the area. These men, suggested for their posts by the headmen or rent contractors of the main villages, approved by the Thanadar and officially appointed at Gonda, were nearly all *Pasis*. The Pasis of Oudh are a low caste of unenviable repute. Formerly they monopolized the position of guards to the refractory land barons. On the principle that it is best to set a thief to catch a thief, they were accepted as village watchmen. The Pasis I encountered looked like ordinary villagers, and it was difficult to imagine them playing the desperate rôle that history assigned them.

Every village watchman carries about with him two books, one for registering births, deaths and diseases in epidemic form for his village, the other, the *Village Chaukidar's Crime Book*. The little red crime book contains rules for guidance, printed in both Urdu and Hindi. In reporting a case, the watchman is to note the name and caste of the plaintiff, the location of the crime with time and date, the exact nature of the crime, name and caste of accused, if known, and the value of stolen property.

Since the watchman himself is illiterate, he makes a verbal report of everything to the thana clerk, who fills out his book for him. He also serves summonses and helps investigate crimes. The vital statistics appearing in the decennial census reports for India are ultimately based on information collected by village watchmen, and the sub-inspector of police depends upon them for first news of all crimes committed within the police circle.

Among factors influencing the general situation around Pachperwa, the proximity of the Nepalese border presented special difficulties. The border has long been a favorite haunt of bad characters. A man can commit a crime on the Indian side and escape into Nepal, and, as the Thanadar put it, at the border he and his pursuer stop and look at each other. Once he himself traced a man with a bad criminal record to a Nepalese village. He learned that all the villagers would welcome his arrest, and he asked permission of his superintendent quietly to carry it out. The answer came back that an officer of the law could scarcely be allowed to break the law. One night in July the Thanadar turned up at my house with the news that he had been attending a police conference in Nepal. He said the Nepalese authorities were just organizing a force patterned after the Indian police force, with circles and inspectors, and that in future there was to be greater coöperation between Indian and Nepalese police officers in apprehending criminals.

Another problem for the police to cope with is the number of potential criminals in Oudh, living in the midst of a generally peaceable and hard-working agricultural population. Large stretches of this territory, three fourths the size of Ireland, have only recently been brought under cultivation, and much of the land is still dense forest. During the rainy season, until the railway made a permanent opening, broad rivers and numerous gullies and ravines near the base of the mountains effectively isolated vast tracts to the north and east. Northern Oudh remained outside the settled influences of the Ganges valley. A century ago it was known as the resort of dangerous outlaws and the home of certain tribes who traditionally followed criminal practices of one sort or another, preying upon luckless travelers, merchants and traders, pilgrims, wedding parties, and unprotected folk wherever they were encountered.

The famous secret society of the Thugs was intrenched in Oudh, though it had ramifications all over India. The Thugs were professional stranglers. They were recruited from among Mussulmans and Hindus, were duly initiated with religious rites and looked upon their victims as predestined to be sacrificed. The goddess Kali was their special patroness. Murders were carried out by Thugs working in bands ranging from a dozen to two or even three hundred members. Every member was assigned his particular rôle. Some performed scout duty. Others, disguised as pilgrims or ascetics, gained the confidence of intended victims, accompanying them on their journeys along the road sometimes for several days. When an opportune moment arrived, often at an appointed place, the wayfarer was strangled with a scarf, robbed, and buried.

With protection in the form of powerful landlords or

chiefs who shared the booty, the Thugs had little to fear, though from time to time bands suffered extermination. By the early part of the nineteenth century, the Thugs were scourging the country on an unprecedented scale. In 1829 Lord William Bentick, Governor General, appointed Captain William Sleeman to carry out a rigorous campaign for their suppression. More than three thousand Thugs were executed, transported, or imprisoned.

The criminal tribes and castes have offered the authorities an even more difficult problem to solve. Scattered over India are certain groups who for centuries have had crime as an inherited occupation. Their origin is shrouded in mist, but they probably represent primitive groups originally excluded from the communities of Aryan settlers. Resisting alike cultural absorption and settled agricultural life, they became wanderers or outcast communities, with crime as their main, if not always their obvious, means of subsistence. Some authorities see a far offshoot of these Indian tribes in the gypsies roving through eastern and southern Europe.

In India, where caste organization has tended to fix occupation and occupation in turn has given birth to caste, communities of hereditary criminals were gradually evolved, associated with fixed brands of crime or criminal practices. Unlike the Thugs, recruited from all castes, these criminal tribes or castes were quite distinct, considering themselves bound to their recognized method of earning a living. One caste, for instance, was permitted by its own rules to thieve by day but never by night. If a member was caught stealing by night he was promptly put out of caste. House breaking was forbidden to members of this group, but thefts at fairs and bathing places were "legitimate." Another caste specialized in cutting pockets out of the long coats and shirts worn by men. Another attacked carts on the road. Others acted as professional poisoners, or stole grain from fields, or committed serious crimes of burglary, in later days taking to robbing freight trains. Still another caste prostituted its women. Sometimes the members of these various criminal tribes or castes carried on honest minor occupations along with their major nefarious ones. They cut grass and made thatch, caught snakes and lizards, sold herbs, castrated animals, moved about helping with the harvesting of crops, made grindstones and curry stones, performed the operation of tattooing.

Since it was impossible to arrest or eradicate whole established communities, a check was placed on their activities by the passage of the Criminal Tribes Act, in 1871. The government enumerated certain tribes and castes for which a rigorous system of registration was henceforth to be observed. The specified tribes are now gradually being absorbed back into the general population. Oudh, as might be expected, formerly contributed its share to the criminal element, and in Gonda district five castes are still classified as criminal and their movements restricted. These professional misdoers, though they are no longer the menace they once were, have bequeathed an unsavory tradition of crime to the countryside at large and have generously furnished the population with potential criminals.

Though Indian civilization, meeting the problem of a heterogeneous mixture of peoples with a curious standardization of social and occupational positions, has apparently fostered and even perpetuated certain types of criminals, a criminal has always been looked upon as a criminal in the eyes of the law. The masses, far from sharing the criminal's mode of life, are peace-loving and socially disciplined to a remarkable degree. Their very peacefulness has made them an easy prey to outlaws and invading armies.

In old times, as one can gather by studying the ancient codes of law and administration, drastic punishment was prescribed for offenders, but Hindu law specifically stated that all men were not equally guilty. Guilt was in accordance with the measure of knowledge. If a man was ignorant, uneducated, of low birth, he was not as guilty in committing a crime as the privileged person. "In the case of theft the guilt of a Sudra is eightfold; that of a Vaisya sixteen fold;

and that of a Kshatriya thirty-two fold; that of a Brahmin sixty-four fold or even a full hundred," declares the *Manava Dharma-Shastra*. The lawmakers, who were Brahmins, did indeed stipulate that under no circumstances was a Brahmin ever to suffer execution or bodily mutilation, but he could be banished, and, like everybody else, he was destined to reap full punishment for evil deeds in some future life on earth, if not in the present one, according to the universal Hindu belief.

In Indian police vocabulary the more serious crimes, such as murder, dacoity—defined as gang robbery with violence— burglary, theft, and riot, are classed as cognizable. A sub-inspector of police is required to investigate and report cognizable crimes to police headquarters, and in these cases he may arrest without a warrant from a magistrate. Lesser crimes are reported at the discretion of the sub-inspector, and he may not arrest without a warrant.

Though official reports showed a high percentage of murders in Gonda district, none occurred in the Pachperwa circle during my stay. The Thanadar said his last murder case had occurred eighteen months before. It had to do with a woman. Women, family quarrels, interparty fights, revenge, and robbery are the most frequent motives for murder. We did have a dacoity, however, and that was bad enough. It took place in a small hamlet three miles from Pachperwa on the night of December 30th, just one week before I moved to the village.

A respectable old Brahmin, incidentally a money-lender, an elderly sister-in-law, and her son were living together. On the night in question they had gone to bed early as usual. About midnight the Brahmin was suddenly roused by a blow on the head. He jumped up, to find himself being struck at from all sides by seven or eight men who were swarming into the room. One carried a flaring torch. In the wild skirmish he somehow managed to dive through the door and rush off for help.

The dacoits turned to the nephew and brother's wife,

whom they beat and roughly handled. They wrenched off the woman's jewelry, a heavy silver collar, bracelets, anklets, and earrings—worn to bed for safe-keeping in the usual village fashion. Then they threatened her with torture unless she told where her brother-in-law had buried his wealth. Dacoits sometimes perpetrate fiendish cruelties. The woman was shrewd. To gain time, she assured them that if they would dig at a certain spot in the cow shed they would find all the household valuables and money. The robbers set about digging and got down two or three feet without coming upon any evidence of the pots of rupees they were demanding. Suspecting trickery, and in order to force the woman to tell the truth, one of them burned her on her arms and the soles of her feet. She stuck to her story, insisting they must dig eight or ten feet before they would find anything. While they were still impatiently digging, the Brahmin, who was not too popular on account of his money-lending, and who had to use a good deal of persuasion to convince the neighbors that his case deserved assistance, arrived with his force of villagers. The dacoits were not eager for open battle and fled, taking with them the booty already picked up, to the value of fifty dollars.

News of this dacoity reached the Thanadar early next morning, and he began immediate investigation. Not one of the three inmates of the house was able to identify a single assailant, but the previous evening another villager had seen and recognized some men making their way toward the village. Inquiries corroborated the evidence, and the Thanadar decided to search the houses of the suspects for stolen property. Luck was with him. In the very first house searched he recovered some of the jewelry. The suspect made a full confession, giving the names of all his accomplices. One man escaped to Nepal, but eventually eight men were arrested and convicted, receiving sentences of imprisonment of from five to ten years.

The gang was oddly assorted. It was made up of two Brahmins, one of whom acted as leader, three other Hindus

—a *Goshain* and two *Kurmis*—and four Mussulmans. It bore out the testimony of the Thanadar that in Gonda crimes of violence were most frequently directed by Brahmins, who outrank others in intelligence, and that Mussulmans came second. He said Pasis occupied third place in the record for violent crime in our region.

Dacoities usually present great difficulties in the matter of detection. The villagers fear them most in the dry season, from November to June. When the rivers are flooded, escape is less easy. Since the men are armed or else work in bands, watchmen and villagers cannot do much to cope with them. They fall upon a lonely village in the dead of night, break into one or two houses, collect what they can of money, jewelry, and household utensils, and vanish before dawn. A few hours later the jewelry has been melted down, the money divided, and the utensils temporarily buried or hidden. They also perpetrate road robberies by daylight.

An able leader is all that is essential for getting up a dacoity. Most frequently he is found to be a man with a previous jail record. He picks and chooses his followers from among the potential criminals in a district. In some cases gangs are permanently organized, with headquarters in some remote ravine from which marauding expeditions are carried out at intervals. In other cases dacoits are brought together under a leader for a particular crime; then they immediately disband and scatter again.

The combined exploits of the Pachperwa police officer and the police officer of the adjoining circle of Tulsipur in tracking down one of these bands was recounted by Fakire, my newsmonger, seated cross-legged on the floor of my living room. It seemed that three dacoities had been committed in a single night, six months before, in a village on the edge of our circle. The robbers, with one woman among them, were sighted by several villagers in turn next day, moving off across the intervening fields toward the Tulsipur forest. Our Thanadar hastily gathered some constables and watchmen and set out in pursuit. Among the various witnesses, the most important was a boy who herded buffaloes. While he was tending his buffaloes in the forest as usual, he suddenly came upon a man at the edge of a stream, washing bloodstains from a big sword. He had actually stumbled among the robbers as they halted for a brief rest. Before he could escape and give warning of their whereabouts, he was seized and forced to go along with them for two days. When they had disposed of their booty, one of them took him out to the edge of the forest and turned him loose. He made his way to the nearest village, half dead with fright, where he found himself more than twenty miles from home. He was able to give the police valuable information. They rounded up nine men in the forest, and the capture of these led to the arrest of seven others. Among the sixteen men convicted, altogether eight different castes were represented. Except for the leader, a convict just released from jail, not one of the dacoits was previously known to the police.

Dacoities are the most dramatic crime of rural India, but they are actually responsible for only a small fraction of the annual losses suffered by the people through malefactors. In our district dacoities accounted for one twelfth, theft for one tenth and burglary for three quarters of the stolen property.

Villagers are heavy sleepers, and they have the habit of wrapping themselves up head and all in a sleeping sheet, as a protection against snakes and mosquitoes. The rainy season, which interferes with the movements of dacoits, is the one most favored by burglars. At this time the noise of wind and rain helps to cover up any little sounds the burglar makes, and he finds mud walls soft and yielding. He can dig a hole through a wall by which to admit himself into a house in a few minutes. Other methods of gaining entrance are by digging through the thatch, lifting the thatch where it rests upon the wall, or climbing over a courtyard wall with the help of a bamboo pole. Even a door presents no real obstacle. It is often badly hung, and a hole dug in the mud wall at the side of the frame will permit a hand to lift the latch from the inside and slip back the bolt.

The burglar's tools are few, a simple piece of iron, shaped for digging by a blacksmith, being the principal one. Occasionally strange use is made of the Indian field lizard. One day the Ayah told me how this little creature, which is scarcely a foot long, is sometimes made to serve the burglar's convenience. It has a very tenacious grip, and once it gets its claws into something it can be dislodged only with much effort. The burglar fastens one end of a strong, fine cord around the lizard, tosses it up on a roof where it can attach itself to a beam, and then pulls himself up by the help of the cord. The Thanadar told me that city house breakers, scaling walls two or three stories high, were much more likely to use lizards than rural house breakers.

Once inside a house, the burglar tosses dried peas about to locate metal vessels or cooking pots in the dark. He cuts into the mud granaries, which are a feature of every village house, and extracts the grain. He takes clothes. If he knows a woman's husband is away, he will try to rob her of her jewelry. Of course a cache of rupees represents the best haul. All villagers who possess anything at all in the way of money or jewelry have a secret hiding place, but it is not easy to find. When the treasure has been buried, the place is smoothed over with a coat of cow-dung plaster, and no trace remains.

The burglarizing of house granaries seemed to be an offense well understood at the police station. One day several women arrived at my house, weeping. They told a tale of two men in their family who had been arrested on an accusation of stealing grain, falsely entered against them by the thekedar of their village. The men had refused to do extra work for the thekedar, the women said, and so in revenge he had had six bags of rice put inside their house when they were all away at the Pachperwa bazar and had then accused them of theft.

I made a point of dropping in at the thana that afternoon and casually mentioned having heard of the arrest of the two men for stealing grain. The Thanadar told his story. The constable on duty at the bazar had observed the men selling rice at a price so far below the ordinary bazar rate that his suspicions were aroused. He had brought them to the police station, and the Thanadar had betaken himself to their village to inquire if there had been any theft of grain. The thekedar said there had not, but no sooner had the Thanadar left than a messenger hurried after him to report that an examination of the thekedar's granaries had revealed a hole cut in the bottom of one, stuffed with rags. The granary, sealed and supposedly full, was found to be entirely empty. The house of the men under suspicion was thereupon searched, and six bags of rice were found hidden in a corner.

The disappearance of the watch confided to Asgar's care, of five rupees from Din Mohammed's tin trunk, of the Tahsildar's trunk, containing a few clothes, a silver fountain pen and, what he valued vastly more, the horoscopes of his two youngest sons, when the trunk was transported by bullock cart, of some bags of peppers from a Bania's shop— these were typical of ordinary village peculations as they came to my notice. But now and then, of course, a serious loss was sustained. After his wife's death the rich thekedar of Baidmao had occasion to draw upon his hoard of 11,000 rupees for funeral expenses. The place where the money was hidden had not been opened for five months. When he dug up his cache, he found 6,000 rupees missing. Since the hiding place was in an inner court and there had been no evidence of open robbery, it was apparent that somebody in his own family was guilty.

To have their standing crops not only destroyed by marauding animals but cut by thieves is a danger all cultivators dread. When the grain is ripe they take precaution to guard the fields by night until the harvesting is over. At this time the fields are studded with little temporary shelters

of thatch, and the men can be heard singing and calling
to each other all night long. Especially when crops are poor
and a general shortage is felt is there likelihood of this sort
of theft. Among people close to starvation the temptation is
great.

Cattle lifting is another catastrophe not infrequently
suffered by the poor cultivator. Certain men make a practice
of moving small herds slowly about the country, following
the seasonal pasturage and ostensibly buying and selling
cattle as they pass about through the villages. Where cattle
are not usually branded, for religious reasons, and fences
are unknown, it becomes a simple matter for the professional
cattle thief to pick up two or three stray bullocks or
buffaloes in each district. The *Banjara* caste bears a bad
reputation for cattle thieving. Banjaras follow a wandering life as carters and cattle traders and are looked on
askance by the stay-at-home villager. Yet he knows well
that there is another and nearer source of danger, namely
the local *thangdar*, a professional receiver of stolen cattle.

This well known individual is most often some wealthy
and powerful rent contractor living in the vicinity. Everybody knows who he is, including the police, but he carries
on his business without fear of molestation. His agents are
most active during the dry months after the crops are in,
when cattle stray about guarded only by children. Somebody
in a village, the watchman himself, it may be, steals a bullock
at night and quickly passes it on ten miles to a confederate
covering the next area, who in turn passes it on to the next
man, until eventually it is turned into the big herd of the
thangdar.

If the owner calls upon the police to assist in recovering
the animal, he has to identify it to begin with, which is not
easy. The owner of the herd can produce twenty witnesses
to swear that the disputed cow or bullock or buffalo belongs
to him. If trouble really threatens, he can get the animal
out of the way by selling it to a Mohammedan butcher at
half price or having it temporarily driven across the border.

By long experience the villager has learned that, if he wants his bullock back, there is only one way to proceed. He does not go near the police station. He loudly bewails his loss and waits until the watchman or the thief, tendering him heartfelt sympathy, confides that he has some idea who the culprit is, adding that if the victim will pay the thief's price of ten or twelve rupees, no doubt the speedy return of the animal can be arranged. Two days later it is mysteriously found grazing near the road.

Incendiarism is another crime in rural India, and this, too, is almost impossible to detect, because accidental fires are all too frequent. Every year from March until the monsoon comes, fires break out, first in one village and then another. Night after night the horizon is red with them. I have counted as many as four red flares all at once, in different directions.

At this season thatched roofs are intensely dry, and a hot wind blows constantly. A chance spark carried up into the roof of a house from a cooking fire reduces a whole village to smoking ruin within an hour. Men and women cluster around the nearest well, all trying simultaneously to draw a jar of water to pour on the devouring flames. The women half sing, half sob, as they run back and forth. An old bearded Mussulman will stand beating his chest in a paroxysm of grief. Frightened children add their howls to the general turmoil. For a short time the burning roofs send up showers of sparks. Then there are only yawning cavities, while the beams blaze on, and the cones of fuel cakes, patiently scraped together and laboriously stacked against the approaching rainy season, become glowing red furnaces. When at last the fire is over, blackened walls of earth remain, a few brass pots and plates, and nothing more. Even the grain inside the mud granaries is destroyed by scorch and smoke.

I watched the forty-five houses of Jagdishpur go one afternoon. A hundred houses of Pachperwa went in another afternoon. Fires on three successive days and nights in April destroyed two thirds of Bishenpur, west across the fields. Many times I saw half burned villages. I saw, too, that extreme poverty has its ironical advantages. After all, there is not so much to lose. Even while the embers of one fire were still smoking, I met people from the nearest village trailing across the fields bearing new rough thatches on their heads for temporary shelter. Who knows if it may not be their turn next? The Banias and money-lenders are on hand to tide the villagers over the first bad time. The estate promises them free wood to rebuild their houses.

Seeing the terrible distress a village fire means, an act of incendiarism is all but incredible, yet it is common. The motive is invariably revenge, springing out of some quarrel, in most cases involving a woman. This was especially true in Oudh, where Mohammedan influence was strong, allowing a freedom in matters of plural marriage, divorce and re-marriage, making for rather uncertain morals. But Mussul-mans were by no means the only culprits. Quarreling was common to village life, and the spirit of revenge was always seeking an outlet. A jilted lover or the injured party in a lawsuit nurses his grievance until the right moment comes. Then on some dark night he goes out and tosses a lighted match on to a roof, not caring whether a general conflagra-tion starts, not even caring whether his own house goes, if only he can bring ruin upon his enemy. Nobody sees him actually perform the deed, and though the whole village is sure of his responsibility, there is no way to prove his guilt.

The Bishenpur fire was like that. A Mohammedan oil presser suspected another of being his wife's lover and ranged a number of villagers on his side. A complaint was carried to the thana, and the man suddenly found himself arrested and locked up. When the Sub-Inspector let him out, he returned home swearing that he would make every person in the village pay forty-one rupees. This was cur-rently said to have been the price for his release. A fire broke out, which the villagers managed to extinguish before it did much harm. Two more fires followed, in one of which a baby was burned to death, and nearly the whole of Bishenpur was destroyed.

Slightly less than half the cases of cognizable crimes investigated in Gonda district each year result in convictions. According to the *Crime Register for Pachperwa* village and its hamlets, with a recorded population of 2,961, just thirty-eight actual convictions for crime had been entered against the name of the village in twenty-four years. The convictions covered sixteen cases of burglary, sixteen of theft, one murder, two dacoities, two cases of receiving stolen property, and the political offense of Devi Prasad, Non-coöperator. Time might have hung heavy on the hands of the Thanadar, if it were not for the far greater number of assaults, quarrels, and woman cases—noncognizable crimes—which he dealt with in his rôle of maintaining the general peace. These were zealously examined into, since incidentally they furnished the police force, from the village watchmen up, with an important source of graft. Practically every complaint brought to the thana, every alleged abuse, real or invented, followed up by the representatives of the law, meant annas or rupees flowing into somebody's pocket.

This fact was gradually borne in on me as time went on. Support came through the testimony of the tahsil officials, themselves well acquainted with the various ways and means of extortion. One of the police constables complained bitterly one day that the thana privileges were not evenly divided. When I inquired what the thana privileges were, I learned that members of the police force claimed a right to purchase grain and ghi and similar articles in the villages at much below market rate, and that all sorts of supplies were regularly brought to the thana as "presents." Carts passing back and forth on the Utraula road skirting the police station customarily gave a bundle of wood, a melon or two, a double handful of grain. A simple soul who came from a village eight miles distant to ask for medicine for his wife's eyes mentioned thana begar—free service for the thana—as the explanation of his presence on that particular occasion in Pachperwa.

More aggressive tactics were mentioned by other villagers. Apparently the red police turban was a symbol of power— opportunity to turn to personal account the elements of stupidity, timidity, or rascality within the community. A child rushed up to my door one afternoon, for example, excitedly crying out that a watchman was threatening to take all his cattle to the pound unless he paid four rupees. The man stood at some distance, obviously ill at ease. The cattle had been eating grass by the roadside, which was against the regulations when the crops were growing. So it was his duty to take them to the pound, he maintained. This did not exactly explain the matter of the four rupees. When I asked him to let them go this time, since they had done no real damage, he consented affably. Impounded cattle cannot be redeemed except upon payment of a rupee a day charged for a buffalo, twelve annas for a bullock or cow, eight annas for a calf. I gathered that the pound, used as a threat, was capable of furnishing a good sum to servants of the law.

The investigation of a fire was another profitable source of income. Whenever a fire occurred a constable promptly put in an appearance and began taking testimony on any dispute which might have led to incendiarism. Whether an accused man was innocent or guilty, whether there was the slightest chance that a case against him could be proved or not, it was understood that his only safety generally lay in speedy settlement. Bribery itself is a cognizable offense, but the person who pays as well as the one who receives is guilty in the eyes of the law, and who then is to make a complaint? Though the villager willingly resorts to the thana when he is in trouble, or wants to get somebody else in trouble, there is no place on earth for which he holds greater aversion at other times.

CHAPTER X

The Fields

On the field recorder's map, Pachperwa sprawled like a thousand-legger, the fat body of the village extending down the center, fields radiating from it in long thin strips. To the eye, divisions were unnoticeable. No fences broke the flat expanse. Only tiny ridges, to retain the water, partitioned the rice fields into irregular squares.

Rice is the most important crop of the low-lying Tarai land, but in northern India rice is grown only in the rainy season. Our fields produced many other things besides rice. In November and December, when the snow-covered mountains dominated the horizon and every morning white mist floated over the fields, masses of mustard flowers flung brilliant yellow scarfs across great stretches of the landscape. As the mustard went, the pulses substituted a darker yellow. A little later, and the color scheme shifted to the melting blue of flax and the hot scarlet and vermilion of chillies spread out to dry on all the bare patches. By the time the chillies had faded to rusty red, the fields were tawny with ripening wheat.

In March, after the wheat was cut, the country quickly subsided to listless brown, except for trees bursting into flower. Along the railway embankment acacias and laburnums put forth delicate yellow sprays. The *nims* bedecked themselves with pendent tassels. Mangoes and jamuns turned to white clouds. Then the rains came in torrential floods. The parched fields drank and drank. And once again the world was lush and beautiful with growing rice.

Upon the regular arrival and adequacy of the southwest monsoon depends the prosperity, if it may be called that, of the agricultural and pastoral millions, 73 per cent of India's population. As the sun moves north each year, a great air current originating in the Indian Ocean sweeps up the Arabian Sea on the west and the Bay of Bengal on the east. It converges upon the Indian peninsula in June and in the next few months deposits nearly all its concentrated moisture. But the rainfall is very unevenly distributed. It is particularly heavy in northeastern India and along the southern slopes of the Himalaya. Other areas, because of local conditions, receive scant rain or none at all. In a normal year our region averaged about five feet of rain, of which all except two inches fell between the middle of June and the end of September.

After the rains, the northeast monsoon sets in. This season, delightful as it is for tourists, causes much misery to cultivators in the north. Malaria is widely prevalent in October and November, and few of the people are adequately protected against the cold nights of December and January. Between day and night the temperature drops at least thirty degrees. I slept under many blankets and an eiderdown quilt and took a hot-water bottle to bed with me. The villagers of Pachperwa huddled under a single cotton sheet and sometimes lacked even this.

Where temperature and rainfall are fairly evenly distributed, as in southern India, early and late sowings of the same crop are the rule. In northern India, the crops vary according to the different seasons. Rice, millet, and maize, requiring intense heat and moisture, are sown soon after the rains commence and are harvested in the fall. They are followed by the cold weather crops, wheat, barley, gram, most of the pulses, oilseeds, and opium poppy, harvested in the early spring. Sugar cane, which is on the ground ten months, is cut between the *kharif* and the *rabi*, as the fall and spring harvests are called. Jute, confined to Bengal, and cotton, for the northern cotton areas, also belong with the autumn crops.

Our village fields produced nearly all the Indian staples, except sugar cane, opium, and cotton, but rice was the principal crop. The cheaper and poorer rice was kept for home consumption, and the more valuable variety was exported. Under favorable conditions certain fields were allowed to lie fallow, but much of the land was double-cropped. Pulses, mustard, linseed, and rape I saw all growing in the winter in fields that were under rice the following summer.

Village life in India resolves itself into a perpetual struggle with the fields. As against less than half the population in the United States living in rural areas, all but ten per cent of the Indian population is rural. But the United States is very nearly twice the size of India, and India, on the other hand, has three times the population of the United States. In the typical agricultural state of Iowa, the density is only 43 persons to the square mile. In the district of Gonda it is 526, and the districts immediately to the east are still more crowded. If forest and waste land are eliminated from the calculation, the density in Gonda actually rises to 750 persons per cultivated square mile. This is greater than in Belgium or England and Wales, two of the most highly industrialized areas in the world. The conclusion is obvious. The average village goes land hungry and the average villager half starved.

In Pachperwa, of course, no villager owned land outright. Broadly speaking, the tenant system I met with prevails throughout Bengal, Bihar and Orissa, the Central Provinces, and the United Provinces. In the Punjab, Bombay, and Madras—north, west, and south—the agriculturist more generally has permanent rights in the land he cultivates. The greater number of tenant cultivators in Oudh now have certain guaranteed rights of occupancy in the land, but the uneconomic size of the average holding, combined with the perennial uncertainty of rain, fails to allow any margin of profit.

My nearest neighbor in Pachperwa was the Patwari, or village accountant, Gomti Prasad, whose house was close to the dispensary. He was responsible for keeping all the intricate details of the village lands. Upon the patwaris' books the government depends for annual crop statistics and periodic land surveys. All cases of dispute over boundaries, occupancy rights, and similar vital themes of village life are referred to his records.

Pachperwa, with its hamlets, not only kept Gomti Prasad exceedingly busy but, such was its importance, served as headquarters for a circle inspector of forty accountants in the neighborhood. This official, an educated Mussulman bearing the Persian title of kanungo, meaning one familiar with prevailing regulations, conducted most of his work in an open shed next to Yasin Khan's house. The work of the kanungos is checked by a government assistant tahsildar. The Hindu in charge of our area once spent some days in Pachperwa, going over records and hearing land disputes. When he told me that altogether 1,583 cases of dispute had been presented to him for settlement, and that by the end of the third day he had already heard 800, with witnesses, I perceived something of the complexity of land administration in India. It was he who casually remarked that not more than two or three patwaris out of a hundred could be called honest. "Not as many as that! Not one!" exclaimed our own estate Tahsildar, who had much faith in God but very little in his fellow man.

After finishing elementary school, the candidate for the position of village accountant prepares himself for his special work by a year's training at the patwari school at district headquarters, where he learns how to keep records and studies simple surveying and map making. Until a few years ago his salary was ten rupees a month. Nowadays, he is supposed to draw eighteen, but Gomti Prasad assured me

that he got only eleven—less than four dollars a month.
But at harvest time the village accountant receives grain
presents from practically every cultivator listed in his books.
The custom hangs over from the day when the accountant
was a village servant. Suspicion lurks in the mind that
records and favors tally with presents. Gomti Prasad must
have been an exception to the rule. I never heard any complaints against him.

One day, at my request, he brought over his map and
books and explained the routine of his work to me. The
map gave the main features of the topography, such as
roads, nalas, and mango groves, the position of the village
houses, and all the fields carefully drawn to scale and
numbered. There were more than 6,000 of these in a compact
girdle around Pachperwa, with a total area of 745 acres.

Gomti Prasad's books were three in number. One was
simply an official record of the name of the village and of
the landlord, a statement of the government revenue demand
and the terms of contract of the rent collector. Until Lala
Babu, superintendent of the Maharaja's elephant department, was appointed thekedar for Pachperwa, while I was
there, the village had been spared a rent contractor for many
years. Tenants had paid their rents directly to the tahsil
treasurer. They were not overjoyed at the change, since the
collector, who receives as payment from a tenth to a quarter
of the rents, can exact labor and certain other taxes from
them. Most unhappy of all, by general rumor, was the rich
Mohammedan tenant who had to give up half his land for
the creation of *sir* land for Pachperwa. Sir land is rent-free
land traditionally apportioned to the thekedar of a village.
The tenant was compensated by receiving an appointment
as rent contractor for another village, but he did not feel
that he had benefited by the exchange. From this and other
sources, a block of a hundred acres was set apart for Lala
Babu. Another one of the records gave a complete list of the
tenants, with area of holdings, numbers of fields, time of
settlement, and exact rentals. The third book presented a

detailed record of each village field, with area, owner, and crops sown.

In the record of tenants' holdings, Gomti Prasad noted in a column headed "remarks" whether the land in question had been sublet or whether another person than the tenant was in actual possession. This column, it seemed, provided leeway for dishonest manipulation of the records, if an accountant was so minded. After prearrangement with a friendly patwari, one man could take possession of a field overnight and start cutting the crops another had sown, protesting that he had sublet the field and producing witnesses to swear for him. If the records substantiated his words, the real tenant might find difficulty in proving his own claims. Or boundaries of fields, mud walls a few inches high, might be tampered with, in actuality and on paper, in spite of the precautionary regulation that all records are to be kept in ink.

Quarrels between tenants were not the result of innate dishonesty but of a pitiful need for more land to cultivate in order to subsist. A typical case came up before the Peshkar. A timid cultivator whose hands trembled and whose eyes kept filling and overflowing with tears was claiming less than an acre of land which another man insisted belonged to him. The second man, a stalwart young fellow, stated simply that he had gone to Rangoon, and while he was away the other one had moved into his fields. My sympathies were all with the first man, but the records, examined and reported upon by an assistant delegated to go to the village the next day, proved him in the wrong. I can still see the old, hardened, trembling hands of that unhappy man, who was asking for nothing but the privilege of being allowed to work.

The size of holdings in any given locality naturally bears a close relation to fertility of soil, pressure of population and rental. In general, the Tarai land, a rich alluvial deposit, like the whole Gangetic plain, is well suited to rice cultivation. Rice is capable of supporting a larger population on a small area than any food crop except potatoes. Consequently the pressure of population in this region was great, land proportionately scarce, and rentals high, considering the uneconomic size of holdings. Villagers of Pachperwa averaged an annual rental of three dollars an acre.

When I asked Gomti Prasad the average size of a tenant's holding in Pachperwa he did not know. Together we worked it out from his records. It came to a trifle more than six and a half acres. Compared with the 145 acres of the average farm in the United States, six and a half acres appeared microscopic. Compared with agricultural holdings in many parts of India it was unusually high. But the figure turned out to be deceptive. If the six tenants who cultivated twenty acres or more were left out, 58 of the total number of 112 tenants had less than three acres, and 49 out of these less than a single acre apiece. One or two had only two biswas, twice twenty square feet.

Another aspect of the field problem making for poverty in India, besides the small size of holdings, is the widely practised subdivision and fragmentation of land. A tenant may have three acres, but it is very unlikely that they are in a compact block. Generally a holding is broken up into a great many noncontiguous fields of different sizes, and the fields themselves are fragmented into tiny plots. The amount of land increasingly taken up in dividing walls, the time wasted by cultivators in going to their scattered fields, and the lack of incentive under the circumstances to undertake permanent improvements, such as the sinking of a well, all represent serious agricultural handicaps.

The subdivision goes back to the precarious conditions under which agriculture has always been carried on in India and to the common laws of inheritance. Usually there are more and less desirable fields belonging to a village. A crop that can be grown in one part may not succeed in another. To give everybody the maximum insurance against want, a system of scattered fields developed wherever land was not actually communal property. According to the Hindu law of inheritance, except in the case of the joint family in which the head assumes responsibility for maintaining all the family members, inheritance of immovable and inalienable property is divided by all the heirs in equal shares. Mohammedan law is much the same with a more elaborate system of division. This means in practice that when a man dies, his sons not only divide his holding, but carry out the principle of division to the point of each taking an equal share in each field.

Subdivision and fragmentation have increased rapidly in the past few decades, partly as a result of imported Western ideas of individualism and private property, before which the joint family and the old communal village, with their coöperative rather than competitive ideals, have broken down. The coöperative farms of Russia, now being forcibly organized by the Soviet government in the interests of modern efficiency, resemble very strikingly the old organic Indian scheme of cultivation. A natural increase in population has also resulted in a reduction in size of holdings. While in the past fifty years the population in the United States has trebled, in India it has actually advanced only 20 per cent. Nevertheless, this increase in an already crowded country, where industrial development has not kept pace, has meant less land for each successive generation of cultivators.

Where village lands are of fairly uniform quality there is little excuse for subdivision, and one of the agricultural reforms most advocated is consolidation, wherever possible, of individual holdings. In the Balrampur Estate only one heir, usually the eldest son, could be named to succeed to a tenant's occupancy rights, but family quarrels continued to precipitate unnecessary fragmentation. Educational work on the benefits of consolidation has to be generally carried out. Following the substantial beginning made in this line in the Punjab, other provinces are endeavoring to popularize the idea, and the Balrampur Estate, under the Court of Wards administration, is trying to persuade village communities voluntarily to consolidate their holdings. In our tahsil, the scheme of consolidation had been satisfactorily worked out in three or four villages.

A day came when the sun was a red hole piercing a heavy sky. It seemed as if all the dust between Pachperwa and the Bay of Bengal went swirling round the Happy House. The wind pushed Din Mohammed at a run, as he brought the breakfast dishes, swathed in towels to keep the sand out. All day the wind kept blowing. Toward night it died down and the stars came out. We sniffed a strange delightful smell —moisture far off. Some hours later I was waked by a dull roar. In a few minutes the trees were dripping, rivers pouring down the steep slope of the roof. The temperature went tumbling down to unfamiliar coolness. By morning I found myself staring with unbelieving eyes at the reflection of mango trees in the moat surrounding my hill. The road had been transformed into a lake, and half the fields were submerged. The next night frogs were singing persistently that though it was only the twenty-ninth of May, two weeks too early, the monsoon had definitely broken.

Time for wrangling over the fields was at an end. All quarreling stopped, even that of monkeys and cuckoos. From the veranda I watched the humped white bullocks with slanting, coal-black eyes being driven out to the fields. Men carried their plows, oddly suggestive of anchors, over their shoulders. The village had come to life.

Fields can be prepared for rice planting only when the rain softens the hard earth. Since the growing season is short, there was little time to waste. First of all the seed beds were carefully plowed and replowed. Then attention was turned to those fields where the rice was later to be transplanted. But rice fields are generally hastily cultivated. Two or three plowings are all the time allows for. After the rice is under way, fallow fields for the autumn sowing receive six or seven thorough plowings.

The behavior of the rain at this time is very important. Pachperwa looked with misgiving on the early arrival of the monsoon. Plowing could be started sooner than usual, to be sure, but what if an early beginning meant an early termination of the monsoon? For two or three weeks the rain behaved exactly as it should—falling in sheets for several hours every day or two with intervals of good weather between. Then a whole week passed with no rain at all. Deep pessimism settled upon the community. "A third of the crop has already been destroyed," was the gloomy pronouncement heard on every side.

I rode out on one of these blistering days. The sky was almost dead white. The fields had split up into great dry cakes. As the elephant plodded softly on, from time to time drawing supplies of water from an internal reservoir and unexpectedly spraying her leathery flanks and me as well, I exchanged words of sympathy over the bad situation with some men I met. Not knowing how else to cheer them, I prophesied rain for the next day. The cloudless sky gave no hint of rain, and it seemed unlikely, indeed, that it would ever rain again. But the following morning I waked to the welcome music of a heavy downpour. It did not stop raining for thirty-six hours—telegraph wires went down, bridges were washed away, and roofs blown off—but the crops were saved.

The Tahsildar sent over word that a small river a few miles west of Pachperwa was in flood. Should I like to go by elephant and see it? The Mohammedan barber Dukhi offered to escort me. We set off about ten o'clock.

Much of the road was under water. The flatness of the country was more apparent than ever. Miles and miles were flooded. One had the feeling that the sky had fallen and smashed itself into an infinite number of pieces. Surrounded by low mud dikes, every field was a brilliant mirror flashing back the sun.

Work was in full swing. Pairs of bullocks were going round and round the fields, each pair followed by a plowman steadying the single handle of his plow. Knee deep in the burning water the plowmen worked, bare bodies thickly splashed with mud. Two to four pairs of bullocks tramped round, one behind the other. The man with enough land to require several bullocks turned them all into one field at a time, drawing upon relatives or hired plowmen to help out, but ordinary villagers pooled their resources, for general convenience, plowing the fields of each in turn. Where the plowing was finished and the churned mud had already sucked up most of the water, the men, two abreast, were standing behind their bullocks on boards and driving round the fields like Roman charioteers, pressing the ooze flat with their own weight. Here and there a microscopic atom of humanity was darkly silhouetted against a lonely world of water, sky and shining mud. Taking strange flamingo steps, it moved slowly forward, scattering seed from a basket held against its breast.

Having had a glimpse of the river, dry a month before, now a respectable little Mississippi, we turned back again. This time we met streams of women winding along the dikes in single file, bringing food to their husbands and sons in the fields. They carried wide-lipped, colored straw baskets on their heads, a flashing brass lota of drinking water miraculously balanced on top. Bullocks were unyoked, and for a few brief moments men and beasts rested. But at this season work waited not even upon death. The road passed within half a mile of Bishenpur, which was just then in the grip of cholera. The Bishenpur men were working in their fields like everybody else.

Three weeks later the rice was two feet high and ready for transplanting. This was another period of feverish activity. The rice had tiny white roots, fine as hair. The older men and some of the women swept it up by handfuls from the seed beds and tied it in bunches with a quick twist of one or two long fresh blades. As soon as a stack was ready, one of the women set off for the outer fields with a towering green pile on her head.

A *gorait*, a humble little watchman of another village who came to serve at tahsil headquarters for a week, and who incidentally pulled my punka at odd hours, described the work. Once the rice is out of the ground it must be transplanted with utmost speed. Each worker is supposed to transplant four pounds of rice plants a day, but the day may be a very long one. He himself often worked in the fields by lantern light. Then he walked a long way home, ate a handful of food, and fell asleep, and was up again at four. If it was raining he felt chilled. Everything was damp, outside and in, including the mud floor on which he slept. His body ached. Sometimes he had fever. If the sun shone, then the shallow water in the fields burned his legs and hands. In the open fields the cultivator has nothing but a few rags between himself and the furnace overhead. Inured to the sun by centuries though he is, he suffers greatly.

The last week in July I went out to watch the transplanting. The fingers of the women are more deft than those of the men, and women did this work. They were strung out in long bending rows, saris tucked well up out of the water. A man on the dike at one corner of the field tossed small bundles of rice plants to them. Separating the plants, they thrust two or three at a time into the muddy bottom, with quick regular gestures like oar strokes, leaving a space between each upright tuft. Under my eyes the field took on a quaintly quilted look.

Laughter and song resounded from every side, for the women sang as they labored. Nonsense, some of the verses were, but the beat of the song timed to the rhythmic gestures was all that mattered:

*"O Rani, you have a magnificent palace, but I have only
    a hut to live in."*

"Who cares for a palace? I like the old hut."

*"O Rani, you have rich garments to put on. I have
    only old rags."*

"Let the rich garments be burnt! I like the old rags."

Or an imaginary barber in his capacity of matchmaker was the theme of the merrymaking:

*"O barber, who has not got a wife, and is there a man
for whom you are seeking one?"*

*"O barber, do you belong to my future father-in-law's
house? If so, will you give me a drink?"*

*"The barber says I am untouchable and he cannot
serve me water."*

"Nevertheless, O barber, I like the Raja."

So they joked, making up verses in turn, or one taking
the lead and the others chiming in on a refrain, not infrequently, from what I gathered, indulging in pointed sallies
at the expense of somebody present. But it was all gay and
happy. Overhead downy white clouds tumbled about in the
blue sky. The purple foothills came down almost to the edge
of the village. Water birds perched expectantly on the
dikes. A pervasive charm hung over the newly planted fields.
Life moved, for one afternoon at least, in perfect harmony
with nature.

The rain continued to fall in sufficient quantities, and in
due course the rice ripened and Pachperwa rejoiced in a
good harvest. Yet between possible drought or flood in the
summer months, frequent failure of winter rains, frosts, and
an overcast, rust-producing January, hail in February
and insect and animal pests all the year round, the fields
give the cultivators many a heartache.

I remember, for instance, how locusts were flying omi-
niously thick when the emerald rice was just up. I first noticed
an extraordinary number of large reddish insects hotly
pursued by a host of small black and white birds darting
hither and thither over my maidan. The Tahsildar thought
they might be moths, and I did not feel qualified to contradict him. While I was having dinner a peon arrived to
correct this statement. They were *tiddis*—locusts—after all.
Two days later I heard a peculiar metallic drone, which
might have come from a thousand distant airplanes. A
smoky yellow tinge spread rapidly over the sky as a swarm
of locusts passed, flying high overhead. Mercifully they

did not light on our fields. A flight of locusts is no mere phrase, but a catastrophe comparable with eruptions, landslides, typhoons, and pestilence. It is looked on as a bad omen. Even the sight of locusts means a year of famine, one old white-beard assured me.

Indian agriculture has been described as "a gamble in rain," but even games of chance have their probable ratios of success and failure. Agricultural records show that the cultivator must expect one bad year out of every five, with serious famine conditions prevailing about once a decade. India has always had to face periodic famines, first in one part of the country, then in another.

What these famines have cost in the past bare figures are powerless to tell. A complete failure of the seasonal rains may mean that literally not a blade of grass will grow over vast tracts of densely populated land. Within recent decades there have been famines extending over areas of from two hundred thousand to half a million square miles and affecting populations of from fifty to seventy millions. Before modern transport was developed there was nothing for people to do but die, after their reserve stores were exhausted, or emigrate to other parts of India. During the famine of 1868–70 in western India, a million Marwaris out of a population of a million and a half left their homes in Marwar and spread throughout the country. Nowadays railways can rush supplies to a famine area, but prices naturally go up, and since population has increased there is no escaping widespread misery. The government has developed a competent system of famine relief which can be set in motion as soon as dire scarcity becomes apparent. Out of the permanent fund maintained for the purpose by every province, able-bodied persons are given employment on public works, while those incapable of supporting themselves by such means receive doles. A famine to-day is marked by a heavy exodus from rural districts to industrial centers. But though millions no longer actually starve to death, as they undoubtedly did in pre-railroad days, a famine year means appalling suffering among people who have no margin of prosperity to draw upon, even under the most favorable natural conditions.

I had plenty of occasion in the village to observe the bad effects of the limited diet, limited both in quantity and quality. Experts estimate that the average Indian consumes a third as much food as the average American. Between thirty and forty millions of the population probably do not have more than one meal a day and live on the verge of perpetual starvation. Diet was the hopeless feature in any attempt to prescribe for the sick people who flocked to my door. "Rice and pulse" or "bread" was the invariable answer whenever I asked what anybody ate, and I learned that the statement was to be taken quite literally. A man's diet depended on whether his land was high or low-lying, whether it produced millet or wheat or maize, out of which the coarse native bread is indiscriminately made, or rice. Rice is, of course, the great Indian staple. Of the total cultivated area of British India approximately a third, eighty million acres, is under rice. India produces well over half the world supply.

The village market offered fresh vegetables and fruits in season, but these were considered luxuries, by no means part of the daily menu even for a vegetarian people. The Hindu religious ideal stands in the way of meat eating for large groups, but in any case the economics of a thickly populated country would prevent the wasteful production of grain- and fodder-fed cattle designed only for the slaughter house. In India pulses supply proteids and generally take the place of the 139 pounds of meat which represent the annual per capita consumption in the United States. Some goat meat and pork are eaten in the villages, but cattle are reserved for work and for dairying. Goats cost less than cows or milch buffaloes to maintain, and goats supply most of the milk used in the villages. The milk from the village cattle ordinarily goes into ghi and cheese, but these are for the comparatively few who can afford them.

Poultry raising is confined to Mussulmans, since Hindus look on hens as unclean and, generally speaking, will not eat eggs. It becomes obvious why India, supporting its great population upon one hundred million fewer acres of crop land and but a fraction of the grazing area available in the United States, turns to intensive cultivation of food grains and subsists—because there is no choice—on meager, unbalanced, and monotonous rations.

Water supply is naturally the most important factor in the agricultural equation. Altogether fifty million acres, a fifth of the total cultivated area, receive artificial irrigation from canals, wells, or tanks. All forms of artificial watering have been known to India for centuries, and some of the great canal systems in present use were constructed hundreds of years ago. Even before improvement and extension in modern times, they watered areas of many hundreds of thousands of acres. Under the British administration, the government has undertaken irrigation projects of first rank, and over half the total irrigated area now receives its water from government canals. A feature of recent development is the extent of arable land, particularly in the Punjab and Sind, made productive under modern irrigation schemes. Several millions of acres of waste land have been brought into cultivation and colonized in the Punjab, where the river system has favored canal expansion. The Sukkur Barrage, across the Indus in Sind, is one of the largest irrigation works of its kind in the world. It is opening up more than three million acres of waste and giving assured water supply to two million acres more, formerly dependent for cultivation on the limited flow of inundation canals.

Purely as a business enterprise, the government canal development has proved itself a most profitable investment. In the Punjab the canals pay 17 per cent on capital outlay, after the deduction of working expenses. For all irrigation works in India, the net return on capital amounts to 7.41 per cent. In addition, there is a large increase in government revenue under the heads of land tax, railways, stamps, and so forth, as a result of the increased productivity of the land and the prosperity that has characterized the young canal colonies.

One hears much of the important contribution to the agricultural prosperity of India of the government irrigation projects, important none the less because they have proved a handsomely paying investment. A little less talked of, perhaps, is the record of increasing poverty and distress over wide areas of Bengal, once known as the garden spot of India, through the unintelligent destruction here of the indigenous canal and drainage system of pre-British days. Sir William Willcocks, the distinguished hydraulic engineer whose name is associated with gigantic irrigation enterprises in Egypt and Mesopotamia, was invited to make an investigation of conditions in Bengal. He discovered that the innumerable small destructive rivers of the delta region, constantly changing their courses, were originally canals which, under the English régime, were allowed to escape from their proper channels and run wild. Formerly these canals distributed the flood waters of the Ganges and provided for proper drainage of the land, undoubtedly accounting for that prosperity of Bengal which lured the rapacious East India merchants thither in the early days of the eighteenth century. In his opinion, silting up occurred during the protracted struggles and disorder of the immediately preceding period of Mohammedan conquest. At any rate, the Company officials completely failed to recognize the remarkable irrigation scheme planned and constructed under one of the early Hindu kings of Bengal. Not only was nothing done to utilize and improve the original canal system, but railway embankments were subsequently thrown up, entirely destroying it. Some areas, cut off from their supply of loam-bearing Ganges flood water, have gradually become sterile and non-productive; others, improperly drained, show an advanced degree of waterlogging, with the inevitable accompaniment of malaria. Nor has any attempt been made to construct proper embankments for the Ganges in its lower course, to prevent the enormous erosion by which villages and groves and cultivated fields are swallowed up each year.

Sir William Willcocks severely criticizes the modern administrators and officials, who, with every opportunity to call in expert technical assistance, have hitherto done nothing to remedy the disastrous situation, growing worse from decade to decade. What is the use of talking about the wonderful work accomplished in the Punjab, where empty regions have been made fertile and opened to colonization for the first time, he asks, when in Bengal, the most densely populated province in India and actually the seat of the capital until 1911, almost an equal area of land has been ruined for agricultural purposes and millions have been reduced from prosperity to dire want?

In the United Provinces wells, responsible for 30 per cent of the total irrigated area of India, play the chief part in artificial irrigation. Around Pachperwa water was everywhere to be struck at fifteen or twenty feet below the surface, and there were no rocks or stones to offer any obstruction to boring. Yet lifting water by hand or bullock power ends by being an expensive operation, and the tenant system is likely to interfere with much investment of capital in the form of wells or any other permanent improvements. A good masonry well costs close to five hundred rupees, a poor one, sixty rupees. As for the modern tube wells with pumping machinery, they are confined to the model farms. At a cost of ten thousand rupees, what humble agriculturist could dream of having one for his handful of acres, even though the provincial government magnanimously offers to pay half the cost of the installation?

Every year the Balrampur Estate devotes some ten thousand rupees to building and repairing wells. With his share of this amount our Tahsildar could put in working order ten wells, but these wells, as far as I learned, were village wells and did not serve the fields at all. Irrigation to supplement the winter rains was restricted to seepage water collecting in holes dug in the corner of a field, here and there, lifted by the bucketful with the help of a sweep made from a tree trunk balanced by a large lump of mud. Slow, back-breaking work, scarcely calculated to yield the necessary eight or nine inches of irrigation, for instance, required for spring wheat. And in times of drought, shallow wells unfortunately have a way of going dry.

The cultivator, particularly the small tenant cultivator, digs a rough channel to catch the overflow from some neighboring stream, resorts to the open pits beside the railway embankment which become reservoirs during the rainy season, to be tapped in later months, or sinks holes in such of his scattered fields as promise to reward the hard labor of lifting irrigation water by hand. Anything more must be provided by God, the government, or a paternalistic landlord.

Bullocks are the backbone of Indian agriculture, and without them Indian rural life would be at a standstill. The man whose holding is too microscopic to warrant his keeping a pair of work animals must resort to the laborious task of hand spading or make some coöperative arrangement with others in a similar position. It is not easy to rent the use of plow bullocks, since the time when they are needed is exactly the time of the greatest pressure of work all round. A pair of bullocks of the type common to our village cost forty-five or fifty rupees. They were small and weak, and one pair of bullocks was required to cultivate every six acres of land under rabi crops or ten to twelve acres of rice land. The amount invested in his cattle is the cultivator's heaviest outlay, one that unfortunately he may be called upon to repeat. In recounting misfortunes that may have overtaken him, a villager never omits to mention the loss of a work animal as a serious disaster.

Outside his bullocks, the whole of the ordinary cultivator's equipment is not worth ten dollars. He has a light yoke and a plow made of a stick of mango wood tipped with iron, a short-handled spade something like a hoe, a clod crusher, a

small sickle, a reed winnowing scoop, a rope—all, with the
possible exception of the rope, locally made, after patterns
that have not changed since the days when the Aryan settlers
first took up agriculture.

The Indian plow does not turn a furrow but merely makes
a V-shaped scratch on the surface of the soil. The scratch
is so narrow that in order to stir up all the earth the plowman has to go over the ground at least three times. Dr.
Sam Higginbottom, director of Naini Agricultural Institute, has made a calculation that in order to plow one acre
the plowman walks fifty miles. With a plow of one of
the improved makes to be had nowadays he could reduce the
walking distance for himself and his bullocks by two thirds
and at the same time cultivate his land more effectively.

But many things stand in the way of the wholesale adoption in India of new agricultural machinery. The cost of
a plow is now about eighteen rupees, a comparatively high
figure, but this is little compared to the fifty-four rupees at
which the Raja Plow sells, one of the most satisfactory of
the improved types. Weight is another important item. I
used to watch our villagers going out to their fields and
returning at night, carrying not only a plow but often
a bullock yoke as well over their shoulders. I persuaded one
old man to weigh his load on the station scales. The plow
weighed sixteen pounds, the yoke fifteen. Since the Indian
fields offer no provision for storing equipment it is very
essential that tools carried back and forth many miles
every day should be as light as possible. The weight of the
machine-made plow with its heavier share is against it,
from the standpoint of the villager. He is also convinced,
rightly or wrongly, that his undersized bullocks cannot possibly draw a heavier plow. This objection does not hold in
western India, where a large breed of cattle is common. Still
another difficulty comes up in the matter of mending a
broken plow. The local product is easily repaired by the
village carpenter or blacksmith, but they have had no experience in tinkering with factory-made goods.

Nevertheless, in spite of all plausible drawbacks, modern machinery suitable to Indian conditions is beginning to make slow headway. The conservative cultivator will be watching the results with shrewd appraisal. A few progressive landowners have invested in harrows and drills, reaping and threshing machines. Cane crushing mills operated by little oil engines are not uncommon. But until a Henry Ford is able to supply India with cheap agricultural implements, and the lowly village blacksmith takes to stocking spare parts and learns to adjust them as needed, progress in this line must necessarily be retarded. Coöperative ownership of modern agricultural machinery is obviously the best solution of the cultivating problem.

Increasing the fertility of the soil and using selected seed are devices for making a limited area produce more and better crops. It is generally conceded that the maximum degree of soil deterioration in India has long since been reached, and that under existing conditions of Indian agriculture, low but stable fertility now obtains. Rice tracts, which are well irrigated, have proved that they can be cultivated indefinitely, though both the land and the output show a deficiency in phosphates. For other land, the Indian cultivator follows the traditional practices of his ancestors. He rotates his crops, sows mixed crops, or lets his fields lie fallow. Pulses and leguminous crops are particularly valuable in this respect. They not only supply proteids, otherwise lacking in the diet of the people, but their root tubercles fix nitrogen, which is taken out of the soil in large quantities by grains. Tobacco and green manures are likewise beneficial to the soil. But the rice yield per acre in India is less than half that of Japan, cotton only a third of the average production in the United States. India, as a whole, according to the League of Nations rating, stands twenty-second in agricultural efficiency among the countries of the world.

The possible increase in yield through the use of fertilizers is well known, but poverty and religious scruples act as deterrents. India does not, for example, commonly employ human waste in the fields, like China and Japan. Most of the dung dropped by India's 187 million cattle is consumed as fuel. Oil cake is used to some extent, but 18 per cent of the total oil-seed production in normal conditions is exported, and much of the remainder is fed to cattle. As a by-product of coal, India now manufactures annually several thousand tons of sulphate of ammonia, but the greater proportion of the product is normally exported abroad since at 140 rupees a ton the ordinary cultivator does not invest. Expensive artificial fertilizers can be used only for highly paying crops such as sugar cane or garden produce. Bone-meal, an important source of phosphate and combined nitrogen, is also lost to India through export. Finally green crops are rarely sowed and plowed in as fertilizer because of the pressure on the land for food crops.

But the evidence of increasing appreciation of fertilizing agencies of one sort or another to promote better crops is apparent in the growing figures of consumption, small as they are. If the economic position of the agriculturist can be raised so that he can afford to buy proper fertilizers, there is little doubt that he will take full advantage of this means of improving production.

Pusa and other experimental and research institutions have made great progress in developing better varieties of the various crops, and already millions of acres in British India are under improved seed. The greatest success has been obtained with cotton. A quarter or more of the cotton acreage is now sown with improved varieties, of American or Cambodian strain. More than a tenth of the wheat area is under improved seed, and the benefit to the cultivator is obvious with his extra profit of several rupees an acre. Experimental work of this sort is going forward with all staple crops.

The practical problem is one of distribution. The small cultivator sets aside a portion of his crop as seed for the following season or obtains seed on loan from his thekedar or the bazar dealer who has bought up his surplus grain at harvest time. Big seed merchants in the sense that they are known in the West do not exist. Some of the provincial agricultural departments and coöperative societies obtain improved seed from model farms and sell it on easy terms. Illiteracy is the great stumbling block. There is no simple way of demonstrating to the vast rural population the advantages of any change in their fixed habits. The higher market price of the improved crops will perhaps prove the best incentive to the adoption of new agricultural customs.

Hampered by poverty, sickness, and lack of education, the Indian cultivators struggle on as best they can. Without capital to invest in fencing, buildings, fertilizers, or machinery, and with holdings far below the minimum size considered as an economic agricultural unit in any Western country, they try to produce the food required for themselves, their families, and their cattle, and a surplus to dispose of in the market in order to pay their rent or land tax and to buy clothes and all other necessaries as well. It is a task beyond human power.

Economic progress in the main is not so much the result of individual initiative and originality as of national policies of protection, encouragement, and education. Alleviation of India's economic ills can come only through an enlightened, self-interested policy of internal development, such as all Western nations follow and such as Japan adopted for herself some decades ago. Unfortunately, as a subject nation, India has had neither the incentive nor the opportunity for normal development. The national life has suffered inevitable restraint under foreign domination. During the era when science has made its most important contributions to human welfare, when by means of new technical knowledge agriculturists have been able materially to increase their output, Indian agriculture has made no such corresponding advance.

It is only within this twentieth century that the government has shown concern to see that India's wretched and starving millions should in some measure share the benefits of modern agricultural knowledge. With a gift of £30,000, to be devoted to some work of public utility, made in 1903 by an American gentleman, Mr. Henry Phipps of Pittsburgh, Lord Curzon opened a government laboratory for agricultural research at Pusa in Bihar. Two years later provincial departments of agriculture first came into being. A Royal Commission on Agriculture in India headed by Marquis Linlithgow—the first of its kind to be appointed—conducted an extensive survey of Indian agricultural conditions and rural economy in the winters of 1927–1928. Tremendous irrigation enterprises now assure a permanent water supply to a vast area of several million acres. Improved types of seed have been developed on experimental farms. Soil conditions and fertilizers are under investigation by experts. Better implements are now on the market, to replace ineffective primitive tools. Every province has its model farms, its agricultural schools and colleges, its staff of trained officials. Village coöperative societies have been organized to provide agricultural capital and, to a lesser extent, market produce. Yet unfortunately most of the new knowledge is still confined to official reports and research institutions. How to get it out to those who actually work on the land is a problem still to be solved. At present the man who follows the plow in the fields is not inclined to listen to the British chief or his high-caste Indian subordinate, a university graduate who has never had a day's practical experience in the fields.

I watched three harvests come and go for the villagers of Pachperwa: two fall harvests, one spring harvest. Certainly very little of modern knowledge had penetrated to our community. Beyond the casual droppings of the plow cattle, the land received no manuring. One field had a little pile of a dark gray powdery substance scattered through it—wood ash, mixed with the ash of cow-dung cooking fires, the plowman explained. For water the villagers depended on the monsoon and *kutcha* wells. But half a million acres in Oudh have been brought under improved wheat stocks, and wheat, oil seeds, and the finest of the many varieties of rice produced in the region, fetched good prices in the export market, largely controlled by the Marwaris.

Harvest time was naturally the happiest time in the life of the village. The countryside was astir with little bands of wandering tribes, camping in temporary thatched huts set up by the roadside. Whole communities moved about, helping to cut the grain in return for a few handfuls a day. The brown monkeys boldly invaded the fields, managing to get something for themselves before they were driven off with shouts and pellets of dry mud shot from bows. The cattle were rewarded for months of ceaseless labor with plenty of straw and chaff, and they even drew rations of grain.

After the rice fields had been stripped and left brown and bare and all the paddy transported to the threshing floors, I watched an old beggar woman going carefully step by step over every inch of a field on the outskirts of the village. Back bent in two, she picked up single grains from among the stubble, dropping them one by one into a cloth gathered in her hand. She was the poorest of the poor, a widow whose children were dead. At other times she begged her food from door to door, but at this brief season of plenty, judged by village standards, even she looked forward to a few meals beyond the day's most urgent need.

If there are lean days and months to come, no one remembers them at this happy time. The whole village turns gay. Weddings are in vogue. The women acquire a new sari or a set of glass bangles, six for each wrist, or a silver ornament or two. Singing echoes from the road as the cartmen come in from distant hamlets and villages, bringing grain to the bazar.

On the threshing floors, great cleared spaces on the edge of every village, the white bullocks go round and round, six or eight abreast, trampling out the grain. Afterward it is stacked in mounds: tall mounds, medium-sized mounds, tiny mounds. This is the time when the hired laborer draws his wages of one fifth of the crop. The money-lender, who has advanced grain for food, pounces upon what is owed him and does not forget to take his interest of so many extra seers for every maund lent. The blacksmith, the carpenter, the barber, the washerman, the field watchman, the Brahmin who performs household ceremonies for Hindus, draw their fixed allotments. They are usually paid for their services according to the number of plows in the village, the plow being a common term of measurement. Literally it is not the plow but the number of pairs of bullocks that counts. By way of indicating its size, a village is said to be a village of so many plows. Pachperwa, for instance, was a village of sixty-four plows. Village servants do not all receive equal amounts. In Pachperwa the blacksmith drew twenty-one *panseries* for every plow, the others twelve. The standard panseri is five seers or ten pounds, but our current measures were all kutcha—that is, considerably under the standard rate. Then the herdsman who may have grazed cattle belonging to some of the individual cultivators with his own herd, is entitled to something from each of them. And finally there are the customary presents to make to the Patwari, to the maulvi, if the cultivator is Mussulman, the temple priest if he is Hindu, and to any helpless person of the community who has to subsist wholly on village charity.

Is it possible that anything can be left, one wonders, after all the debts and the little presents have been paid?

CHAPTER XI

Bazar Day

I NEVER had to ask if it was Wednesday in our village. This was the day of the weekly bazar, when the usually quiet road in front of the Happy House changed into a congested thoroughfare. Then, too, on bazar day the Doctor and I were visited by three times as many people as on ordinary days.

So that they might spread out their displays in good time, a few early birds started arriving Tuesday night. Others, from Utraula, spent the whole night on the road, reaching the village as the sun came up. Still others sent their things on by train and had them transported from the station by local cartmen. Most of the village shopkeepers also moved the contents of their shops out into the big mango grove in which the weekly market was held.

As the bullock carts moved past the house in a steady stream, each surrounded by its own little private dust cloud, I grew aware that however much one's bones may protest against this springless mode of travel, the archaic simplicity of the Indian bullock cart is an unceasing delight to the eye. The two ponderous creaking wheels possess that beauty of form perfectly adapted to purpose, the dignity of fulfillment. The white or the pearl-gray bullocks obey the peculiar trilling call of the driver, perched just behind their tails, and the cart moves forward as if the speed mania had not yet taken possession of men. But motor lorries have invaded India, and in the name of efficiency modern methods of transport are destined to drive out the ancient bullock cart.

Along with the Wednesday carts of the traders, throngs from the thickly scattered hamlets for miles about came trailing on foot, carrying woven trays or large flat baskets, a few pounds of grain tied up in a cloth, whatever they had to barter for salt or sugar or spices or cloth from the world outside the margin of their village. For every fifty barefoot villagers only two or three had shoes. Now and then came one who sat with legs out sideways over the fat saddlebags of a low-caste donkey, or who proudly held aloft a white or black sun umbrella, as he bestrode a little country pony. A deep-toned bell, tolling solemnly, announced a passing elephant.

All the morning the crowds flowed toward the bazar, attaining their greatest density about noon. At this time the noise from the mango grove reached me as a confused roar. During the middle of the afternoon the tide turned and began flowing in the opposite direction again. At sunset, bearing odd-shaped burdens on their heads, figures silhouetted through thin white draperies took on the unreality of a shadow show. The little ponies acquired silver halos. Hours later, stragglers were still going by, some of them evidently having paid a long call at the wineshop. Lanterns traced erratic patterns across the dark, and songs with sliding minor intervals echoed from nowhere in particular. The next day all was quiet orderliness once more.

The first time I went to our Wednesday bazar, escaping the Ayah's vigilant eye, I set out, as I thought, alone. Afterward I learned that the Tahsildar, seeing me from a distance, had ordered one of his men to follow at a discreet distance and render help in case I got into trouble. Just what sort of trouble he imagined possible I do not know. The only result of the adventure was the disappointing discovery, which held good for all subsequent visits, that aside from vegetables the village market contained absolutely nothing worth buying, from my point of view. Most of the stalls dealt in raw food, cloth, or small, cheap importations.

The Mohammedan Station Master was always offering

his service to elucidate anything and everything about Indian life and customs for me. One day, between trains, we made a thorough tour of the market. The usual haze of dust from milling animals and men had spread through the mango grove and along the edge of the village. Empty carts stood around, tilted backward, and unyoked bullocks wandered about or lay placidly under the trees. The ponies were tied to trees or had their front legs hobbled. One was wearing a peacock feather braided into its forelock, and necklaces of blue beads or tiny brass bells decorated some of the bullocks. Plenty of donkeys, hobbled like the horses, strayed at random, taking astute nibbles from the vegetable booths when the attention of the dealers was engaged with a prospective customer trying to get a purple eggplant for one cent instead of two. To add to the general confusion, a local herdsman took it into his head to drive his whole buffalo herd from one side of the grove to the other at this moment of greatest congestion, but it never occurred to anyone to complain over the matter of a little extra dust or unnecessary crowding.

The dealers were grouped according to trade, in the traditional fashion of the East. In the large cities as in the villages of India, you still generally find the cloth merchants gathered conveniently in one place, the shoemakers in another, the brass workers or goldsmiths in another, just as you do in China or, to a lesser degree, in Japan. Group organization in India has gone even farther. There are casual references in the Buddhist *Jataka* tales to villages of carpenters, villages of blacksmiths, villages of potters, to which the populace of neighboring cities and districts resorted when in need of their particular products. Villages of outcastes and of primitive tribes and Brahmin villages are still not uncommon, though for the sake of practical economies isolated communities of craftsmen have given way to the ordinary communal type of village, like Pachperwa.

At our bazar the fruit sellers lined both sides of the road along the part of the grove nearest to the village, and just beyond them, extending almost to the house of the dwarf potter, was the place of the vegetable sellers. Both piled their wares on the bare ground, indifferent to the dust of scuffing feet. The great lumpy green jackfruit, familiar in cold weather, the oranges, guavas, custard apples, and papayas had now disappeared. Mangoes had not yet come. The fruit dealers all sat behind monotonous mountains of small round watermelons. As for the vegetable sellers, they had little to offer at this season but onions and potatoes.

On the far side of the ditch dividing the road from the open fields on the west were the basket weavers, selling round baskets two and a half feet in diameter and a foot high, suitable for Bania stalls or bullock feeding. They also had basket scoops shaped like dustpans, flat trays and winnowing fans. All these goods were of the simplest and coarsest make.

Scattered about in the vicinity of the fruit and basket dealers were the traders in oil. Bottles standing on the ground indicated their stock in trade, but bottles cost money, and the thrifty village folk usually brought their own. The *Telis* dealt in all kinds of oil, mustard oil for lighting, cooking, and rubbing on the body, castor oil for burning, scented rape-seed oil for the hair, kerosene oil for lanterns, nim oil for medicine, linseed oil for greasing cart wheels. The only imported oil to be had in the Pachperwa market was the BOC—Burma Oil Company—product, used for lanterns. The Telis bought seeds, giving oil in exchange. One woman was weighing off a basket of bullet-like rape seeds against stones of various sizes placed in the other side of the balance, while another woman squatted in front of her, carefully watching the operation. Stones, bricks, half bricks, silver rupees, baskets, gunnysacks of standard size and oil tins all serve as rural weights and measures in India.

The gallon oil tin originally designed for kerosene has won an important place for itself in Indian village economy. *Ahirs* make use of empty tins for ghi, and anybody and everybody uses them as water carriers. Fitted with covers by the local iron and tin smith, they furnish the Bania with ratproof food containers. The Ayah stored her clothes in one. My own watering can was a transformed oil tin.

A variety of dry articles such as salt, sugar, grain, spices, dyes, cosmetics, and matches were displayed at the stalls of the many traders, spreading along the front of the village. Two merchants dealt only in salt. Under their little awnings they squatted beside mounds of coarse salt piled on pieces of gunny cloth. Three or four grades were to be distinguished. One consisted of rough lumps the size of marbles, gray with dirt. Another kind was broken into rocks a foot or more in diameter and the color was that of beautiful translucent pink jade. The two other kinds resembled the first, but were cleaner and finer. But the less clean and less fine salt cost more, because, as one of the Banias explained, the percentage of salt in it was higher. Refined salt, like refined sugar, was entirely unknown in the village. Sugar came in the form of brown baseballs—crude cane-juice boiled down and pressed into shape by hand.

To my untrained eye most of the Banias' sacks with tops neatly rolled down displayed only an indistinguishable and uninteresting collection of brown roots, powders, and dried leaves, but these were the spices without which Indian cooking is considered flat and tasteless. A lumpy little thing as long as my finger, brown outside and bright yellow within, was the ubiquitous *haldi*, or turmeric. This is the base of all curry preparations. It is also used in religious ceremonials and is the source of a yellow dye. Saffron, much prized as a flavoring for rice, also was to be had from the Banias, but its costliness put it beyond the reach of most villagers. Other bags contained unhusked grain, areca nuts, sunken-cheeked coconuts stripped of their shells, indigo, sulphur, red lead, antimony, dried fruits, bits of sandalwood, and camphor chips—all necessary, useful, or desirable from the village standpoint.

Perhaps the oddest article for sale was money, in the

form of unminted chunks of copper and tiny white shells.
The Gorakhpuri pice, as they are called, are small, roughly
squared bits of copper, worth a half cent, still current in
Oudh along with the minted copper coins of government
issue. Cowries are also accepted as a money token, but their
value depends on the rate at which the Bania sells them.
Now that the railways have cheapened importation and the
cash-rent system has fostered the use of standard metal
currency, shells are little used except for keeping tally.
Haweli Singh, owner of the Pachperwa brick factory, purchased them for his foreman, who counted out two cowries
for every brick carried across the yards by the child workers
of his factory. Translated at their current exchange back
into money, 384 cowries equalled one anna. Each child had
to carry ninety-six bricks to earn one cent.

Included with the food vendors were four other groups of
traders, the sellers of sweets, pan, tobacco, and meat. Meat
was not sold actually in the bazar, where its presence would
have been considered contaminating by vegetarian Hindus,
but way off at one side. Mohammedan cartmen from Utraula
were in the habit of bringing supplies of mutton with them,
either to sell to Mohammedan butchers in Pachperwa or to
dispose of privately. It was rumored that sometimes they
smuggled in beef to well-paying Mohammedan customers.

Tobacco was also a Mohammedan monopoly of trade, but
the tobacco stalls were scattered thickly in among the Bania
shops and were patronized by Hindus and Mussulmans
alike. Ever since its introduction into India by the Por-
tuguese at the beginning of the seventeenth century, tobacco has been popular with all classes except the Sikhs and
orthodox Brahmins, who are supposed to abstain from smoking. Nowadays cigarettes are coming into vogue, but the
Indian smoker's favorite apparatus is still the water pipe.
Tobacco for this and for the small clay chillum, also very
popular, was grown locally in our district and prepared with
pungent spices. The tobacco sellers' booths were adorned
with huge balls of tobacco paste variously spiced, the

cheapest quality selling for a cent and a quarter a pound. They also offered snuff and smoking equipment.

A strange feature of the bazar was the almost complete absence of vendors of prepared food, such as swarm about Chinese fairs and market places. Hindu custom does not sanction promiscuous eating. But parched grain is excepted, and many people brought along a little gram or corn and dropped in around noon at one of the numerous grain parchers' shops in the village, giving a portion of the raw grain to the shopkeeper in return for having the rest parched in hot sand. Curds were also sold by Ahir women and sweets by the *Halwais*, one of whom specialized in sherbet. A number of pan sellers, cross-legged on low benches, carried on a brisk business at their little stands. They were preparing the pan as fast as their fingers could work. First they spread lime on half the astringent pan leaf and then catechu in a thin brown wash on the other half. Next some chopped areca nut was sprinkled on top, and usually a pinch of tobacco or camphor was added. The leaf was finally folded into a little triangle, called a *bira*, perhaps fastened with a clove and handed to the customer. Two biras cost a quarter of a cent. Pan chewing is an Indian equivalent for gum, and the use is so universal that the cost of any small trifle is frequently estimated in "biras."

The bazar boasted several dealers in metal. The iron dealers sold chapati irons, water jars and buckets, tongs, nails, hinges, raw iron, and corrugated sheet iron. Another group dealt in brass and aluminum cooking vessels and drinking receptacles, another in anklets and bracelets of German silver or white metal. A few silversmiths were also on hand. At the market their chief stock in trade consisted of all sorts of small charms, in the form of gold or silver plaques or cylinders to be worn around the neck or on arm bands. A Mussulman ordered a verse of the Koran, a Hindu some favorite health-protecting mantra, which was written on a bit of paper, rolled up, and sealed inside the charm. Every mother desired to have one for her child, but every-

body wore a charm of some sort. Charms not only avert the
Evil Eye, sickness, and dire calamities, but they are supposed to bring success in cherished enterprises.

The thread dealers made the necklaces on which the charms
and ornaments were strung. They sat in a long double row
under the mango trees, all out of proportion in number, it
seemed to me, to the other traders. There must have been
fifty of them. They sold thread of all kinds, including loosely
twisted skeins of cotton from which Brahmins make the
sacred thread worn by the "twice-born" castes among
Hindus. Colored woollen balls for dressing the hair of little
girls, buttons, small mirrors, and bead necklaces completed
the list of their wares. Glass bangles, earrings, and forehead spangles belonged to another section of market vendors.

The cloth merchants were many, spreading over a large
part of the grove and carrying on heavy trade, both in piece
goods and ready-made clothes. String fences were put up
for displaying *kurta* and *kurti,* the shirts worn by men and
women respectively. These were generally of white shirting
with narrow stripes, similar to the ordinary shirtings sold in
London or New York. There were also short sleeveless jackets
for women, put on over the head. They were invariably red,
with a bold appliqué design of black cloth. The trend of
the times manifested itself in the cheap machine lace,
stitched in rows, which some of them displayed. Full-
gathered skirts of dark striped material, with bands of contrasting colors around the bottom, were also to be
purchased ready made. Such skirts are worn by country
women, though the graceful sari is more universal. All the
ready-made clothes are cut and sewed by Mohammedan
tailors.

A great many Banias sold cloth by the yard and white
piece-goods in the form of saris, dhotis, and scarfs. In among
the cloth Banias of the bazar were also a few country
weavers, selling coarse dhotis of hand-woven unbleached
cotton.

The last important group of traders dealt in manufactured articles belonging to the class of small luxuries. Nearly every country in the world, with the exception of the United States, contributed to the bazar trade of our little Indian village. Outside of England, which dominated the cloth trade, of course, Germany was easily in the lead in manufactured articles as represented in the Pachperwa market. I noted German trade marks on safety pins, erasers, buttons, lanterns, knives, mouth organs, packets of needles, locks, torchlights, toy pistols, penholders, and, by far the most important, aluminum pots and bowls and tall cups. Next in order came Japan, with tin combs, tin flutes, knitted undershirts, colored socks, pencils, buttons, black cotton umbrellas, and crochet cotton. China sent socks and some gaudily embroidered silks and satins, occasionally used for men's coats. Belgium offered us "Great Mogul Playing Cards." England also sent a single glass bottle of fruit drops, more playing cards, buttons and laundry soap, manufactured according to expectation by "Soap Makers to H. M. the King." From Paris I came upon a card of steel key rings. Italy contributed the most varied assortment of buttons—bone, pearl, and tin—but Italian and Japanese artificial silk, beginning to make serious inroads upon the silk trade in India, had apparently not yet penetrated into our rural life. Most of the storm lanterns came from Austria. Czecho-Slovakia completely controlled the field of brass rings set with paste, glass-and-brass shirt studs, brass cuff links, and stamped tin boxes with tiny keys.

When I jokingly told the Station Master that my national pride was hurt at finding nothing from the United States in the bazar, he reminded me that two tailors of Pachperwa used Singer sewing machines. A night or two later he made a special call to inform me that he had been thinking the matter over and that, having in any case long contemplated the purchase of a phonograph, he had now decided to order one from Lucknow, of American make. He hoped thus to make up, on behalf of the village, for the noticeable lack of American products.

Bazars are held on regular days in different towns and villages all over rural India, and many traders from neighboring cities make a point of sending representatives who spend their whole time traveling about from one market to another. The people of the countryside flock in for their week's supplies, bartering anything they may have to dispose of in exchange or bringing along a carefully hoarded rupee or two, out of which they may recklessly squander a few annas on some treasured trifle. Even those who have nothing to spend turn up for the general excitement, the gossip, the occasional chance to witness at somebody else's expense the tricks of an itinerant magician, a stray snake charmer's performance, a tumbler, or a poor, irritable dancing bear put through his paces by a wandering showman. Though each person spends very little, and scarcely an article in the bazar costs more than three rupees, in aggregate the bazar trade mounts up to a considerable sum. The records of the *Zilidar*, the official who collected bazar rents and taxes for the Balrampur Estate at Pachperwa, showed that on the particular day of my visit 480 shopkeepers in all transacted a volume of business amounting to 5,580 rupees. On bazar days preceding important festivals, such as Moharram, the amount of business doubles that of ordinary Wednesdays.

The estate levied customary charges of ground rent for stalls, cart tolls, and a tax on the volume of the business itself. Rent for stall space in the mango grove was charged at the rate of a half cent a day, but in order to save the trouble of collecting this sum every week a contract for bazar rents was auctioned off by the Tahsildar once a year —most recently it had brought 205 rupees—and the contractor assumed responsibility for the weekly collections, naturally being entitled to take the surplus for himself. Then, every cart coming to the village or bazar paid one cent, but this toll collection was also farmed out. The temple priest of the New Bazar had contracted for the right to the cart tax, for 525 rupees. Everything over and above was supposed to go to the upkeep of the temple. Finally, the regular trade tax levied on all outside dealers who took space at the bazar was a half cent for every dollar of business. The Zilidar or his assistant was always on hand on bazar day, circulating around the market and keeping a watchful eye on every transaction involving possible estate dues.

The same general business tax was applied by the estate to the Marwari tradesmen of the permanent bazar, who paid shop rent to the estate at the rate of six rupees a month. All paid a half cent on every dollar's worth of goods sold. Every night they reported the total of the day's trade registered in their books to the Zilidar, and he in turn kept a record and collected the dues at stated intervals. The Marwaris paid still another tax to the estate, on grain bought from the cultivating tenants. Every grain cart coming to the New Bazar with the standard load of six bags of grain, equal to eighty-two pounds each, had to give up the financial equivalent of six pounds, four for the estate and two for the weighmen. The Zilidar worked with a staff of one assistant, two peons, and eight weighmen, checking the records of his men by a check of the daily freight exports of the different traders at the station.

Wednesday market brought home to me the dependence of the village on the outside world for nearly all its principal necessities and trifling luxuries, aside from the barest of bare food. Of the total bazar sales, a third at the lowest estimate stood for articles of non-Indian origin. In a new country like the United States, which has never known the craftsman tradition, this would have been expected. In India it meant a serious change in the whole economic life of the country, a dislocation between the past and the present.

Even in a rural community where the people raised their own food staples, more than one third of all they spent in cash, eliminating land rent and payments on debts, also went for food, something less than a third for clothing, and the remainder for household necessities like cooking utensils, little indulgences like tobacco and glass bangles, investment in the form of ornaments. All authoritative surveys based on actual wage incomes for India reach the conclusion that well over half the family budget of the poor classes goes for food alone. By the time the cost of clothing and other compulsory expenditure is deducted little or nothing remains for amusements, medical care, education, or anything commonly associated with well being.

Before the expansion of railways facilitated the easy movement of foodstuffs and the flooding of the country with foreign manufactures, the Indian village lived simply, storing its surplus grain, producing for itself out of necessity nearly everything essential to its existence. Nowadays village life has acquired a different basis. The villagers find themselves with less food and more currency, underemployment and more importations.

The most striking index of changed conditions was the amount of imported cloth to be seen in the Pachperwa bazar, with the corresponding prosperity of the cloth Banias contrasting with the general destitution of the weavers.

Weavers are mentioned in the ancient *Rig Veda* hymns, showing that India had its weavers before the dawn of history. We had in Pachperwa eighteen Mohammedan families, including six families of *Dhuniyas*, or cotton carders, and twelve families of *Julahas*, or weavers, still following their hereditary callings. The Julahas are thought to have been originally Hindu weavers, perhaps converted wholesale to Islam in the early days of the Mohammedan invasion, but according to their own legend they are direct descendants of Adam. When Satan first made Adam conscious of his nakedness, he promptly invented the art of weaving and taught it to his sons.

Two of the village weavers, Habibullah and Jahangir, made a fairly good living. The rest were having a hard struggle to survive. But the carders were even worse off.

With the increasing use by hand weavers of mill-made yarn in place of the uneven handspun thread, the carders have lost the spinning market. Preparing cotton for *razais*, or quilts, and for the padded jackets worn by a few villagers scarcely keeps them occupied. Fourteen Hindu *Kori-Chamar* families lived in Pachperwa. Their hybridized caste name indicated that they were in a transitional stage, sinking from the weaving caste to that of the untouchable leather workers.

One day I asked a Kori-Chamar boy of the village if he knew how to weave.

"No," he said. "My father could weave, but I never learned." Ajudya skinned dead cattle instead.

The product of the country looms is coarse and plain. Nowadays taste favors the finer and less durable fabric of the mills. None of our local officials or shopkeepers was ever to be seen wearing anything but a machine-made dhoti, seldom anything but a shirt of imported cloth. The cultivator, on the other hand, knows that the Julaha's dhoti at one rupee and four annas wears twice as long as the Bania's at two rupees, and he still generally buys from a local weaver. But the women have almost all adopted mill-made saris.

A weaver at the bazar said that both men and women in his family worked on his two looms. Weaving was easiest, he explained, in cold weather. In the rainy season the thread became damp and sticky. He could make two dhotis a day in good weather. With the material for one dhoti costing one rupee, his earnings at best came to sixteen cents a day.

Gandhi's campaign to revive the hand-spinning-and-weaving industry in India is not, as often represented, a sentimental revolt against machinery, but a desperate effort to offer some slight immediate relief to the half-starved rural population of India. Without a subsidiary industry, agriculture alone cannot lift the burden of poverty from the backs of the masses. Formerly weaving offered this subsidiary industry. Scarcely a house was without its spinning wheel, and India manufactured not only all the textiles required for home consumption but exported silk and cotton fabrics in large quantity to the Western world. Indian muslins were a chief article of trade with Rome in the first two centuries of the Christian era. When the first Europeans made their way overland to India in the sixteenth century they found Indian weavers producing muslins sheer as cobwebs, exquisite gold-brocaded silks, woven materials of infinite variety and beauty, never surpassed in any country. The tradition still survives. In Benares and many other localities weavers still turn out exquisite work.

Why, asks Gandhi, should India import textiles and yarn from foreign countries to the value of approximately two hundred and fifty million dollars a year? Let the Indian mills go on expanding slowly, as they should and must, but for immediate relief stop the annual export of two million bales of raw cotton. Let the people of the villages, whose work is distinctly seasonal in character, leaving them with nothing remunerative to do for from two to four months out of the year, at least spin and weave enough cotton to clothe each household. Let the village looms again hum. As conditions are now, the people can have both food and raiment only if they produce their own cloth. If each family annually saved only five rupees by this simple scheme, it would be an appreciable amount where the budget is as low as it is in rural India. Gandhi's critics have suggested nothing better to alleviate the present hunger of millions.

The economic policy of the British government in India, starting with the days of the East India Company, has always been compass-true to British interests. First, the Indian weaving industry was encouraged because of the enormous profits at which Indian goods could be disposed of in the English market. Pepper, saltpeter for gunpowder, indigo, and drugs also contributed to the great fortunes built up from the India trade, but textiles represented by far the most significant item. Since England produced little that India wanted, bullion was exported to pay for the goods purchased in India. At the beginning of the eighteenth century the export of bullion amounted to a million pounds sterling a year, and India's hand-loom calicoes, chintzes, muslins, and silks were threatening to destroy England's woollen industry. The trade was killed by an enactment prohibiting the further use or sale in England of Indian silks and calicoes.

Then came the industrial revolution in the nineteenth century, but when India, too, built mills and began to compete on a modern basis with foreign manufacture, the principle of free trade was applied to India. All customs dues were wiped out in 1882. This step brought about a financial stringency for the government of India requiring a reimposition of tariff. In 1896 a duty of 3½ per cent was placed on imported woven goods, but to prevent this duty from acting in any sense as a protective measure an excise tax of 3½ per cent was simultaneously imposed on the Indian mill product. Imported cotton yarns and twists remained on the duty-free list. In 1917 government revised its customs schedules and raised the general *ad valorem* tariff from 5 to 7½ per cent, but retained cotton goods at the old rate until the following year, when for the first time they were placed on a par with other imports. Five years later the general duties were again subjected to revision, and the duty on cotton piece goods was fixed at 11 per cent. Then it became 15 per cent. Not until 1926, however, was the excise duty on Indian mill goods finally abolished.

Along with the unpopular tariff policy, forcing products of European manufacture upon the Indian market and holding back industrial development within the country, the government monopoly of salt has attracted particularly bitter opposition. The salt tax, which existed in the form of octroi duties in pre-British days, falls on a primary necessity and is paid by the poor. Through its own agencies or a licensing system, government control is now exercised over the salt production for the whole of India. On rock salt mined in the Punjab, on brine salt obtained from Sambhar Lake in Rajputana or from the Rann of Cutch on the Gujarat coast, on sun-evaporated sea salt from Bombay and

Madras, a uniform duty is imposed, fixed at a cent a pound in 1888, now standing at half a cent. This half-cent duty and other salt levies yield an annual revenue of about $30,000,000. But in terms of village life the salt tax becomes a severe hardship. Villagers live almost entirely on grain food. They require salt for their cattle as well as themselves. In spite of the fact that the per capita income in India is perhaps not even twenty-five dollars a year—compare this with what it is in the United States—villagers of Pachperwa paid from a cent and a quarter to two cents a pound for rough, dirty, unrefined salt—very little less than one pays for refined salt in New York City. According to official figures the incidence of taxation is 3½ annas—seven cents per head a year—which may not at first seem unreasonable. Relative to income, however, it is a heavy burden.

On March 12, 1930, Mahatma Gandhi, accompanied by a little band of seventy followers from his ashrama at Sabarmati, started to march to the coast two hundred miles away to manufacture salt in defiance of the government monopoly. That march may one day be recorded in history as more portentous than the Boston Tea Party. Thousands and hundreds of thousands of supporters fearlessly took to making illicit salt. The police, aided by the military, were utterly unable to cope with Gandhi's Salt Army. Gandhi himself was arrested on May 5th, and interned for an indefinite period (he was released again January 25th), and all the important leaders of the Nationalist campaign soon followed him to jail. But the movement launched could not be arrested. Starting with popular resistance to the salt tax, it spread to the boycott of foreign imports, particularly cloth, and to the nonpayment of land taxes. The strength of the movement is its nonviolence. Gandhi's spirit, permeating his followers, has been capable of absorbing the lathi blows that have disgracefully rained down on heads and backs of unarmed men and women in this painful aspect of India's struggle to be free.

The steady rise in agricultural prices over past decades

is frequently cited as proof that the Indian cultivator is better off to-day than formerly. A hundred years ago rice and wheat sold in Oudh at 200 pounds to the rupee. Now the rupee buys less than 15 pounds of wheat and 11 pounds of rice. The exchange value of the rupee a century ago was double its present stabilized rate of 1s. 6d., but its purchasing power was obviously many times greater.

Theoretically the tremendous enhancement in the value of agricultural produce ought to benefit the cultivator, but outside specially favored areas like the canal colonies in the Punjab, village conditions in India do not indicate prosperity. Middlemen and large exporters reap the lion's share of the profit, as they do everywhere. As land values have jumped, the tenant cultivator has been pressed for higher rent. The small proprietor, on the other hand, has been tempted to mortgage his land. Recent legislation has stopped the further alienation of land to non-agricultural classes, but large areas have already passed from their hereditary owners to the money-lenders, as formerly they passed to the rent collectors in Bengal. Former cultivators have thus been forced down into the ranks of tenants or landless laborers. With the general shrinking in the size of the individual holding, a smaller surplus crop remains to sell at higher prices. To pay rent or the interest on debts, or to marry a daughter, the cultivator of three acres, in the flush of harvest optimism, often sells more than he can spare. When he runs short later in the year he is obliged to buy back his own grain from the market dealers, dearer than he sold it. If prices have gone up from the selling point of view, costs have also gone up more from the living point of view.

Meanwhile the village artisans, thrown into direct competition with machine-made production, are being pressed to the wall, while the village life suffers that general stagnation which inevitably follows the closing of free channels of development. The last available census figures show that only about 10 per cent of the population of British India is supported by industry. Except for about two million persons employed in factories, this 10 per cent is made up of those who supply personal and household necessaries and simple implements of work, the village artisan class. The government census reports give indubitable proof of India's retrogression in indigenous industry. Each decade shows that agriculturists have increased in proportion to the total population. "Industries have substantially decreased, and of the principal forms of industry the textile workers have dropped considerably, as also have potters and workers in wood and metal," says the 1928 *Indian Year Book*. Hand technique does not survive anywhere in competition with the machinery of the modern world, but in other countries the transition from one stage of production to another, though not achieved painlessly, has at least been made as smooth as possible by the support and encouragement given to the young industries by the governments concerned. Industrialism has absorbed the handicrafts, and the factories have taken care of the former artisan class and at the same time provided occupation for the natural increase in population.

It is not hard to understand why India resents the economic policy of her foreign rulers which has effectually transformed her from a manufacturing to a consuming country as far as world trade is concerned. The reiteration that the consumer benefits from the generally cheaper price of imported articles falls on the deaf ears of Indian economists. They see Indian industry seriously paralyzed and the Indian people among the poorest in the world, as a result of British policy, and they quite agree with Sir Austen Chamberlain, former Secretary of State for India, who in 1917 expressed the view that "India will not remain and ought not to remain content to be a hewer of wood and a drawer of water for the rest of the Empire." Yet it is significant that in spite of a backward economic state, India, exceeded only by China in population, has been ranked by economists actually as the sixth industrial country in the world.

Coming back to my own little village, typical artisans were there, still plying their ancient trades in the ancient manner, but the unsettling influences of the times was upon them. Except for the goldsmiths, the blacksmith family, and the five families of carpenters, who made the village tools and were supported in turn by dues of grain, the artisan class rested on a precarious footing. And even the more fortunate suffered from foreign competition.

For example, the blacksmith bought his iron in the bazar, ten pounds to the rupee, also tin and galvanized sheets. The chances were nowadays that his iron at least came from the Tata Iron and Steel Mills at Jamshedpur, in Orissa, but the market supply of hooks, nails, hinges, locks, and other small articles, which he formerly provided, were all imported from abroad. He must have been aware that many minor tasks were slipping from him. Iron was a commonplace commodity in ancient India. A marvel of the metallurgical skill of Indian ironworkers fifteen hundred years ago is the famous wrought-iron pillar at Delhi, weighing six tons, bearing a Sanskrit inscription of the Gupta period. Countless primitive smelters were worked all over India until modern processes of production, cheap sea freights, and the development of railways helped the foreign manufacturer to stamp out the native industry. Only within the present century have Indian iron and steel works, fostered by government bounty and protected by a tariff under a new national policy, been able to recapture part of the market. Metals and their manufactures still rank second, however, in the list of Indian imports, coming next to cotton manufactures.

Another destructive invasion has occurred in the Indian dyeing industry. Rajab, the dyer of Pachperwa, was busy during the winter months block-printing cotton cloth for quilts, and just before the Mohammedan mourning procession in the month of Ramazan he worked feverishly, stamping patterns on pieces of paper for the decorative coffins which would be carried in the procession. But there was Jumai, also a dyer by caste, who knew nothing of his trade.

The collapse of the old hand-loom industry mortally injured the dyer's profession, but the more recent invention of artificial dyes ruined his art. I bought forty yards of white material in the bazar one day and took it to Rajab to stamp and dye, before having the tailor make it into curtains for the Happy House. A few days after the curtains were up I noticed the colors were already beginning to fade. Rajab explained that none of his colors, except black and red, were *pukka*. He had supposed I knew. He did not even have a fast blue, though indigo was grown in the province. Practically all his dyes were cheap importations from Germany.

The lacquer bracelet maker, a Mussulman, still made a few bracelets, but he survived mainly by selling glass bangles, which he himself bought elsewhere. Indian glass was known in Rome two thousand years ago, and the bangle industry was a flourishing one in the sixteenth century. Lacquer, too, early developed into a fine art. Then Germany entered the field with glass and celluloid, and of late Japan has seriously encroached upon the bangle trade. The bracelet maker of Pachperwa eked out his existence by manufacturing fireworks, for which he held a required government license. Hindus greatly enjoy the display of fireworks at weddings and other celebrations. The bracelet maker, after first showing me how he heated his stick lacquer and rolled his bracelets, offered to make some fireworks for my special benefit. He led me to a small isolated shack perched on top of the slope beside the more distant of the two village tanks. Here he kept a store of saltpeter, sulphur, charcoal, and powdered iron. Using some old account sheets for paper to wrap his powder balls, he made a "bomb," which went off with a loud bang. Then he made a "flower pot" with gold and silver stars, mixing German and Indian varieties of iron. He could also make simple Roman candles and colored flares. But the business was not important, he said sadly. He could not make more than twenty rupees a year out of it.

Germany again, with hardware, has affected the prosperity of potters, brass workers, and coppersmiths. Aluminum pots cost less than brass ones, if wearing quality is not taken into consideration. In the Wednesday bazar were many stacks of ugly things made of "alimoonia," as the village folk called it, only one or two of shining substantial brass. Pachperwa did not boast either brass or coppersmiths, but the humble potters, twirling their flat wheels and calling clay pots and bowls into existence beneath deft fingers, kept a place in the village economy only because their pots were cheapest of all.

The one group of skilled and prosperous craftsmen remaining in Pachperwa appeared to be the goldsmiths. With charcoal fires, bamboo blowpipes, and delicate tweezers they produced all sorts of ornaments of gold and silver—earrings, nose rings, toe rings, anklets, bracelets, collars, girdles, head ornaments—in traditional patterns, often displaying exquisite workmanship. The gold of the Indian ornaments has always been kept exceptionally pure, much purer than the 14-karat standard of the West, and the silver, too, has been of fine grade, because ornaments have represented the conventional dowry of women and a means of permanent investment of savings where no other adequate savings-bank system has been developed. The use of debased metals is increasing, unfortunately, and in place of the solid ornaments formerly worn, much shoddy stuff is now beginning to make its appearance. Along with Japanese tin flutes and Belgian playing cards, the Pachperwa bazar offered a large assortment of Czecho-Slovakian imitation jewelry.

The few remaining articles produced in the village were the handiwork of low castes, for the most part unskilled workers. One *Mochi* made shoes. A little encampment of gypsy stone cutters in the grove beyond Bargadwa cut rough grindstones. Baskets and mats of various sorts were manufactured, including reed awnings for carts and bazar stalls. Leaves were gathered in the jungle and sewed with their own stems into plates and saucers. The schoolboys used reed pens carved with designs by the Kurmis, our principal cultivating caste. Some wood turners manufactured hookahs and legs for cots. The carpenters turned out wooden sandals. Apparently every household was familiar with the art of making thatches upon a foundation of pliable arhar stalks and of twisting grass rope. But such articles answered only the most elementary of needs. They afforded no margin of profit by which the village as a whole could raise its standard of living.

We did, however, boast a real industrial enterprise in Haweli Singh's brick kiln. During the sunny winter months and until the rains, at just the time when agricultural work was slack, Haweli Singh was able to give employment to sixty or seventy people, brick molders, firers, carriers. His brick molders, drawn from the earth-working caste, were paid at the rate of one rupee for every thousand bricks, and a thousand bricks could be made in one day of hard work with the coöperation of the man's whole family working for nothing. One person dug the clay out of the bottom of the pit, another trampled it to the proper consistency, the wife rolled it out with sand and tossed the roll to her husband, seated on a flat space of ground above her. He pressed it into a wooden mold, ran a string over the top, shook the mold slightly, and turned out one brick, ready to be sun-dried or fired. The ant-like chain of unskilled laborers, mostly women and children, who transported the bricks to and from the furnaces on their heads, filed past the checker and received their two cowries per brick. The women earned about six cents a day, the children half as much. But that six cents stood for something above the average allowance for food for one day for one person, and in the case of many families, particularly those of the wretched hired plowmen, it meant an incalculable boon.

Everywhere in India to-day the necessity of relieving the pressure upon the land and of creating subsidiary means of earning for agriculturists is keenly felt. Nearly every province now possesses a department of industries, and three provinces have quite recently passed financial measures making funds available on loan for industrial development. Technical schools for teaching modern methods of work are maintained out of provincial revenues. India is at the beginning of a new age.

The villages no longer offer even bare subsistence. The cotton mills of Bombay, the jute mills of Bengal, big railway repair shops, coal mines and iron and steel works, dockyards and irrigation projects are drawing enterprising individuals away from the overcrowded land. But they cannot solve the problem of employment in a country with a vast population like that of India. The hope of the future would seem to rest mainly in the development of small industries in the rural areas, such as flour mills, sugar refineries, paper mills, match factories, glass factories, and the thousand and one small enterprises which, taken together, make up the vital industrial life of the modern nation.

Machinery is of the age, and twentieth-century India cannot possibly do without it, save at the cost of exploitation from without and starvation within. Yet the inevitable is not always an unmixed blessing. One fears for the creative tradition and the instinctive love of the beautiful, which have enriched Indian life through countless centuries. The blight of modern industrialism has already left its mark on the countries of the East. In the wake of this dragon, grass withers, trees are scorched, and the spirit loses much of its sensitiveness.

Money-lending

$\mathbf{M}$Y FIRST personal contact with the world of money-lenders came through Mahabali Singh. He was not at all the sort of person I expected a Hindu money-lender to be. Mahabali Singh was fat and jolly, very clean and pious, and always to be singled out on the village street by the broad-brimmed, gray felt Stetson hat he wore.

The hat, an astonishing article of apparel in Pachperwa, was explained when Mahabali Singh came to pay a friendly call two weeks after my arrival. He began talking a queer jargon of Hindustani and English. I could scarcely believe my ears as I took in that I was being addressed in an unmistakable Negro dialect. It seemed that Mahabali and his wife had lived for twenty-eight years in Trinidad, where he owned a grain shop. It was there he had acquired his accent, the hat, and a contempt for Indian village life.

"Dis here place no good! Dat place fine!" he summed up.

Anyway, here he was in Pachperwa, still dealing in grain in a small way and carrying on a money-lending business. He wanted it made clear that as a money-lender he was not to be compared with those "mean Punjabi fellows," who charged "plenty much interest." He himself commonly took only 37½ per cent, a half-anna per rupee per month. At the time, I was not impressed with Mahabali Singh's leniency. As I came to know more of village money-lenders, I perceived he had some reason to feel virtuous.

We had no bank of any sort in Pachperwa. Even Balrampur, a town of seventeen thousand inhabitants, could not cash a foreign draft. Village financing was entirely in the hands of the money-lenders. Grain, spices, and cloth were as often taken on credit at a fixed rate of interest as cash. A charge account simply meant an interest-bearing debt. The Marwaris of the New Bazar, the more important cloth Banias, the village grocers, all who had money to spare, were in the habit of lending.

It was not for many months that I somewhat tentatively began a specific study of the village money-lending problem. One day I sent Mewa Lal, a chaprasi of the tahsil, off to the New Bazar and Fakire in the other direction to the Old Bazar, with instructions to gather a complete list of all the money-lenders in the village and their rates. Between them, they brought back a record of forty-nine money-lenders, though they acknowledged a few had probably been overlooked. This meant at least one to every sixty persons in Pachperwa, including its hamlets. In British India three times as many money-lenders, in proportion to population, reside in the Punjab as in any other province, and in the Punjab they officially number one to every five hundred inhabitants. Pachperwa appeared to be vastly more prolific in the matter of money-lenders.

Ours belonged to a variety of castes, but nearly half were Banias, the traditional money-lending caste of India. Mahabali Singh was a *Khatri*, representing a respectable mercantile caste of the Punjab. Khatris claim the distinction of having supplied Akbar with his famous finance minister, Todar Mal. The founder of the Sikh religion, Guru Nanak, was also a Khatri. Two Sikhs, Haweli Singh and his brother Daula, and the four Punjabi wood contractors in Pachperwa were very much to the fore on the list of money-lenders. So were all the Marwari traders. There were also a blacksmith, a grain parcher, three pan dealers, three members of the wine caste, and two *Babhans*—a local name for Brahmins. Trading and money-lending Brahmins are debarred from performing priestly offices or receiving religious gifts. Some Brahmins will not eat with them, calling them false Brahmins. Legend has it that in ancient times a certain King of Magadha, wishing to have a sacrificial feast, ordered his prime minister to summon a *lakh* of Brahmins to the palace. Unable to find so many, the minister, concerned for his head, distributed sacred threads to a lot of low-caste people, and thus created the required number of Brahmins overnight. Afterward this group followed its own practices. In spite of the fact that taking interest on money is forbidden by the Koran, we had four Mohammedan money-lenders, dealers in leather or tobacco. In addition to these people of the village and bazar, practically every rent contractor in the tahsil—nearly all of them were Mohammedan—carried on a grain-lending business, too easily converted into money-lending.

Fulfilling a very essential service in a country where irregularity of agricultural conditions is always to be reckoned with, money-lenders were not only tolerated but approved by ancient Hindu lawmakers. Manu made exact rules regarding the rates of interest. On cash loans interest was not to exceed double the sum lent; on goods in kind, five times the value. Later 50 per cent on cash and 100 per cent on grain came to be accepted as the proper limit of interest.

High as these rates appear, the village money-lender probably has more chance to practise extortion to-day than he did in the organized society of two thousand years ago. Many causes have tended to increase rather than to diminish his power, the two chief ones being the decay of village life, which no longer exercises a restraining influence upon members of the community, and the shift from a personal to a legal basis of jurisprudence.

Mr. M. L. Darling, formerly commissioner of income tax for the Punjab, devotes an interesting chapter to money-lenders in *The Punjab Peasant in Prosperity and Debt*. He shows what happened after suits for debts, originally settled before the village executive or council, who considered the simple fairness of a case, were turned over in 1874 to the newly created civil courts to be tried by professional judges generally drawn from the city or town population. These judges looked at the technical aspect of a case and rendered a decision according to the written document. The amount of interest was according to individual agreement and might be compounded indefinitely. One blacksmith, who mortgaged a small plot of land in 1896 for 26 rupees at 37½ per cent, ten years later found himself with an accumulated debt of 500 rupees. In 1918 a decree was given for the amount in full. It has been reckoned that a debt of one pound compounded at 60 per cent will become 100 pounds in eight years, if permitted to accumulate.

Another development, growing out of the increase in land values resulting from the spread of railways and the general security of property under British rule, was the incentive the money-lender now had to acquire land for real-estate speculation. Formerly the money-lender was content if the owner or cultivator of the land remained in his debt. Communal ownership made the mortgage of land all but impossible. With the new emphasis on private property all this changed. The money-lender offered better rates on secured as against unsecured loans, and the small peasant proprietor became as wax in his hands.

Expropriation was advancing so rapidly by the close of the past century, particularly in the Punjab, that drastic measures were necessary to save the small cultivators from widespread dispossession. The Punjab Land Alienation Act of 1900 forbade the sale of land to any nonagriculturist and also forbade the holding of a mortgage by such a person for more than twenty years. The transfer of land to the trading money-lenders is now checked by legislative acts in force in a few areas of India, but unfortunately this legislation has fostered a new type of agricultural money-lender—equally rapacious and with even greater interest in securing a personal lien on land.

The Usurious Loans Act, passed in 1918, was also designed to improve the legal position of the cultivator. He cannot now be arrested for debt nor evicted from his holding. His bullocks, implements, and seed cannot be attached. If he is sued, the courts have power to examine the merits of the case and decide what is fair interest, regardless of the agreement. But the Usurious Loans Act is generally acknowledged a dead letter. The money-lender still has the advantage, since he can dictate his own terms to those who have to depend on him. He can always refuse to lend anything, thus forcing the villager to any agreement he cares to exact. Since the money-lender is in most cases the person who buys the villager's grain, sells him his daily necessities, or employs him in the capacity of a field laborer, his victim has no alternative but to get on with him as best he can. I knew one man who had turned over his plow bullocks on demand to cancel a debt to his thekedar. He had never heard of any law making the confiscation of work animals illegal.

Mortgage rights did not crop up in Pachperwa where nobody owned land except the Maharaja, and even he, by rules of inheritance, could not alienate any part of his estate. Loans were generally unsecured, rates high. Manu's stipulation that interest should be charged according to caste, no longer applied literally, was a custom in practice. The lower a man ranked in the social and economic scale, the poorer he was, and the fewer his visible assets, the higher his interest.

The village money-lenders were divided into a sort of hierarchy. The Marwaris, with Jokhi Lal at their head, were aristocrats. They refused to have dealings on a small scale with little people. Ordinarily they served the village thekedars, the richer tenants, and persons of consequence. To those in good standing, with an assured income from land, especially favorable terms of 25 per cent were quoted. Lesser traders served the poorer element of the countryside. The Punjabis and the Sikhs bore an unsavory reputation of trading on dire necessity, charging extreme rates of 150 per cent, and Yasin Khan certainly ran them a close second. The commonest rate in Pachperwa on an unsecured loan was 75 per cent, the interest always paid in advance each month. On clothes it was from 75 to 100 per cent. On grain it was one eighth of the amount lent, to be repaid at the next harvest. This worked out at 25 per cent for the year. Generally loans were for six months. If not repaid at the expiration of the period, the debt was renewed, depending on the humor of the money-lender, at the same or more severe terms.

The *sowkar's* willingness to lend without security has rested in the past on the static character of Indian village life. One or two sons may leave home. Daughters marry and go off to their husbands' villages. But the ancestral fields and the family house remain intact from generation to generation. A pivotal gray-haired member of the family is always present to substantiate ownership. When the money-lender meets his debtor half a dozen times a day and is familiar with every detail of his income and expenditure, he knows the right moment to press his claims. The villager, for his part, does not always look on the money-lender as his enemy, but rather as a friend who helps him out of immediate difficulty. He is a neighbor and a human being. Extend credit another month or so? Certainly. Why not? Only, of course, pay the extra interest.

The money-lender is also safeguarded by the traditional sense of honor which binds the sons or even the grandsons to repay a loan if the father dies without having settled a claim against him. Refusal to pay would be an act of disrespect to the dead. Paper contracts and outside compulsion of alien law courts are lessening this sense of moral responsibility in India, but simple, illiterate villagers still generally accept unwritten obligations as a matter of course.

A stocky little man from the village of Manpur used to turn up for medicine now and then. His country speech was not easy to understand, but bit by bit I learned his story. For performing odds and ends of village service he was credited with forty or fifty local maunds of grain each harvest. To make the allowance stretch farther for a family of mother, wife, and child, he took, instead of rice or wheat, a larger supply of a certain cheap pulse, *aksah*, often used as cattle food. In terms of selling value his grain allotment represented an income of about thirty dollars a year, a fraction over eight cents a day. A seventh of the grain went to a cloth Bania to buy the four garments he had to have in a year—two dhotis and two little cotton jackets—and the saris of the mother and wife. Ghi and milk were unknown luxuries in his household. He laughed when I asked if they had sugar. If the harvest was good and he had any grain to spare, they bought spices and salt; otherwise not. Nor was anything spent even for an oil lamp such as villagers use. The only light was the cooking fire, and they all went to bed when it grew dark. But he had invested not long since in two eight-anna baby pigs, which his wife now tended. Later, when the pigs produced a litter, he would sell the young ones to other low-caste Hindus and realize three or four rupees on his investment. Oh, yes, one other item in the account. He tried to give his wife two rupees eight annas a year for ornaments!

This man was one of those unfortunates who had fallen heir to a father's debt. A village servant like himself, the father had died owing eighty maunds of grain to the thekedar. Somehow, over a number of years, the son had managed to pay off this heavy load of debt through work. "Now I am free," he repeated many times. It was true he owed five rupees to a money-lender on his own account, but at the coming harvest, if all went well, that debt, too, would be canceled.

More usually the poor villager gets so hopelessly entangled that he can never extricate himself. The hired plowman near the bottom of the economic scale cannot support a family in bad years on his only wage—one fifth of the crop from the six to ten acres he cultivates. Enticed into service with an initial cash loan and then forced to borrow merely to subsist, he is unable to accumulate anything and spends his life virtually as a bond slave. One master may buy him from another by paying off his debt, but he remains in the same position of slavery. Slavery is the universal state of field laborers in Oudh.

Now and then one hears of villagers turning upon a money-lender and beating him mercilessly, burning his house or even murdering him. And there are cases in which a simple-minded money-lender is exploited by shrewd if illiterate borrowers. The widow often finds it difficult to collect her dead husband's accounts. Kunji Bania, a wizened little old money-lender of Pachperwa, haunted the tahsil all winter. He used to carry a mountainous pile of account books in a cloth on his back. His plaint was that, unable to recover hundreds of rupees he had lent, he was now penniless. Most of his accounts were old, and since legally no claims for recovery are now valid unless made within three years of the time a loan expires, his case was hopeless. In a neighboring district a man told me a sad story of lending seventy rupees, the savings of a lifetime, to a fellow villager in return for a mortgage on his fields. He himself was a cowherd, ignorant of the fact that a tenant has no right to mortgage his land. The debtor had defaulted and disappeared from the village. When the cowherd attempted to take possession of the fields he was confronted by the real owner, and the court, to which he took his trouble, found his claim worthless. The poor man was still trying to fight for his lost fortune. When I met him he was again on his way to the big world of magistrates at Gorakhpur.

Nearer home, my own servant Jumai showed me that the money-lenders occasionally have something on their side. Jumai owed ten rupees to various traders in the village, and though the ten annas of monthly interest he was expected to pay taxed his resources, they taxed his disinclination to hand them over more. Jumai evaded creditors by spending everything he earned at once and then displaying empty hands. One afternoon he burst into an eloquent tirade, as usual forgetting to pull the punka while he inveighed against life's injustices. He had gone to Hira Bania, seller of general supplies, at noon, asking for the loan of one rupee for only four days, and Hira Bania had actually refused because Jumai could not produce the anna of interest in advance. Knowing Jumai as well as I did, I could not help feeling that Hira Bania had displayed uncommon good sense.

India's total rural indebtedness, placed at not far short of half a billion pounds sterling, is much less than that of the United States and proportionately below that of Italy. But it is an intolerable burden in comparison with the capacity of the people to pay, and only a fraction of it represents productive investment.

Attempts have often been made to estimate the per capita income in India through surveys of given areas. The most recent investigations officially carried out give 100 rupees as the average income for the whole population of Madras, 100 rupees for urban localities, and 75 rupees for rural areas, in Bombay. If twenty-five dollars is accepted as near the true figure, it is obvious that with incomes of wealthy landlords included in the estimate, a large proportion of agricultural families subsist on vastly less, perhaps eight or ten dollars per head a year.

Another long-distance view of the general poverty is obtained from the income tax returns for India. Every individual, every unregistered firm, and every undivided Hindu family with an income equal to 666 dollars, derived from any source other than agriculture, pays a graduated government tax, beginning at a minimum rate of 2½ per cent. Likewise every company and registered firm, whatever its total income, pays a tax of slightly more than 9 per cent. Yet the total number of income tax returns for British India is under a quarter of a million. In the United States corporation and individual taxes yield more than two billion dollars a year normally. The expected revenue from this source in India, with nearly three times the population, is but sixty million dollars. Exactly ten persons in Pachperwa were subject to a tax on their incomes, according to the

Brahmin collector who arrived one day to inspect account books. All of them lent money. One out of every four persons paying an income tax in the Punjab is a money-lender, and this proportion probably holds good for India at large.

Without reference to price scales, income estimates for India can scarcely convey any adequate idea of the condition of the rural masses, but the very fact that millions can sustain life on three or four cents a day shows that the standard of living is desperately low. In the annual statement prepared for Parliament in 1927-28, by the Director of Public Information on behalf of the government of India, appears the statement, "There is a vast amount of what can only be termed dangerous poverty in the Indian villages—poverty, that is, of such a kind that those subject to it live on the very margin of subsistence."

There was plenty of "dangerous poverty" even in a "rich" village like Pachperwa. Household servants received their food, a garment or two a year, and wages of two rupees a month. The wage of casual labor was six cents a day. In the average family of five, certainly not more than two persons contributed anything to the family budget. The husband might be at work in the fields while his wife tended a parching oven or shop. The children collected leaves for oven fuel, dung for household fuel, grass for cattle. As the sons grew up to be earning members of the family, more children arrived, and the old people had to be taken care of. But the fields did not expand; the shop yielded only the same small return. Any man who attained a fair degree of prosperity, from the village standard, found a host of poorer relatives crowding in upon him. Dukhi was tenant of twenty acres, but he supported a household of eighteen—his wife, a widowed daughter and her children, a widowed sister, two hired plowmen, two servants, and several nephews. Teja Khan, rent contractor for Bargadwa, maintained a household of forty-five persons.

The ordinary village house gives an idea of the rural

standard of living. I have been in countless village houses. They seldom boast more than two or three small rooms, with a protected corner apart for cooking and a tiny court. Goats or a cow are likely to share the family living quarters in cold weather. The walls of the houses are of mud, the roofs of thatch. The dirt floor is quite bare. Not a picture nor an ornament is to be seen—unless an image of Ganesh or Lakshmi reposes on a little shelf. There are neither tables nor chairs, books nor papers, nothing in the way of furniture except possibly a square wooden bench, or a low board seat. There may be one cot. Most of the family sleep on the floor, rolled up in sleeping sheets. The stove is a clay horseshoe six inches high, or two bricks overlaid with a thin iron sheet. A flat-topped clay granary the size of an ice box may be seen at one side of the room. A few clay pots, an iron kettle or two, one brass drinking vessel, a grinding stone, a wooden husking mortar and pestle complete the furnishings of the house. The house itself is worth from fifteen to twenty-five dollars. All its contents, including tools and implements of work, are worth perhaps ten dollars. Nobody is likely to have more than one change of clothes. Three outfits stand for luxury. The same clothes are worn day and night by the poor. A thin cotton quilt for cold weather or a woollen shawl is reserved only for those upon whom Lakshmi smiles. "Luxuries indicating a rising standard of living," of which one hears a good deal nowadays, are likely to consist of a cotton umbrella costing fifty cents, a lantern of equal value. Such is the average village house as I saw it. Its stark nudity explains why the money-lender prospers in India.

The Kanungo of Pachperwa, the official supposed to know most intimately the economic condition of the people, estimated that 75 per cent of the community were indebted to their thekedars or to money-lenders. His statement agrees with figures given by other authorities. Mr. Darling found that 80 per cent of proprietors and tenants were in debt in the Punjab. I sometimes asked villagers who came and went about the tahsil if they owed anything to a sowkar, how much they owed, when and why they had borrowed. They never seemed to mind my questions. They appeared flattered to have me show an interest in their affairs. I found that nearly everybody owed something, even if it was only four or five rupees. Usually a man's debt increased with his standing. This was due not to extravagance but to increasing pressure put upon him, more poor relatives to look out for, bigger dowries demanded for his daughters. The man with nothing did not find it easy to borrow, but the one who cultivated ten acres had no difficulty in raising a loan. Except when money was borrowed to buy cattle or when seed grain was taken on loan, nearly all the debt incurred was to meet living expenses. Almost nothing stood for productive investment. Food and clothes, weddings and land rent, these were the main causes of debt, and they went on repeating themselves from year to year. One of our grain parchers, with twelve acres and a household of sixteen persons to support, owed 100 rupees—cattle, rent, a wedding. He had owed this sum for five years and had already paid back 125 rupees in interest. The people are economically crippled. With no margin of reserve, debt is inevitable, and high rates of interest make it permanent. The situation is hopeless.

The failure of the government up to the present time to develop a modern banking system in India to finance the principal industry of the country and to meet the requirements of three quarters of the population is a serious indictment of its financial management and outlook. The Imperial Bank of India, created in 1921 by amalgamation of the three Presidency Banks of Bengal, Bombay, and Madras, is the government bank. It controls currency and note issue, receives deposits, and advances money upon proper security, and incidentally pays a 16 per cent dividend, but it can make no loan for a period longer than six months. Short-term credit is of little use to the agriculturist. The exchange banks, branch agencies of foreign banks with their head offices abroad, monopolize the export finance of India and to some extent lend support to internal business. Joint stock banks, of recent origin, primarily serve the interest of the small percentage of the population engaged in trade or industrial enterprise. None of these agencies of credit reaches out into the rural areas.

Until 1904, when the first Coöperative Credit Societies Act was passed, agriculturists languished for any organized system of cheap credit. Lord Curzon's government undertook the organization of coöperative agricultural credit societies, and a year or two later the idea was expanded to encourage the formation of noncredit societies of a coöperative character. The success which has marked the coöperative movement in India during its short history is one proof of the great need for organized banking facilities in rural areas, and it points the way to the only feasible solution of India's credit problem—the credit of the Indian people. "If coöperation fails, there will fail the best hope of rural India." This, at least, is the conclusion that was reached by the Royal Agricultural Commission under the Marquis of Linlithgow, after two years of intensive study of Indian agricultural conditions.

In spite of the immense labor of teaching coöperative principles and organizing societies among illiterate villagers, some 67,000 primary village societies are functioning in British India, with a membership of more than 2,250,000 and a working capital of $85,000,000. In addition, 11,000 more societies are registered in the Indian States. Although all but a handful, comparatively speaking, are purely credit societies, the noncredit organizations have initiated important work in fields where coöperative enterprise can bear fruitful results. Thrift societies, societies for compulsory education, for the supply of agricultural implements and improved machinery, for the promotion of consolidated holdings, for cattle breeding and insurance, have all come into being. Coöperative sales shops have also been started. In Bombay Presidency weavers have organized societies of their own, with coöperative buying of raw material and sale of finished products. Irrigation and milk societies are another expansion of the idea, and in Bengal anti-malarial societies have lately tackled the problem of rural health. The movement to supply rural credit at reasonable rates of interest is well launched, and if it is properly fostered the money-lender is doomed.

Yet the fact remains that the vast majority of the people are still groaning under the oppressive exactions of the money-lenders. To one village provided with a society, nine have none. The development has gone forward in some provinces and lagged behind in others. At present the movement is strongest in the Punjab and Bombay, among the nine major provinces, with Madras next in order. In the Punjab 10 per cent of all rural families are represented in the membership of coöperative societies. In the United Provinces, the families represented number less than 2 per cent. This means that from 90 to 98 per cent of the rural population of India are dependent on money-lenders, are still forced to pay from 25 to 150 per cent interest on loans, still stagger under indebtedness that eats up all the surplus of favorable times and keeps living down to the lowest standard known in any great country in the world.

It happened that before I left Pachperwa I had an opportunity to see a coöperative society formed in my own village. The suggestion originally came from William Massey, the Indian Christian school teacher who returned to the village for his vacation. I immediately wrote Kanwar Jasbir Singh, who gave us his blessings and made the practical suggestion that we get in touch with Pundit Ganesh Dutt, head of the Central Coöperative Bank of Balrampur. The pundit suggested that I ask the Tahsildar to call a meeting of tenants from some four or five villages, also inviting the attendance of thekedars and all influential persons who might be expected to sympathize with the movement. He and his staff would then come and address the meeting.

Meanwhile I began to sound out some of the thekedars

and others of the community. The Station Master was
familiar with the coöperative idea and thoroughly approved
of our plan, but not being an agriculturist his influence
scarcely counted. The Peshkar did not know what it all
meant, but since his family was heavily in debt he had no
use for money-lenders and was eager for any scheme to
loosen their hold. The faithful Dukhi said he would support
anything I told him to. When I spoke with Teja Khan, the
thekedar of Bargadwa, he asked many intelligent questions
and in the end promised to lend his whole-hearted support to
the movement.

One day several rent contractors from surrounding villages
chanced to be sitting in front of the Peshkar's quarters.
All of them acknowledged that they buried their spare
money. One was investing his surplus, when he had any, in
land in Nepal. Another explained that his family practised
charities; this year they were sinking a well. Still another
said he was engaged in building a small temple. They listened politely while the Peshkar outlined the coöperative
plan as best he could, and they agreed to come to our meeting, but one of them, Nagesher Singh, expressed grave
doubt about the advantage of a village bank. It was convenient to keep your money just where you could lay hands on
it when you wanted it. Personally, he would not care to trust
his to other people's handling. A few weeks later Nagesher
Singh would have spoken less confidently. He was robbed of
several thousand rupees, which proved that a hole in the
ground was not a safe hiding place after all.

The time of the meeting was finally fixed for an afternoon
in late July. Tenants of ten villages had been summoned,
and in the space in front of tahsil headquarters at least
three hundred villagers, including a dozen thekedars,
assembled. It appeared not all had come voluntarily. One
man, at the close of the meeting, complained that when he
told the peon who summoned him that he would like to go
on with his plowing until the others had assembled, the peon
beat him. He produced in evidence a bruised arm, a torn

shirt, and two pieces of a broken stick. I could not help wondering at the futility of expecting violence to induce the coöperative spirit in anybody.

Chairs were placed near the big tree, and here, facing the curious audience squatting on the ground, Pundit Ganesh Dutt, two assistants who had come with him from Balrampur, the Tahsildar, the Peshkar, and I sat in a solemn row. The chief assistant presently arose to make the first address. He did not begin with technicalities. He told them instead how poor they were—I wondered if they needed to be told that—and how they had to give up a large portion of all they could produce to the money-lenders. There were but two ways to improve this deplorable state of affairs: lower rates of interest on the one hand; on the other, higher profits obtained through good seed, better implements, more efficient methods of cultivation. "We have come to bind you, village by village, to a central point, from which forces will be radiating to look after you and your children. We are willing to advance you loans at a very cheap rate of interest, payable in easy installments at the proper time and season. If you will unite and form a society in your village, according to the plan that will now be explained to you, the time will soon come when you will no longer have to depend on outside help. All working together, you will help yourselves." Thus he began the speech, carefully memorized.

Then the working basis of a coöperative society was laid before the villagers. Each village must have its own separate organization. A minimum of sixteen persons must apply for membership. No one can become a member except by the purchase of one or more shares, but none is permitted to hold more than twenty shares. Shares cost 20 rupees, and payment may be spread over ten years, in half-yearly installments of one rupee. As soon as a man has paid his first rupee he is entitled to full membership with the privilege of making a loan.

When a village signifies its desire to form a coöperative society someone is sent from the nearest central bank, with which the primary society will hereafter be affiliated, to examine the status of the village and the proposed membership. A list of members with a tabulation of property, income, and debt is prepared. On the basis of the total assets the bank figures out the maximum advance it is willing to make the society in one year, generally one half. A most significant proposal made by the Balrampur Central Bank representatives was an offer to liquidate all debts to moneylenders owed by members of the village coöperatives under its jurisdiction. Immediately upon registration in a coöperative society members could draw funds to pay off their indebtedness, and the debts would be transferred to the books of the society, at its own cheap rate of interest.

After the bank survey is completed, Pundit Ganesh Dutt went on to explain, the members elect their own panchayat to manage the affairs of the society, choosing those they consider the most trustworthy, intelligent, and influential. New members are admitted by a vote of three fourths of the society at a general meeting. The panchayat decides the maximum credit to be allowed each member. Since all members are jointly responsible to the extent of their whole property for debts incurred by the society, the governing body in no case permits an individual member to borrow in excess of assets. When an application for a loan is made, the applicant must state the purpose for which he is borrowing, and it is at the discretion of the panchayat to grant the loan or not. Money may be borrowed for any purpose, such as the purchase of bullocks and seed, or even for weddings and personal expenses, but it is expected that primarily a loan will be devoted to agricultural purposes.

At the beginning, a central bank supplies the funds out of which a society lends to its individual members. The rate at which the Balrampur Central Bank offered to lend to a primary society was 12 per cent. The society lends to its own members at 15 per cent, entering the difference to its own credit. A society in good running order soon becomes independent of the central bank and lends to members out of its own paid-up shares, interest and money which may be invested by members. Those who invest with the society are entitled to draw interest at 6 per cent, and they may receive dividends not exceeding 10 per cent on shares fully paid up.

While the bank officials were outlining the coöperative scheme in detail I watched the faces before me, pleasant, childlike faces. At first I could see little evidence of interest. Probably very few in the audience had ever heard of a bank. When the speaker directed his remarks to a particular group that group listened politely. The moment he faced in another quarter, roving eyes indicated attention was no longer fixed on what he was saying. But gradually some conception of the purpose of the meeting began to percolate through the cloudy consciousness. Here and there someone asked a question. Little knots entered into animated discussion among themselves. What would happen if a member defaulted? How could the society make him pay his obligation when it fell due? Would the treasurer keep the funds, or would they be deposited in the central bank for safe keeping?

Finally Pundit Ganesh Dutt stood up and asked how many villages would like to consider forming a coöperative society. Seven out of the ten represented, including Pachperwa, signified a wish to have one. When I saw my money-lending friend Mahabali Singh in the background I felt a twinge of conscience, but he was one of forty-nine, while the village folk numbered hundreds. Some weeks later, when the rice was transplanted, one of the Balrampur officials returned to carry out the necessary preliminaries. By this time the number of villages had dwindled to four, but I was more than satisfied. Once a society proved its usefulness in one village, neighboring villages would be sure to take up the idea.

It is beyond the ordinary layman's province, and certainly beyond mine, to discuss in detail the vexed question of Indian currency and monetary policy. Since 1893 one finance commission after another has been discussing it and making recommendations. But even the authorities do not seem able to agree among themselves, and Indian national opinion always has an ingrained suspicion that British recommendations will necessarily be in the interest of Britain, not India. So the tug-of-war continues, a fruitful source of disagreement and discontent. In the Legislative Assembly at Delhi questions are constantly being asked about banking and currency policies, the stabilization of the rupee at the fixed rate of one shilling sixpence, the disposal of India's reserves, the interest on debt, cost of supplies purchased abroad, salaries, pensions and so forth, all payable in sterling by the government of India in London. Nor do suave answers generally succeed in turning away wrath! Originally, the policy of keeping large funds in London was to guard against a drop in rupee exchange as a result of a fluctuating silver market. But nine years out of ten the balance of trade is in favor of India, and India has bitterly resented a policy which has permitted and encouraged the withdrawal abroad of large sums from the national exchequer.

Another long-standing quarrel centers in the privileged position that the Foreign Exchange Banks have acquired. There are some eighteen of these, all under foreign register, and even the government of India cannot exercise an effective control over them, according to the terms of their charter. They have their head offices and many branches outside India, in England, the United States, Hongkong, Holland, Japan, etc. Since they are under no compulsion to reveal what proportion of their deposits are kept in India, they may even, if they wish, transfer abroad money belonging to Indian depositors, for instance, to meet an emergency in China. They have practically a monopoly in financing India's foreign trade, with their net-work of branches all over the world. It is easy to understand that Indians may well find it difficult if not impossible to compete with foreign nationals resident in India, who will naturally be given preference by the banking institutions of their respective countries. Closely associated with this foreign monopoly in finance are shipping, marine insurance and warehousing interests, all of which operate to the disadvantage of Indians wishing to do business abroad. Some foreign-owned banks have opened branches in the interior cities as well, and encroached upon this field of financial enterprise also, with respect to the movement of crops from the interior to the ports, or from one part of the country to another. The entrenched position of the foreign banks in India has thus very seriously interfered with the development of a sound modern banking system for India under the control of Indians.

One unofficial critic, Sir Daniel Hamilton, long ago stoutly proclaimed that no banking and credit system for India can ever be sound unless it rests on the sound financial condition of the people. Sir Daniel Hamilton, representative on the Viceroy's Council under Lord Curzon, helped to frame the Coöperative Credit Societies Act. Twenty-five years of experience as a landowner in India in direct touch with the agricultural population gave him a practical grasp of rural problems and the needs of the people of India. His own scheme is designed to fit those needs. He points out in a small book, *The Rayat and the Statutory Commission*, that so far the government has made no provision in any of its bank proposals to finance agriculture, the one great industry of the country, and the millions dependent on it. He challenges the contention of Sir Basil Blackett, former finance member of the government, that the financial position of India is the envy of other nations:

> Sir Basil mistakes the government of India for India. Government may borrow at 4.69 per cent, but the people's rate is 46.9 and oftener more than less. This is the wrong which only a banking system suited to the people's needs can put right; and until it is put right, nothing will be right, whatever the paper constitution may be.

It is the old Scottish credit system, applied coöperatively —credit extended not on the basis of deposits but of goods to be created—that he proposes. Government outlay on irrigation works has shown the manner in which production can be multiplied. A water supply guaranteed to the small cultivator outside government irrigated tracts, through wells and tanks and small works, proper drainage, afforestation to prevent erosion, good seed, and better implements and fertilizer, all require capital. But where is the man whose sole assets are "an acre or two of impoverished land, a pair of lean cattle, an eight-anna plow, a dry cow, a two-rupee goat" to find any capital?

The coöperative movement has already shown a way out, but it needs the whole weight of the government to develop it into the people's bank India sorely needs. Sir Daniel Hamilton calls any policy of building up a large central gold reserve antiquated, more appropriate to the past century than the future. He has proposed an All India Bank to be linked with provincial coöperative banks into a concern to finance India, apart from the mercantile community. Resources are immediately available in the currency reserves, which, now drawn off to England, could sensibly be used as backing for paper credit money, "the note being the people's check." With a coöperative society organized for every village, the people could be dealt with in groups rather than as individuals, and the group would see that credit went only to those of its members who could be trusted to repay. Besides making large supplies of credit money quickly available, a paper currency would develop the deposit habit now conspicuously absent in India. Silver rupees can be buried, but paper does not keep well and is much safer in a bank than in a hole in the ground.

So long as India maintains her favorable trade balance gold and silver will tend to accumulate in the country. One currency expert estimated some decades ago that the stock of gold bullion useless for commercial purposes then lying in India was equal to two and a half times all the gold money in circulation in the United Kingdom. India normally absorbs every year astonishingly large quantities of gold which are imported from abroad. Yet important as this potential reserve is, its presence in India does not contradict the general poverty of the masses. Evenly distributed among the total population, all of the so-called hoardings would mean less than seven dollars a head. Whatever small share finds its way down to the people is put into ornaments, which serve as an emergency capital, since they can be sold or pawned. India's annual gold absorption is less than the yearly bill for perfumery, cosmetics, and toilet preparations in the United States and is just twice our chewing gum bill.

Once India develops a modern banking system, plenty of this "dead capital" will undoubtedly come to light. The people will develop habits of thrift when they begin to see a return on their investments, and the government will then reap its harvest in taxes. Money will be available for nation-building services which are now starved for lack of funds. "From the base to the apex the financial system will belong to the people. The people, federated, will own the village societies; the village societies, federated, will own the Central Banks; the Central Banks, federated, will own the Provincial Banks; the Provincial Banks, federated, will own the All India Bank."

"India would seem by nature to be destined to be a creditor country, if only her people wills it so," Sir Basil Blackett has said. Sir Daniel Hamilton would agree with the first half of this statement, but I am inclined to think he would amend the second half. He would say that it is the duty of the government of India to provide the Indian people with the right sort of banking system to stimulate prosperity, if they provide the productive labor. "The rayat is a small man, but multiply him by 300 millions, organize his credit and his labor, provide him with a banking system, and he becomes a giant, able to move the world," says Sir Daniel.

BOOK THREE

CHAPTER XIII

Caste

Pachperwa boasted some thirty wells, most of them kutcha, that is holes fifteen or twenty feet deep, with boarded or bulging brick sides in which bushes or even young trees sometimes grew. Water is a crucial test of caste, and my first lessons in village caste ideas were learned at the tahsil well from which my own water was drawn.

One day I noticed my Dom sweeper filling his red clay jars at the well. I felt glad that in my locality the harsh restrictions in force in southern India, where "untouchables" are widely forbidden the use of public wells, were not observed. The next morning I enthusiastically expressed approval to the Tahsildar.

"But he should not have taken water from that well," was the answer. "I think nobody was looking when he did so. Many people here would object. He should go to the other well back of the tahsil." Though nothing more was said in my presence, I knew that the sweeper was told not to repeat his offense.

A little later I was watching the gardener manipulating the well-sweep. Along came the sweeper. He squatted down silently in front of the well, and silently he waited. Presently the gardener drew up two extra bucketfuls and emptied them into the jars held out. No words were exchanged between the two men, and, as the sweeper walked off, he did not even say thank you. To me it seemed rather absurd that a man should be forbidden to draw water at the well because of his low caste and yet that a man of higher caste was willing

297

to draw the water for him. I puzzled over this until I got an explanation. There have never been any restrictions among Hindus in regard to gratuitous service. A high-caste man who serves another, whatever his caste, is only fulfilling a recognized ideal of service. On the other hand, without knowing anything of germs, the ancient Hindus were vaguely aware that food and water were sources of contamination, and the fear that someone who followed an unclean occupation might pollute what one ate or drank was largely responsible for the early ideas of dietary exclusiveness, later crystallized into caste rules.

Arriving in India, one expects to pigeonhole every Hindu in one of four traditional groups: the Brahmin is the thinker and priest; the Kshatriya, better known to-day as the Rajput, is the ruler or fighter; the Vaisya is the trader or producer; and the Sudra is the servant. It came as a surprise to me to find that though the Brahmin and the Rajput are recognized castes, the other two groups are scarcely ever mentioned by name to-day. Ask any villager his caste and he will tell you simply that he is a bracelet maker, a herdsman, a goldsmith. Whether he belongs to the Vaisya or Sudra group is often difficult to ascertain. But to the descendants of the ancient Aryans alone, the three higher groups, belongs the appellation of "twice-born." They were the only ones formerly permitted to hear or to study the sacred scriptures, this spiritual teaching giving them their second birth. The sacred thread, worn by male members of the "twice-born" castes, is a symbol of spiritual initiation.

In Vedic days the social division was a twofold one, to begin with, between the light-skinned Aryan conquerors and the primitive, dark-skinned original inhabitants of the Indian peninsula. The psychology of the conquerors was much like that of the white invaders of North America, or of the British in India to-day, who still generally refuse to admit Indians into their clubs. They despised those whom they had conquered and ostracized them socially.

The Brahmins were largely responsible for the gradual stratification of Hindu society into caste as the term is understood to-day—marriage restricted within a group, interdining forbidden, occupation determined by birth. The high-born pioneering Aryans were particularly concerned that their women should not be lost to the group by marriage with the *dasyus*, the "slaves" or "enemies," as the aborigines were called. But caste never was, nor is it now, as inviolable as one might suppose. At the time when Buddhism began to flourish, marriages between Brahmins and Kshatriyas were not unusual. Manu's Code allotted four wives to a Brahmin, one from his own caste and one each from the three lower grades. A Rajput could have three wives, one from his own and two from the lower castes. A Vaisya was limited to his own and the Sudra group for his two wives, and a Sudra was restricted to one wife from his own group. The law permitted a man to marry down, a woman to marry up. But the children of mixed parentage did not enjoy the same status as those born of two parents of equal rank.

All the innumerable castes into which Hindu society is now split up—the census lists 2,300 of them, and subcastes are legion—represent the kaleidoscopic shifting of social relations. Castes have gradually evolved from a number of different causes. Some represent descent from a common ancestor, others have a regional origin, still others are purely occupational in character. Vastness of territory, made vaster by primitive modes of transport and communication, permitted small groups to crystallize without disturbance from outside. As new occupations came into existence, new castes sprang up. The process of caste formation is going on even to-day. Every new census brings forth some new groupings.

It took me weeks of assiduous work to learn that Pachperwa boasted sixty-one different castes. After hearing me vainly ask some of the local officials about the village castes, Hassan Kuli, chaukidar for twenty-five years in the New Bazar, acted as my private census enumerator, in return for a package of permanganate crystals.

"What is your caste?" was a question many times on my tongue. It was always a suitable way of opening conversation with a stranger. Gradually I came to associate the various caste names with the traditional occupations, but often a stray visitor would name a caste quite outside the known categories. The four ponderous volumes of William Crooke's *Tribes and Castes of Northern India* were an invaluable textbook. There was, for instance, a leper whose eight-anna quarrel with Jumai I was called upon to arbitrate. He was a *Khair*, whose caste work was collecting catechu in the jungle. Another man, who said he was a *Bhand*, once came to my door. Bhands are professional jesters. Like *Bhats*, or bards, they are employed to entertain rajas or rich men. One of their specialties is parodying Europeans for the private amusement of Indians. But they have fallen on evil days and now make a precarious living doing anything they can.

A stout man going along the road in front of the Happy House one morning was pointed out as a *Mahabrahmin* who lived in a village eight miles to the east. Sheobalak enlightened me on the subject of Mahabrahmins, a subcaste of Brahmins very much looked down on by the others. It is they who perform the official purification ceremony after a death in Hindu families. On the tenth day after the cremation the Mahabrahmin is feasted; on the eleventh day the relatives formally take food in the house of the deceased. After this, except for certain personal observances of mourning, the death pollution is removed. Every Hindu family in Pachperwa and the surrounding villages on the occasion of a death had to send a present to this Mahabrahmin. Such men grow very rich, in defiance of the ancient rule that a Brahmin is not to concern himself with this world's goods. Balrampur boasted ten official Mahabrahmins. According to custom they divided the month so that three consecutive days fell to each, and the Mahabrahmins in turn had the right to receive the mourning perquisites from all deaths occurring in those days. When the Junior Maharani, mother of the Maharaja of Balrampur, died, the fortunate Mahabrahmin of that day received clothes, furniture and jewels, to the value of ten thousand rupees.

Everyone is struck by the obvious differences in physiognomy to be encountered in India. Generally speaking, the Indians of the plains, both Hindu and Mussulman, are small in stature, but Sikhs, Punjabis and Pathans from the northwest—all of these were represented in Pachperwa—possess magnificent physiques. The pure Brahmin type is marked by thin lips, a high-bridged prominent nose, and deep-set, penetrating eyes. Just as the outcastes show the devastating and benumbing effect of centuries of social ostracism, so the Brahmins unconsciously manifest an unmistakable superiority, too often accompanied by haughty intolerance, born of their long caste monopoly of the intellectual inheritance of India. The Rajputs still hold a reputation for being among the finest fighters of the world. Our Rajputs, most of them landlords or rent collectors, were men of unusually fine build, tall, strong, light skinned, and handsome. The Tharus, with their high cheek bones and eyes set flat in the face, bore a first-cousin resemblance to Nepalese, Tibetans, or Mongolians.

Brahmins and Rajputs together number some twenty-five millions to-day, about one tenth of the total Hindu population. They may be considered as the more or less pure survivals of the ancient Aryans. The forty to fifty millions of "untouchables," roughly one fifth of the Hindu community, include the descendants of the aboriginal Dravidians and all those whose occupations have been classed as unclean. Between these two extremes lies the bulk of the population, Hindus of mixed origin who follow the numerous trades, professions, crafts, and agricultural callings. Apart from the Hindus are the Mussulmans, roughly a fourth of the population, five or six million Christians—mostly in southern India—and the small communities of Parsis, Sikhs, Jains, and Buddhists. Practically all the Buddhists now live beyond the Indian peninsula, in Ceylon and Burma.

The castes themselves offer great complexity and variety.
Some castes predominate in certain parts of India and are
entirely unknown in others. Some number millions, others
may be represented by a few thousands or even hundreds.
Only six castes have above five million. In round numbers
Brahmins lead with fifteen millions; the caste next in order
of size is that of the Chamars, with twelve millions; the
Rajputs follow with ten millions; the Ahirs number nine
millions. The two other leading castes of India are the *Jats*,
a fine cultivating class of seven millions centering in the
Punjab, and the Marathas, distinguished for their military
prowess before they were defeated by the British in the
wars of the eighteenth century. There are fifty-four other
castes in India with more than a million members each.

A caste exists, as a matter of fact, for every conceivable
occupation or possible division of labor. The divisions are
sometimes incredibly fine. Blacksmiths, for example, are sub-
divided into separate castes including the producers of ore,
those who sell iron, the makers of sharp-edged tools such as
razors and knives, sharpeners, horseshoers and the ordinary
village blacksmith responsible for making and repairing
agricultural implements. Likewise there are coppersmiths
who deal in raw metal, those who make molds for vessels of
various sorts, who cast the vessels, who engrave them and
who sell them.

The sixty-one castes of our village could well be grouped
under half a dozen main types of occupation. First of all
there were the cultivating castes, of whom the Kurmis were
the most numerous and industrious. Special gardening castes
also came under this category. Among the laborers, considerably lower in rank, were Koris—ex-weavers—Chamars,
and earth workers, originally of the salt-producing caste,
before the government monopoly largely destroyed their
trade. The herdsmen were divided into Ahirs who tended
cattle and sold milk and ghi, and Gadariyas who acted as
goatherds. Fishermen, collectors of jungle produce, bird

catchers, leaf gatherers, and plate makers, sawyers, basket and mat makers, were all represented by separate castes.

The group of traditional village servants included those families essential to the community life—carpenters, blacksmiths, barbers, and washermen. Another caste was that of the palanquin bearers, who also acted as private servants. Chamars under their original occupation of leather workers, who skin dead animals and carry off carcasses, and scavengers further contributed their despised but necessary services to the village.

The craftsmen were an integral part of the community. Weavers and potters did not command much respect, but the village dyer and the bracelet makers were in somewhat better standing. The shoemaker suffered obloquy for working in leather. The goldsmiths, though not a popular fraternity, had prestige because their art still called for skill and their ornaments were still in demand.

The various tradesmen constituted another large and important group. One might also make a separate classification of the professional and religious castes. The village accountant, the head teacher, and the clerical staff of the administration were drawn from the Kayasths. To the Brahmins was reserved the priestly service at the village temple and shrines, the prerogative of officiating at all ceremonies in Hindu households, and the profession of astrology.

Out of the sixty-one castes in Pachperwa, twenty were Mohammedan. These Mohammedan castes were to all intents and purposes exactly like Hindu castes. The bulk of the Indian Mussulmans, most of whom are descended from low-caste Hindu converts, have retained much of Hindu social structure. Although more flexible than Hindus in regard to rules of eating, the Mussulmans of the village did not marry outside their particular group. So we had our Hindu and Mohammedan potters, carpenters, oil pressers, confectioners, barbers, bracelet makers, and bird catchers. The Mohammedan Halwais did not sell sweets, however, but specialized in tobacco.

Other callings fell exclusively to the Mussulmans. Because of the Hindu abhorrence of taking life, even though plenty of Hindus eat meat to-day, the butchers in India are Mohammedan. By the same logic, since Islam forbids spirituous liquor, the wine dealers are drawn from the Hindu fold. Although a Hindu will buy tobacco, uncooked vegetables, fruit, and grain from a Mussulman, he will not buy pan, which has a certain ceremonial significance in Hindu life. Mussulmans monopolize the shoemaking and tailoring trades, and they are the carders of cotton and the weavers —at least, in the part of India with which I became most intimately acquainted.

Besides these groups with distinct caste affiliations, the Mussulmans also divide themselves into sectarian and regional groups. Shias and Sunnis represent the two chief religious divisions of Islam. Most of the Indian Mussulmans are Sunnis. In Oudh, where the last reigning family was Shia, Lucknow has remained the Shia center of India, and Mohammedan officials of the region are likely to be Shias. The Shias generally consider themselves superior to the Sunnis.

Pathans, supposed to be descendants of the Afghan invaders of India, and Mohammedan Punjabis were other distinct groups. The Maulvi of Pachperwa claimed descent from the Prophet through his daughter Fatima—forming one of that group of progeny calling themselves *saiyids*, now scattered throughout Asia and even more numerous than the descendants of William the Conqueror. All Mussulmans not falling into one of the special classes already mentioned were classed as *Sheikhs* or *Fakirs*. The Sheikhs claim that their community contributes very nearly one half the total Mohammedan population of India. In village parlance these two names carried the suggestion neither of Bedouin chiefs nor of "holy men" on beds of spikes. The Sheikhs do not follow a caste occupation, but in rural districts they are commonly cultivators. Fakirs follow begging as a profession, but since there is so much competition in begging in India, sometimes they work. Among my servants the Ayah and Din Mohammed were Sheikhs, Asgar Ali and Fakire were Fakirs, and Jumai belonged to the occupational dyer caste but had never practised the art.

In an ancient country like India, where tradition plays such an important part in the life of the people, every caste has invented a mythology to gild its origin. Since the pre-occupation of the Indian mind has always been with religion, even the lowest castes boast that they are descended from some god or saintly *rishi*. The imagination of a primitive folk is not always poetic or refined. Parvati, Shiva's consort, while picking flowers, pierces her finger with a thorn. Shiva washes away the blood with a drop of sweat, and out of this sweat the first Mali, or gardener, is created. An attendant in Shiva's court is called upon to sweep the stairs to the Throne of Heaven. His descendants become sweepers. Blacksmiths trace their ancestry to Visvakarma, architect and master craftsman of Indra's heaven. Many castes of later origin have a semi-historical background. The Bhats, or bards, are supposed to have come into existence during the time of Timur. The Emperor spent seven years mourning the death of his only son. At last a court retainer composed a long, amusing poem to distract his patron. In spite of himself the Emperor laughed when he heard it and declared that henceforth this man and his descendants were to be entertainers to make men forget their sorrows and responsibilities.

Caste rank is outwardly determined by whether or not one of the "twice-born" will take water or *pakki*—food cooked with ghi, butter, oil, or milk, but not boiled in water—from a member of the caste or touch him. Generally speaking, our so-called "respectable" castes of the village included carpenters, pan sellers, milkmen, the Kurmi agriculturists, blacksmiths, gardeners, barbers, confectioners, and goldsmiths. Certain other castes were on the border line. Some of the "twice-born" would accept water from them and some not. These included fishermen, shepherds, grain parchers, potters, and tailors.

Below these came a group from whom the "twice-born" would not take water, but who were not considered literally untouchable, such as carters, wine dealers, oil pressers, earth workers, and a few tribal groups like the Tharus. Still lower were castes regarded as untouchable but not wholly degraded, since they did not eat beef—washermen, bamboo workers and a number of others of questionable occupation.

At the very bottom came the "untouchables," who ate beef, vermin, and dead animals, the scavenger Doms and the Chamars. Anyone who will sink so low as to commit the unforgivable sin of eating beef is an outcaste in the true sense of the word, from the Hindu point of view. This abhorrence explains why Hindus also refuse to accept water or food from Mussulmans and Christians. "May you eat beef!" is the most potent curse flung by one angry Hindu at another. For such as these no Brahmin household priest will officiate.

The popular proverbs of the countryside, with their shrewd appraisal of character, have spared the foibles of no caste. The Brahmin, the Bania, and the Kayasth are all held up to scorn for their greediness, selfishness, and deceitfulness, ascetics for their hypocrisy, the barber for his inquisitiveness and talkativeness, the goldsmith and the tailor for their dishonesty, the carpenter and the shoemaker for their procrastination, the weaver for his dullness, the lowly grain parchers and oil pressers for the airs they put on with prosperity.

A number of the familiar sayings have been collected by Sir Herbert Risley, and some of these I found current around Pachperwa. Because of his respect for religion, the peasant attacks religious hypocrisy in such sayings as: "When a man cannot get a wife, he turns ascetic!"—"When his crop has been burned, the Jat becomes a fakir." The Bania, to whom the peasant is always in debt, gets little shrift: "A friendly Bania, a chaste courtesan!"—"The dogs starve at a Bania's feast." The following proverbs speak for themselves: "The carpenter's face is the equivalent of unpunctuality."—"The tailor's 'this evening' and the shoemaker's 'next morning' never come."—"The oil presser's daughter puts on airs and wonders what oil cakes can be."—"The goldsmith will even filch gold from his mother's nose ring." Other proverbs have an ironic thrust: "The Dhobi knows who is poor in the village."—"The potter can sleep sound, no one will steal his clay."—"To eat Dom's leavings!"

It is easy to understand why certain occupations are looked down upon, but the obloquy attached to others is often derived from obscure emotional or religious antipathies. The work of scavengers is naturally filthy, and the Doms have added to their occupation of scavengering the unpleasant monopoly of tending the burning ghats of Benares. They are also executioners in jails. Washermen, like sweepers, are degraded because of the nature of their occupation. Since everything associated with death is contaminating, the great leather-working caste is also beyond the pale. Even professional drummers are polluted as a class because of contact with the skin coverings of their drums. Incidentally, catgut strings on musical instruments are taboo for high-caste Hindus. The *vina, esraj,* and *sitar* all have strings of silver and other metals.

The mucous discharges of the body are looked on askance, perhaps because in some obscure way Hindus have long been aware that these are a dangerous source of infection. Only the lowest caste people will play wind instruments. Licking the flap of an envelope or a stamp is against all rules of Hindu etiquette—an insult to one's correspondent. This feeling also explains the metal dishes used in India. They can be scoured more effectively than the ordinary unglazed earthenware of the village. Leaf plates solve the problem of guest dishes at feasts.

In northern India the attitude toward outcastes has never

been as extreme as the attitude in southern India, where 93 per cent of the population is Sudra and 4 per cent Brahmin. Traveling along the west coast near Calicut, I once heard a man on the road utter a doglike yelp and then repeat his peculiar cry a moment later. This was a case of "unapproachability." He was warning high-caste Hindus of his polluting presence. The exact mathematical distance at which a pariah causes pollution to a caste Hindu, forcing upon him the inconvenient necessity of taking a purifying bath and changing his clothes, has been fixed by long-established custom. The non-Brahmins of southern India are now demanding and obtaining simple human rights formerly denied them. They have many champions of their heartbreaking cause, among Hindu reformers as well as missionaries and government officials. Mahatma Gandhi as usual has expressed his attitude very practically by adopting into his own family and cherishing as a daughter of his own a little outcaste girl.

But it must be remembered that ordinary interchange of hospitality as practised in the West plays no part in Indian life. No castes intermarry or eat freely with one another. Since a raja does not eat with a Brahmin any more than a gardener eats with a goldsmith, the "untouchable" sweeper scarcely experiences a special feeling of ostracism because he too is barred from eating with any save his caste fellows. The potentialities of this attitude were brought home to me when my own sweeper refused point-blank to accept food from me.

In Pachperwa the Chamars and Doms, though they lived in a quarter by themselves, had their work and place in the village life and walked around with their heads up. The sweeper's shadow disturbed no one, though it was true that he was not expected to use certain wells. He came and went freely. His daughter-in-law, as stout as he was thin, and generously tattooed and braceleted, used to stand and gossip with the crowd of village folk who spent much of their time near my house. At the dispensary the Doctor, a Rajput, and the compounder, a Brahmin, never dreamed of questioning a man about his social status.

Where people are largely dependent on well water, the question of obtaining water presents complications which scarcely arise under more modern conditions. The ordinary well of the Indian countryside does not have even a sweep, and a man who wants water must fetch his own rope and jar or depend on another's. The idea of purity has come to be associated with the person who offers the water rather than with the quality of the water itself.

I once made a journey with a Brahmin—the pundit from Nautanwa—to the ruins of Kapilavastu, the city of the Buddha's youth, only twenty-five miles from Pachperwa. From the nearest station on the railway line, it took ten hours to go and come by elephant. A high wind was driving the dust in clouds about our heads as we sat cross-legged in a red-flounced howdah, listening to tales told by the white-bearded mahout. In the middle of the afternoon the dust suddenly swirled down upon us in such choking fury that we had to take refuge in a grove and wrap our heads in thick scarves. We were on the edge of a tiny cluster of huts. By this time we were both terribly thirsty, having had nothing to drink since early morning. There was a well a hundred feet in front of us, but my Western ideas of sanitation made it impossible for me to drink unboiled water from an open well in an Indian village.

"If you cannot drink, I must not drink either," the pundit remarked.

"Why not?" I asked in astonishment.

"It would not be polite, I think," was the gracious answer.

I assured him that I should feel much better to have the thirst of one of us quenched, and finally he consented to climb down from the elephant and go in search of a man of the right caste to give him water. The village turned out to be composed entirely of low-caste people, but a boy volunteered to run to a small settlement near by and bring back one whose brass lota and service the pundit could accept.

The caste rules in regard to food I soon discovered were incomprehensibly intricate. Food is generally classed as pukka and kutcha, literally good and bad, according to caste prohibitions. "Good" food is food that castes of allied social status will eat together or in public—*puris*, vegetables cooked in ghi, curds, parched grain, spices, fruits, sweets, milk, and pan. Such food may be accepted as a present even from one of lower caste, provided his caste is in reputable standing. "Bad" food, on the other hand, is all food prepared with water, particularly grain food, which forms the staple of the Indian diet. If a man accepts this from any save a caste fellow he is liable to outcasting. The hookah is also taken as a symbol of caste intimacy, and Hindus are debarred from borrowing a smoke from any outside their caste. When a man has been put out of caste he is said to be deprived of *pani-hookah*, water and the water pipe. Children are wisely freed from observing caste rules about food until at the age of seven or so they are considered old enough to conform.

The *Shastras* give three regulations to be observed in regard to food. First, food must be by its nature pure. Onions and garlic are taboo because they are considered exciting. In the second place, food, to be pure, must be prepared under special conditions. The place where it is cooked, the dishes used, the person cooking it, and the circumstances under which it is eaten, all enter into consideration. Behind all the elaborate taboo of to-day undoubtedly lies a sound concept of sanitation. Because of this sanctity of the Hindu kitchen, caste Hindus were forbidden to travel abroad without paying the penalty of being outcasted, until within a few decades. Even to-day any high-caste Hindu who has been living abroad is required to perform a purification ceremony on his return before he can be accepted back into the fold of an orthodox family. Thirdly, the food should be free from dust, flies, and other sources of contamination. Since Indians have not been trained in modern ideas of sanitary cleanliness, they pay little attention to this condition. Water from insanitary wells and fly-ridden sweets from the bazar do not trouble the Indian mind.

Hindu exclusiveness in regard to food has given a very special stamp to daily life as one sees it in India. It explains why, except for sellers of sherbet, milk and curds, and purveyors of sweets, you see few or no food vendors in the streets of India, and why there are no Hindu hotels and inns. At the *dharmasalas,* or rest houses, every Hindu provides and cooks his own meal.

Although caste complicates hospitality for Hindus it simplifies it for the foreigner. There was practically no question of my entertaining anybody in the village. In all the time I was in Pachperwa I gave two formal dinner parties— that is, I paid for them. One was my house-warming feast, the other a dinner for the nineteen members of the tahsil staff who bought tickets for my cow, when the Tahsildar arranged to raffle her and her calf before my departure. This last dinner was held on the veranda, the guests squatting on a large white cloth on the floor. Halwais came from the bazar and prepared the food under the Peshkar's supervision. Leaf plates were furnished by a man of the proper caste, and none of my Mohammedan servants had anything to do with the feast or its preparation. The raffle party was in a gay mood and for the moment I had forgotten caste rules. I half started to sit down with my guests, though not of course intending to eat with them. The Peshkar rose in horror just in time. "If you sit down here none of them can eat anything," he exclaimed.

There was also the very special occasion when the Sub-Inspector of Police came to call with his wife and four of his children. The Thanadar's wife, a tall gaunt woman suffering from tuberculosis, was dependent on my little visits to bring variety into her secluded existence. One day she remarked reproachfully that though I had asked her to come to see me, I had never made definite arrangements. So the party was promptly arranged for nine o'clock the following evening.

I knew that sweets without grain, fruit, and pan were all the hospitality I could offer. Sheobalak, my Halwai friend, prepared the sweets, trimmed with silver leaf. The Station Master put in an order with the conductor of the night train to fetch some melons from Gorakhpur, and bananas were ordered from Balrampur. This time the Peshkar, who was of the same caste as the Thanadar, lent me his guest set, consisting of many small brass bowls and brass plates of graduated sizes and he also sent a brass jar of drinking water. Ram Lakhan, my small Hindu servant, was to be on hand to pass the refreshments.

About half-past nine an advance guard in the shape of the head constable arrived to say that the others would soon be leaving the thana. At last I saw a lantern staggering along on the far side of invisible fields. It came jerkily on, and in due course the constable, two servants, the children, the Thanadar, and his wife arrived at my door. For the first and only time I saw the Sub-Inspector's wife arrayed in all her glory. She was wearing a thin white sari embroidered with black flowers. Her arms were weighted with gold bracelets nearly to the elbows. She wore several gold collars, a head ornament, large dangling earrings, and three slender nose rings, the largest a thin circlet at least a foot in diameter. I could see that the Thanadar was a devoted and generous husband.

When Ram Lakhan passed the laden trays, the Thanadar stuttered effusive apologies for all the trouble he was causing, but evidently he had come prepared. His able news scouts had already reported the arrival of the melons and the loan of the Peshkar's dishes. His servant now produced a lota of water that had been brought along, so the essential mouth rinsing could be performed before and after eating. Although they were orthodox Hindus, the Thanadar confessed that times were certainly changing. His own father and mother would never have dreamed of eating anything, even pan, sitting on the same cotton rug with me. They would have taken nothing in my presence unless we were seated on the ground, which absorbs impurities.

The Thanadar's wife did not miss anything on this rare opportunity for escaping her own prison walls of brown mud. My clothes closets, as usual, received extravagant admiration. We even went on a tour of the servants' house —after they had been warned to make themselves invisible —and the kitchen. Hindu women keep their brass kitchen utensils brightly scoured and their kitchens immaculate. From the Hindu point of view Western food habits are revolting. For one thing the average Westerner openly relishes beef, pork, and chicken. This explains why no one but a very low-caste Hindu will ever cook for a Westerner in India. Cooks in foreign households are either Mussulmans or Christians. I was glad to see, when the door was unpadlocked, that Din Mohammed had left everything in excellent order. The keen black eyes of the wife of the Sub-Inspector took in appreciatively the screened food boxes and the waist-high brick stove, so much more convenient than her own little horseshoe-shaped *chula* of clay, scarcely six inches high.

The Mussulmans are comparatively free in the matter of food, though Shias and Sunnis will not eat together, I was told. More than once the Station Master dropped in for a cup of cocoa, and once I persuaded the Persian sanitary inspector to share a late breakfast when he arrived unexpectedly in cholera season. But all Pachperwa stood aghast when Dr. Saxena, a Hindu of good caste, took tea with me. This historic event occurred during the fourth month of my residence in the village, and it was the first and only time a Hindu actually "broke bread" at my table. Dr. Saxena scorned the rules that had no direct bearing on hygiene and sanitation, but his own conservative household in Gonda, he said, observed all the orthodox traditions. His wife permitted herself no laxity, but realizing the difficulties for a man constantly traveling without a servant in the rural areas she accepted another standard in these matters for him.

All matters pertaining to a particular caste have been crystallized by centuries of convention, but organization varies greatly from caste to caste. The Brahmins and the Rajputs have no central governing body. Rules for their life conduct were codified by Manu, and these rules they still observe in principle. The craftsmen, following their hereditary occupations like the craftsmen of the Middle Ages, submitted themselves to a body of elders invested with governing authority. The more flexible trading groups also found it advantageous, as commerce expanded, to enter into closer association and in course of time formed well-knit economic units with all the aspects of caste. The agricultural, pastoral and hunting groups, because of the nature of their occupations, remained but loosely organized.

Brahmin exclusiveness, Kshatriya expediency—expediency still dictates royal alliances in modern Europe in exactly the same way it governed such alliances in India—craftsmen traditions, the advantages of economic union, tribal affiliations, the tendency of lower social groups to imitate the example of the higher ones, and finally, the absence of swift transportation systems which gave communities greater stability than they possess to-day, lie behind the slow stratification of Hindu society into castes. The castes in one respect resemble fraternal orders. All the members are on equal footing and express their views and vote in a very democratic manner. Caste fellows contribute to marriage expenses of poor members; they take charge of funerals for individuals who have no families. No caste can interfere in the internal affairs of another. Even a Brahmin has no right to dictate what rules a Chamar is to observe within his own sphere. The poise of the lowliest Hindu springs, I imagine, from the consciousness that in performing his own caste duties and in obeying his own caste laws he is fulfilling all that can be asked of him. In India one almost never encounters social maladjustment—

a painful effort on the part of someone to fill a position in society for which background and training are inherently lacking.

With the exception of the Brahmin and Rajput castes, most Hindu castes are governed by panchayats, consisting of the male members. Local panchayats control caste affairs within certain areas. An elected *sarpanch* or *chaudhari* serves as the headman for a given term. Caste meetings are held on occasions of funeral feasts and weddings or at any time when caste members naturally come together, and from time to time general conferences are held to discuss current caste problems. When Kayasths held a panchayat meeting at the schoolhouse after the wedding of Devi Prasad's sister, they invited me to attend. The main question discussed was the marriage age, and Kayasths were urged not to permit marriages for girls of their own caste under eighteen or for men under twenty-four. I also attended a general Marwari council at Gaya, quite by accident. In this case the meeting had under consideration the all-important matter whether the caste would modify its laws to allow widow remarriage. The proposal was overwhelmingly defeated by the conservative element.

The panchayat exercises final authority in all matters of dispute. It also has the power to consider offenses against caste and to punish by fines or outcasting. If a member is convicted of having flagrantly broken caste rules in regard to marriage or food, he is generally forbidden to take part in any caste ceremonies until certain conditions have been fulfilled. Outcasting is not final in the case of minor offenses. For these it is customary to exact a monetary fine, which may range from two to five rupees, and two dinners to be given to the brethren by the offending member before he is reinstated in the caste. My milkman told me that a caste brother of his in a neighboring village had married a Chamar woman. He was put out of caste—that is debarred from pani-hookah privileges—until he sent her away.

Whenever I began to study some particular phase of

village life, strange facts came to light. It was Asgar who confided that the sweeper had originally belonged to the Kurmi caste but, having married a Domi, he had been degraded to the level of a Dom. Stranger still, in a village two miles away lived a one-time Brahmin, now married to a Dom woman. He had been outcasted, of course, and was actually doing scavenger's work in his village.

Dukhi was head of the Mohammedan barber's caste of Pachperwa. Dukhi was a whole panchayat in himself. He described at length a dramatic crisis of the year before. The thekedar of a certain village near by had insisted that the village barber should shave him twice a week instead of the customary once. Since he was not offered even an extra anna, the price of a shave for non-agriculturists not paying grain dues, he saw no reason why the fastidious thekedar should be humored. A feud developed, ending with the barber's ultimate insult—he walked off, leaving the thekedar only half shaved. A grand meeting of the barber brotherhood was called and the affair discussed from beginning to end. The rebellious barber was upheld in his position, but a compromise had to be effected. He and another barber exchanged hereditary villages. This was the first time, according to Dukhi, that such a radical innovation had been introduced into barber customs.

When a man or woman is outcasted for some offense too serious to be expiated, the unfortunate individual is completely ostracized from the group. The outcasted man's own family cannot eat with him. He has no choice left but to become a convert to another religion, to go to a distant place and hope that the caste community there will not learn the truth, to take the risky course of pretending to belong to a different caste, to join some lower caste or to live outside the Hindu social order altogether. In private many rules are broken, particularly those in regard to food, but an out-of-caste marriage focuses public attention and can scarcely be ignored. Association with a prostitute counts as a moral offense, but not as an offense against caste. Prostitutes are a caste by themselves. In our region some of the low-caste vagrant tribes, like the Beriya, prostituted their women, and Mohammedan prostitutes—most of them nautch girls from Gonda—visited the countryside singly from time to time, when they were employed for *tamashas* of one sort or another. When caste marriage rules are flagrantly disregarded, which is not often under the circumstances, the higher caste person sinks to the rank of the lower, if he can gain admittance to it, or he becomes an outcaste. A great many groups, particularly the vagrant gypsies, are constantly recruiting members from the higher strata of Hindu society.

The caste system troubles the Western mind because it is a negation of Western ideas of democracy and freedom. Caste is certainly responsible for the social and economic disfranchisement of more than forty million people, between a seventh and an eighth of the total population of India. It entrenches the Brahmin aristocracy in a position of advantage, restricts individual initiative, prevents competition, automatically limits marriage to caste unions, and surrounds such innocent necessities as food and water with artificial prohibitions. To the Western mind a division of society into fixed compartments and the unchangeable determination by birth of each individual's position are looked upon as wholly irrational and unjust. The astonishing submissiveness of the Hindus to the self-imposed limitations of caste are beyond comprehension.

Indian reformers recognize that serious abuses have grown up around the caste system, but they do not believe that reforms are to be effected only by destroying the Indian social structure and substituting for it some alien Western scheme of organization, especially since no two Western countries have yet agreed on a "best scheme." The Hindu solution is far too deeply rooted in Indian tradition and religious thought to be applicable to another country, but it has given India the most highly evolved plan of social coöperation, through specialization, that any society has ever evolved for itself.

It is everywhere the natural tendency of people to break up into groups. In the West we call the groups "classes," and the basic difference is an economic one. If a man can change his economic status he can change his class. Economic competition, though it permits individuals to rise, precipitates an endless struggle for supremacy in which the most are inevitably doomed to failure.

Obviously ancient Aryan society must already have developed, before the period of the great migration, that specialization of labor which is a feature of the modern caste system. Before the age of industrialism a son almost universally followed in his father's footsteps. Observing his father hammering out metal vessels, weaving, turning a potter's wheel, or making beautiful ornaments of gold, he acquired a natural aptitude and a sensitive understanding for all the tricks of the craft. These were supplemented at the proper age by initiation into the little secrets which gave his father and his father's father their skill. Modern industrial schools with their mechanized efficiency try to give much the same sort of training.

The Brahmin lawgivers, perceiving that people were unlike in qualities and capacities and so had different contributions to make to the social body, set about codifying caste as they found it existing in more or less fluid state in ancient India. They recognized three qualities or tendencies innate in humanity. There are those in whom the *sattva* quality, of truth and illumination, predominates, those in whom *rajas*, or the active quality, predominates, and those characterized by *tamas*, or inertia. In theory caste was based on a profound reality. In practice when caste was made hereditary, it began to develop inevitable injustices.

The lawmakers, in assigning fixed duties to different groups, made a theoretical adjustment between duties and capacities and laid down rules of conduct appropriate to the supposed state of spiritual evolution. Likewise there was an attempt to make the conditions of the environment conform to the needs of the particular group. The Brahmin, for example, who was to study, teach, and perform religious ceremonies, was to be supported by society, just as modern Western society endows educational institutions and lavishly bestows scholarships and fellowships in acknowledgment of the fact that students cannot do their best work if they have to divert part of their energies to the problem of earning a living while they are studying. At the same time, the Brahmin was subjected to rules of self-discipline and asceticism far more austere than those decreed for any other social group. Spiritual knowledge was not to be passed out to anyone, but only to those whose disciplined lives fitted them to receive it.

Under the impact of modern life many changes are at work in the social structure of India. Caste in its economic phase has met the needs of a simple society, but it is not adapted to the age of machinery. To begin with, the mastery of a machine process is of an inferior order. It does not ordinarily require the skill involved in hand production. Machinery irons out the differences between capacities more quickly than anything else. India is entering the inevitable stage of industrialism, and already factory hands are recruited from many different castes.

The growing population of India is another factor. Traditional caste work no longer offers adequate support to millions. A community of fifteen million Brahmins is more than large enough to supply India's need of priests, and the opportunity to be a king or warrior is increasingly restricted. Nowadays Brahmin tax collectors, Rajput policemen, Kayasth doctors, and Vaisya deputy collectors are found working side by side. In village life a general loosening and overlapping of occupations is noticeable. It came as something of a shock to me to find Brahmins performing all sorts of menial tasks. In Pachperwa the Brahmin Tahsildar's cook was a Brahmin. The station water boy who used to bring my three pounds of ice from the morning train in a box of sawdust on his head was a Brahmin. The mail carrier, the compounder at the hospital, one of the constables, and several of the tahsil messengers were Brahmins. More astonishing, I heard of a Brahmin in Calcutta who owned a shoe factory.

The modern industrial age, which coincided with British rule in India, has dealt blow after blow to the caste idea. Railways attack the caste system at the root. Third-class carriages do not discriminate between the Brahmin and the Chamar. Both sit side by side on the wooden benches. Schools, hospitals, casteless government service, the example and influence of the dominant European community, all are factors influencing the present situation. That many of the minute regulations in regard to caste practices have long outlived their original significance is acknowledged by increasing numbers.

Gandhi and many other reformers are carrying on an agitation to abolish "untouchability." Under the stimulus of new ideas of nationalism and a fresh religious emphasis, outcastes and Brahmins have actually eaten together on more than one occasion in recent years. The Benares Hindu University will not admit any student who objects to the presence of an outcaste. The Brahmo-Samajists, in Bengal, do not recognize caste. Referring to the depressed classes, the Simon Report makes this significant statement: "Never has education among the classes falling within this category received such encouragement as it has since the transfer of education in the provinces to the charge of [Indian] Ministers." It is significant that lately the enrollment of pupils from this element of the population has increased from 377,000 to 802,000. Many exceptions to caste rules are now almost universally taken for granted. Ice sold at railway stations is not water. Bottled water and piped water are also widely accepted. Imported food in tin boxes is not food in the Indian sense. Biscuits of all sorts are acceptable on railway journeys.

I discovered that I myself was having a revolutionary

influence on the Peshkar in these matters. With intense interest, he would inquire of Din Mohammed, the cook, just how he prepared everything I ate for my dinner. Then he would give instructions to his own cook to prepare his food in the same way. Boiled vegetables instead of vegetables fried in ghi seemed utterly insipid to him, yet he ate them heroically in the belief that they might be better for him. When he visited his family they told him I was fast making a European out of him. Instead of sweets for breakfast, he now demanded fruit.

In spite of his expressed annoyance with the elaborate Hindu food ritual, his own kitchen arrangements illustrated the preposterous lengths to which caste conventions are sometimes carried. He could not afford, on his salary of thirty rupees, the high-caste cook he should have had. So of necessity a compromise was worked out. The cook did not touch his food after the fire was lighted nor approach the fire. I could not conceive how the poor man could prepare a meal under such circumstances. To satisfy my curiosity the Peshkar invited me to come as far as his kitchen door. The cook was carrying out caste regulations to the letter. The fire needed replenishing, and he flung a stick with dexterous aim half across the room. He tossed the peeled potatoes into the pot of boiling water. When the rice needed more water, he used a long-handled dipper, not venturing within three feet of the fire. Only when the fire had been extinguished, could he touch the cooking pots.

"Do you really think he observes all these rules if you are not watching?" I asked.

"Oh, yes," said the Peshkar confidently. "It would trouble him to have me break the rules of fooding." I was not so sure.

Escapes from at least the economic restrictions of caste are possible through many doors. For those who succeed in acquiring an education there is government service. For the masses there are the mills and factories. Christianity and Islam, which free their adherents from "untouchability" as well as limitations of work, have both drawn their converts, and there is always an open door for the avowed "renouncer," willing to give up society and the world altogether for the sake of finding God. No one asks the caste of a sadhu. He has none, and he is bound by no caste rules.

The Hindu believes fervently in transmigration. He is convinced that he travels from birth to birth, gaining experience through a beginningless round of birth and death, until ultimately he reaches perfection and becomes free. Transmigration is neither to be proved nor disproved. It is a working hypothesis of the scheme of things, like heaven, or any other attempt to satisfy the deep-seated belief in a continuance of life in some form beyond the postern gate of death, and to rationalize the facts of this life as they are experienced. To the Hindu mind we are working out our own destinies, slowly uncovering the divinity within our own natures. The conditions of one life are too limited to learn all that life has to teach, and so the Hindu postulates many lives, millions of them, it may be. The deathless soul puts on one body after another, selecting the environment that will give the particular experience it needs to help it in the process of unfoldment. Out of the infinite range of experience the soul draws to itself the necessary experiences through which its gradual awakening takes place.

If one tries to imagine one's self an outcaste of the Hindu social order, it is apparent that the concept of many lives before and ahead, all logically related, would at least give a very different attitude toward existence than the conviction that this fraction of immediate perception is the whole. The Hindu believes that by living this life well, to the best of his capacity and understanding, he will have better fortune in the next. It is like breaking a railway journey you know will be continued, by alighting for a few minutes at a wayside station. But the law of cause and effect works both ways. A fortunate Brahmin, in spite of the previous progress he must have made to be born a Brahmin, will find himself degraded or handicapped in a subsequent life if he fails in his duties as a Brahmin. This attitude explains why Hindus accept their caste with as little question or resistance as most people accept their sex or race.

The evils of the Hindu caste system are all too obvious, but it is only fair to recognize that caste has contributed important benefits to India. It has furnished stability to the social fabric for at least three thousand years. No country except China can show an equal continuity of civilization. Is it possible to deny that caste has had much to do with the preservation of India? Caste has at least provided everybody with some recognized occupation and the necessary training to pursue it. It has kept alive high standards of craftsmanship and artistic skill. It has emphasized the ethical obligation of the individual to subordinate himself to the society in which he lives. It has deliberately thwarted competition and prevented energy from being dissipated in the endless struggle for material or social supremacy. Out of the stern prohibitions in regard to intermarriage and interdining, a saving barrier has been created around the Hindu home, protecting the vital life of the people from the complete disruption that must otherwise have come as a result of countless foreign invasions and a thousand years of alien rule. These are no small services, though they are commonly ignored by those who insist on seeing caste only as a dividing and oppressive influence.

CHAPTER XIV

Wedding Drums

A THUDDING of drums broke the quiet of a February afternoon. A little procession was passing along the cart road at the end of the tahsil path. Four men carried a boy in a red palanquin. Others straggled alongside the *doli*, and two drummers brought up the rear, big rounded drums criss-crossed with leather thongs slung from their necks. "A bridegroom," the Tahsildar announced, and he called out to the procession to stop.

The center of attention was a bewildered little boy with fresh sandal paste streaked across his forehead, a red turban, and a red cloth drawn about him like a shawl. He was certainly the unhappiest bridegroom I had ever seen. I asked how old he was, and the father replied, "Ten." They were of the Ahir caste and were on their way to the village of the bride, four miles farther on.

Although this was a February marriage, February is not an auspicious month for weddings. Rama and Sita, who experienced so much suffering and misery, began their married life in this month. The months are conveniently auspicious after the spring harvest, from the middle of March to the middle of June, and in November and December, after the autumn harvest. Soon wedding drums were no longer a novelty in Pachperwa. All through the hot season the drums sounded on my road. After a while I ceased to run down the hill every time I heard them and hold up processions to take photographs.

The bridegrooms' processions were all more or less alike

except that some were larger and noisier than others. A tatterdemalion band of drummers, flute players, and cymbal players—in any event drummers—marched along either before or behind the doli. The *barat*, the procession of male relatives and family friends, was made to cover as much space as possible to emphasize the importance of the bridegroom's family. A relative or old family servant bore the gifts for the bride in jars or baskets swung from a shoulder pole—jewelry, vermilion in a small wooden jar for marking the part in the bride's hair, some saris, including the one the bride would wear during the wedding.

But all the interest centering in the bride's clothes in the West, in India is transferred to the clothes of the bridegroom. He becomes suddenly metamorphosed from nobody into somebody, an astonishing figure in a turban of auspicious color, red, yellow, or pink, and a strange dress of one of the same colors. He is also adorned with puja paste, put on his forehead by the family priest.

Our village bridegrooms ranged in age from nine or ten to full maturity. The doli itself was usually a simple boxlike affair, roofed, but open at the sides. One day there was much excitement in Pachperwa when a doli arrived from Tulsipur with glass windows on all four sides through which the bridegroom stared in self-conscious pride. Glass, except in the form of bottles, was unknown in Pachperwa. Borrowed elephants sometimes lent special glory to a wedding procession, the bridegroom riding in state in an ornamental howdah.

Mohammedan bridegrooms, in dresses like those of Hindus, and with the same reinforcement of musicians and friends, were distinguished only by long transparent veils hanging in front of their faces. Generally, too, instead of being carried by palanquin, they sat astride horses led by wedding retainers. Unaccustomed as most of them were to this aristocratic mode of travel, they suffered accidents now and then. Once I saw a bridegroom ignominiously spilled from his little pony into the dust of the New Bazar.

With all the glamour of the wedding processions, something was missing. No woman ever took part. All this drumming and tootling, these gay clothes, this excitement, were solely for the bridegroom, more often than not a mere child.

It is only as recently as the year 1930 that child marriage in India has ceased to have legal sanction. The earliest attempt on the part of the government of India to interfere in the domain of Hindu marriage relations was a law enacted in 1892 forbidding the consummation of marriage for girls under thirteen. Since a child bride often went to her husband's family before this age, enforcement was difficult, if not impossible. At the beginning of the century, two states under the control of Indian rulers, Mysore and Baroda, passed laws designed to restrict child marriages within their territory.

Adherents to the cause of a later marriage age are drawn from all groups—the Brahmos of Bengal, the Arya Samajists of North India, even certain high-caste orthodox Hindus, whose custom of forbidding widow remarriage has made them realize vividly the tragedy of lifelong widowhood that may overtake their daughters. Western reformers have naturally joined the ranks or led them. The present Child Marriage Act, passed by overwhelming majority in the Legislative Assembly, is applicable to all communities. It makes it a criminal offense to arrange, solemnize, or participate in the marriage of a girl below the age of fourteen or a boy of eighteen, and the penalty for infringement is one month's imprisonment or a fine of 1,000 rupees. The political upheaval into which India has lately been thrown overshadows every other phase of life in the country, but the law is there to stay, an epochal landmark on India's road of social progress. When I was in Pachperwa, however, child marriages were still celebrated with tranquil ignorance of impending reform.

The wedding months slipped along, and I was growing almost tired of listening to Fakire's nightly enumeration of the weddings that had occurred in surrounding villages. One evening he appeared at the window screen after dinner. "The wedding procession has started," he announced.

"What wedding procession?"

"The Halwai wedding to which you are invited."

Fortunately my social engagement book in Pachperwa was not overcrowded. Throwing a scarf over my head, for the sake of propriety, I followed Fakire, who led the way carrying a stout lathi and a lantern.

We could see a mass of twinkling lights ahead of us. They were colored flares, burning out one by one. We arrived just in time for the end of the fireworks. Two strange figures resembling mounted knights formed the center of a haphazard procession starting up the main road of the village. Rajab, my friend of the Mohammedan "color-pouring" caste, suddenly seized my hand and pulled me after him, dodging in and out of open shop fronts.

Except for a torch or two the street was lighted only by the moon, so when Rajab almost pushed me into an iron-legged chair in front of a house, it took me a second or two to make out that I was at a familiar confectioner's shop. A crowd of women massed behind me sang the bridegroom's welcome. Rajab and Fakire and I had outdistanced the procession itself, which was just now arriving. The first knight, all in red with a huge red turban topped by a basket frame from which strings of straw flowers dangled, was riding a nervous little horse with bristling mane. The pleasant-faced grandmother who had often beckoned me to sit down in the shop and eat some sweets offered the "door welcome" to the bridegroom, waving over his head first a butter churn and then a husking pole, intimate symbols of domesticity. As soon as she had finished with the first knight she repeated the ritual for the second knight, garbed in orange, who rode another bad-tempered little steed. At this point I was warned to duck and avoid a shower of small stones which the women and the bridegrooms' party began flinging at each other, in mock antagonism.

Fakire explained in my ear that this was a double wedding of the two motherless daughters of the Halwai household with two brothers from Utraula. The first lad was a handsome boy of sixteen or seventeen, but the fat-cheeked little brother of twelve had a pouting expression, as if he did not in the least enjoy being married. Of course there was no sign of the brides. After the formal welcome, a presentation of money to the red and orange bridegrooms was in order. A mysterious white-coated gentleman whose tongue seemed a bit thick—and got thicker during the night —volunteered in what was intended to be English that the brides' family was giving only a paltry five rupees. Then the bridegrooms rode away again, the crowd dispersed, and the street relapsed into an empty little lane, in which the alchemy of the moonlight turned the mud to liquid silver.

Rajab suggested that I should follow the bridegrooms, and somebody was ordered to bring along the chair. As we turned the corner past the shrine where the trunkless elephant stood, we came upon the bridegrooms' party, established in temporary headquarters in front of the residence of one of our wine dealers. My chair was set down in the middle of the road on the assumption, apparently, that I was going to sit there and stare at the bridegrooms, but though I was made to feel welcome, I thought I should prefer to return to the Halwai shop. Everything looked just as it did on ordinary days. I could see no preparations for the wedding. The stout older brother of the brides, smiling affably, said the actual ceremony would not take place until midnight. Just then the friendly grandmother appeared in a saffron-tinted sari, took me by the hand, and insisted that I join the women's procession. A minute later, linked arm in arm with the Halwai grandmother, I found myself in the odd rôle of leading a Hindu wedding procession through the village of Pachperwa.

A band was playing full blast, and the women—this time the brides' friends and relatives—were all singing. Above the drums and clashing cymbals their song rose and fell with trembling modulations and little minor waterfalls of sound.

Scores of children accompanied us. Everybody in Pachperwa knew that I had come to the wedding, and even the dogs joined the procession.

We trailed up and down some alleys and came out in a clearing near a grain parcher's shop. Into the tiny room we all crowded, or at any rate as many of us as could get in. Eyes were glued to every opening, and a row of eyes peered through the crack between the mud walls and the sagging roof. The parching oven rose from the middle of the floor; jars of sand stood about. A flickering light from the open mouth of the oven, into which dead leaves were being thrust, threw a red glow over all the shrouded figures.

The smoke from the fire made my eyes smart terribly, but I did not dare close them for fear of missing something. The woman at the oven was ceremonially anointed with oil, and red lead was painted along the parting of her hair. Then, as she squatted near her fire and sifted the hot sand from the parched rice, all the women began cursing. One of the women explained that they were saying "bad things" about the grooms' relatives, particularly their uncles. Marriage ceremonies among the lower Hindu castes reflect many evidences of the primitive marriage by capture. A mock enmity is set up between the bride's people and the groom's. The pelting of the bridegroom's party with small stones, and this use of *gali*, or insulting language, directed against the bridegroom's family, were curious survivals that had long outlived their meaning. At last the parched grain, which was to be used later in the evening, was stowed away in an enormous cloth, and we marched back with it through the village, children yelling, musicians dinning, women singing, dogs barking.

A further interlude for feasting was declared, during which I went home to rest. Fakire fell into a deep sleep and required vigorous shaking to bring him back to life at midnight, the time when we were to return for the actual wedding. The village was now dark and silent. Cots with mummy-like forms and naked children sprawling in grotesque attitudes lay on both sides of the road. One had the feeling of walking down the middle of a great dormitory. In the faint light of a single lantern I saw more mummies lying about in the shop on the board benches where sweets were displayed in the daytime. Two or three vague figures, propped against a wall, took turns at a gurgling hookah.

"Not for another hour or so," the Halwai announced calmly. "The bridegrooms' party have not finished eating." There was nothing to do but retrace our steps. This time they promised to send word when the right moment arrived.

From my bed on the veranda I waked with a start. "Huzur, the *shadi* now begins," a gentle voice was saying. In the moonlight, standing at a respectful distance, I recognized the drug seller of the New Bazar. It was just half-past two.

The same women with whom I had gone in procession to the grain parcher's earlier in the evening were now gathered outside a house along the way. They called to me to join them. They were fetching two washerwomen and two barber women to dress the brides. We all went on together to the Halwai house. Passing through three pitch-black rooms, we came out in a small open court. My chair reappeared once more, placed against a wall of the court. Almost at my feet were two festooned water jars, each supporting a saucer of dry barley. On top of the barley saucers were other saucers of oil with lighted wicks—the sacred marriage fire. Two posts erected beside the jars and joined above by a straw rope served in this poor little household for a marriage pavilion.

I heard a splash. In a corner of the court one of the two Dhobins was dumping jars of water over the head of a slim girl of fourteen. The grandmother stood by. Not satisfied with the casualness of this bath, considering the special occasion, she told the woman to rub the bride more thoroughly. A new yellow sari was produced and modestly put on above the wet one, which was then allowed to drop to the ground. The bride was directed to step on a tiny up-

turned saucer placed in front of her and to crush it with
her heel. Nobody needed to explain the symbolic meaning of
this act. The childhood home lies one way and another way
the home of the new husband's father, to which, before long,
the bride will be going in her covered palanquin.

The bride smoothed back her wet hair with her hands. A
white muslin cloth was draped about her, making her look
like a little cocoon, and she was turned over to one of the
barber women, who painted five neat red stripes across her
insteps and a broad line around the soles of her feet and
tinted her toe nails pink. In the gleam of the oil wicks I
saw big tears rolling down her cheeks.

"Her mother is dead," a pocked-marked woman who sat
near me remarked loudly several times. "Don't cry, child!"
Unexpectedly she sobbed herself, while the child's tears continued to fall.

Meanwhile the second bride, the eleven-year-old sister,
was brought out and submitted to the ministrations of the
second washerwoman and barber woman. She, too, was crying—more audibly than the older girl.

The Pujari who always officiated at the shrine near my
bungalow now came into the court, wearing a faded red
scarf around his shoulders. He inspected a brass plate of bel
leaves, uncooked rice, turmeric, and other puja essentials.
He commanded certain missing things to be brought and
seated himself on the ground near the two jars. The shrouded
little bride sat down opposite. Obeying instructions given
by the Brahmin, she reached out a hand and dropped a bel
leaf or bit of rice at the foot of the auspicious barley jar.

Nobody except me paid much attention to proceedings.
No men were present. A crowd of neighbor women—among
whom I noticed one or two of the Bania caste—filled the
covered end of the court. The women chatted and moved
around restlessly, and when their babies waked up and cried
they nursed them.

At last the red bridegroom entered with a few of his party.
He sat down on a low board, facing the bride, who was

huddling on the floor, supported by the barber woman. He cast a curious glance at the shapeless bundle in front of him, wondering, I suppose, what sort of wife he was marrying.

The grandparents, acting in place of the brides' parents, the bride, the groom, and the village Pujari all had parts to play in the puja that followed. Suddenly my eyes fell on the Pujari's bandaged leg, and I could not suppress an inner shiver. Our village priest was a leper. The toes of one foot were just beginning to look oddly blunt and worn off. He had one open sore. To see him in this rôle, passing rice and leaves to the bride and groom and lifting water in his cupped hands from a brass bowl and pouring it into theirs, appalled me, but the village folk have no conception that leprosy is infectious.

The white-coated pundit who had ostentatiously attempted to explain things to me earlier in the evening in a broken jargon of English now reappeared. Whenever the Pujari stumbled a bit in the Sanskrit marriage ritual this gentleman jumped into the breach. Several times he corrected the Pujari's grammar, and once proceedings stopped altogether while a hot argument was waged about some nicety of the Sanskrit text. When the little orange brother was at last brought in and made to sit facing his bride the Pujari moved over to them, while the pundit finished off the first pair. The ceremony for the younger children was conveniently telescoped, so that all four were ready for the finale at the same time. Neither brides nor bridegrooms had uttered one word throughout the ceremony. I imagined the elder girl might still be crying under her crumpled white covering, but the little sister slept soundly through most of her wedding. Whenever the Pujari wanted her to take leaves or water in her hands, the barber woman, who was holding her, had to wake her up.

The Sanskrit monologue had been relieved at one point when the brides' offerings of copper kitchen pots—a small set for the small sister—were produced and surveyed critically by the pundit representing the bridegrooms. "Where is such and such a thing?" he would demand haughtily, as if he had discovered an attempt on the part of the brides' family to cheat. Somebody would reach down inside one of the large caldrons and fish up a lota or small bowl, which mollified him. The bridegrooms' trays of folded clothes, jars of red ointment, and silver jewelry were also brought in. The jewelry was examined with interest by the women present, who silently passed it from hand to hand.

The moment had come for the last act in the mute drama. The red bridegroom and the orange bridegroom stood up, took the jars of vermilion from their gift trays, leaned over, and, for the first time looking under the veils, traced the red lines of wifehood down the parts in the brides' hair. Then the garments of bride and bridegroom were symbolically knotted. Together, the bride bending over while the bridegroom guided her from behind, they made the seven turns around the ceremonial jars bearing the sacred fires. After every turn a small boy, brother of the brides, poured over the covered heads several handfuls of parched rice. A mock struggle ensued, relic of old days, in which each bridegroom in turn pushed the brother away.

"Become thou now my partner, as thou hast paced all the seven steps," the Pujari chanted, speaking for the bridegrooms. "Thy partnership have I gained; apart from thee now I cannot live; apart from me do thou not live; we each shall be an object of love to the other. Combine I now thy mind, thy action, thy senses with mine." The weddings were over.

Long before, the stars had gone out. The crows had arrived and were perched on the thatched roof, waiting the auspicious moment to hop down and clean up the puja rice. As daylight returned, the little court resumed its drab appearance. An animated discussion began over the pathetic division of annas and pice—so much to the washerwomen, so much to the barber women, so much to the Pujari and the pundit, so much to a quiet figure in a corner addressed as "Chaudhari," who turned out to be the father of the bride-grooms.

The Halwais' invitation may have broken the ice, or possibly a modest present sent to the brides by the hand of Fakire the next day was the explanation. From this time on unsolicited invitations to other village weddings began to come in. Some of these were more impressive than the Halwai wedding, but my first village wedding was a typical one.

Except for Devi Prasad's sister, who must have been eighteen or twenty and who married a man of twenty-five, all our marriages were those of children. The boys ranged in age from ten to thirteen, the girls were usually two or three years younger. Mussulmans, who are generally credited with marrying later, in our rural community did not seem to do so. One day Allah Baksh, the Station Master, invited me to make a donation to the Mohammedan station servant to help him marry off his two daughters, the younger of whom was just eight. I bluntly refused on the ground that I did not believe in child marriages, but the station servant borrowed the money somewhere, and the joint wedding came off. A wedding for two, it seemed, did not cost much more than a wedding for one and so was an economy. Double weddings, usually two sisters married to two brothers, were popular for this reason. My satisfaction that Asgar Ali, dishwasher-in-chief at the Happy House, was not yet married at fourteen was short-lived. When I presented him with twenty rupees upon my departure he promptly announced that he would now be married. Negotiations with the bride's family had reached the stage where the marriage was to come off as soon as Asgar's family paid fifteen rupees to the bride's family and presented in addition four "cloths."

I came in touch with only one tragic marriage between an old man and a little girl. This, as it happened, was not a village affair, but concerned the palace at Balrampur. Palace walls in India can neither shut misery out nor happiness in. One of the Maharaja's relatives, a man of more than fifty, had no heir. His wife herself proposed that her husband should take a second wife, and she chose her own thirteen-year-old niece to fill the post. A stranger might make trouble, she explained, but a member of the family— and especially a child like this—would not upset her position in the household. She met the situation with dignity, yet it was whispered that when the new bride was taken away on a journey, while she remained behind, it was a bitter cup for her to drink.

I once spent an hour with these co-wives. The first wife had grown plump, like most zenana women, for want of exercise. She held her green silk sari well pulled over her head and closed in front of her face, a big black eye shining out through a small aperture. The second wife sat on a gilded blue velvet sofa. Her sharp little face was plainly visible through a transparent orange silk veil hanging all about her. Her thin arms were decorated with heavy gold bracelets, so heavy they had to be held up by chains attached to the shoulders. A pearl necklace and a large pearl head ornament gleamed through her orange veil. Pearl drops dangled from her ears, and a diamond stud sparkled in her left nostril. She did not wear a sari, but a silk and velvet bodice and a full flaring skirt with a band of gold brocade that made it stand out stiffly around her slippered feet and chased silver anklets.

What did these two feel within the recesses of their own hearts? The one who saw herself replaced as she was beginning to grow old by this new favorite decked in dazzling splendor treated the child wife with gentle motherliness. The little wife, if she felt an inward shrinking from her marriage, hid her deeper emotions with the trained reserve of the well bred Hindu woman. Married to a man more than four times her age, she was all too likely to pass the greater part of her life in the plain white garment of a widow. Then there would be no more golden jewels, no more silken splendor. Perhaps she was too young to think of this. I hoped so.

Such ill assorted marriages occur most frequently in the cases of rich old men who use their money to bribe parents to sell them their young daughters, but the villages of India do not specialize in rich old men. Practically all the husbands and wives I met were as suitably matched in age as husbands and wives are anywhere in the West. Old ones had grown old together. Children were still children together. But I did come upon a few unusual cases of marriage in which the girls were from four to six years older than their husbands. The fathers had offered tempting dowries for the privilege of marrying their daughters into families of high standing.

On a day after Pachperwa had been set astir by news that the daughter-in-law of a neighboring Rajput thekedar, an eighteen-year-old girl whose husband was a boy of fourteen, had jumped into a well, Dukhi and an old sadhu of the village happened to be sitting on my maidan. The sadhu remarked sagely: "Such a marriage between an old girl and a young boy is bad. If the girl is nine, the boy should be eleven or twelve. If the girl is twelve, the boy should be fourteen." Ordinarily the father, according to the common saying, looks to the family position of the future son-in-law, the mother to his financial position—she wants assurance that her daughter will be well taken care of—and the girl herself to his youth and physical charm.

Dukhi could speak of marriages with authority. In spite of changing times, the barber is still a traditional matchmaker in India, and Dukhi boasted that he was responsible for at least a thousand marriages. I was surprised to learn that in our community a Mohammedan *Hajjam* was as likely to arrange a wedding between two Hindu families as his confrère, the Hindu *Nau*, was to arrange them between Mussulmans. For his trouble the barber, who also attends the bridegroom and makes himself generally useful during the wedding, receives a small money present and a share in the feast. A poor family may give no more than a rupee or two, but from a rich one he may receive as much as twenty. Since even a fair-sized village like Pachperwa is not likely to have more than ten or fifteen weddings in a year, and perhaps none at all if there has been a crop failure, the barber scarcely grows rich as a marriage broker.

The barber, according to Dukhi, inherits his clientèle from his father. Naturally he knows the community he serves very well. The barber's wife, moreover, in her capacity of hairdresser to the women, also commands strategic sources of inside information. It is strictly against custom for a boy and girl of the same village to marry, a wise precaution against consanguineous marriage. Hence the barbers' panchayat becomes a matrimonial clearing house in which husbands of one village are offered for brides of another. A barber tells the father of a suitable boy that he knows of a rich and virtuous family of the proper caste in which there is a beautiful girl of marriageable age. Dukhi acknowledged with a burst of laughter that literal truth did not play a part in preliminary negotiations. Having interested the boy's parents, the barber then visits the girl's household and describes the boy's qualifications in equally superlative language. Many questions are asked, and sometimes special stipulations are made: an educated family may insist on an educated daughter-in-law, or emphasis is placed on a light-colored skin. There are bargaining points on both sides. If a widower is seeking a second wife, he is not so desirable a husband, and the bride's family can offer less dowry. If the girl is unattractive, or if either the girl or the boy have physical defects, compensation must be offered in some form, usually of financial bearing.

After the preliminary points have been agreed upon, a meeting is arranged between the parents or between the two fathers, but before the final settlement can be reached, the important matter of horoscopes must be examined. A pundit is summoned to compare the horoscopes of the boy and girl. There are thirty-six points in which these may have possible agreement, and it is considered essential that they should agree in at least thirty-two of them. Marital affinity is believed to rest on physical fitness, the governing aspects of health or temperament, qualities of character, compatible levels of spiritual evolution and devotedness. All these factors are accepted in the Hindu view as being established at birth for each individual. If the exact moment of the birth of each party is known, the astrologer of the village—generally the village pundit or priest—is able to work out the affinities according to his tables and declare whether the proposed marriage is auspicious or not. Marriages are classified, on the basis of the various possible combinations, as best, second best, third best, bad, very bad, and fatal. A marriage is possible under the first three classifications, but no Hindu family would risk marriage if the horoscopes indicated one of the unpropitious combinations. In this event, there is nothing to do but begin the search for a suitable mate all over again.

In most cases the girl's parents take the initiative. According to the Hindu scriptures, parents have not fulfilled their duty as parents if they have not arranged for the marriage of their daughters. There is much less concern over a son's marriage. For one thing, if he belongs to one of the "twice-born" castes, he is supposed to go to school, and age is less vital as far as he is concerned than for a daughter. He can be married at any time. But his marriage will bring money into the family, and for this reason the family barber on the boy's side keeps a watchful eye out for good "prospects."

When all has progressed smoothly, when the financial arrangements have been settled and the horoscopes have been found to agree, the pundit is again consulted and the actual day and hour of the wedding are fixed. First, however, the betrothal ceremony takes place. The girl is not present. The pundit representing her family, and possibly her father or brother, will go to the bridegroom's house, bearing half the dowry. The bridegroom receives a *tika*, or mark upon the forehead, which seals the betrothal. Once the tika ceremony has been performed, the wedding is obligatory.

Yet all rules have their exceptions. As I was sitting, one May afternoon, under the big pakar tree with the Tahsildar, while he tried cases, a strange drama began to unfold, involving three families of the Ahir caste. In each family were a son and a daughter, and the six children had been paired off to be married. The weddings were scheduled to take place that very evening, and of course all the preliminary ceremonies had been held long before.

One of the three fathers presented himself excitedly before the Tahsildar at about five o'clock to complain that the father of the girl who was to marry his son had suddenly refused at the last moment to permit the marriage to take place. The girl's father, in the offing, stepped forward to explain that the boy had fits and was dumb. The other vigorously denied this, producing a witness who testified that the boy was perfectly normal. Knowing that the statement of a village witness fluctuates for all sorts of reasons, the Tahsildar promptly sent a messenger to fetch the boy, and the little fellow, perhaps twelve years old, was soon produced. He replied to the first question put to him by the Tahsildar, showing that he was not dumb, but immediately some sort of fit took possession of him and he refused to say another word. With a queer unfocused look, he simply stared at his own hands. It was obvious to us all that he was an imbecile. The girl's father triumphantly claimed that he should not be forced to marry his daughter to an idiot, even if the tika ceremony had been performed. The Tahsildar, orthodox to the bone, acknowledged the sacredness of the betrothal ceremony, but at the same time he was unwilling to countenance such a marriage and decided against the boy's father. Meanwhile the third father had sided with the first. He now insisted that he was no longer willing to marry his daughter to the second man's son. Accordingly, two of the weddings were canceled, and the only one that came off was that of the first man's daughter and the third man's son. It was sunset when the matter was settled, almost time for the wedding processions to begin.

In rural areas where the population remains rooted in traditional villages, a matchmaking canvass of the surrounding district is not difficult, though the fact that many castes restrict marriages to a particular subcaste, or even to branches within the subcaste, complicates the whole matter. Marriages are almost universally arranged between families of villages not more than a hundred miles apart. Cities, with their growing populations, present a new problem and meet it in a characteristically new fashion. Nearly all the newspapers, including the English dailies, carry a column of matrimonial advertisements. They are inserted by matrimonial agencies on behalf of clients or by families themselves. In a matter-of-fact way the salient points are set down. A man may advertise for a wife, specifying the caste and giving the age limits between which he will be satisfied. He will state his own salary or income and, if he is a university graduate, that important fact will certainly appear. A girl's family will present the qualifications of the bride they have to offer. Invariably she is "beautiful, educated, and accomplished," and a husband "of good family" is desired for her.

Even a casual study of these notices reveals the changes creeping into the supposedly inflexible social customs of India. I have read advertisements in which it was definitely stated, "No objection to a virgin widow." Not many years ago such a thing would have been unthinkable. "No restrictions as to caste" was an even more remarkable statement. It was perhaps made by an individual or family outside caste.

Affiliated families may not need the help of a barber or a newspaper to marry off younger members. As long as the supply of sons lasts in one household and daughters in another, the problem solves itself. In the Peshkar's family, for example, such joint marriages had been arranged. But he liked to tell how he himself had actually chosen his own wife.

Because of the family tie, he could visit in his sister-in-law's household. When there was talk of his marriage to a younger sister, he made an excuse to go and inspect the proposed bride, and he came to the conclusion that he preferred another sister. After much family discussion he was permitted to marry the one of his choice. "So my marriage was American style," he said with a laugh. The sacred duty of finding a husband for a daughter or a sister falls upon the head of the household, and the fulfillment of this responsibility is a perfectly legitimate reason for asking for a leave of absence from any sort of work. Once an educated Indian gentleman in government railway service, riding in the same compartment with me on the way to Balrampur, quite seriously informed me he was taking a month's leave of absence from his official duties because he had to search a husband for his sister.

The much-remarked high cost of Hindu weddings is practically all borne by the bride's household, and a wedding all too generally plunges the bride's father into debt. It is not income that determines the amount of the dowry to go with the bride, but the social position of her family. The bridegroom is expected to present the bride with jewelry, but her father must also endow his daughter with ornaments, in addition to paying the stipulated dowry to the bridegroom's father. The father of the bride must also bear the wedding expenses. The *stri-dhan*—the bride's jewelry—remains her own property for life and can never be taken from her. She herself can, however, and often gladly does, sacrifice her inheritance on the altar of family need. A mother donates her jewelry to pay for her son's education or sells it to save her husband in a financial crisis. Countless contributions of jewelry for the national cause have been offered to Gandhi by women in his audiences whenever he has toured India.

The fixed necessity of securing a husband for a daughter naturally raises the cost. A desirable son-in-law for whom there is lively competition fetches a very high price.

One of the Balrampur estate officials, a Vaisya, drawing a salary of 200 rupees a month, confessed he could not marry his daughters under 4,000 rupees apiece. Since he had five of them, two of whom yet remained to be married, his problem presented startling difficulties. I wondered how he could possibly spend almost two years' income on a single wedding and yet manage to live. His answer was that he had borrowed, mortgaged his property, and spent the dowries brought into the family by two daughters-in-law.

Another estate employee, a Kayasth, was a member of a family all but ruined by the father's foolish passion for alchemy and a daughter's marriage. It was hard to believe that the mild old gentleman whom I met two or three times had actually spent twenty years of his life and ten thousand rupees trying to turn copper into gold. A university graduate had been desired as a husband for the daughter, and university graduates cost at least ten thousand rupees. To obtain one the family property, consisting of three houses, had been heavily mortgaged. Fortunately there still remained one unmarried son, also a university graduate, through whom the family fortunes were somewhat restored. I received a pink and perfumed invitation, printed in gold, to the wedding, performed near Lucknow with sumptuous splendor.

On a still more ostentatious scale the Peshkar's family celebrated a wedding at their ancestral home a mile from Balrampur. The family was land poor and heavily in debt, but because of prestige—they were related to the Maharani of Balrampur—the wedding was conducted with that lavish extravagance for which the Rajputs of Oudh are particularly noted. It cost 30,000 rupees. A thousand guests were invited, for whom tents had to be set up and food provided. Thousands of cooking pots were supplied. The most famous dancer of Lucknow entertained the guests for a bagatelle of 3,000 rupees. A band was brought on from Lucknow. A special train facilitated the arrival and departure of guests.

In this instance the money was furnished by a rich uncle, formerly a tahsildar of Pachperwa.

The most costly wedding of all, however, was that of the Maharaja's sister, celebrated after my departure, shortly before famine swept the whole of the Gonda district. It cost the estate twelve lakhs—more than four hundred thousand dollars. The irony of the situation was that this drain was as inescapable, under existing conditions of social pressure, as the famine itself, to the relief of which thirteen lakhs were contributed by the estate. The strain of marrying a daughter and protecting her rank at all costs is the principal reason why girls are not always welcome in Hindu families. It is also an explanation of the female infanticide which used to be practised among certain castes in India. Exposure of infant girls was practised particularly among the Rajputs, who observe extremely rigid rules, forbidding the slightest social inequality in marrying their girls. Infanticide is now, happily, a thing of the past. Surreptitious instances that come to light are no more frequent than the cases of abandoned infants in the West.

One of the reforms most advocated for modern India is a reduction of unnecessary expenditure for weddings. In Rajputana an organization of wealthy Rajput families has agreed to keep the expenditure for a wedding within one year's income of the bride's father. From time to time some courageous family of established position will attract publicity for the reform movement by donating to charity what has been saved by a simple wedding. It is largely at the top, among the educated people, that social changes of this sort are beginning tentatively to be made, but in time they will make their influence felt among the masses.

Yet where life is pared down to such meager standards as it is for the Indian millions, the very expense makes the wedding acquire tremendous significance. No individual or nation is without its special form of extravagance and self-indulgence. What seems silly or futile to one is a favorite indulgence—almost a necessity—to another. American wedding customs, as I once tried to explain them in Pachperwa, deeply shocked my listeners. The flexibility struck them as utterly lacking in dignity, and the Hindu wedding, with all its elaborate ritual and prescribed traditions, seemed infinitely the more civilized.

I was brought up suddenly against a consideration of the fundamental ideals of the Hindu marriage. To begin with, Hindus do not look upon marriage as a private affair in which the happiness of two particular individuals is of first importance. Marriage is viewed as a social institution evolved for the purpose of safeguarding the permanence and stability of the family. Therefore society retains the right to make the laws governing marriage and divorce. Chance and whim, which play so large a part in Western matings, are looked on askance in India as a very uncertain foundation upon which to build the marriage relation. If marriage is to depend on love, and love depends on chance and whim, it may very well happen that the chance will never be favorable or the whim may change. Love is as integral a part of Hindu married life as of Western married life, but with this difference: in India love follows, rather than precedes, the actual marriage ceremony.

The real flower of enduring love must always spring from a common understanding growing out of experiences and responsibilities shared together and the emotions these give rise to. Through unselfishness, devotion, and service called out in the marriage relation, the individual rises in spiritual perception. For this reason, marriage offers an opportunity for realization of an ideal quite independent of the possible failure of one member of the partnership. India does not absolve either husband or wife from continuing to strive for the ideal, whatever the shortcomings of the other may be. Against the Western ideal of dynamic self-expression stands the Indian ideal of dynamic renunciation—not pallid negation, but willingness to sacrifice the smaller for the greater end. It is an austere ideal from which the young West is likely to turn away.

This Hindu ideal of marriage is not to be understood as some remote speculation drawn from the realm of abstract philosophy, but as a warm and living perception close to the Indian mind and heart. It has many times been put into conscious words for me by educated Hindus. Many more times it has been borne in upon me from entirely unconscious sources. The epic poetry belongs as much to the illiterate masses as to the scholars of India, and under a village tree or within the mud walls of a humble village home, all the trials and triumphs of life are vividly projected in stories of heroes and heroines, both real and imaginary, peopling this ancient land. These furnish a never ending source of instruction and inspiration, keeping the ancient ideals ever fresh in the heart.

Abhorrence for the practice of child marriage outweighs everything else in the Western mind in considering the whole question of the Hindu marriage. It is commonly forgotten how recently our own grandmothers were accustomed to marry young. The circumstance that in a tropical climate physical maturity takes place much earlier than in a cold climate is also overlooked. And the statistical fact that actually 60 per cent of Indian girls are not yet married at fifteen is wilfully ignored. Nor do child brides, except in rare cases, go to live with their husbands immediately upon marriage. Years may pass before consummation. The older marriage state for women in the West has come about primarily from no cause more sacrosanct than education. When compulsory education was introduced in the free countries of the West a little more than a century ago, a change in the economic position of women occurred, and the marriage age automatically rose, as it will rise in India when the same "modernization" takes place.

Everything in India must sooner or later be referred back to the Vedas, and those who have become most vividly aware of the drain on the vitality of the nation exercised through child marriage have ceaselessly pointed out that the Vedic marriage texts clearly show that the Aryan marriage of earlier times was consummated only between physically mature persons. The rule that a girl was to be given in marriage before the age of puberty was a subsequent innovation. The Brahmin teachers and lawmakers, always seeking to interpret life in its finer terms of spirit, saw that chastity—self-restraint—was inseparable from the concept of the highest type of union. To protect women's honor, child marriage was sanctioned in post-Vedic religious codes and gradually put into practice among the higher ranks of the Hindu population.

It was not, however, until the Mohammedan power was established in India in the fourteenth century that child marriage attained anything like wide prevalence. Large numbers of conquering Mussulmans, most of them soldiers, were a constant threat to the safety of Indian women. Hindu fathers saw to it that their daughters were married as soon as possible, to protect them from falling into the hands of the conquerors. To religious, historic, and economic reasons, must be added still another. The family and not the individual being the social unit in India, the wife has to merge herself into her husband's family. Obviously the adjustment to the new environment is less painful if she still has the flexibility of youth.

The going-away of a bride is a moment of poignant intensity. When she puts on the dignity of a wife she loses the freedom of the child. In her own village she has run about unveiled. Now, in the first few years to come, her life will be subject to rigid rules of propriety.

A few covered green litters of departing or arriving brides passed along the road in front of the Happy House. Sometimes a shrouded bullock cart was substituted. These passages had not the glamour of the bridegrooms' processions. Often, very often, there was a sound of wailing—no real tears, perhaps, but a conventional lamentation, *crescendo, diminuendo, crescendo, diminuendo*, from the women accompanying the bride's palanquin or riding with her in the curtained cart. At the station the palanquin would be brought alongside a zenana intermediate or third-class compartment. Curtains would be held protectingly, but a fleeting vision could be had of a red or yellow sari as the bride climbed into the compartment. As the train glided out of the station the shrill wailing of the bride mingled with the wailing good-byes of relatives and friends.

The tears are not because she is going to a life of unalleviated sorrow, oppression, and unhappiness, but because of the finality of the departure. Her own parents will never spend one night under her new roof. In the Aryan tradition a woman is given in marriage, not sold—even the acceptance of hospitality from her husband's family might be interpreted as a bride price. She herself will return but rarely to her parents' home; in some cases, never. She is saying good-bye to all that is known and familiar, to cross an irrevocable threshold.

CHAPTER XV

Mothers of India

FOR a foreigner to meet—much less to know—Indian women is by no means easy. For a foreign man, it is practically impossible. Purdah customs stand in the way, and language is also a barrier. Wherever one travels in India some Indian man will turn up who can speak English well enough for all practical purposes, but outside the cities one finds very few women who know anything but their own vernacular. Another obstacle is that the women are far more conservative and orthodox than the men. But in a village the women naturally are more accessible. As soon as I had acquired an elementary use of Hindustani I found most of the barriers down.

Purdah—seclusion of women—was not adopted in India until after the Mussulmans introduced the custom, and it did not really take root until the commencement of the Mogul period, in the sixteenth century. Even to-day it is practised much more extensively by Indian Mussulmans than by Hindus. The stronghold of purdah is the Northwest Frontier Province, the Punjab, the United Provinces, and Bengal, where Mussulmans make up a large part of the population, if not an overwhelming majority. In Bombay and Gujarat and southern India purdah is not generally practised. Among Hindus, again, it is only the higher castes or the rich who keep their women in seclusion. One of the great blessings of poverty in rural India is that village women, millions of them, go about quite freely, helping their husbands in the fields or tending the little shops, bargaining vociferously on market day, going to the village tank to bathe, journeying endless times to the well, making pilgrimages to holy places.

Where families are well off purdah women are not denied the privileges of education. There have been and are to-day purdah princesses noted for their intelligent and able statesmanship. Many Hindu women have become Sanskrit scholars. The modern high-caste girl, if she is not permitted her freedom, usually has a chance to attend a zenana school if her parents can afford the tuition, or a tutor in the home will teach her at the same time with her brothers. She may even have an English governess and learn French and English. Fashionable purdah parties break the monotony of the old seclusion.

Women's associations of one sort or another are becoming popular wherever intelligent leaders have undertaken the initial work of organization. The *samitis*, as they are called, with their lectures, classes, social service, and training in cottage industries, have been rapidly spreading over India in the past decade. Important subjects like child marriage and education for women are discussed with passionate earnestness, and at national conferences leading women come together for the purpose of organizing social welfare and educational work. Last but not least the range of interest has been widened to include politics.

Sarojini Naidu, at one time President of the Indian National Congress, elected Mayor of Bombay, appointed by Gandhi third in line to succeed him in the event of his arrest as leader of the movement of nonviolent civil resistance, and herself imprisoned in consequence of her activities, is perhaps the best known woman in India. But there are many others who have taken their places beside her. Mrs. Gandhi, faithful, brave, self-sacrificing, shows what the Indian woman can accomplish in her own quiet way. In Gandhi's big meetings provision has always been made for a purdah section, and the nonviolent program advocated by Gandhi makes a strong appeal to women. Shrouded though they may be, hundreds of thousands of Indian women have listened approvingly to political addresses in the past decade. Indian women marching in nationalist processions, taking part in salt demonstrations, addressing huge mass meetings, picketing liquor and foreign cloth shops and going to prison are portentous signs of the increasingly active part women are destined to play in Indian national life.

In the ordinary poverty-stricken Indian village the woman who observes purdah has few or no opportunities for leading anything but a narrowly restricted existence. She goes nowhere, unless on a rare pilgrimage or a visit to her parents. She sees no one except her immediate family and a few neighbors. Year in and year out the stream of life flows imperceptibly on, or flows not at all, within the narrow compass of bare mud walls. Fortunately, in and around Pachperwa, purdah was practised by only a microscopic fraction of the community—the wives of the small officials, of the Marwari bazar traders, of the thekedars, of Brahmins, and a few Banias.

Though the Marwari ladies could not come and see me, from time to time I had brief glimpses of them. My first call was an informal one by way of a back door. I had been visiting our little Sanskrit school. On the way home I noticed a small open door in the back wall of Nattu Lal's courtyard. With smiles and friendly gestures a woman invited me inside. She was the wife of Nattu Lal, one of the big cloth traders of the village. Her daughter-in-law was spinning at a low wheel of dark, polished wood, turning the wheel with one hand while with the other she deftly twisted the carded cotton fluff beside her into thread.

Mrs. Lal took my hand affectionately, beamed with pleasure and drew me down beside her on a *charpai*. How long was I going to stay in Pachperwa? Why had I come? Was it really true I had no husband? Why had my parents not married me? How old was I? How had my parents let me come so far alone? Personal questions show interest in a visitor, and in India it is rude not to ask them. She wanted to tell me, too, that she had already seen me. When once I had come to the cloth shop in front, she had peeked through a crack at me, but of course she could not speak to me then. Also she had heard all about my house, and she was filled with curiosity to see it. There it was, five minutes' away, but a foot-thick wall stood between, and Mrs. Lal behind the wall could only picture in her imagination the wonders outside.

On a rare occasion when the Marwari women came out of their seclusion I was privileged to be present. Jokhi Lal sent word by his one-eyed servant that there was to be a puja for Sitalamai, the smallpox goddess, at the shrine in the New Bazar at eight in the morning. I arrived just in time to see fifteen or twenty women and as many children emerging from a side door of Jokhi Lal's house, with a great clinking of anklets. Over the heads of all the women and drawn down in front so that nobody could even so much as peek at their faces were brilliant-colored opaque veils. All of them wore long full skirts and long-sleeved bodices. The babies, eyes charmingly shadowed with kohl, were bedecked with gay velvet caps, gold-embroidered, or vermilion or purple silk bonnets of a meretricious pattern borrowed from the West. The little girls looked like miniature replicas of their mothers.

Bearing trays of food, the brilliant colored procession moved across the strip of sunlight to the leafy shade of the shrine. Holy water was sprinkled and food was presented to the goddess, together with some nim leaves, sacred to her. Having appeased the dread deity responsible for the deaths of so many children in the first hot months of every year, the procession clinked back through the little door.

Jokhi Lal extended me an invitation—or was it permission?—to go with the women, but by this time the door was already closed. An old servant opened it cautiously and conducted me into a narrow passage. There he left me while he went to announce my arrival. I could hear a great buzz.

When at last I was permitted to enter the courtyard I found all the women as completely swathed behind their rainbow-colored veils as they had been in the open bazar. This strictly orthodox group treated me almost exactly as if I had been a man. In their eyes there was not much difference.

Target of all their hidden, inquisitive eyes, I felt painfully uncomfortable. My own clothes, amid all this silk and brocade, struck me as immodestly skimpy and commonplace. My uncovered face seemed a bit shameless, my absence of jewelry almost a reproach, and I realized that my hat could not possibly disguise my short hair. In spite of the veils I caught glimpses of nose rings with pearl or diamond drops, jeweled collars, heavy gold bracelets, and other valuable ornaments. In contrast I could not help noticing the small, mean courtyard surrounded by mud walls, dhotis drying on the overhanging thatch, brass lotas and water jars standing about, a string bedstead or two tilted carelessly against a wall. Conversation did not progress well. I felt impassable chasms between us—but my camera saved the day. Each woman wanted to be photographed with and without her children, but each insisted on holding her veil as tight as ever in front of her face. There was nothing to do but patiently photograph their clothes.

The Marwari women were at least strengthened by numbers, though their soft fatness showed how much they needed healthy exercise. Their houses joined, and doubtless they saw one another from time to time. Their own households were large, and there were numerous daughters-in-law and plenty of children. But other women in the village who observed purdah were worse off.

The Thanadar's wife, who was a victim of tuberculosis, often complained of the general conditions requiring women of her social rank to remain invisible. There she lived, month in and month out, deprived of the companionship of any other woman at all, her whole world bounded by the four dilapidated walls of one tiny courtyard. "My wife is weep-

ing because she has not seen you for such a long time," the
Thanadar used to report at least weekly. Melons, oranges,
mangoes, pan, would be hospitably produced whenever I
dropped in, and little Talu stood on one side of my chair
and little Dhuni on the other, to peel the oranges or slice
the melons. "You are so free," she once remarked thoughtfully, "and you can earn your own living. But what should
we do if we did not have our husbands to feed us? We should
starve." She believed in education, for girls as well as boys,
and every afternoon one of the teachers from the village
school came to instruct Talu, who showed me proudly how
she could now both write and read. For herself there were
no diversions of any sort. At times, especially in the hot
months when she lay gasping on her cot in the stifling court,
the senseless cruelty of purdah, in a village of all places,
oppressed me heavily.

Next door lived the Mohammedan *munshi* of the police
station and his childless wife of twenty-five. She, too, observed purdah—confined to a house of one room and court,
shared with four goats. She had not been outside this house
for more than two years, and she and the Thanadar's wife
next door had never even seen each other. How she ate me
up with her eyes and patted my hand and begged me over
and over to come as often as I could! And there was the wife
of the Brahmin constable, who once sent for me. I knew the
minute I saw her, lying on her bed with great dark circles
around her eyes and with wrists burning my fingers, that
she had not long to endure. Within a month permanent
release from purdah came for her.

Another of my purdah acquaintances in the village was
Haweli Singh's wife. She lived just back of the Old Bazar
in a two-roomed house with gaping cracks where doors hung
askew. The Singhs were from Gujarat, where purdah is
not usually practised, but since the better class people followed the custom in Oudh, the wife of Haweli, as of his
younger brother who lived with him, had to remain shut

up in Pachperwa. When they went home every summer they immediately came out of their enforced seclusion, which they disliked thoroughly.

In spite of the friendly welcome to their houses the village women extended me—those who observed purdah as well as those who did not—they were all extremely reticent about calling upon me. I was all the more astonished, therefore, to receive a surprise visit from two women late one night. Certain queer sounds drew me out to investigate. There was Mahabali Singh, the fat tradesman who had lived many years in Trinidad, behaving in a mysterious way. When I caught sight of two swathed forms standing a long way off under the trees I understood the reason. He summoned them, and the women scurried quickly into the shelter of my house. It was the dark night of the moon, they explained, and so they could come to pay me a call.

It was a great adventure. Mahabali's wife was a kindly faced woman who spoke a little English and who was never tired of telling me how fine Trinidad was. "Not dirty, like this place." She and Mahabali had very clear ideas about the superiority of Western medicine and the disadvantages of purdah. "Purdah ladies get sick," she repeated many times. The toe rings of her companion, the wife of a nephew, fascinated me. She had one on each toe, and all were joined together with little silver chains. Over the instep were silver plaques fringed with tiny balls. In addition, she must have been wearing at least twenty pairs of anklets, many thin ones and several heavy ones of worked silver. Hindu women, except princesses and sometimes vulgarly ostentatious Marwaris, never wear gold on their feet, since gold is reverenced and is not to be defiled by contact with the feet. Mahabali's wife, however, carried off the honors in jewelry. She was adorned with a long necklace of American gold eagles! I counted twenty-six of them, and a double one at the end—a fortune in rupees! This necklace and Mahabali's battered old Stetson redeemed American prestige in Pachperwa.

Of other purdah women I met, there were those of one

or two goldsmith households, of the Patwari's family, the wives of some rich Mohammedan thekedars and many others who came in covered bullock carts or by *palki*, seeking help for their ills. Among those I never saw, though they were my nearest neighbors, were the Doctor's wife, the Jamadar's wife, and the Tahsildar's wife, who once came from Balrampur to spend two weeks at the tahsil, when her new daughter-in-law was ceremoniously brought home.

Except for the purdah women—and these, after all, were exceptions—the life and interests of the village women were no more circumscribed than the life of the whole community. If the women could not read, neither could most of the men. If they spent their days in the fulfillment of small tasks, what else were their husbands and sons doing? In the ceremonies of family life, however, which are so vital to the Hindu, in the stark realities of sickness or famine, of injustices to be suffered, in the joys of human relationships, in the serene pursuit of the ideal of service and sacrifice, which India holds high above rights and privileges, the women played their essential parts.

The custom of sons bringing their wives into their parents' households means that usually there are a number of women to share the domestic tasks. In the patriarchal home of Teja Khan forty persons were fed daily. A man of his position had plenty of servants, but his wife and daughters-in-law, like other Indian women, would never have dreamed of delegating the cooking to servants. The Indian wife takes extreme pride in her ability to prepare pleasing dishes, and many times these women of the higher social classes sent me presents of food they themselves had prepared. Even for those living on a bare margin of subsistence, there will be occasional feasts in which a woman can display her art. Purchase of supplies is also within the woman's purlieu.

The care of the house is simplified by the absence of furniture, rugs, books, and ornaments. Sprinkling takes the place of dusting, a fresh coat of mud that of sweeping.

Water for cooking, drinking, and washing must be fetched from the well. Pots and pans must be scoured. The village woman, squatting by her doorway and polishing a brass drinking vessel or plate with earth, ashes, straw, and water is a familiar sight. It is the woman, too, who husks the rice and grinds wheat or maize into flour. The thumping of husking poles and the monotonous hum of grindstones are sounds inseparable from village activity.

To the lot of women and girls—it is one of the first tasks into which little village girls are initiated—falls the unpleasant drudgery of manufacturing the endless dung cakes used for cooking. The dung must be collected, mixed with straw, and plastered against a sunny wall to dry, then stacked in mounds. It is filthy work and economically unsound, since the manure is five times more valuable as fertilizer than as fuel. But what else are the villagers to do? In an estate like Balrampur they are not entitled to cut wood, and the cost of charcoal or coke is at present prohibitive, though F. L. Brayne, formerly Deputy Commissioner of Gurgaon District in the Punjab, who has made a practical study of village reconstruction problems, believes that coal, which is plentiful in India, could be supplied for cooking purposes to villagers at a cost within their means.

Household labor, bearing and rearing of children, and tending of the sick do not leave women with time heavy on their hands. They have comparatively little sewing to occupy them, since fashion has conveniently stabilized draped garments and the tailors monopolize the shirt-making industry, but jackets, bodices, quilts, caps, and similar articles may be made at home. I used to see one or two of the Marwari women embroidering velvet caps for their sons or veils for themselves with gold and silver thread. Devi Prasad's sisters had somehow picked up the art of crocheting lace. "For our petticoats," they replied when I asked the use. Petticoats were a stylish innovation. Few village women wore them.

Fine basketry afforded another outlet for inherent artistic

talents. The baskets, of patterns and shapes often very elaborate, were made of bright-hued grasses which the women dyed. Baskets were constantly being offered me as presents from friendly villagers. Women's work also included the painting or drawing of conventionalized designs on floors and walls for domestic ceremonies and the dyeing of saris. But the real self-expression of the Indian woman is in living the old ideals of womanhood no home is too poor to inherit.

Behind customs easy to condemn from a superficial standpoint is almost invariably a basic ideal to which one may well do reverence, and this Indian woman, so frequently an object of patronizing pity in the eyes of the West, becomes transfigured when the point of view is shifted from the details of what she does to what she is.

The bride of fourteen or fifteen, entering her husband's home, is welcomed by her mother-in-law and all the women of the household with singing, and by her husband in the touching words of the ancient Aryan ritual: "O bride, live thou long in the house of thy husband and enjoy thou the companionship of thy husband evermore. May there be happiness in our home for both bipeds and quadrupeds." But India reserves homage for something deeper than the transient charm and grace of youth. Love and affection the bride may have, but honor and respect will be reserved for her later years.

At the time of the Swing Festival in August, symbolic of Krishna's playtime, I happened to be in the house of an orthodox Hindu family in Balrampur. The house was overflowing with women, too many to count. Crowded into the square court were the grandmother and her daughters, the youngest of whom was only nine years old, the wives of at least two sons and several neighbor women. The swing was suspended from the veranda roof, a substantial affair big enough to hold four or five of us at a time. The women insisted that I share the delights of swinging with them, and they looked at me with pitying amazement when after ten minutes of dizzy flying back and forth, I begged to be let off.

On the floor against the wall was the new bride of the oldest son—a second wife, the first having died the preceding year. Her pale gauze sari enfolded her like a golden cloud. Through it glinted many gold bracelets and elaborate ornaments. The soles of her little bare feet were charmingly rose-tinted. But the fourteen-year-old bride took no part in the festivities. In the mad swinging, the saris of the others flew back from their hair, but the bride's sari remained discreetly drawn down over her face as she huddled against the wall. The others chattered and laughed and sang until my head ached, but she spoke not a word. It is unbecoming for a well bred Hindu bride to talk in the presence of elders or to uncover her face before them.

A bride shows great deference to her husband's parents, the higher the caste, the more exacting the etiquette. A Brahmin bride is expected to go to her mother-in-law after dinner, greet her by saying, *"Pailagan!"*—"I touch your feet!"—and then massage her legs gently. The same greeting is used by members of lower castes in addressing Brahmins, or by any younger Brahmin to an older one. Or the new wife, sitting down at her mother-in-law's feet, will slowly lift the colored border of her sari to her forehead three times, in a beautiful and gracious gesture. These are the old ways of India.

With her father-in-law and her husband's older brothers, a young wife must observe strict propriety of manner. She will not even speak in their presence, and she will never appear with her face uncovered. They for their part treat her with prescribed formality. For self-evident reasons in a joint household, the rule has been established that an older brother may not even touch the wife of a younger one, nor so much as let his shadow fall upon her or hers upon him. The bride is subject to other restrictions. She is not permitted to cook or serve rice to the older members of the family, nor are offerings of prepared food acceptable from her in the ritual of worship. During the daytime she and her husband are not expected to meet or talk much together, far less make any noticeable display of sentiment for each other. From the Hindu point of view this would be the height of bad taste.

In all these prohibitions and duties the bride will have been duly instructed by her own mother and the older women in her household before she left home. If anything is amiss in her training, her mother-in-law will undertake to teach her, as she would her own daughter, whose place she has taken. The young wife emerges from her period of discipline only when her status changes to that of motherhood. Gradually she then wins greater freedom, until in the end, in her later years, she dominates the household with her influence. Duties and privileges in the Hindu social scheme alter with altering conditions, and the fullness of life is achieved, not in trying to make all stages identical, but in passing from one stage into the next. Variety of relationships and their ritualistic aspect give Indian life a peculiar richness in spite of—or is it because of?—the discipline and restraint from which no individual is ever wholly free.

Motherhood in India is fadeless, and it becomes sanctified with the passing of time. If the Western woman is courted and petted more especially in the first third of her life, the Hindu woman attains a compensating position of dignity and influence in her later years, when her sons literally take the dust of her feet. Youth and beauty draw affection naturally—society does not have to be forced to admire them. Romantic beauty has been celebrated as fervently in the literature of India as in that of any country in the world. But where the social emphasis is on transient physical charm, the individual woman's position can never be secure. By placing the emphasis on tested qualities of character India assures all women a permanent position within the group.

So far as I know, general figures to show at what age Indian women bear their first child do not exist. If there were any such figures I should distrust them. In the villages age does not matter much, and census figures collected by the village chaukidars display a marked predilection for round numbers. Who is to keep track of exact ages? For girls there is a strong tendency to understate ages. If a girl is not yet married, though of marriageable age, the parents are concerned to give out an impression that she is younger than she is. Indian girls are unquestionably more advanced in physical development than Western girls of the same age. Girls of but twelve or thirteen, according to their mothers, invariably looked three or four years older to me. Aside from hospital records—and hospital deliveries are the exception—no reliable information on the subject is available. From personal experience I can say that out of several hundreds of village mothers I saw, only one was a child mother—a girl of thirteen.

The primitive taboos surrounding birth for Hindus apparently contradict the idea that Hindus really reverence motherhood. Ignorance and poverty seem to me largely responsible for the distressing lack of sanitary care shown the mother. Village houses are small, and it is by no means easy to set aside one room out of two or three for the private use of any one member of the family. Somewhere at the back of the house, as far away as possible, is a tiny room or hut for childbirth. If even this accommodation is lacking, some corner must be used temporarily. When I went to see the sickly week-old baby of one of our goldsmiths I found the mother secluded behind a flimsy screen of dhotis strung across one end of the single room.

The *dais*, or midwives, drawn from among the outcastes, have no medical training or supervision to prepare them for their work. In our district women of the Chamar and Kori castes acted as midwives. The idea of pollution attached to birth is so strong that in the past no Hindu woman of respectable caste would think of serving the community in this capacity, nor would any woman permit a male doctor to officiate at a delivery. An older woman of the household generally attends the mother, but anyone who has anything to do with her during this period is not allowed to prepare food or draw water for the rest of the family. The professional dai remains for from six to twelve days, when her place is taken by a washerwoman—one degree higher in the social scale. For the birth of a first child the young mother almost invariably returns to her own home, where her own mother, with the assistance of the midwife, can be counted upon to care for her to the best of her limited ability.

Within the dark out-room are no conveniences or sanitary provisions of any sort. The midwife wears her oldest and filthiest clothes. The expectant mother may lie on a string bed, if the family can afford to donate a bed to the cause and throw it away afterward. More generally she lies on the ground, an explanation of why so many women die of pneumonia.

The ignorant methods of the dais are responsible for the high mortality among both mothers and new-born infants. The instrument most commonly used for severing the umbilical cord is the ordinary *hansiya,* or sickle. It is a carrier of tetanus, which causes many infant deaths. Villagers know from sad experience that the twelfth day is often fatal to a new-born child, but they do not know why. Their own way of warding off disaster, as well as of celebrating birth, is to employ some one to beat a drum at the door. The noise is supposed to frighten away *bhuts*—evil spirits —or any other perverted creatures eager to do mischief to the helpless infant. When a son was born to the Jamadar at Pachperwa the whole tahsil was in an uproar. Two drummers were employed to keep up a constant noise in his compound day and night, and the Peshkar fired his rifle a few times.

Here was a good opportunity to obtain first-hand information on the subject of village midwives. I sent for the dai, who turned out to be a young woman of the Kori caste, considerably cleaner and more intelligent than I had expected her to be. It seemed that Pachperwa boasted two dais, each handling about seventy births a year. This particular woman, according to her own account, as soon as she had delivered an infant, threw it in the air several times to make it breathe. Then she rubbed it with earth to clean it, oiled it all over, and covered it up. I inquired casually if she made use of a sickle.

"Yes," she replied.

"Do you wash it?"

"Oh, yes!" Such unexpected cleanliness astonished me, until a second thought came.

"Do you wash it before or after using it?"

"After," was the calm reply.

I took my cue from a talk I had had with the district health officer. "Any old thing will do, a stone, a shell, a piece of glass, a grass cutter, if it is properly sterilized beforehand," he had insisted. "All this fine advice about surgical scissors and knives is ridiculous under existing village conditions. The main thing to impress on them is just the idea of sterilization."

"You know how often babies die in the first few days?" I went on. "Well, if you will make a fire and boil water and put the hansiya in and leave it there half an hour, keeping the fire burning all the time, the babies won't die! The babies die because they catch sickness from a dirty hansiya that has been lying on the ground."

"But no one would like me to do it that way," said the dai in a bewildered tone.

"Do they like their sons to die?" I persisted relentlessly. She agreed that they did not. "Very well," I concluded dramatically, "they won't die if you boil the hansiya!"

The Ayah, stalwart champion of my medical knowledge, made the dai repeat my directions word for word. She appeared to be impressed. Nobody else knew this mysterious fact I had imparted to her, she said, and she would tell all the dais in the surrounding villages. Though I did not have any great confidence that the little discourse would do much to change rooted customs, I did feel certain that the next

time a village baby died of lockjaw the midwife would remember what I had said.

A poster tacked up on the wall of my clinical veranda
graphically pictured a dirty midwife and the tragic results
of her ignorance, and beside it hung another poster showing
a model midwife tending a smiling mother and a healthy
baby. The posters were part of the official propaganda being
carried on nowadays in every province to promote infant
welfare work. Training schools for licensed midwives, the
first step toward reform, are slowly coming into existence.
Moreover, the girls now receiving school education are likely
to know a good deal more about elementary medical matters when they grow up than their mothers and to demand better care for themselves at the critical time of childbirth.

What, after all, can be expected from a village midwife
paid from sixteen to thirty-two cents, a few handfuls of
rice and possibly a sari for bringing a baby into this vale
of tears? The standard rate was four annas for a girl and
eight for a boy, the Ayah said. The dai corrected her. It
was eight annas for a girl and a rupee for a boy. The Ayah,
for all the ten children she had borne, was now an old
woman of forty-five, who had not kept up with important
economic changes.

An admiring and affectionate household renders homage
to the Indian baby, as soon as its existence has become a
reality. A high-caste father may not, it is true, see his new
baby or its mother for a month, but once the birth taboo
is removed, the baby begins to wind its little fingers around
his heart. If it is a son, there is reason for special rejoicing.
A son will remain in the family house, share the economic
burdens, and sustain and comfort his parents in their old
age. One day he will light the funeral pyre for his father,
and he will make oblations to the departed ancestors. The
baby receives an astrological name from the family priest
on the twelfth day, but for long it will be known only as
Gold One, Little King, Jewel, Moon, or some such adoring

reference to the infant majesty. The astrological name is reserved for ceremonial purposes. The parents themselves give the child its ordinary name, but Hindu social etiquette forbids naming a child after any elder in the family.

Clothes are mostly dispensed with, but an amulet tied around the neck is essential, and anklets with silver bells and a pair of tiny silver bracelets, lost in the creases of the little wrists, may also be added. Parents often have a superstitious dread of providing anything for a new baby. Even the love of one's own baby can be selfish love, can make one neglect others and forget the worship of the gods. So custom decrees that relatives and friends present the baby with what it needs.

Like most Indian babies, the Peshkar's son at six months was more precocious than a Western baby of the same age. I saw it only once, on the occasion I visited the Peshkar's family home. The four wives of the four brothers were present, as well as the Peshkar himself, before whom the wives were not required to show any particular reticence, since he was the youngest son. I was permitted to hold the baby on my lap. It stood up in an abbreviated lavender jacket and scrutinized me with great kohl-ornamented eyes, quite obviously recognizing me as a different species from any to which it was accustomed. The day was a landmark, pronounced by the pundit auspicious for the baby's first journey beyond the family courtyard, but the Peshkar had lost much of his faith in pundits. He had paid them hundreds of rupees to name auspicious moments for everything in the life of the elder son, and all the little "firsts" of the Hindu baby had been observed with proper ceremonial— the first time it had taken rice, the first time it had its hair cut, and so on—and yet it had died of smallpox. The women might believe in the pundits if they liked.

One of these childhood ceremonies I attended three nights after my arrival in Pachperwa—the ear-piercing puja for Dhuni, the Thanadar's little boy. The ceremony took place

in the courtyard of his house at five in the afternoon, with
a goldsmith, a barber, and a Brahmin officiating. While the
pundit recited his Sanskrit mantras, Dhuni, in a new bronze-
colored satin coat with brass buttons and a green and pink
turban, stoically submitted to the goldsmith's needle. All
the time Talu, his small sister, sat beside him, stuffing sweets
into his mouth. Later we were entertained with fireworks,
music, a great feast and a dramatic performance which
lasted until midnight. Dhuni would never wear earrings, but
presumably his Rajput ancestors had worn them in the past,
and nearly all Hindu children, boys as well as girls, have
their ears pierced at the age of seven or nine. The only
explanation I heard was that it improved the health.

The real power of the Indian mother springs from the
intensity of her devotion to her family and the life of
patient sacrifice she leads. Though the village woman is
ignorant of how to care for her child according to modern
rules of health—she will feed it whenever it cries and give
it wrong things to eat and let it stay up too late—her unselfish devotion leaves an enduring impress on the child. I
recall the voice and expression of one Hindu man telling how
his mother used to fast when there was illness in the family,
as well as regularly two days every month. On these days,
the eleventh of the waxing and waning moon, she would eat
nothing until after the moon had risen. From the top of a
little hill near the house the moon could be seen rising a
quarter of an hour sooner than from the house itself. The
children always watched impatiently for the first silver
gleam above the horizon. Then they would scamper down
the hill shouting, "Mother, Mother, the moon has risen. Now
you can eat." Those fasts, in later years, symbolized for
the son the mother's tender concern and deep religious feeling. Every Hindu cherishes similar memories of his mother.

Over and over again I was struck by the simple dignity
of the Indian woman. I cannot remember ever having seen a
distinctly silly or vain woman in Pachperwa. The graceful

sari drawn over the hair and falling to the bare feet, in its utter simplicity, lends an ineffable dignity to the wearer. Kohl about the eyes, henna-stained palms, or soles tinted with lac, are seen now and then, but neither rouge nor powder. Older women do not try to appear young, and sex vulgarity is peculiarly absent. A woman's pride rests in the fine red line freshly painted each morning in the parting of her hair—sign and symbol of her wifehood.

The wife of one of the estate officials at Balrampur invited me to tea one day. Too orthodox to permit me to use her dishes, she had borrowed the silver tea service from the Maharaja's guest house. She knew no English, and I am unaware whether she could even read or write. What I remember is her concern because her husband was overworking. To meet the pressure he found it necessary to rise at four and go through his file of documents. She, too, rose at four, and busied herself with her household tasks. "How can I rest, knowing that my husband is working so hard?" she asked simply.

By contrast, her own youngest child, little eight-year-old Janki, sang me a bit of modern sophistication picked up from playmates at the zenana school she attended. Her father wrote out the translation:

> *"Dear, teach me a little English and bring me petticoat, gown, hat; it looks odd to wear* langha *and* dupatta, *which are like trappings for an elephant, and I do not like them. Bring me a sari from Germany.*
>
> *I cannot walk now with wooden clogs. Bring me pumps and shoes; get me high-heeled slippers.*
>
> *I cannot bind my hair with threads. They look like snakes, and I am going to tear them up and throw them away. Get me hair ornaments.*
>
> *Heat has annoyed me greatly to-day, and I am so upset that cooking is impossible. Bring food from the hotel. Get me biscuits worth one rupee.*
>
> *I will put on a hat, petticoat and boots and go bicycling. Bring me spectacles.*

> *I cannot walk even ten steps, and I want a motor car
> for driving.*
> *I cannot bear the weight of gold ornaments, and I do
> not like toe rings any more. Get me a wrist-
> watch.*"

And so the demands of modern "civilization" were made,
through countless verses. Janki herself did not wear a
sari. She wore a shapeless little dress trimmed with machine
lace and little stovepipe drawers hanging halfway down her
legs and black shoes and stockings. Janki was "modern."
What, I wondered, would she be like in years to come?

Are Indian women happy? The laws of Manu brought
upon them social restrictions alien to their earlier freedom,
but even Manu, in his dictatorial code, insists that the happiness of women is essential to the well-being of society.
"Where women are honored, there the gods are pleased;
where they are dishonored, religious acts become of no
avail!" "In whatever family the husband is contented with
his wife and the wife with her husband, in that house will
good fortune assuredly abide!" "The house which is cursed
by a woman perishes utterly."

Many times among the village women I came upon acts
of self-effacing love. One woman came to the house day
after day, leading her husband who was suffering from an
acute case of trachoma and a bad infection of the face. They
lived too far away to make the journey daily, so they moved
to the village, finding hospitality at the house of a family
of their own caste. Morning and afternoon this faithful
wife brought her husband and took him away again. Her
painful efforts to understand the directions for his care, the
tender solicitude she showed for him, were touching. And
there was another case of an ugly little woman of forty or
so, a *Lunia*, also suffering from trachoma. Here the devotion
was on the husband's side. I did not dare give her my argyrol
or silver nitrate to take home with her. If a drop of something benefits, why not hurry up the cure by using the whole
bottle, is too often the village psychology. This low-caste

woman and her husband walked sixteen miles to and from
Pachperwa two or three times a week, in the hope that I
might render her a little assistance. Such cases of devotion
on the part of the wife for her husband, the husband for his
wife, the mother for her children, were countless among the
Indian villagers with whom I lived.

But even in Pachperwa there were exceptions to the rule.
We were not wholly without sin. The mother of the Pujari
who tended the Shiva shrine at the tahsil—not the Devi
shrine near my house—arrived one morning with red eyes,
displaying a badly bruised shoulder and two swollen fingers.
She had had some kind of quarrel with her daughter-in-law,
and her son, when he came home, had taken the wife's part.
He had beaten her with a lathi, she said, and twisted her
fingers.

Finger twisting was too much for me, and I promptly
undertook to administer a rebuke. The Pujari was in the
habit of bringing me a flower or two from the shrine as he
passed by. The following morning when he arrived with a
marigold, I coldly refused it, saying I could not think of
accepting anything from a man who beat his mother. I added
that I did not care to see his face again. Audible murmurs of
approval from the audience of sick people on the lawn
greeted this remark. After vainly trying to insist that his
mother had fallen and so hurt herself, the Pujari, properly
humiliated, slunk away. The next day he and his mother
appeared together. To my surprise she came forward and
begged me, with tears in her eyes, to forgive her son. He
stooped quickly and took the dust of her feet, likewise honoring me. More flowers were humbly proffered. This time I
accepted them, and peace was restored.

A favorite story in Indian literature is that of Savitri,
who wrested her husband out of the clutches of Yama, King
of Death, through the power of her goodness, her austerities
and her love. Every Hindu woman knows Savitri. A King
and Queen of ancient times were blessed with a daughter
after many childless years. The little Princess was named

Savitri—Dawn—in honor of the goddess to whom the pious parents had addressed their prayers. When the time came to think of Savitri's marriage, no desirable suitor having presented himself as yet, it was agreed that Savitri should go on a pilgrimage to various holy sanctuaries, seeking spiritual guidance. She set out with a long train of elephants and attendants, in the fashion becoming a princess, and traveled through the forests where saintly hermits had their abode. One day, through the curtains of her palanquin, she spied a handsome young man, carrying a load of faggots, who turned out to be the son of a blind king driven from his throne and now living in exile in the forest. Savitri quickly returned to her father's palace, announcing that her heart had found him she sought. She would marry the young Prince Satyavan.

The name had no sooner fallen from her lips than a seer who dwelt at the court, the great Narada, began to tremble. Narada foresaw that one year from that day Satyavan's destiny condemned him to die. If Savitri married Satyavan, she would become a widow. Vainly her father strove to dissuade her from her fatal choice. "A young girl marries only once; only once can her father say to her, 'I give thee.' Once I have chosen a husband, I do not choose a second time," she replied. And since she was not to be deflected from her decision, the marriage was celebrated with fitting observances.

Savitri was accepted with joy by Satyavan and his parents. Laying aside her jewels and rich robes, she went to share their simple forest life. The happy year drew to a close, the secret of impending doom still locked in Savitri's breast. As the time drew near, Savitri fasted and performed severe austerities in the hope that she might soften the heart of the gods. On the fatal day, when her husband went to the forest to chop firewood she begged permission to accompany him. Fearfully she watched and prayed. Suddenly a strange weariness overcame him. He lay down with his head on her knees, and the pallor of death began to spread over his features. At the same moment a shadowy presence emerged from the deeper forest.

Detaching the soul of Satyavan from his body, Yama, Lord of Death, bound it with his cord and started for his own realm. But footsteps followed him. Turning, he saw Savitri in tireless pursuit. Even Death was touched. "Choose any boon save the life of thy husband," he said, "and return from this fruitless journey." First the sight of her blind father-in-law, next the restoration of his lost kingdom, Savitri exacted from Yama, but still she followed. Once more he pleaded with her, this time begging her to choose something for herself. Before her own death, then, might she know the blessings of many sons, was Savitri's request. Yama acquiesced, and she then reminded him that a widow does not remarry. Unless he gave back Satyavan his promise could never be fulfilled. So, by her dauntless love, Savitri won her husband from Death himself.

Brides who go from their parents' homes are often enjoined to be "Savitris," but not all of them are spared the sadness of widowhood. The ban against remarriage is a matter of caste law only. It is effective for about one fourth of the Hindu women, but the influence of the Aryan marriage ideal is inescapable, and whether caste law permits widow remarriage or not, Hindu society does not look with approval on the woman who takes a second husband. The custom works merciless individual hardships, especially tragic for those virgin child widows doomed to a life of nunlike asceticism. Of these there are a third of a million under fifteen in India. Yet the women of the West who never have a chance to marry and who must keep up an endless struggle to support themselves in a none too sympathetic world likewise experience frustration. In India, no woman fails in having at least one chance to marry.

The position of a widow depends very much on circumstances. If she has grown children, particularly grown sons, she remains the honored mistress of the household. Legally she has the first lien to support in the property of her husband. Surrounded by her sons and their wives and children, she continues to be a directing force in the household, and her life is not necessarily an unhappy one.

The terrible rite of sati—immolation of the wife on the funeral pyre of her husband—which takes its name from Sati, Shiva's consort, who cast herself into the fire rather than hear abuse of her husband even from the lips of her own father, has all but passed from the pages of modern history. Historically, sati is known to have been practised in parts of India as far back as the time of Alexander's invasion, but neither the Vedas nor Manu gave any sanction for the cremation of living wives. Widow-burning was embodied in a code in the sixth century A. D., in this text: "If a woman's husband dies, let her lead a life of chastity or else mount his pyre." Immolation was supposedly not practised by any woman with young children, and it was to be a voluntary act of devotion on the part of the wife, but pressure of public opinion, and even physical force on occasion, compelled widows to follow their husbands into the flames. In northern India, particularly in Bengal, sati involved the sacrifice of thousands of women.

The English were not the first or only rulers to fight it. The Moguls required a woman to obtain permission to sacrifice herself from the governor of the province in which she resided, and the governor was instructed to do everything he could to dissuade her from her intention. Widow-burning was forbidden by Albuquerque at Goa after his capture of this western port of India in 1510. It was forbidden in parts of the Maratha domain. In Bengal, Ram Mohun Roy, founder of the Brahmo Samaj, carried on a ceaseless fight to end sati. Missionaries everywhere, of course, supported the crusade against it. Finally, in 1829, under the administration of Lord William Bentinck, widow-burning was definitely and successfully put down.

Remarriage of Hindu widows was legalized in 1865, but caste law still controls Hindu marriage customs, and though public sentiment is slowly beginning to support the idea of remarriage, at least for virgin widows, widows among the higher castes do not marry a second time. Among the Brahmo Samaj group, the Arya Samajists and the Social Reformers, as well as for other independent educated groups or individual families, virgin widow remarriage is now a possibility, though the numbers of such marriages so far may not have exceeded a thousand for all India. Whenever one occurs it is still considered worthy of record in the columns of the *Indian Social Reformer*. But a beginning has been made. The tragic sound of the widow breaking her glass bracelets is a little muted.

The young childless widow often returns to her own home —usually, in fact, among the poorer people. Whether she returns to her own home or remains with her husband's family, she is expected to follow a life of austerity. Jewelry is no longer for her, and she will wear only a white sari without border. There will be no vermilion streak in the parting of her hair. Sometimes she will even cut her hair short. Her food is a simple diet, without meat, fish, or highly spiced dishes. She will eat but once a day, and she will cook for herself. She will take no part in the household festivities. And possibly—this is the ideal—through leading an ascetic life of self-sacrifice, she will find spiritual consolation for her earthly bereavement.

A widowed sister or aunt is often a source of quiet strength in a Hindu home. It is she, more often than not, who is the family doctor, who cares for the sick, who cooks and cleans and performs countless little services for the others. Sometimes she is reduced to the unfortunate position of family drudge. Sometimes, too, when circumstances free her from other responsibilities, a widow devotes herself to study. The sacred literature is open to her to-day, and the Indian woman living the traditions of India holds the key in her slender fingers to all the wisdom of the sages.

We did not have many widows in Pachperwa, and not a single child widow, I am glad to say. Our population had a large Mohammedan element. Islam is without scruples on the subject of widow remarriage, since one of the Prophet's own eleven wives was a widow. Under Islam, also, marriage is a legal contract, not a religious sacrament, as it is under Hinduism. All but a fraction of our Hindus, moreover, belonged to lower castes, for whom remarriage is permissible. Of the widows I knew best, one was Mrs. Massy, the Christian *padrin*, who spent her time keeping her little house immaculately clean, looking out for the orphan boy she had adopted, helping the sick, and being kind to the village idiots. Her life was patterned very much after the ideal set up for the Hindu widow. Another was a young woman sadhu, who from time to time came to the village. Her garments were of coarse white homespun, and she had cut off all her hair. She carried a drum, which she beat softly as she sang religious songs to the little groups always ready to assemble at her tapping. One of Devi Prasad's sisters was also widowed, a sweet-faced woman with a ten-year-old daughter. She had an elementary education and there was talk that if the village ever opened a girls' school, Devi Prasad's sister might take charge of it.

At Mahabali Singh's one afternoon, I noticed a little girl clasping a small thick volume. Mahabali's wife said it was a copy of the *Hanumanji*. She took the book from the child's hand and began reading aloud. I ventured the opinion that there could not be many women in the village who could read. "Oh, yes, plenty can read," she insisted. She promptly led me to the house of a goldsmith a few doors away, where all four women of the family acknowledged shyly that they could read. Then Devi Prasad's widowed sister arrived with her daughter. All the women and the two girls sat upon a large wooden bench in the zenana courtyard of the goldsmith's house and read together from a fat volume of the *Ramayana*.

They made a charming picture, earnestly bending above the old worn book, the sunlight falling over them and touching their green and yellow and white saris with flecks of gold. As I listened to the chanting of the beloved lines, the drab little court seemed to put forth a graciousness and beauty of spirit. Oh, yes, plenty of other women could read, at least ten more besides themselves, they assured me. Even those who could not read knew by heart long passages from the epics and countless songs and legends learned from their own mothers and grandmothers.

And suddenly a comparison of Pachperwa illiteracy and New York literacy thrust itself upon me. From time to time I had been receiving packages of American magazines, sent out to relieve my supposed monotony. The unillustrated ones presented no problem, but for a long time I racked my brains in vain on what to do with some of the illustrated weeklies and monthlies. Nothing was ever wasted in Pachperwa, and sheets of paper, even printed paper, had a thousand uses. For one, the pan seller of the bazar wanted them to line his booth with, and for another Ram Lakhan wanted them to transform into bridegrooms' crowns. Pictures, of course, could be read by any one, and I knew that the village would be deeply shocked by those in my American magazines. It was essential, to save my reputation in Pachperwa, to get rid of those sophisticated representations of love-making, bathing beauties, and I know not what else. But there simply was no place to throw anything away. The ground was as hard as a rock. The charcoal stove was in the kitchen under Din Mohammed's jurisdiction. At last, in the dead of the night, when all the servants were safely asleep, I rose and at the far side of the house, on the path of red brick dust, I made a little bonfire of the telltale evidence of what my civilization contributed for the edification of the literate masses. The illiteracy of the village seemed infinitely preferable. Those legends that in India take the place of daily newspapers and ash-bin reading matter are the true poetry of the people.

In and out of them move all the great characters—both men and women—who have inspired India for thousands of years. Could a group of Western women in one breath name their ideal woman, I wonder? In India the answer would spring instantaneously from all the millions of Hindu women—Sita—Sita—the central star in the great galaxy including Savitri, Kunti, Draupadi, Damayanti, Sakuntala, Maitreyi, and many more. Sita is not merely a legend, but a living force in India. Hers is a name that has been spoken millions upon millions of times. Her presence intangibly pervades every household. She is the undimmed, unchanged Hindu ideal of womanhood.

CHAPTER XVI

The Outside

"WHEN it is day here, it is night there."—"How long does it take to go to your country?"—"How much does a ticket to your country cost?"

These were practically the only observations or questions by which Pachperwa expressed curiosity about my country. Even the four school teachers, when they called in a body to collect the photographs I had taken of them, did not get beyond remarking, "When the sun is shining here, the moon is shining there." Once the Peshkar did actually inquire what kind of government we had in the United States, but he was more interested in knowing how much it would cost an Indian to live there.

"About four hundred rupees a month," I told him.

"Then Indians cannot go to your country, I think," he remarked sadly.

The ordinary perspective of the village did not extend far into the "outside," as any place beyond the confines of the village was called.

Among the villagers Dukhi was by far the most promising candidate for a class in world geography. He imagined that the United States was really part of the English "continent." He was surprised when I told him that England was a small island and that a whole ocean lay between England and America. He became vastly interested in the comparative sizes of India, America, England, Germany, China, and Russia. I drew a rough map of the world for him, which he bore off, saying he was going to explain all these astonishing facts to the other villagers.

"But New York cannot be so fine as Pachperwa!" he insisted with splendid bravado. He took a sheet of paper and a pencil from my table, pretended to write a letter as an actor dashes one off on the stage, and waved the news to America that I was happy and comfortable and would not be coming back. My parents, or any others concerned about me, should come to Pachperwa, he concluded.

In spite of general ignorance, Pachperwa here and there poked a finger into the unknown. Looking up from my letter-writing, one morning, I noticed a woman standing a long way off. Presently I heard a soft drawl which bore a faint resemblance to the words, "Good-morning," uttered close to my ear. The woman was now standing at the door, apparently paying me a call, so I smiled encouragingly and called the Ayah to help in linguistic difficulties. In spite of several brave efforts on my part to talk Hindustani, my guest remained obdurately silent. At last, with a touch of annoyance, she demanded: "Don't you speak English? Didn't you hear me say 'good-morning'?" I nearly fell over in astonishment. "Of course," I replied meekly. A village woman speaking English was a mystery that roused deep respect.

She was born in British Guiana, where she married her husband, who as a young man had answered the call of a recruiting agent for the Guiana sugar plantations. Six years ago she had come to India and settled here, since her husband was a native of the vicinity of Pachperwa. Mother, father, and brothers were still in British Guiana. Her own three children, however, had all been born in Pachperwa. "Two is a girl and one is a boy," she parenthetically informed me.

Her foreign residence had given her a feeling of haughty contempt toward the village. "Dis very poor place. Dis no good place," she reiterated many times, complaining that in Pachperwa she was compelled to talk "coolie talk." If she could see a ship she would certainly get on it and return to

British Guiana. The people of the village were "no good."
Once when her husband, a carter, was away, she had waked
to find a thief trying to take her ornaments from her. Seiz-
ing him firmly, she called for help until the neighbors rushed
in and tied him up. Duly impressed by her courage I remarked, "You are very brave."

"Oh, yes, me *very* brave!" she agreed. "Me not afeared
*onny*thing." With this, she came to the point of her visit.
Would I speak to the Deputy Sahib so that her husband
might take up some land as a tenant?

All this time the Ayah was standing in the background,
awestruck that a village woman should have knowledge of
my tongue. "Mussulmani or Hindu?" she inquired. The
woman merely pulled back the edge of her sari and showed
a fringe of silver rings through the rim of her ear, just like
the Ayah's own. A Hindu woman of the village would have
worn a single big spool-like stud of glittering glass and
wood, or a pendent earring of silver with dangling balls.
To me, the chief surprise lay in the fact that her English
was spoken with an unmistakable Negro accent. To find
African English in my tiny village way off at the foot of the
Himalaya was an astonishing incongruity. More than this,
I began to notice that there was something a little peculiar
about this woman—lips fuller, nose flatter, nostrils wider,
than the average, even though Dravidian characteristics pre-
dominated over Aryan in Pachperwa. Also, the woman's
attitude was different—the way she caught the thief, the
scorn in her voice when she repeated, "Dis place no good,"
her general independence of manner. The conviction came
to me that here was actually a blend of African and Indian.

Saturday afternoon. Long lines of Indians squatting on
an embankment beside an irrigation ditch, each with something to sell, potatoes, beans, fruits, spices, rice. Crowds
swarming everywhere. Women in bright saris, arms, ears,
neck, ankles weighted with heavy silver jewelry. At the far
end of the embankment a small house, or "office." Coolies
passing in a long file before the babu seated at a table on

the veranda, receiving their week's pay according to the number of their "tasks." So many rows of sugarcane cultivated or cut, so many shillings—an average earning of two a day. Palms stir languidly, and the tattered banana leaves reflect the sun like broken mirrors. Here and there the scarlet canopy of a fire tree. At the opposite end of the plantation is the spacious jalousied house of the red-faced English manager, surrounded by a tiny garden. Some distance away are the coolie "lines," gaunt and ugly, like railway sheds or warehouses. They are divided into single rooms, one room to a family. A little farther on rises a small octagonal-shaped temple, freshly whitewashed. A Brahmin priest, austerely polite, forehead strangely decorated with gold leaf, arms filled with great pink lotuses he has just brought from a pond near by, effectively blocks the doorway. None but a Hindu may enter here. All around stretch rustling acres of sugarcane.

Such is the typical plantation of British Guiana, where Indians recruited from many parts of the homeland and their descendants to-day make up one half of the total population of three hundred thousand in the colony. The rest are African blacks and a handful of whites. It chanced to be British Guiana that gave me my first contact with Indians, but India itself was then a mystery. "Unless you know the background, you can understand nothing of all this!" the British Governor declared. Even so, that brief glimpse of a transplanted India was never forgotten. Here in Pachperwa I found myself remembering one particular incident with special interest.

During the last war, no ships could be spared to take immigrants home. The first "coolie ship" in several years was to leave for India in the fall of 1919, and many more passengers than the four hundred the ship could accommodate had entered their names. The Immigration Inspector, swamped with applications, was carefully "trying" each case. An old man, very thin, with a short dhoti and a crumpled white rag of a turban, a large, opulent woman in a yellow sari, wearing much gold, and a small girl in a broad-brimmed sailor hat and a blue sailor suit trimmed with white lace, presented themselves before the Inspector. They wanted to go "home." There seemed to be some hitch. It was the child. The mother was dead, the Inspector elucidated. These were the grandparents. He wanted them to leave the little girl behind with the father or with some friend. "Here," he went on, "she can go to school. She will marry well. But what sort of chance will she have back in that village in India?" The woman's eyes blazed, and she poured out an angry torrent of words. The old man said nothing, but tears began to flow down his gaunt cheeks. He took the end of his dirty turban to stanch them, but they rolled between his fingers and splashed to the floor. For twenty homesick years he had worked unremittingly in the cane fields and had hoarded his golden harvest for a day of return. Was the dream now to be shattered? For without the child, he stubbornly insisted, they would not go. The Inspector gave in with a sigh: "They are so much better off here, but they won't believe it until they have been back in their village a few months. Then they'll want to take the first boat back again. Meanwhile some unscrupulous relative will have made away with all their savings."

"Unless you know the background, you can understand nothing!" As this village woman with the soft drawl stood there at my door in Pachperwa, I knew that at last I had come to the "background."

Others who had been "outside" turned up from time to time. Among my patients was a quiet little fellow with gray hair and a kind, passive look. He had lived twenty-two years in Jamaica. After we had thoroughly discussed his stomach ache, he brought up another trouble. With a saving of seven gold sovereigns he had returned a month ago to see his father and relatives in a village three miles from Pachperwa. A brother had invited him to share his house. "Me papa marry two times, me have two mammas, me brother he belong second mamma." The brother had offered to take care of his gold, but yesterday, when he asked for some of his own money to buy clothes, the brother had refused to give him any. I suggested that he had better see the Thanadar, but he was afraid the Thanadar would "slap" his brother, whom he did not want slapped. He only wanted his money back.

A thin, sharp-faced young man with oily black hair also put in an appearance. He hailed from Trinidad, where he had spent eighteen years. An elder brother had first made the venture; he had followed. On his return to India he had deposited the two thousand rupees brought home in a postal savings bank. At present he was recruiting Indian labor for the tea plantations of Assam. The suave agent informed me that the tea coolies could earn as much as sixty rupees a month. They were required to sign a contract for only six months, and they received railway fare. He himself drew a salary of fifty rupees a month and a bonus of three pounds for every contract signed through his efforts. Sometimes he was able to get one man, sometimes two, sometimes seven. The tea plantations of Assam, as he painted them to the villagers, were paradise.

The Mahabali Singhs were always looking back affectionately upon their years in Trinidad. Compared with Pachperwa, Trinidad represented civilization to them. In Trinidad, for instance, there were tramcars. Those christened tramcars of the West Indies with advertisements plastered on their sides, drawn along wabbling tracks by mules and driven by lazy Negroes—the whole somnolent atmosphere—did not seem a synonym for thriving industry to me, but compared with bullock carts even those tramcars represented a forward step in transportation.

I could see Mahabali Singh in his grain shop in Port of Spain, with black cobwebs among the rafters in spite of all the business in clinking shillings and crowns going on over dull brown bags—buying low, selling high, with the astuteness of his caste. Mahabali was a Khatri, and Khatris have a reputation for being among the shrewdest traders of India. He was a good-natured, friendly soul. Though he complained that he could not compete with the big grain dealers of the New Bazar, his Falstaffian paunch seemed to indicate that his household did not lack for ghi and sugar and milk. He must have made a good deal of money in his many years in Trinidad, and no doubt it was hidden away safely under his floor. It was the business opportunities in the West that appealed to him.

His wife's reactions were more social. The village was dirty. There was so much sickness here. In that foreign country there were fine hospitals and schools and good roads —not deep-rutted tracks like these. And the people here were so ignorant. They did not know that cleanliness was the secret of health. Flies everywhere, dirt everywhere, sickness everywhere. Over there it was much better. Mahabali would have liked to return to Trinidad, but now that he owned his house in Pachperwa he could not afford to give it up, paying the estate its premium.

Again the village reached out unexpectedly and touched the hem of the distance. Asgar was telling about his family. Just how many of them were there, I asked.

"Eight children—six living and two dead." After a pause he added, "And one sister in Fiji *tapu.*"

This was news. I had never heard the sister mentioned. Asgar, it seemed, was very small. He remembered only that once his sister had given him a custard apple. Then he remembered waking up one night to find his mother crying and his father very angry: All they said was that his sister had gone. She was then nineteen. Her husband had died previously, and at the time she was working as a servant for a former clerk of the tahsil. The munshi, when she disappeared, could offer no explanation. She must have run away with two men from "outside" who had been staying at his house. Years passed. At last a man returning from Fiji to a neighboring village brought back information that she was living there, married. Asgar's story was that she had been forced to go to Gonda with the two men, the munshi sharing in the plot, and that she had then been taken to Fiji and sold to somebody as a wife. In most of the colonies wives are at a premium. Anyway, according to the neighbor's report, Asgar's sister was now well off, and at this late date there seemed no reason to mourn her possible abduction.

So they went out by handfuls, Indian villagers, to the West Indies, British Guiana, Fiji, South Africa. There was a Sikh contractor, a friend of Haweli Singh's, who came to ask aid in drafting an application for a position as supervisor in the railway works at Gorakhpur. He had been in Mauritius. Sikhs, who hail originally from the Punjab, are especially great wanderers, turning up as lumbermen in Canada and Washington, policemen in Shanghai and Hongkong, contractors in Africa, engineers or taxi drivers in the big cities of India. Seventy per cent of the students in the engineering college at Lucknow are Sikhs. Not long after Narain Singh's visit, Haweli came along, wanting me to fill in an application for his passport. He was thinking of going somewhere, he announced, to Mauritius or Kenya, maybe to Canada or New York. At any rate, he wanted to have a passport in his vest pocket.

To-day 2,400,000 Indians are living abroad, most of them within the British Empire. In the early days shiploads of Indians were transported every year to work on the English plantations in the colonies. After the abolition of slavery in British Guiana in 1834 the plantation owners there found themselves hard pressed to secure necessary labor. The first shipload of Indian coolies arrived in 1838. Through a system of private enterprise, for which the control of the various colonial administrations was later substituted, Indian coolies were rounded up in different ports and shipped off so many times a year to meet the demands of the planters. They were brought over under a modified form of slavery, the indentured labor system, probably with little or no idea of the actual conditions they were to face or the terms of their contracts. Recruiting agents were none too scrupulous in enticing men to sign up for a "coolie ship," and there is reason to believe that, before the suppression of slavery in India in 1843, some of the emigrants did not embark voluntarily. But famine, a cash bonus, and glowing promises were persuasive factors.

The sea voyage must have been the worst part of the venture. Several hundred coolies were crowded between decks with inadequate ventilation, no berths, and no space for exercise. The food was often impossible. If the emigrants complained too vociferously, cruel and inhumane punishment might be meted out to them. Before the opening of the Panama Canal in 1915, the two months' journey to British Guiana and the West Indies around the Cape of Good Hope was marked by a high mortality, in some cases as much as 17 to 20 per cent of the coolie passengers. The adjustment to different climatic conditions was also costly, mortality among the newcomers averaging 10 per cent a year. Those who survived and settled down found themselves better off economically, but at the cost of losing their cultural traditions.

When their numbers became significant, in some countries they were subjected to humiliating social and racial discriminations. The indignities suffered by the Indians in Kenya and in South Africa originally stimulated Gandhi to take up his first great experiment of nonviolent resistance. Denial of the right to the franchise, restriction upon the holding of land, compulsory segregation and a head-tax have been some of the unjust handicaps which Indian settlers in South Africa have had to face.

Reports of Indian commissions sent out to investigate the conditions of the Indian communities in the various colonies stirred up such indignation at home that a general restriction and in some cases a complete cessation of emigration was adopted by the Indian government. Since 1922 the whole emigration policy has been revised. Emigration is now permitted only under certain fixed rules. The Indians in Fiji, Kenya, and the Union of South Africa meanwhile have been carrying on their struggle to better the conditions under which they live. When the foreign channels for emigration were cut off the tide of migration turned instead to Assam and Burma, but the crowded districts of the United Provinces, especially the eastern districts of Oudh, are still choked for an outlet.

Besides the cultivators who had been drawn overseas as coolie laborers, I came upon a few villagers who had a different sort of world experience. Gobare Gir, the Goshain who tended the Shiva shrine in the tahsil, began a long story one day about a "big battle." It was some time before it dawned on me that tucked away here in Pachperwa was a veteran of the last war. He had served in Mesopotamia and Persia and had been wounded. Though he could point to the scar of a bullet wound in the leg and other slashes on his body, he did not know the name of the place where he had been injured. He did know, however, that he had spent two years in a hospital in Basra. Very proudly he informed me that he had received a medal. The next morning he brought it to me. It was of copper, not much larger than an English penny, and it bore the sounding inscription "Great War for Civilization." But Gobare Gir, as far as I could make out, fought for the practical consideration of twenty rupees a month. His ideas of "civilization" were very hazy. At best they did not extend beyond artillery, tanks, and airplanes. He had managed to save two hundred rupees. Quite evidently he was filled with regret that the war, a providential source of income to himself, had come to an untimely close. His peace-time earnings of two rupees a month for performing his simple duties at the shrine he found inadequate.

Another door out—for Indian Mussulmans—was the annual pilgrimage to Mecca. Every year ships carry some 25,000 Indian pilgrims from Bombay and Karachi to the Red Sea port of Jidda. According to the Station Master, at least thirty pilgrims from our vicinity set out every Mecca season, the date for the *Haj* shifting by eleven days from year to year. A barber living at Motipur, a mile from Pachperwa, was entitled to great distinction because he had been twice to Mecca, and a holy man, known as a *mir*, who dwelt by himself beside a large tank near Bargadwa, had also twice made the long journey to the Holy City. The two *Hajjis*, however, instead of sharing their honors in friendly fashion, were bitter rivals. The Mir claimed that he had walked to Mecca across Baluchistan and Persia, taking three years to complete his first journey. When Fakire told me about him I expressed a hope that he would be so kind as to come some day and recount his Mecca experiences, but he rejected my invitation with dignity. "He sits all day under his little roof reading the Koran," explained Fakire, a trifle apologetically. But I was assured that the barber would have no such reluctance in relating his adventures, and the Station Master promised to bring him after mosque the next Friday.

"I shall come early because it will take at least three hours," he said with satisfaction.

"Oh, no, it won't," I quickly put in. "An hour will be plenty of time."

The Hajji Barber, better known as Hajji Nahnu in Pachperwa, made a striking appearance. His cotton shirt of huge white and black checks reaching nearly to his knees gave him a bold and jovial look. White trousers cut in at the ankle, a white cap and a bag of barber's tools, like a little wallet, completed his wardrobe. His hair and beard were jet black, and he wore spectacles on his nose. The Station Master and his three brocaded sons sat on chairs, but the Hajji Barber, as became his position, squatted on the floor. While he talked he kept snapping his fingers and thrusting his hands out dramatically with all the fingers spread. Between paragraphs, while the Station Master translated, his eyes roved everywhere, taking in all the details of my house.

The first time he went to Mecca, seven years ago, he had accompanied a rich thekedar of a neighboring village in the capacity of servant. Having learned the ropes, three years later he was again invited to go, this time with an enterprising old lady of Ramnagar, whom he called "aunt" —mother of the thekedar Bismillah—who undertook the pilgrimage upon her husband's death.

I began with sordid questions of cost. "It costs five hundred for a poor man like me, but a rich man will pay at least a thousand rupees. Your Honor would have to pay fifteen hundred," translated the Station Master. The Hajji Barber had an excellent memory. He had paid eighty rupees for his steamship ticket on the first trip, which took twenty-one days, and forty-five rupees for the return ticket. The second time, prices having risen, it cost him one hundred rupees for the out-trip and sixty-five for the return. Shipowners know that pilgrims have no money when they start home, so concessions are made. On the first pilgrimage he had waited to buy his food supplies in Bombay, only to discover that Bombay prices were sky high. The next time he prudently laid in supplies at Pachperwa. Experience had taught him another valuable lesson. The first time he had taken all his cooking pots and necessaries in one big bundle, for which he was charged six rupees excess baggage on his arrival in Jidda. When he went again, he tied up his things in small bundles, which could be distributed to advantage among the twenty-six members of the Pachperwa party, and there was no extra charge.

All the pilgrims had to be vaccinated at Bombay and undergo medical inspection before they were permitted to sail. The ship provided medical attention, but not, alas, for the Hajji Barber's seasickness. At this point he gave a dramatic exhibition, so that I might clearly understand the nature of his sickness. On board he did the cooking for the party under his wing. The day before landing at Jidda all of the pilgrims put on their pilgrim clothes, consisting of two pieces two and a half yards long of unsewn white cloth, purchased at Bombay. They wore no head covering, but were permitted to keep on their shoes. At Jidda the Pachperwa pilgrims joined a big company of five or six hundred other pilgrims under the leadership of a maulvi, each pilgrim paying the maulvi ten rupees for his services as guide. They set out after five o'clock evening prayers to march the forty-five miles from Jidda to Mecca. They walked all night, rested during the day, and walked through the second night. Torches made of oil-soaked cloth lighted the way. They reached Mecca, lying in a depression below the rim of desert hills, at four in the morning. "It looked very fine," said the Hajji Barber. "I was filled with astonishment."

Here the party was split up into groups and housed in different parts of the city. The cost of lodging depended on proximity to the Kaaba. The poor filter out to the periphery of the city. Like everyone else, the Hajji Barber had performed all the proper ceremonies at the Holy City. As soon as he had had his bath he went to the Kaaba, entering the court of the Great Mosque by the Baba Salaam. "There are forty-two gates, but it is by Baba Salaam that one must enter," he said impressively. Then he made his seven turns around the Kaaba. There were too many people for him to get anywhere near the sacred Black Stone set in the wall of the sanctuary, hidden by a curtain.

Next there were prayers to be said at special places. After this he ran back and forth between Mecca and the hill to which Ishmael's mother went in search of water when her son was born. There was nothing to eat but sherbet bought at stands. The sun was hot, to be sure, but on pilgrimages one gladly stands discomfort. Having completed these preliminaries, he was duly shaved, all except his beard and one little lock on the left side of his head, and was free to wear his Indian clothes again until the three mad days of the real Haj. Then, once again submerged among the vast crowds, he struggled to touch the Black Stone, prayed endless prayers, drank of the sacred Zum-zum water, and at Mina threw his forty-nine pebbles, spending the night on the hill of Mujalfa. And the Haj was over, save for three days of feasting on goat's flesh and other delicacies. After Friday prayers the general exodus of pilgrims commenced

—a few going on to Medina, the most retracing their steps to Jidda, where they scrambled for passage on the steamers waiting to take them to Egypt, India, Java, and the Philippines.

He half closed his eyes, trying to remember what had impressed him most in his pilgrimage. It was the sight of the Kaaba, he finally announced. And next to this, the intoning of the Koran and the calls to prayer from the seven minarets of the Great Mosque. There was no such reading of the Koran at any other place in the world. It made tears roll down his cheeks, and no thought could dwell in his consciousness except that God was God and Mahomet was His Prophet.

As for the material treasures he brought home to Pachperwa, there was first a sealed tin of Zum-zum water. One drop of this made a whole jar of ordinary water holy. He also brought some rosaries, a package of dates, some black for the eyes, and a small square of the Holy Cloth that had covered the Kaaba. At the completion of the Haj this had been cut into bits for the pilgrims. He paid twelve annas to his maulvi to secure a few inches. He had eaten the dates and given the antimony and rosaries away, but he was keeping the two-piece garment he had worn as a pilgrim for a burial shroud. Before long he would go again, and he would not come back from his next pilgrimage. His three sons were now grown, and he had no special tie or duty to stand in the way of dying at Mecca.

I thanked him for the interesting account of his experiences and congratulated him on being one of the two men of the community who had actually made the great journey twice. "He says," remarked the Station Master, "that the other Hajji, that Mir, is an impostor. Both men were on the same ship, and from something that slipped out in the course of the voyage, he is convinced this other man never made the journey by land. But he says so to impress ignorant people."

Not long after, when I was riding along on an elephant, I saw a lonely little hut under a soft thorn tree on the bank above a large tank. The mahout remarked that a sadhu lived there. In the village Mohammedan and Hindu ascetics were indiscriminately referred to as sadhus. As the hermit came to the door of his hut I knew he must be the barber's rival. He was wearing a shirt and skirt of exquisite apricot color which set off his black hair and beard glistening with oil. He and his little house were immaculately clean. He greeted me with dignity, asking me to descend and accept the shelter of his roof from the hot sun. He also brought the mahout a drink of water, passing up to him a brass jar. The front of the house was entirely open except for a low half wall. The roof of thatch was supported by peeled posts. Within was a platform of mud, swept very clean, which evidently served as a seat of meditation by day and a bed by night.

It was easy to see why the Mir and the loquacious barber were not on friendly terms. For two years now he had lived alone in his little hut. He said he had forsaken the world, preferring solitude in which he could occupy his thoughts with God. He took no care for the body. For companionship he had his holy books.

"But how do you get your food?" I inquired.

"God provides it," he replied. "People come, and they bring all I need. I have never wanted for anything."

No doubt the sanctity of his life and his fame for having gone overland to Mecca drew followers to him. Incidentally he received gifts for reading the future and finding answers to all sorts of questions. He was the baba, I learned later, whom Asgar was so eager to have name the thief who had stolen his watch. He was reserved, mysterious, austere, to all appearances concerned with holy things. His manners were those of the saint. I was quite ready to believe that he spent most of his time meditating upon God. As we rode away he climbed to the top of the embankment and stood watching us wind our way across the fields, an unforgettable picture in his pale-pink, wind-blown skirts, silhouetted against the blazing sky.

The old lady who had been to Mecca with the barber excited my interest. She was one of five women then living in the vicinity to have made the pilgrimage. The Hajji Barber offered to bring her to see me, since she did not observe purdah. It seemed more appropriate for me to call on her, and the barber duly arranged a visit for eight o'clock in the morning, the customary visiting hour in our rural society. It was a little after six when we set out. I rode on Champa, the baby elephant, and the Hajji Barber, merrily singing, strode in front, a pair of black checked pantaloons tucked up to his knees. Fakire marched behind with his faithful lathi. The early morning air was very pleasant, though the sky looked as if it might spill some rain on us before we returned. The mahout was full of complaints. He and his elephant had taken part in a Bania marriage procession in the New Bazar the night before, and he had received nothing, not even food. I tried to soothe his feelings with mention of forthcoming bakshish. The barber, however, was in a cheerful mood. As he walked briskly ahead of little Champa he was singing after this wise:

"It is delusion to think in terms of Kaaba or Temple. O God's Light! Whether candle of Kaaba or torch of Temple, it is all one. I lie prostrate before the door of God's House. Neither I was, nor will I be, separated from the threshold of the Beloved. O ungodly people! It is senseless to oppose the followers of Mahomet. The Beloved pervades everywhere, in Kaaba and in Temple."

When we arrived at Ramnagar the whole village swarmed into the open space in front of Bismillah's house. The house was of the usual type for a well-to-do thekedar— two long wings with projecting roofs, facing an open court. A white sheet had been laid out upon the ground and in the middle a table was spread with what looked like a Thanksgiving feast. The chair before it showed where I was expected to sit. As I slid off Champa, Bismillah Khan came forward and held out two rupees as a ceremonial offering.

Thanking him, I touched the money, and back went the rupees into his pocket, to the bitter disappointment of the mahout.

The *dali* overwhelmed me—several pounds of husked rice, squashes, tomatoes, and a cauliflower, four huge mangoes —a messenger had gone all the way to Balrampur to purchase these—a dozen eggs, two live hens, and three pomegranates. The eggs were reposing on a beautifully woven round plate of dyed straw made by Bismillah's wife. I felt some relief when I found that I was not expected to eat anything on the spot. The dali went home with me, on the heads of the barber and a servant of the thekedar.

The old Hajjin now appeared on the scene. She sat on a low chair near me while a solid bank of onlookers walled us in. I liked her at once. Her white hair was visible under her *orhni*, or small head-covering, but she looked very lively and as sound as a hickory tree. Her purple cotton trousers gave her an almost saucy appearance. Her son said she was eighty, but Indian villagers have a disconcerting way of adding anything up to twenty years to the age or taking off twenty with equal indifference. At any rate, the Hajjin looked like a woman who, having decided to go to Mecca, would certainly go there.

Mecca was a fine big city, but not so big as Bombay, she maintained. She had made the journey from Jidda by camel, and in spite of the desert heat she had not felt specially tired. As souvenirs she brought back some antimony for the eyes —that from Mecca was better than any that could be bought at home—and some Zum-zum water in a tin resembling an oil can, produced for my benefit. Unfortunately the water had dried up before she could get it home. She had also bought some rosaries, six for six annas—"Oh, no, six rosaries for eight annas!" corrected the Hajji Barber. One of them was shown to me, blue glass beads with a few red and white ones worked in, "Made in Germany" stamped all over it. Recently she had gone on another pilgrimage in India to

Agra, Ajmir, and Delhi. Allah willing, she would go again to Mecca and Medina some day.

The next time, I told her, she would undoubtedly make the journey from Jidda by motor car. I had just been reading in my newspaper from Allahabad particulars of the first pilgrim ship getting under way for the new Haj. Announcement was made that eighty-seven motors were now in service between Jidda and Mecca. Yet I preferred to think of the Hajji Barber and his old lady moving slowly along with the band of pilgrims through the desert night, their way lighted by flaring cloth torches, instead of racing to Mecca in two hours in a rattling motor car.

In ways like these, something of the outside world percolated through to the village. Those who had had the experience of foreign travel were sure of an appreciative audience when they returned home, and if they drew upon a fertile imagination in describing the marvels they had seen, so much the better. Their stories knocked at the door of imagination and set others wondering.

CHAPTER XVII

Silver Lining

ONE day there was rejoicing for a certain member of the tahsil staff, who was also a rent contractor for three villages. He had unexpectedly had his official salary raised from fifty rupees a year to a hundred. To celebrate his good fortune it was suggested to him that he should give a nautch party, and I was asked to come.

The nautch was to be staged in the open veranda of the Mohammedan chaprasis' house, and I had only to step across the tahsil grounds. Chairs had been placed for the Tahsildar and me at one end of the large white floor cloth. The rest of the audience squatted along the walls. Among the outside guests were two or three Marwaris, the Brahmin compounder from the hospital, and the head schoolmaster. As usual the Ayah and I were the only women present.

The first number on the program was a song and dance by a *Paharin*—a hillgirl from Nepal. She was scarcely the theatrical nautch girl of Western imagination. Her broad Mongolian face and slim body had a certain appealing quality hard to define, perhaps a perfection of racial type. No one except an artist would have thought her beautiful. Her eyebrows were plucked into a slender tapering curve. Her freshly oiled hair, parted on one side, combed smoothly back and braided in a large coil at the neck, gleamed like lacquer. Her clothes were shabby. She had anklets with little bells, red glass bangles, a microscopic gold button in her left nostril, and earrings of brass loops strung with glass beads. Her orchestra consisted of one man sawing at a *sarangi*, the crude prototype of the violin, and a boy tinkling minia-ture cymbals.

She sang in a hoarse, overstrained voice, feet clinging to the ground, heels stamping rhythmically, bells jingling to the beat of the song. She postured with her arms, repeating ever the same graceful but stereotyped poses. First she sang a village song, then a mountain song, and then an Urdu poem, set to music. With her mountain song her dancing grew livelier. She whirled first to one side and then to the other, until her tinseled skirt undulated all around her, and now and then she made sudden swoops to the ground. Be-hind her a man held a rag torch, fed with oil from a slim-necked, fat-bellied bottle. He followed carefully every move-ment of the dancer, always keeping the torch directed toward her face, which remained as impersonal as if carved out of wood. When she sat down at the end, wrapping herself in a dark red shawl, for the first time her face became human. Suddenly it looked sad. She bowed, saluted us with folded hands, and disappeared through the crowd.

The play that followed was performed by a little troupe of six actors accompanied by four musicians from a village a few miles away. There were three such theatrical com-panies in our tahsil, including our own little company of Pachperwa, in which Asgar Ali had starred before he be-came my dishwasher and lamp tender. The rôle of leading lady on the present occasion was played by a young *Kahar*, of the palanquin-bearing caste. His dark-skinned face, coated with liquid white, had an ashy gray look. What appeared at first as perspiration turned out to be a sprinkling of gold powder.

All the actors sang their parts. The plot of the play was simple to follow. Scenery was entirely dispensed with. A man of noble birth and his beautiful wife had gone on a journey. Overtaken by night in a jungle frequented by dacoits, they found themselves in a dangerous situation, but at last, overcome by sleep, the husband lay down while the wife, in true Indian style, remained on guard. No sooner had he pulled a red cloth over his head than four robbers appeared on the scene. One bore a large sword. Another, with a black rag tied about his head and a puttee wrapped around one leg, carried an ancient blunderbuss at least six feet long. A tall fellow with a wig of coal-black hair falling below his shoulders flourished a lathi. The leader of the gang, also with long hair and a ferocious beard to his waist, was adorned with an ill-fitting khaki coat and a cartridge belt.

Aroused from his slumbers, the hero battled artistically, he and the robbers advancing in turn and making passes at one another, until the robber chief finished him off with magic. The poor wife at this juncture fainted dead away and did not come to life until the robbers had departed with the valuables. As she was then lamenting the loss of her lord, singing that she would now commit sati, the robber chief, miraculously reformed into a "holy man," returned with a rosary around his wrist and a pilgrim's staff in his hand. Overhearing the fatal decision, he restored the husband to life by the same magic with which he had killed him and commanded his companions to hand back the stolen jewels.

During the robber act, I noticed that one of the villains in the play kept edging out toward the audience and whispering something to Asgar Ali, who remained stolidly indifferent. At last, quite audibly, the robber informed Asgar that Jawahir, my cook in tent days, wanted him immediately in the kitchen. Annoyed at being left alone to guard camp while Asgar and the Ayah were enjoying themselves at the play, Jawahir had sent his irate summons by the actor, since no one else could get across to the other side of the temporary stage. Asgar finally tore himself away. The audience, to judge by the faces, enjoyed every minute of the play, and I could see genuine emotion at the lady's grief over the supposed death of her husband. On the whole the acting was not bad, but the real merit of the performance lay in the fact that the villagers could entertain themselves.

Most village plays are based on well known legends and stories, and even illiterate actors are quite capable of transforming themselves at will into familiar heroes and gods. Any incident from the epics is a suitable theme. Manners and customs are satirized in short extemporaneous interludes, and in these a clever actor does not spare an opportunity to raise a laugh at the expense of some local character. Our Pachperwa company included, among others, a Mohammedan tobacco dealer, Asgar Ali and Sheobalak, the Hindu confectioner, and the chief music was a Hindu baba's harmonium. The village companies perform on all sorts of special occasions—puja ceremonies, weddings, celebrations of one kind or another. The whole village attends, and the host pays the bill. It is certainly not excessive. For the tahsil entertainment I witnessed each actor received a rupee.

The village story-teller is another of the time-honored institutions. The Tahsildar once arranged a story-telling evening on my behalf. One of his own peons, he said, was a skilled teller of tales, and there was another man in the village who often entertained with his narrative art. The peon turned out to be an old fellow I had noticed many times because of the way he parted his brown and white beard down the middle of his chin and tied the two ends back with string behind his ears. He was generously turbaned and well wrapped up in a plaid blanket; for this was January, and at night we all huddled gratefully over a charcoal fire. Next to the peon squatted a bareheaded young man whose identity I did not know, and then came the village story-teller, shivering in a cotton sheet.

The Tahsildar asked the villager what sort of story he would tell us. He had two stories, he replied, one about a legendary king and the other about the historical Raja of Ujjain, Vikramaditya. Both were long. One alone, he announced, would take all night to tell. A little alarmed, I asked if the peon did not know a shorter one. The old chaprasi, with ill disguised eagerness, immediately launched into his tale. He did not look at us at all, but faced the young man, seated between himself and the villager. It now appeared that this person was a professional listener. He kept his eyes glued to the face of the story-teller and at every pause said, "Mmmmmmmmmm," thus expressing attentiveness and a desire to hear more. It took the Tahsildar a full half hour to translate the peon's short story—a moral tale about a king and a Bania and the Bania's beautiful and virtuous wife, who resisted dishonorable overtures made by the King in her husband's absence. When the turn of the village story-teller came the professional listener hitched himself around and continued to say "Mmmmmmmmmm" at every pause in the new story, which dealt with a raja, distinguished by great wisdom, humility, and courtesy, who eventually succeeded in reaching Indra's palace, where beautiful, celestial nymphs danced and sang for him. The story covered altogether sixteen episodes. At the end of an hour or two the Tahsildar suggested to the villager that he might speed up the end, but this was beyond his capacity. He could tell it only in the literal sequence in which he had learned it. The Tahsildar's patience was exhausted, and we never got beyond the ninth episode.

The story-teller himself was a tenant cultivating two and a half acres of land, yet two lakhs of rupees tripped lightly off his tongue. He was perfectly at home in palaces, and he thoroughly understood the kingly virtues and responsibilities. It was quite evident that he was lost in the fine world he was fashioning with his own words. He had learned this tale, he told us afterward, from somebody now dead who used to tell it in the village years before.

Itinerant entertainers also turned up to reap small harvests of pice for amusing the village. Men with trained animals, jugglers, tumblers, snake charmers, fortune tellers, magicians, were familiar in Pachperwa. Every bazar day was sure to find one or another of them on hand.

The bear trainer announced his arrival with a penetrating rattle, made by shaking a *damaru*, a tiny hourglass drum with a leaden ball on a string. As soon as a crowd collected, the bear would be made to go through its tricks. These bears were the medium-sized black fellows from the Himalaya with a white V under their chins. Obviously they performed out of fear. The bear stood up on its hind legs, while the trainer sang various little songs, and directed its movements by a rope fastened through the nose cartilage. If the song described a mother rocking her baby, the bear would hold up its front paws and sway back and forth with an imaginary child. Sometimes it would dance a "shimmy," to the great delight of the children. The climax of the performance was invariably a simulated struggle between the bear and his master, in which both rolled over and over on the ground. Then the bear would salaam the audience, and annas would be in order.

I soon acquired a reputation for being a patron of the juggling arts. Whenever a traveling entertainer appeared, he was led to my hill, the whole village following at his heels. One hot afternoon the familiar whine of a gourd flute sounded through the still air. Up the hill came, not the snake charmer I expected, but a Mohammedan juggler who said he had come from Balrampur. With a bushy white beard and a gigantic white turban on his head, he had a theatrical presence suited to his part. A lean helper marched behind, carrying the tricks in a red cloth and the rolled mat on which the juggler was accustomed to sit. Plucked out of the village to help was a potter's boy, an alert little fellow with a twinkling eye and a contagious grin.

I installed the stranger in front of my shisham, and the audience crowded upon the veranda and overflowed on the lawn. First the juggler began to bring up marbles out of his mouth. He would utter a loud cry like "*Om!*" and then, face turned toward the sun, sleeves rolled up and hands folded in his lap, he would open a cavernous mouth and spit out large wet marbles, one after another. There was nothing false about them. They rolled solidly along on the mat. Now and then he would cough up something extra, like a wooden top, which he set spinning for us. Somewhere in his interior he seemed to have pouches like a squirrel or a monkey, for he produced at least ten marbles and two tops.

Then he went through the rest of his repertoire. He changed a rupee into a lemon, made three balls roll uphill and a clay bird in a bowl of water dip and reappear at command. He pulled yards of string out of the astonished village boy's dhoti—roars of laughter from the audience! He filled a tin box with straw, set fire to it, and, removing the lid, shook out a handful of sweets which he tossed to the enchanted children. As a climax, he offered to bring up his lungs. *"Nai achchha! Nai achchha!"* exclaimed the Ayah with horror, covering her face. But I was quite ready to face the ordeal. He coughed a few times, puffed out his cheeks until they seemed ready to burst, and with spasmodic jerks produced a three-foot string of a transparent sausage-shaped something, which he then slowly sucked in again. The performance met with flattering applause, and the urchin who had taken part was the hero of the afternoon.

Village poverty does not permit much in the way of expensive toys. The potter, for an anna apiece, made little clay carts with wheels that actually turned on a wooden axle. On certain days the ground about his door was covered with clay carts. He also made crude mud dolls. More elaborate ones, carved from wood, could be ordered from the carpenter. I saw one top in the village. Most of the children's games required nothing more elaborate than pebbles and a stick with which to scratch some checkerboard pattern in the dust. The children themselves were curiously dignified for their years. The little goatherds and buffalo tenders and grass cutters had a solemn air of responsibility. In the schools the children nowadays have to be taught to play games. But wrestling and lathi fencing, kite flying and contests between fighting birds, offered a variety of amusements for both the younger and older children of our village.

Card playing among certain groups of men was also popular. The Doctor, the Patwari, and the school teachers made a card table out of the well curb near the hospital, and here they were to be seen with their feet comfortably tucked up, playing cards nearly every evening. Another group of players used to sit on a string bed outside one of the Bania's houses in Pachperwa. That they played for money I took for granted. Both Hindus and Mussulmans share this vice, though the Hindus claim to be the most ancient gamblers in the world. In the *Mahabharata* it is related how Yudhisthira the Truthful, eldest of the Pandavas, staked and lost his kingdom and his wife Draupadi in a game of dice, bringing misfortune to the house of Pandu, and likewise how Nala was enticed into gambling away the kingdom of the Nishadhas to his jealous brother Pushkara.

A spontaneous outlet for every villager and for all the moods of the village was music. I can still hear the vibrant song of a cartman I never saw to my knowledge, who used to drive his lumbering cart along the road past my house at night. His voice had a strangely moving quality. It made no difference that I could not understand the words. Another cartman's song heard in the district I was fortunate enough to have translated. The Tahsildar and the Peshkar and the Station Master, as a matter of fact, all helped me collect the songs of the village folk, but they constantly pointed out that the illiterate villagers misused words and as often as not made an unintelligible jumble of their songs. This one was called a *biroh*—a type of song expressing the pangs of separation:

> "*O people, we have to go on a journey, and the destination is far; let us join in the worship of God today.*
>
> *When Death comes it waits for nobody, it comes with a chain to carry the soul away.*
>
> *The soul leaves by one of the ten gates of the body; rich or poor, it is all the same to Death.*
>
> *Vain is the lamentation of father and mother! When the time comes, Death bites like a serpent and is gone, and none can stay him.*

*All the riches of the world and all the armies of the
world are useless to the soul when it leaves the
body.*

*Brothers, worship God to-day and, being at one with
Him, know peace.*

*The wisdom of the sages is this: Worship God as Rama,
Lakshman, and Sita before life ebbs away."*

Song wove itself in and out of the daily life of the village
in an ever recurring pattern. The brick makers at Haweli
Singh's factory, in their huts of loosely stacked bricks, entertained themselves at night by singing. Asgar announced
his return from supper by a lusty caroling. Unlike Ram
Lakhan, who had real musical feeling, Asgar was content to
make a cheerful noise. In the hot nights before the rain,
when the *popiyas* called intermittently from the mango trees,
and none of us could sleep much, I listened to the tahsil
peons singing hour upon hour—strains that came plain-
tively through the darkness, broken into infinitely small
fragments of sound.

One day a particularly energetic burst of song drew me
outside to find a Mohammedan sweetmeat seller going the
rounds of the tahsil with candy mangoes and custard apples
nestling among fresh green mango branches fastened to his
staff. His song did not, as I supposed, advertise the merit
of his wares. He sang whatever came into his head. One
song was a puritanical attack on the tendency of women in
these degenerate days to wear expensive finery. "No longer
do they wish to wear coarse garments to the *melas*. They like
fine saris with colors. In this way they lose their honor,"
sang the itinerant Halwai from Sitapur.

Religious mendicants did not go from house to house
knocking at the doors, but stood outside and sang. Both
Hindu ascetics and Mohammedan fakirs have an endless
repertory of devotional songs. The one group will sing of the
delights of Paradise and the splendor of the Durbar of
Allah; the other, of the intimate relation between the devotee
and God, or of God in his varied forms as the child Krishna,

Krishna the cowherd, Rama the Lotus-eyed, Shiva the Great God. The people learn these same songs and sing them after the wanderers have passed on.

The songs of three great religious poets who lived in the fifteenth and sixteenth centuries are still sung to-day all over India. Devotees of Rama and Sita find their greatest source of inspiration in the songs of Tulsidas, best known for his popular translation of the *Ramayana* from Sanskrit into Hindi. The worshipers of Krishna chant the songs of Mirabai, who lived during the reign of the great Mogul Emperor, Akbar.

Akbar was fond of music, and at his court he kept a famous singer and maker of songs, Tansen, said to have gathered his melodies from listening to the songs of the humble cultivators as they drew water at the wells. One day Akbar, according to the legend, asked if there were any better singer in all India, and Tansen answered that Mirabai, the great devotee of Krishna, was his superior. The Emperor disguised himself as a sadhu and went with Tansen to the temple where Mirabai sang daily. While she was singing ecstatically, unconscious of the world, Akbar placed his own jeweled necklace around her throat. Her husband, Rana of Udaipur, as soon as he saw the costly gift, accused her of having a lover and drove her away. Later he was warned in a dream that his raj would be destroyed if he did not bring her back, and Mirabai, touched by the sufferings caused by famine, returned, though she had dedicated herself to the adoration of Krishna. At the end of her life, singing before Krishna's image at Dwarka, she suddenly vanished into the image.

Kabir, the other great song maker, was the adopted son of a Mohammedan weaver. He became a disciple of Ramananda. For him the barriers between Islam and Hinduism did not exist. Hindus and Mussulmans alike sing the songs of Kabir, whose body at his death was disputed between them, and Sikhs, too, honor his memory, since Nanak, the founder of Sikhism, was a disciple of Kabir. In his songs, which have been translated by Tagore, he preached only the one invisible Unity:

> *"I laugh when I hear that the fish in the water is thirsty:*
> *You do not see that the Real is in your home, and you*
> *   wander from forest to forest listlessly!*
> *Here is the truth! Go where you will, to Benares or to*
> *   Mathura; if you do not find your soul, the world*
> *   is unreal to you."*

> *"O servant, where dost thou seek Me?*
> *Lo! I am beside thee.*
> *I am neither in temple nor in mosque."*

When the spring crops were ripening toward the end of February and cultivators spent the night guarding them against thieves and animals, they sang songs of the Holi season, celebrating Krishna's playtime and his sport with the milkmaids of Brindaban. These songs were especially popular with the Ahirs, who worship Krishna, the Divine Herdsman, and claim descent from him.

> *"In the lanes of Brindaban Krishna promised to meet us.*
> *He has gone to Dwarka while we are waiting for him*
> *   with garlands, which are fading.*
> *In the lanes of Brindaban Krishna is patrolling like a*
> *   thief.*
> *He drinks our milk and breaks our pots, and curd flows*
> *   like water in the street."*

In a land where life is regulated by an almost ritualistic adherence to tradition, music, too, follows a definite pattern. The *ragas* are the Indian equivalent for scales, and every raga represents a particular group of notes, giving rise to a distinctive and recognizable melody. Since quarter tones and even smaller fractional notes are used—the octave ordinarily includes twenty-two notes—plenty of melodic variety is possible, but harmony, as it is known in the West, is lacking. The rhythm in Indian music is much freer than in Western music, with phrases of variable length and different time beats.

The many ragas—one authority lists seventy-two of them
—are perfectly discernible to the trained Indian ear. Moreover, love of enduring patterns in life has decreed that certain ragas shall be sung or played at particular seasons of
the year or particular times of the day or night. The *Kajli*
is the raga of the rainy season, the *Chaita* is a summer song,
the *Bhajan*, a song of devotion, *Basanta*, a spring song,
Megh, a song of exuberant joy in anticipation of the rain,
Bhairava, a song of ascetism and reverence, *Panchama*, a song
of calm night. In imitation of the classical ragas popular
ones have sprung up. The *Dhobia Rag* is shouted by the
washerman as he slaps his clothes on a board.

Though Pachperwa did not boast any musicians who could
play the vina, sitar or esraj, flutes of metal or bamboo, brass
horns, cymbals, sarangis, and a dozen different sorts of
drums were constantly shattering our rural quiet. Among
the instrument players the drummers were certainly the
most ubiquitous. Their skill in manipulating complex
rhythms filled me with admiration. An Indian can produce
rhythm even out of a clay pot, and pot drums were, in fact,
a pulsing undertone of life in Pachperwa. Slapping on a
bare thigh would serve as an accompaniment for a song, if
nothing else was available. Thus I grew used to associating
music in some form with every mood of the village and every
significant incident of village life.

Yet my baby phonograph was not popular among the villagers, except with Ram Lakhan, who listened attentively to
violin, song, and orchestral records and expressed very posi-
tively his preference and dislike for certain selections.
Western music, with its elaborate harmonies, did not appeal
to the Indian villagers. They found it too complex, too
"noisy," to suit their tastes.

For sheer excitement and joy, a mela offers inexhaustible
diversion to the Indian countryside. This combination of fair
and religious festival is held at a fixed time in association
with some particular shrine or sacred bathing spot. The
greatest of the Indian melas is the Kumbh Mela, which

occurs every three years at four sacred cities in turn, and which is attended by several million pilgrims, but the Magh Mela, held in January at Prag—or Allahabad, as it is called by Westerners—is the most popular of the annual melas. The Magh Mela lasts for a whole month, and its principal feature is the bathing at the confluence of the sacred Jumna and Ganges. For the accommodation of the million pilgrims, tents and temporary shelters are erected. Pennants and flags fluttering from tall poles show where hostels have been established, many of them by charitable associations or rich patrons, for pilgrims coming from different localities.

It is the ambition of every pious villager, especially in the United Provinces, to go to at least one Magh Mela, as well as to visit the great shrines sanctified by associations of thousands of years—Brindaban, Hardwar, Ayodhya, Benares, Gaya. For Mussulmans the tombs of holy saints have the same attraction. But the poor villager cannot afford to undertake a long journey away from home very often, and so for the most part he has to content himself with some local mela, in which trading usually plays an important part.

In March I began to hear much of Debi Patan and its three-day annual fair soon to take place. Debi Patan was close to Balrampur—the railway fare from Pachperwa was only twelve annas. All the Pachperwa traders and those of surrounding villages rented booths to display their stocks. Haweli Singh obtained the contract for the sacred tank in which sacrificial goats and buffaloes for the goddess Kali, whose temple was the center of the mela, would be given their ceremonial baths at so many annas per head. The proceeds from ground rents and other taxes, amounting to something like five thousand rupees each year, went to the Balrampur Estate.

I had promised to take the Ayah to Debi Patan. The only train left at two in the morning. Accompanied by the Peshkar and his cook and a bodyguard of tahsil peons, we walked to the station by lantern light. On the platform, many people were rolled up asleep, waiting for the train. I saw the man from Trinidad, now a recruiting agent. He said he was on his way to the mela to sell 250 rupees' worth of red peppers. The Thanadar was there, too, taking a miserable prisoner to Gonda.

The sun was just rising when we arrived at Debi Patan. Thousands were camping in the bare fields or wandering about the grounds of the mela, which had been built up with rows of temporary booths until the place looked like a small city. A special feature of Debi Patan fair is the horse mart, and long lines of horses were staked out at a corner of a grove. Little black and white Nepalese ponies brought down from the hills were much in evidence, but there were also finer horse breeds. The Peshkar managed a shrewd piece of business, selling his old horse and buying a new one at a bargain price of less than twenty-five dollars. All day, as the Ayah and I wandered about, we encountered friends. The village tailors were there in full force with their sewing machines, stitching muslin caps. The cloth merchants unrolled their bolts of cloth and displayed fancy saris and dhotis. The goldsmiths were plying a brisk trade. The Ayah discovered that her brother from Balrampur had set up a food booth, and she thriftily exacted a free meal from him. The fun for the crowd was principally in the sights and in the driving of anna bargains. After a few hours the dust and heat and crowds sent me back to the Public Works Rest House, but the Ayah was indefatigable.

Much is said and written of Hindu-Moslem ill-will and communal strife and tension, especially at times of political crises. In towns and cities during Moharram the authorities take special precautions to prevent communal conflicts. People are forbidden to carry lathis, and ordinances limit even the length and thickness of the walking sticks that may be carried at this time. But I could see almost no traces of bad feeling in my little corner of India. The Tahsildar said that fifteen years ago communal clashes were almost unknown. They have come as a result of modern political developments. In Pachperwa it was hard to tell whether Moharram was a Hindu or a Mohammedan festival. The ten days of mourning for Ali's two sons, the martyred Hassan and Hossein, were transformed into a gay little fête during which Hindus, along with Mussulmans, wore their best clothes, stayed up all night, ate as much as they could afford to buy, and amused themselves with those fantastic paper and bamboo cenotaphs, called tazias, which were carried in the Moharram procession.

For weeks before Moharram, the villagers were feverishly making tazias. Stacks of square papers replaced the cloth in the dyer's shop, and these Rajab was busily engaged in stamping in different colors and patterns. The whole village was hard at work pasting Rajab's papers or sheets of colored isinglass on skeleton frameworks of bamboo, and in making lantern-like domes to top off the marvelous skyscrapers ten or twelve feet high. If you are rich, you furnish half a dozen tazias to the Moharram procession. If you are industrious, you make and sell as many to others. In any case everybody, Hindu as well as Mussulman, hopes to turn out with something at the last second. This was Kalu's moment of triumph—Kalu, chief artist of Pachperwa. I came upon him, very proud and pleased with himself, putting the finishing touches to his masterpiece. He had used transparent oiled green and red paper and had painted all his strips with charming friezes of flowers.

Tazias are supposed to have been invented by Timur in the fourteenth century. Not being able to take part in the annual pilgrimage of mourning to Kerbela, he ordered a miniature tomb of Ali, the Prophet's martyred son-in-law, to be carried in the Moharram procession at Delhi. Nowadays Ali's sons, the popular heroes Hassan and Hossein, have their little coffins, like twin beds, inside the gay paper tombs. Balls of mud stuck on matches at the ends of the silver or gold paper coffins represent their turbaned heads.

The drums were going a full week before July first, when Moharram commenced. Every night I could hear them— the thump-thump, thump-thump, thump-thump of the *dhol*, the t-t-t-t-t-t-t-t-t of the little cup-drum of clay, at intervals the trembling clash of cymbals. After Moharram had really begun, the music was even more insistent. Instead of an hour or two, it lasted half the night. Lying in bed, I could distinguish one set of drums going full blast at Bargadwa, one at the New Bazar, another in Pachperwa. They seemed to inspire the frogs with a spirit of rivalry. Frogs and drums, drums and frogs, mosquitoes singing incessantly, the windy whir of bats' wings flicking overhead—haunting memories of Moharram nights!

On the eighth night of the festival there was a tazia procession around the village, and the next night the tazias were displayed outside the houses on square benches. Usually the village was very dark. The lights were too faint and small to cast more than a pale blur. On the night of the procession the main street was dotted with torches. A crowd of men surged along, holding aloft a towering tazia, its gaudy walls rising in three narrowing stories and crowned by a gold paper dome. By the magnificence of his tazia a man rises to sudden fame. This particular one was the work of Haidar Julaha, an ex-weaver. The Maulvi, in his long white gown, smoking a cigarette, acted as stage manager, though no words could be heard above the mad beating of drums. A sturdy old man marched in front, holding a large book from which he chanted the tale of the beloved martyrs. With his free hand he beat his hairy breast in a somewhat mechanical way, keeping time to the double thump of the big drums. Behind pushed a crowd of men, women, and children, Hindus and Mussulmans indiscriminately mixed. Many of them carried tall "spears." Spears not being permitted in disarmed India, bamboo poles, wrapped in red, green, or white cloth and with cloth pennants fluttering from the tips, were substituted. The women at the end of the procession were singing a doleful chant of mourning.

The next night I again went struggling through the mud with the Thanadar and his chief munshi to view the display of the tazias. Through an opening in a mud wall we had our first glimpse of a group of them lighted. Four tazias stood on a platform under a canopy, with a lantern swinging aloft, like a ship's light, from a pole supporting the canopy. This was the display mustered by a Hindu household of grain parchers. Across the way a woman was lighting tiny clay lamps in front of a modest tomb of plain red paper. She was a Luniya, or earth worker, Hindu again. Then we visited Nepal Bania's tazia—he was one of our money-lenders. At the next house a *Barai*, or pan seller, had three tazias set up in a row. Farther on, a Teli, observing the Hindu mode of remembering the dead, had placed two little dishes of milk before the tombs. It really seemed at first as if only Hindus were having tazias, but before finishing our rounds we saw plenty made by Mussulmans.

Everybody in Pachperwa expected—and took—a holiday on the tenth night of Moharram. Asgar Ali and Din Moham-med joined one of the bands of men and boys going about singing from village to village. They did not return until five in the morning. These night wanderers were all men and boys, but before dawn bands of women and girls began to trail along the road, singing the traditional lament for the death of the martyrs. Looking out through the mos-quito net of my bed, I observed that the dingy saris of ordi-nary days had vanished. The women had blossomed out in bright, freshly dyed saris and all sorts of tinkling finery. Small boys were adorned with gay satin or velvet vests and caps—purple, green, magenta, orange—and even a few men were in festive garb. I saw one wrinkled old fel-low, with a white beard, in a brilliant purple dhoti.

As I was dressing, I heard what sounded like a Persian caravan outside. Some thirty or forty strange figures, like masqueraders, were stalking about the house. They had wigs of red and white cloth braided into long ropes hanging below their waists, and belts of jingling bells, and in their hands they carried bunches of peacock feathers or whisks of split bamboo. These gentlemen, I learned from the Ayah, were the sipahis, or guards, of Imam Hossein and Imam

Hassan. Men falling seriously ill often made a vow that they would serve as a sipahi at Moharram in the event of recovery, or a mother made such a promise on behalf of her child. The sipahis march with the tazia processions, plying their peacock brushes or bamboo whisks to chase away flies, real and imaginary. Among the group on my lawn I was amused to discover Mewa Lal, one of the Hindu chaprasis of the tahsil.

The climax of Moharram was reached on the eleventh day. This was the time when tazia-bearing processions, starting from all the neighboring hamlets and villages, converged at Pachperwa and marched on to "Kerbela" for the final burial of the tazias—in village phraseology they were "made cold." Every group of inland villages in India where Mussulmans make up a fair proportion of the population has its own "Kerbela," named for the sacred city in Irak, dedicated to the annual burial of tazias. In the vicinity of great rivers and along the seacoast tazias are not buried but are drowned.

The Station Master came to fetch me as drums announced a procession approaching from the New Bazar. A group of boys at the head of the procession staged periodic circular dances. Sweetmeat makers and pan sellers mixed with the throngs of pallbearers carrying the colored tombs. We all moved on to the thana, where five different processions were scheduled to meet. Ours was the first to arrive, so while we waited—all the officials had appeared to share the hospitality of the thana—the boys repeated their dance, singing a plaintive little melody of which the words were: "Don't cry, Mother. Here in Paradise, amid cool streams and singing birds and blossoming trees, we are happy." Thus Hassan and Hossein considerately comforted the Prophet's daughter Fatima. "Are there any Hindu boys among them?" I asked the Thanadar. He laughed. "There are only five Mussulmans. The other fifteen are all Hindus."

Presently a gay procession came winding across the flat fields from Bargadwa. It was headed by a magnificent tazia fifteen feet high. This one, murmured the crowd in awed voices, purchased by Teja Khan at Balrampur, had cost the whole of twenty rupees. Tazias were now pouring in from all directions. All of them were set down on the ground to give the crowd a proper chance to admire them. Meanwhile a champion fencer, armed with a lathi, had challenged anyone to try a bout with him. He was a Mohammedan greengrocer, ugly of face but lithe as a panther. His movements, as he twirled his lathi, reminded me of a slow-motion film. His challenge was accepted by an old man, and a knot of spectators formed to watch the match. The champion easily parried the lusty blows of the other, making no obvious effort even to return them, but suddenly the old man went down on one knee, defeated. It turned out that the pair were father and son.

Once more the tazias were shouldered and the mile-long procession got under way. Since the sun had now almost dropped to the horizon, most of the village aristocracy went home. I was eager to stay to the finish and so I went on with the crowd, under the wing of the Thanadar, along a zigzag path which wound across the tops of the dikes through the half-submerged fields. For weeks the mountains had been hidden, but in the rain-washed air the snowy ranges suddenly stood out once more, flushed with heavenly pink.

Presently we reached our destination, a patch of ground near a mango grove a mile west of the village. It was pockmarked with yawning holes, dug the night before. Into these the tazias were lowered, story by story, if they were too tall. Some had single burial, others were interred in trenches. Everybody began to throw handfuls of earth on them. Little boys took running jumps, smashing down the frail frameworks with irreligious joy. Several bore off bits of tinsel or colored paper rifled from the graves. Altogether there must have been several hundred tazias. Though the same burial ground was used year after year, in the open pits there was no sign of last year's wreckage. The rains soon rot everything away. Thus Moharram came to an end in Pachperwa.

Why people in our little village in far-away India should concern themselves about two Arabs who happened to be killed in the fortunes of a political and a religious war of the seventh century and metaphorically, not to say literally, beat their breasts over them, is hard to say, but for Mussulmans, of course, the anniversary is as sacred as Christmas or Easter is to a Christian. In Pachperwa, as far as I could see, time and distance had subtly altered the original spirit of the Day of Martyrdom. It had turned into one of the happiest holidays of the year.

The traditional ceremonies of the Hindus are likewise a source of endless joy. In the framework of changing seasons, they celebrate, always with a religious emphasis, the moods of nature which play such an important part in pastoral life. The little marked events of every household also make many special days among the ordinary ones—weddings, births, the name day of a child, the ear-piercing rite, the *upanayama*, the ceremony of investing boys of the "twice-born" castes with the sacred thread. All these and countless others are occasions for a Hindu family to feast or fast. The village pujari or the family priest recites appropriate texts. Relatives or caste fellows are invited to the house. This ceremonial aspect of Indian life offers an escape from drab monotony. On a larger scale, the Hindu calendar also generously provides the countryside with all sorts of pujas in honor of the gods and.goddesses—as the saying is, "Thirteen pujas to twelve months."

On Basanta Panchami, in February, most of the Hindu women of the village appeared in yellow saris, turmeric dyed. I had seen them drying, for a week or more, on the thatched roofs. Basanta Panchami is a day dedicated to Saraswati, who, in her rôle of goddess of learning, receives the homage especially of students and scholars. Books, reed pens, and musical instruments are symbols used in her worship. In the school yard one of the Brahmin pundits chanted mantras invoking the presence and blessings of Saraswati, and the boys observed her worship at a little temporary shrine.

In March we celebrated Ganesha Chaturthi. On this day many of the women fasted until the moon rose and then worshiped Ganesh with an offering of sessamum mixed with brown sugar. Mothers hope that by honoring Ganesh, the model son of the gods, they will be blessed with worthy sons. Someone—perhaps the pujari, if he is engaged to do so—will tell the Ganesh legends: how, for example, when Ganesh as a boy once struck a cat, he found his mother Parvati ill on her bed when he returned to the house, and he was then taught by her that the Mother dwells in all female forms. Or how Ganesh and his brother Kartik, god of war, competed for their mother's necklace as the reward in a race round the world. Kartik sped off, mounted on his peacock. Ganesh, on his mouse, merely encircled his mother —and won the necklace.

In March, too, fell the Holi festival, supposed to commemorate Krishna's play with the milkmaids of Brindaban, really a sort of spring festival, in origin not unlike the Western May Day. It is observed by all Hindus, but more exuberantly by the lower classes. A feature of Holi is a great bonfire. The wood for this is collected by boys who enjoy a license for the occasion to carry off anything they can lay hands on. The old Doctor of the dispensary, sitting on my veranda the afternoon before Holi, told me a long story about the bonfire. A certain king compelled all his subjects to substitute his name in their worship for that of God. The young Prince Prahlad, a fervent devotee of Krishna, refused to obey his father's edict, thus incurring his wrath. With the name of Krishna on his lips, Prahlad successfully overcame all his father's attempts to do away with him. Finally as a last resort the king's sister, Holika, jumped into a fire with Prahlad, but when the fire had burnt to blackened ashes, Holika had been utterly consumed while there sat the boy serenely in the midst of the charred ruins.

The Thanadar promised to come early the next morning and take me to the bonfire. He assured me I needed his protection. Whatever religious significance the festival once had, nowadays Holi has turned into a time for crude tomfoolery. Men and boys in the morning throw dust and filth at one another and at any woman who dares to venture out, in the name of the reviled Holika. Later they squirt colored water out of bamboo syringes, sparing no one. A less pleasant feature of Holi is the singing of more or less obscene songs. Women and girls generally remain invisible on this day to escape insult.

True to his word, the Thanadar arrived promptly at nine, drenched with pink and yellow dye which the Peshkar had just thrown over him. We set out through the mango grove and were joined on the way by Haweli Singh, duly bepinked, and the Thanadar's little girl. When we reached the large tank east of the village, only charred and smoking embers of the Holi fire, representing the pyre of Holika, remained. I was expecting to find things rather lively, after what I had heard, but all the men and boys, with a handful of small girls among them, were engaged in nothing more mischievous than washing down all the village animals in the tank—cows, horses, buffaloes, donkeys, elephants, goats, and sheep.

Half an hour later, safely home again, I heard a strange uproar coming straight up my hill. I went to the veranda, to be greeted by a crowd of at least a hundred men and boys, whose clothes, faces, hands, and hair were all stained vivid pink. Beneath the dye I began to pick out familiar faces. There was Haweli Singh again, with his curly beard now a deep magenta, and there was Jokhi Lal, glowing beyond one's utmost dreams of rosiness, and there, if you please, was the Thanadar himself, as pink as anybody. All were laughing and enjoying themselves hugely. A contingent of musicians kept up a wild accompaniment, while the whole crowd, armed with squirt guns filled with pink water, were sprinkling one another to their heart's content. "I have brought them all here! I have brought them all here for you to see them!" the Thanadar kept shouting above the din, and I shouted back my delight that he had had the happy thought to do so, wondering with a little alarm if they intended to aim their squirt guns in my direction. They were very polite, however. Several of them came forward, one at a time, and asked permission to put a red thumb-print on my forehead. This, it seemed, was a friendly sign that they accepted me into the village life. They also asked if they might not put some pink dye on an old garment, so that I could take it back to America with me as a memento of Pachperwa. Much to their joy, I donated a handkerchief to the cause of international friendship.

That same afternoon I was invited to attend a celebration at the temple for ushering in the Hindu New Year of the Samvat era. At four o'clock, when the Thanadar appeared again with a cortège of now clean and recognizable neighbors, the Holi mood had disappeared, save for expectancy of the fine feast all would indulge in that evening. The brilliant dyes, I was relieved to hear, in view of the wreckless spraying, all came out in the wash. That week all the village washermen did a heavy business. I saw mine going off with a bundle the size of my kitchen on his back.

At the time of the Durga Puja, the great harvest festival, I was many miles away from Pachperwa, at Almora in the Himalaya. The Durga Puja, or Dasara, is the puja for Durga, the Mother, worshiped throughout India. It is perhaps the most elaborate of all Indian festivals, with its joyous celebration of the "homecoming" of the Mother from Kailash, Shiva's snowy abode. This is the time for processions, feasts, present giving, and display of one's best finery. Incidentally it is Rama himself, King of Ayodhya, who is credited with originating the Durga Puja, when he invoked the aid of the goddess in his campaign against Ravana, the demon king who carried Sita off to Ceylon.

Hence it has become a custom to act the *Ramayana* during the Dasara festival, a performance usually continuing through ten or eleven days.

The setting for the *Ram Lila* in Almora was perfect. A great open court was cut out from the side of the mountain, and hundreds of spectators crowded around the sides or perched on the flat stone roofs of surrounding houses. Wisps of white clouds trailed across the stage in the cold mountain night. A section of the court was set aside for women, and the brilliant green and red and turquoise-blue and saffron of the softly flowing saris glowed jewel-like in the artificial illumination of the court. The actors were boys, most of whom played the same parts for two or three years in succession.

There was a delightful casualness about the performance. No one minded if the prompter read out the lines when they were forgotten by King Dasharatha, Bharat, Lakshman, Sita or Hanuman. Some of the little actors fell asleep and had to be roused again. But there were tremendously exciting moments, when Parasu Rama shot off Shiva's great bow, when Hanuman, in a red suit with a long tail and a monkey mask, went jumping to Lanka, and when, on the last night, the gigantic wood and papier-mâché images of Ravana and his confederates, paraded through the streets of Almora all afternoon, were dramatically burned, sending showers of sparks up toward the stars. Back in Pachperwa, the *Ram Lila* was being celebrated, too, not with all this elaboration, perhaps, but in simple village fashion. It was Asgar Ali, my own Mohammedan boy, who generally played the part of Sita.

CHAPTER XVIII

God in Pachperwa

Almost from my first day in the Village of Five Trees I was aware of the invisible presence of God. I bumped into him twenty times a day. He was the explanation of everything, giver of good fortune, weaver of the net of kismet, scapegoat for the village troubles. He played a part in almost every conversation. Before long I found my Anglo-Saxon reticence breaking down: I, too, talked of God in familiar fashion. To have ignored God in Pachperwa would have been impossible.

"God save Miss Sahiba," the Brahmin postman always ejaculated piously as he handed me a letter. For all my comings and goings, the Station Master made special petitions to God to keep me safe or praised him for having done so. "It all depends upon God," said the Peshkar resignedly, discussing the prospects of his future promotion to the rank of tahsildar. "Ram, give me food!" "Ram, send rain!" groaned the low-caste gorait, pulling the punka during one of Jumai's periods of rest. "If God wills, he will get well," the compounder at the hospital remarked as he stared down placidly at a fever-stricken man who had crawled to my door.

The villagers were named after gods with delightful informality. The Tahsildar bore a name common among Brahmins, Jagannath, "Lord of the Universe." The Peshkar was Raghuraj, "King of the Raghus," one of Rama's many titles. Rama and Krishna were the commonest names of all. Two of my acquaintances were called Mahadeo, "Great

God," and my friend the confectioner was Sheobalak, "Shiva's boy." Hanuman Bania supplied our staples. In English we should have had to address Devi Prasad, our village Non-coöperator, as "Blessing of the Goddess." One simple cultivator walked around unselfconsciously as Bhagavan, "God." Many a little Lakshmi, Vishnu's consort, played about the village streets. The Mussulmans were also partial to names of religious significance. The Station Master was called Allah, Jumai was sanctified as "Friday" —the Mohammedan holy day—and his brother, who most certainly did not live up to what might be expected under the circumstances, was "Godly." Since there is virtue in the name of God, as well as everything that suggests him, why not take advantage of an easy opportunity to have his name constantly on the lips?

The Mussulmans of the region were descended for the most part from low-caste Hindus, converted a century or two before. They were called Nai Mussulmans, "New Mussulmans." Observing the five daily prayers of Islam, attending Friday mosque, not eating pork, fasting during Ramazan, and mourning in Moharram were the outward manifestations of the Prophet's followers in Pachperwa.

On all days except Fridays the mosque was like a Protestant church during the week, starkly deserted, gate inhospitably shut. But on Fridays it came to life. The zeal of the devout did not abate even under the blazing sky of May and June. It was on a June Friday that I went to mosque with the Station Master, who had previously asked the Maulvi Sahib's permission to bring me.

The service began at the hottest hour of the day, one o'clock. Leaving my shoes among the scuffed, worn ones heaped promiscuously at the entrance, I crossed the scorching cement courtyard in stockinged feet. I was very glad to sit down on a stool at one side. The only other woman present was an old soul who squatted on a bit of gunny-sack at the back of the court. The Station Master washed his feet and arms and punctiliously rinsed his mouth with water poured from a brass jar in a corner by Illahi Baksh, the shaggy old man who called the prayer hours. Then, twisting his round felt cap sidewise so that the brass "Station Master" adorning the front would not interfere with his prostrations, he took his place in line with the five hundred other worshipers and performed his private prayer ritual.

When the Maulvi in a snowy turban and long white gown mounted the three steps of the pulpit within the open-faced mosque and began to chant verses from the Koran, the whole congregation sat down on the strips of matting stretched across the court and listened attentively. According to the Station Master, the Maulvi Sahib was a man of parts who would have been better appreciated had he come from "outside." Unfortunately he had always lived in Pachperwa, like his father before him, and the villagers accepted him as a matter of course. The Maulvi chanted for half an hour, and then the Moslem prayer ritual was repeated in unison. Thumbs were placed behind ears, hands were folded over the stomach, bodies were bent so that the hands rested upon the knees, a kneeling posture was assumed, and finally the complete prostration was performed, with the forehead pressed to the ground. It was as if the rows bowed before some great wind.

The Mussulmans of the village, like Mussulmans everywhere, observed a dignified indifference to their surroundings when the prescribed hours for daily prayer came. Not all Mussulmans, of course, showed equal ardor. Asgar and Fakire never prayed at all, so far as I could see, and the Mohammedan women of the village, whatever may have been their practice inside the houses, did not pray openly. The purdah tradition stood in the way of their public demonstrations of piety. But Dukhi was inveterate in the matter of his prayers. He developed a special fondness for saying them on my lawn. He even kept a straw prayer mat hanging from a nail on the north wall of the Happy House.

His barber father, he confessed, was not religious, but his mother was very particular about her prayers, and she had given him his prayer habit at the age of twelve. Though he was now somewhere around seventy, it was his custom to rise before dawn, bathe, go next door to the small mosque in Bargadwa, and repeat the ritual of his prostrations sixteen times, after which he "read" the Koran for a while. He meant he recited verses by heart. Dukhi did not know how to read or write, but he had paid the Maulvi two hundred rupees to teach his daughter to read the Koran in Urdu, and another two hundred for each of her three children. By the time these extra devotional exercises had been performed, it was sunrise and time for the first prayer, so he had to go through his performance all over again, contenting himself on this occasion with only four repetitions. With twelve prayers at two o'clock, eight at four, seven at six, and nineteen at midnight—which Dukhi insisted was his routine observance—he claimed a grand total of sixty-six prayers a day. His own pious choice dictated the precise number of his religious exercises. Besides saying prayers, he expressed his religion by radiating kindly feelings toward everybody. He laid down the injunction that a good Mussulman should not lie nor steal. "And then," he concluded, "when he goes to paradise, Allah will give him a house like yours to live in, Miss Sahiba. But if he be wicked he will be thrown into the everlasting bonfire."

Mohammedan fervor rose to a climax on three occasions during the year—Ramazan, the month of fasting, Bakrid, when animal sacrifices were offered, and the first ten days of Moharram, the period of mourning.

During the whole of Ramazan all strict Mussulmans, the sick and children excluded, did not eat anything nor allow a single drop of water to touch their lips until after the sun went down. They were supposed to put their minds on God, but it seemed to me that the fasting produced a good deal of irritability. This period was especially difficult for those who had to travel. Presently I made the discovery that these days the Station Master's wife was cooking simple food which the Station Master was offering every evening

to all Mussulmans on the westbound train, when it stopped
at Pachperwa at seven o'clock. "Just a little something to
break their fast," he explained. His pious act of serving
food nightly during Ramazan to forty or fifty persons was
a part payment of his debt of gratitude to God. Did he
not owe to God his good fortune of being Station Master
at Pachperwa with a salary of fifty rupees? His relatives
did not remember God, and it was to be noted that they
were all in bad straits.

Bakrid is the day when animal sacrifices are offered by
Mussulmans in commemoration of Abraham's sacrifice.
Usually goats are sacrificed, but with special permission and
under carefully restricted conditions cows also may be
slaughtered. Cow *qurbani*, like the playing of music by
Hindus in front of mosques during worship, is one of the
chief causes of Hindu-Moslem animosity, and in the
cities Bakrid almost inevitably ushers in a communal clash.
The quarreling over these sacrifices is often cited as proof
of fatally irreconcilable difficulties between the two communities, but since cattle are slaughtered daily in India
for beef-eating Europeans and Mussulmans without causing
riots, it is evident that the exercise of a little tact and self-
restraint on both sides would solve the problem.

Pachperwa was outside the range of trouble on this score,
because all killing of cows was prohibited in the Hindu estate
of the Maharaja of Balrampur. The day commenced with
early morning prayers at the mosque. Afterward goats or
sheep were sacrificed in the homes of those who could afford
to make a sacrifice, and Bakrid wound up with general feasting, in which Mussulmans sent bits of sacrificial meat to
friends and with prodigal hospitality offered other bits to
guests. Teja Khan sent me a sheep's leg, which I in turn
passed on to the servants. In general council it was decided
they would have it in the form of *kebob*. When I asked
what they would do for the skewers on which to roast the
meat, the Ayah, with a burst of inspiration, produced some
spokes of a broken umbrella I had recently discarded.

The automatic simplicity of the Moslem ritual of worship and the genuine democracy of the mosque, where all men stand together as brothers, explain the peculiar strength of the body of seventy million Indian Mussulmans. The emptiness of the mosque is wonderfully soothing. There is nothing to distract the eye, no image to stir a response, no music to awaken subtle emotions, nothing upon which to divide. The rules of conduct, the prohibitions and injunctions, are not too many, and they have all been clearly laid down by Mahomet. Ultimate responsibility for life remains with the invisible High Command. The greatest of Islamic virtues are faith and submission, and with these the followers of the Prophet take flight for the Infinite. Allah is great, and Mahomet is his Prophet.

In sharp contrast to the more or less uniform practices of Islam, Hinduism, with its diverse forms of worship and its varied rituals, is immensely bewildering. The Hindu religion is not organized, like Christianity. There is no such thing as a Hindu Church, no one fixed creed, no congregational worship at temples. One can be a good Hindu without ever entering a temple. A Hindu can even be a devotee of Christ or Mahomet and still remain a Hindu so long as he renders obedience to the rules and regulations of Hindu society. What exactly is a Hindu, then? The answer is not limited to what a Hindu believes. To be a Hindu in the accepted understanding of the term, one must simply be born in a Hindu family, obey the caste laws, and refrain from eating beef. But every act of a Hindu is supposed to be performed religiously. Even the Thugs had their religious codes.

This is why the religious life of Hindus is very commonly confused with their social codes and taboos, such as "untouchability" or child marriage. The Western world, obsessed by the blindly rigid aspect of any scheme of life in which the touch even of a British viceroy would pollute a jar of drinking water for a Hindu villager, generally fails to perceive that for *being* and *becoming*, the Hindu enjoys unlimited freedom. No one has ever been burned at the stake or put to the sword or crucified under Hinduism for any religious idea he may have held, and the followers of Zoroaster, Christ, and Mahomet have all alike found hospitable welcome in India—the land of religion. From the absolute monism of the *Vedanta*—in which the idea of God apart from the Self is looked upon as a superstition—down to the worship of stocks and stones, a Hindu is free to accept whatever spiritual outlook most appeals to him.

Hinduism does not depend for its sanction on any historic personality. It finds its validity in the unchanging principles embodied in the *Vedas*. The authors of the *Vedas* were rishis, or seers, most of them nameless, some of them kings, a few of them women. They are not looked upon as prophets to whom a revelation of God was given from without. By the power of perception alone, they "realized" spiritual laws, which may be rediscovered and experienced by all human beings. Because the *Vedas* were already venerated at a very early date, the form in which they have come down from remote antiquity has not suffered alteration; but commentaries upon commentaries have been written to explain abstruse passages. Six different schools of Hindu philosophy have arisen, each of them basing its existence on a different interpretation of the same texts.

Common to all of them, however, is insistence that religion is actual realization within one's self of the ultimate Reality. The method to be used for this realization depends on the stage of spiritual evolution. For those who are still in a spiritual kindergarten, requiring symbols in order to grasp abstract ideas and ideals, India supplies millions of gods and goddesses. If the image helps toward God, then by all means use an image, say the spiritual teachers of India. Few, indeed, are those who can do without some symbol of worship—whether it be a dove, or a lamb, or a cow, a cross or a shrine, a painting or an amulet, some piece of sculptured stone, holy words, which are themselves but symbols.

Holiness is not in the object itself but in the mental association with it, so the object is not important.

The residences of gods and goddesses in Pachperwa were not imposing—they reflected the poverty of the village. The whitewashed temple in the New Bazar, dedicated to the beloved trio, Rama, Sita, and Lakshman, was very simple. Not even carved stonework like that in the temple at Ramnagar, three miles west. A white marble *linga* and a small image of Nandi, Shiva's sacred bull, nestled beneath the slender roof of a Shiva shrine at one side. The temple images were clothed in ragged finery. Only at night, when oil lamps were lighted in front of them, did the gilt no longer show its tarnish, the silken and tinsel rags lose their dusty look.

Twice daily, at eight in the morning and six in the evening, puja was observed at the temple. One of the eighteen Brahmin boys studying at the little Sanskrit school conducted by the pundit struck the gong in the temple veranda. It was not a musical sound that came forth, but a hard, exciting, metallic clang, recalling an engine bell. The temple priest went through the rites of god-worship, offering water and flowers, blowing a conch, waving a light before the images. Perhaps he put them to bed and assisted them to get up again each morning. Gods are often dressed and undressed, bathed and fed, in India. But I never saw any one attend the puja. It was not a ceremony that concerned any except the priest, whose duties were those of temple servant. Hindus merely dropped in informally at the temple—those that wished to—with the comforting sense that Rama would accept their personal worship at any time convenient to themselves. The temple never gave me the feeling of peace I experienced at the mosque, but neither did it convey the same static feeling. The mosque was empty. The temple was a dwelling place in which God and man shared one friendly roof.

The various shrines scattered about the village were little

more than mud platforms with offerings of clay elephants, mounds of earth smeared with vermilion, rounded stones, sacred trees. The Shiva stones of Pachperwa were smooth boulders, not very large, brought from mountain river beds and set here and there by the road or in some triangular corner where two lanes ran together. Water might be poured over them as an act of remembrance, but no ritual of worship was obligatory. Men on their way to the fields, women fetching water from the well, children playing in the lanes, as they caught sight of the familiar, formless symbol of the Great God, remembered Shiva and perhaps felt a sense of intangible protection. The stones served no other purpose.

Asgar and I set out one afternoon to visit all the shrines of Pachperwa. There was Sitala's shrine in the New Bazar, dedicated to the smallpox goddess. In front of Mahadeo's sweetshop, where red and yellow hornets dangled their long legs over his brass plates all day, was the tumble-down brick and mud shrine of Matahi Mai, the Taker of Troubles, to whom offerings were sometimes made on the occasion of a bereavement. A trunkless elephant stood guard, a big fellow more than two feet high. His broken trunk worried me, and I asked if it could not be mended. The potter who had made the elephant was away making pots for the Governor's camp, I was told. As soon as he returned, the elephant would certainly be supplied with a new trunk. But he remained trunkless to my last day in the village. Another shrine pointed out was a *kadam* tree, in season adorned with soft pink balls of flowers. Sometimes goats were offered here to Kali, but the only goats I ever saw under the tree were live ones tethered among the gnarled roots. In the Mohammedan butchers' quarter were three clay mounds close together, a shrine to Deohar, as the collective village godlings are called. Offerings were made there by Hindu bridegrooms. Still another shrine belonged to Samai, a purely local goddess. At least fifty children tramped with me across the sun-dried fields when I went in search of Samai's headquarters. We came to a spot beside the path where a little four-cornered spider web of bright woollen thread dangled from a slender stick. Beneath were a pair of clay horses three inches high. The colored spider web, explained the children, was the chariot of the goddess, and the horses were the steeds to draw it. It was a small affair to have come so far to see. Nobody could tell me much about Samai. As far as I could make out, she was a goddess charged with the village health.

My own shrine, as I came to call it—the one under the five trees, not more than twenty yards from the Happy House —was dedicated to Devi, Shiva's consort, who goes by as many different names as Shiva himself—Parvati, Sati, Kali, Durga, Devi, all of them really symbolizing the concept of the Mother.

Scarcely a day passed that a puja of some sort was not held at this shrine. A family group would assemble with the puja necessities, rice, vermilion, bel or mango leaves, a brass plate, *kusa* grass, turmeric, wood for a fire, water. Later came the village Pujari, who held the right to officiate at all village pujas. He arranged the offerings on the plate, placed four small banana stalks upright in the ground to mark the four corners of a holy square of ground, lighted the fire and sat down, facing north. The person offering the puja likewise sat down, facing east, and the others arranged themselves at one side in a flexible line that bent or broke in accordance with the restless movements of the children. The Pujari recited the appropriate texts by heart or read the mantras from a palm-leaf manuscript. They might be addressed to Suraj, the sun, to Mahabir-Hanuman, the devotee of Rama, to the Nine Planets, to Ganesh, or to numerous other deities. The pundit himself sometimes sat on the shrine, and when Brahmins were fed as a part of the act of worship they generally sat there to partake of the food that was offered. But as soon as the puja was over, the crows and monkeys took possession.

One big fellow often gave a ludicrous impression that he was imitating the Pujari, with whom, incidentally, he was on very friendly terms. He used to bare his teeth and make a feint of springing at Din Mohammed or anyone else who noticed him. He had us all thoroughly intimidated, but often I saw him sitting quietly hunched over in meditative attitude among the clay elephants by the side of the Pujari, as the latter read his sacred texts. It would have been easy to imagine him subdued by holy influence.

Nearly every Hindu who passed the shrine made some little gesture of respect. The villagers would stop, step out of their shoes, fold their hands together respectfully. Many touched the shrine with the right hand and then touched their own foreheads, repeating this gesture two or three times. Once I asked the washerman, who was scrupulous in his shrine observances, what deity he worshiped there. "Devi, Ram Chandra, Bhagavan," he answered inclusively.

Pujas at shrines are for special observances, usually an expression of thanks for some blessing such as recovery from sickness, sometimes a petition for help in time of distress. The Jamadar held an elaborate puja at my shrine when his little girl was sick, and when the cholera visited us the Peshkar, in spite of his disillusionment in regard to the efficacy of pundits in general, hired the pujari of a small village near by, for which his family served as rent collectors, to come every day for a week and recite prayers for his special benefit. But simple worship is practised daily in almost every Hindu household. If a whole room in the house cannot be spared for religious ceremonies, worship and meditation, then a corner is set aside as a sacred place. Maybe there is only a god-shelf on the wall. Even this is not essential. The pious old cook of the Tahsildar chanted his prayers every morning while he scrubbed his teeth with a nim tooth-stick at the well.

In the household of one of the "twice-born," portions of the Vedas will be recited. The Tahsildar spent an hour in religious meditation and reading each morning and evening. After his name he always wrote *Dwivedi*, a title of honor he was privileged to use because one of his ancestors had once learned to recite by heart two of the Vedas. Since the Rig-Veda alone contains one thousand and seventeen hymns, the feat was not to be despised. To-day there are still many scholars in India—I heard of one blind one—who show marvelous powers of memory for reciting the sacred literature of the Hindus.

The ritual of household worship—of remembrance—is a matter of personal choice for each member of the family. Whatever aspect of divinity appeals most will be selected for worship. Different members of the family may favor special deities, but to none is honor denied. It is much as if one member of a Christian family called himself a Catholic, another preferred to ally himself with the Methodists, another were an Episcopalian, but all lived together peaceably—if such a thing can be imagined—acknowledging themselves bound by the higher concept of their common ideal, Christianity. The silent repetition of one's particular mantra, simple offerings of water, leaves, flowers, or milk, either to an actual image or some temporary symbol of divinity set up and destroyed again as soon as the act of worship has been performed, the chanting of hymns, a conscious effort through the practice of meditation to realize spiritual truth—these sum up typical ways in which ordinary Hindu men and women express their religious devotion.

Way back in the days when the Rig-Veda hymns were being composed, six or seven thousand years ago, the Aryans, awed by the majesty of the mightiest mountains on earth, by tremendous storms, by thunder, by the scorching sun of the plains, by the great sweep of broad rivers, prostrated themselves before the *Devas*, the "Shining Ones," of the terrestrial, atmospheric, and celestial regions. They gave names to these manifestations of power: Varuna was the deity presiding over the sky, Indra was lord of heaven, Agni, lord of fire, Vayu, lord of the wind, Savitri was the dawn, Surya, the sun, Soma, lord of sacrificial drink, Yama, god of death.

Though the Vedic gods still have a certain tangible reality

through the hymns addressed to them, recited even to-day, they have been supplanted in the popular mind by later conceptions of divinity—Shiva, Vishnu, and Kali, whose devotees make up the three principal sects of modern Hinduism. Shiva himself has been transformed for the masses from a dread deity representing the destructive forces of creation to the "easily pleased" giver of all blessings. Vishnu, the preserver, is familiar in his two human incarnations, Rama and Krishna. Kali symbolizes the active principle of creation and is worshiped as the Mother of the Universe.

Yet even in the early Vedic period the Aryan mind was possessed by the thought of an ultimate unity. First one and then another of the gods was lifted to a position of preëminence. Varuna, Indra, Agni, in turn became the favorite. One of the ancient hymns chants: "Who is the god to whom we shall offer our sacrifice? He who gives life, He who gives strength, whose command all the Bright Gods revere, whose shadow is immortality, whose shadow is death. He who through his power is the one king of the breathing and awakening world. He who governs all, man and beast. He through whom the sky is bright and the earth firm. He who measured out the light and the air. He who alone is God above all gods."

But the mystic Hindu philosophers did not stop even here. They carried the idea of unity above the One God as standing apart from the created universe. They came out with the bold declaration that God and his creations are indivisible, and this eternal, all-pervading unit they called the *Atman*, the Self. Sankaracharya, the great ninth century interpreter of the Vedanta—"end of knowledge," another name for the *Upanishads*, since they are accepted as the last of the Vedas—defines God as "Absolute Existence, Knowledge, Bliss." From God as Existence, or Being, comes all that *is*— the material world is God perceived in and through the senses. From God as Knowledge comes all that is classed as knowledge—everything included in the realm of thought, or capable of being known by the mind, is God in this aspect.

From **God** as Bliss come human love and joy—and in experiencing these we understand in a small measure what the nature of infinite love may be. This same Existence-Knowledge-Bliss is the essential and real nature of every living thing, and, consciously or unconsciously, man is continually evolving toward the perception of the real within himself. Divinity, perfection, are within, but they are overlaid, covered up, contracted—in Hindu phraseology—and they have to be made manifest. The real nature never changes. The apparent difference between an atom of protoplasm and the greatest mystic is not of kind but of degree of manifestation. In this ultimate knowledge doubts vanish, desires vanish, all contradictions meet.

The astronomer concentrates on the stars and "the stars roll forward and give up their secrets to him." Knowledge is not in the stars but in the astronomer. And for him who concentrates upon God, knowledge of God will be distilled. Religion, to the Hindu, is not a creed, not a system of ethics, not an explanation of the universe, not an attitude toward life, but an actual realization, a direct perception, accompanied by intense awareness, of the ultimate Reality —call it God or Atman or Self.

Even the enlightened Western scientist cannot make his personal reactions to life conform with his scientific views, and the ordinary human being in the West is quite humanly filled with unscientific prejudices. The Hindu villager is scarcely to be blamed because he cannot live in the impersonal Atman, but even villagers, who cling tenaciously to their little Ramas and Krishnas, have an astonishingly clear appreciation of the unity of God. The Tahsildar gave me a naïve explanation of the countless deities of Hinduism. Just as the King-Emperor in England could not be expected personally to manage all his countries and so appointed a viceroy, who in turn appointed governors, who appointed commissioners—even he himself had a staff of subordinates under him—so God delegated the various departments of the universe to his assistants. Why did the wind change from east to west unless the Wind God directed it to do so? Why did the rain stop or fall unless Indra gave orders? To my tentative suggestion that the West had scientific explanations for all these phenomena he replied: "Very well. You may say that magnetic attraction holds the earth spinning around the sun. But who made the sun with the power of attraction?" As for God, he was not a Christian god nor a Mohammedan god nor a Hindu god, but just God. And there was nothing else to say about him!

The many-sided world is the school of experience provided so that the self may learn to know the Self and in that knowledge find lasting joy, and here, incidentally, is the answer to the question why the world is as it is, why there must be suffering and pain and disease and sin and death. Environment, physical and social, is the stimulus to which we react, and through which inner consciousness is awakened. In our own limited lives we can look back and be grateful for many experiences which at the time seemed insufferably hard to bear. From them was born understanding which was like a key to a door that had been closed. So, be patient. Do not try to judge the whole by this fragment within the realm of immediate consciousness. Step by step you are enlarging your consciousness, and with increasing consciousness comes increasing joy, foretaste of what will be experienced in the final merging of the little self into the infinite Self, when it ceases to think in terms of its limitations, when it can suffer no more pain because there is no more "I."

When the West says, all men are born free and equal, what is meant is that all men should have free and equal opportunity to fulfill their highest capacity. The effort of society is to control the environment in such a way that opportunities will be equalized. The Indian outlook is different. Practical observation shows individuals to be at all levels of development, and India does not believe that the environment can ever be standardized to suit the varying capacities and needs of all these different individuals. Evidence is against the possibility of complete evolution for the individual within the limited compass of one lifetime. As an explanation of human inequalities on the one hand, and of the ever changing environment on the other, the Hindu postulates prolonged existence, extending from birth to birth and covering innumerable lives, until emancipation comes with spiritual knowledge. What the West explains and accepts as heredity, India defines as the sum total of the soul's previous experiences gathered on the road of its evolution. "For whatsoever a man soweth, that also shall he reap," is only in a narrow sense to be accepted as a law of reward and punishment. It is really the law of evolution. We are not thrust into life as helpless victims of circumstance. The soul takes birth in the particular environment which will yield the next experiences it needs on its evolutionary path.

This doctrine of transmigration—*Karma*—almost universally accepted by the Indian mind, is a working hypothesis set up to explain the evolutionary process by which the individual is to achieve his majestic and inescapable destiny. Hinduism teaches that salvation, ultimate freedom, is not to be attained by some and denied to others. It is to be won by every living thing, through the difficult upward climb by way of experience, to real knowledge and enlightenment. The mercy of God is not capricious, lifting one of his creatures up and thrusting another down. It is stable, expressing itself in man's innate capacity for spiritual growth, in the appreciation that can never wholly be killed for higher values, the steadfast conviction born of experience that the higher type of life is worth living for its own sake, the peace and invincibility that come to one who has attained. Nor does the Hindu, with his relentless insistence on ultimate self-responsibility, look with indifference on his neighbor's suffering as superficial observers or critics sometimes assert. He is quite as sensitive to love and quite as ready to acknowledge the necessity for disinterested work as anybody. Love and unselfish work, as a matter of fact, he has always acknowledged as the two most direct paths to God.

The religious education of the Hindus is kept alive by the poetic and imaginative legends which preach moral conduct in concrete terms. The makers of the god-tales delight to present the gods with human qualities. They are very human in their attributes. They are full of pranks, and they are subject to understandable passions and emotions, such as anger, flattery, or pride. It is not to the great but to the humble—a woodchopper, a butcher, a cowherd, even a thief —that the gods most often reveal themselves in Hindu mythology. They mingle and talk with ordinary men, assuming the form of a holy beggar, an old man on the banks of the Ganges, a child, but always the legends under their poetic or fantastic imagery have a profound meaning. Faith, love, being true to one's *dharma*, or duty, are rewarded by mystic visions.

Hindu mothers are never at a loss for a god-story to tell their children. All the ceremonial days in the Hindu calendar associated with particular gods are so many days of religious remembrance. On these occasions the family priest recites the *katha*, or story, of the particular god being honored. The ordinary village pujari will perhaps recite in a perfunctory way, but a priest from "outside" may be engaged to visit a well-to-do household, and friends will be invited to hear his skilled rendering of the familiar tales. He may stay a whole week. Meanwhile the women take pride and pleasure in cooking all sorts of special dishes for him. He receives a money present in accordance with the family means, and his mere presence is looked upon as blessing the household.

From the great characters depicted in the epics and the *Puranas*—the later popular religious literature—a Hindu derives his spiritual inspiration. Rama the ideal king and son; Sita the pure, the ideal woman; Mahabir-Hanuman the ideal worker; King Janaka the ideal householder; grandfather Vishma the warrior saint; Karna the giver, the hero; Krishna the child, Krishna the friend, Krishna the charioteer, Krishna the beloved; and, above all, Shiva-Mahadeva, the "blue-throated," who has swallowed the poison of life for mankind, god of gods, ascetic of ascetics, giver of all knowledge, utterly indifferent to the relativity of things. These are living realities for the simple people who live in the destitute villages of India. Images and concrete symbols for their worship have been enthroned in the temples. The emphasis is not even on beauty of form or expression. Nothing is too lowly, nothing too majestic to represent Shiva. A wayside stone is good enough for the village Shiva, eternally snow-covered Kailash equally acceptable.

The more humble one is, the greater the chance of attaining that blissful experience of God's actuality, the end of all religious thought in India. Many are the tales in which children are unexpectedly blessed with visits from the gods. A Brahmin boy, very simple and direct, is instructed by his father to present the daily offering of food at the family shrine during his absence. The boy offers the food, expecting the god to eat. When there is no response he pleads with the god, since he has been told to feed him by his parents and he will be punished if he fails in the duty assigned him. Still there is no response, and at last he angrily threatens to strike the image if it does not partake of the food. Whereupon the god enters the image and eats. When the parents learn what has happened the father wants the miracle repeated. Suddenly a voice is heard to say: "My child, you are simple and pure in heart, and that is why you have seen. You believe, but your father doubts. To such it is not given to see the gods with their own eyes."

In February, Shivaratri was observed by many Hindu households in Pachperwa. This is a special fast day in honor of Shiva, when simple offerings of water and bel leaves are made to his symbol. The Brahmin postman told me the legend of Shivaratri, as it has come down in the *Maha-bharata*. A frightened hunter, overtaken by darkness on a fast day sacred to Shiva, climbs a tree to escape the wild beasts. Trembling, he shakes down some leaves, which chance to be bel leaves, on an unsuspected shrine of Shiva below. As he thinks of his family, who have gone hungry on this day because he was unable to bring home any game, he sheds tears, and these also fall on the shrine. Old Shiva declares that such a devout worshiper, who makes offerings to him of his favorite leaves and water on a dark night, is certainly deserving of the highest reward. When the time comes for the hunter to die, messengers of Shiva arrive to conduct his soul to Shiva's abode. When he is next born on earth, after a long sojourn in Shivaloka, it is as a king and a great devotee of Shiva. Shiva points the moral of the story to Parvati. If the hunter, who did not intentionally perform the puja or observe the fast, could not be prevented from obtaining the fruits of these good actions, how much greater will be the reward for those who devoutly fast and worship him.

To catch sight of the profound truths hidden away under the guise of mythology is not easy, especially for a foreigner, to whom many of the terms and concepts are necessarily bewildering. The Himalayan vision of the Vedanta and the little ways of the poor, ignorant, illiterate village folk have to be tied together by such flimsy bridges of understanding as one is able to build. What astonished me was to find that poor, ignorant, and illiterate as the villagers were, they possessed a measure of insight that reflected the far source of their inspiration. It was they who taught me much of the deeper wisdom of India.

The path of *Bhaktiyoga*, devotion, is recognized as one of the four principal paths leading to illumination, and the history of India overflows with the names of great devotees. It requires no effort to concentrate on what one loves, and the *Bhakta* preaches that with sincere love the simplest and humblest may find his way to God. There is another path, that of *Karmayoga*, or unselfish work, and this is the great doctrine of the *Bhagavad-gita*. "To work you have the

right, but not to the fruits thereof." They belong to God.
The one who performs his duties without self-attachment
and without any concern of gain to himself, living for
others, will achieve the same union with God as the sincere
devotee. Give what you have to give, but do not bargain
with the world for a return. So long as you are concerned
with the results of your work, your mind cannot be at peace.
Every condition of life carries with it its own duties. Those
for the householder, as opposed to the homeless *sannyasin*,
are hospitality and the faithful performance of simple tasks.
"For it is better to do thine own duty, however ignoble, than
to do the duty of another," Krishna tells Arjuna on the
battlefield of Kurukshetra.

Love and unselfish work are two paths. *Jnanayoga* and
Rajayoga, discrimination through knowledge, and psychic
control, are two others. Love and work come naturally to
most of mankind—it is only necessary to raise the love to
its highest potentiality or to acquire the proper attitude
toward work to make them spiritually effective. But the
power to discriminate between the ultimate essence and
transient appearance is not so easily won. It requires intense
concentration, and the sort of discipline, physical, mental,
and spiritual, which makes concentration possible. In the
Chandogya Upanishad, Uddalaka, trying to open the mind
of his twenty-four-year-old son Svetaketu, but newly returned from school—"having then studied all the Vedas,
conceited, considering himself well-read and stern"—begins
his instruction with emphasis on the necessity of discriminat-
ing the essence from its varied manifestations. "By one clod
of clay, all that is made of clay is known, the difference
being only a name," he teaches. His discourse on the nature
of the all pervading Self leads up to the great Vedantic
declaration: "And That thou art, O Svetaketu."

The austere path of Jnanayoga is one to which the
average man is not attracted. It offers nothing in answer to
the instinctive need of most people of an object to worship.
Through sheer force of concentration the adept slowly at-

tains the ultimate knowledge, realized from within and not from without, which constitutes the only real freedom. A powerful will is necessary to begin with, and an intense desire to know truth. Vivekananda, one of the dynamic spiritual leaders of a quarter of a century ago—a great preacher of the Vedanta—illustrates this essential condition, after the usual method of teaching in India, by telling a story. A young man sought out a sannyasin of holy reputation and asked for the instruction that would make him realize God. The holy man merely requested the youth to follow him to the river. Once there, he seized the religious aspirant and held him under the water, gasping, until he was almost suffocated.

Then, releasing him, he asked sternly, "What did you want most when you were under the water?"

"Air," was the reply.

"Very well, when you want God as you wanted air you will find him."

Nothing in Western life precisely corresponds to the spiritual discipline laid down for the followers of Rajayoga. Acting on the principle that the vital force of the individual is a small part of the universal force called God, the follower of Rajayoga attempts to transcend his own limitations by psychic control and merge himself in the unity of the whole. Certain mystic powers are supposed to come to one who adheres faithfully to Rajayoga practices. All India believes in miracles—miracles, that is, only to the uninitiated—and these miracle makers as a rule are those who have mastered the science of controlling their own inner forces. I was often told in Pachperwa of "saints" who could at will suspend bodily animation and remain buried alive for indefinite periods, who could make the pulse beat at one speed in one wrist and at a different speed in the other, who could fly through the air, make themselves invisible, or sit in meditative posture on the surface of the Ganges.

The Brahmin priests, as executives indispensable in every ceremonial of social life, wield great authority over the masses, but they are not necessarily respected for their spirituality. The function of the spiritual teacher, "the eye-opener," is reserved to the *guru*. He is one who possesses spiritual insight and understanding and who can help others in their path. He may belong to any caste or be outside of caste altogether. Sometimes guruship is passed on in a family, and a traditional guru will serve a regular clientèle, but freedom to choose one's own guru has always been allowed. One may, if one wishes, have more than one. But the spiritually inclined do not rest until they have found the guru of their need. So deep rooted is the institution of the guru—the secret of the continuity of India's spiritual life is wrapped up in it—that even ordinary villagers talk of having their gurus whom they reverence profoundly. The relation between guru and disciple is looked on in India as more sacred and enduring than any other human relationship, not excepting that of husband and wife, mother and son.

Naturally there are gurus and gurus. The ideal guru is one who has direct spiritual realization, who is perfectly sincere and who identifies himself completely with the spiritual welfare of his disciple or disciples. Through his power of discrimination he understands the needs of his disciple and sets him on the path of his proper evolution. The simple villagers, however, are all too likely to be exploited by charlatans wearing the garb of holiness and wandering about the countryside.

It was the pundit of the temple school who gave me some insight into the Indian values of things. The gifts that may be made to mankind, he said, are four in number, and they are to be classified in the following order: lowest in the scale of benefits is the gift of food, since the satisfaction it renders can never be anything but temporary; the gift next in order is the saving of life or the curing of the sick, because in themselves these cannot assure lasting happiness or well-being; third in importance is the gift of secular knowledge, which lifts men to greater freedom through greater mastery of the environment: best and highest in the scale stands the gift of spiritual enlightenment, which makes men really free. The gift to mankind of a Buddha or a Christ transcends time and space. It comforts the hungry and the sick and makes them forget their misery. It inspires those who have, to share their blessings with others who have not. It travels down centuries and filters into all the corners of the world.

Understanding that this spiritual enlightenment, greatest of gifts, can be disseminated only by those who have actually realized the deeper knowledge within themselves—just as every teacher must actually know what he is trying to teach before his teaching can become effective—India cheerfully assumes the burden of supporting all those who are willing to dedicate their lives to a search for the ultimate knowledge, sham "holy men" along with real seekers. The aspect of the economic drain involved in taking care of some five million wandering ascetics does not impress itself on the Indian mind. What of it—if one among them attains that supreme knowledge, even the small rays of which serve to light and warm humanity!

According to ancient code, the wandering ascetic is not supposed to spend more than three nights in the same village, but the rule is not strictly observed. Some of our sadhus stayed around for weeks. Although all ascetics do not wear the ocher-colored robe, many of those I saw used it. Another mark of the holy man was the pilgrim staff. Every sadhu carried some sort of staff—a polished crooked stick, iron tongs, an iron rod with rings at one end, a trident. He also bore a begging wallet in the form of a cloth bag resembling a large envelope, an hour-glass-shaped gourd with the top cut so as to make a handle, or a brass imitation of the gourd, a wooden bowl, or a bowl made from a polished double coconut. He wore wooden sandals on his feet. His locks were generally long, but sometimes the hair was twisted into a grotesque knot over one eye. His forehead or his whole body might be smeared with ashes of his sacred fire—a Shiva devotee—or his forehead might be marked with the special symbol of the religious order or sect to which he belonged. He might even be naked, save for a strip of cloth about his loins. But all were alike in one respect. They came empty handed and went away fed, leaving their spiritual blessings behind.

I could not be persuaded that one sadhu who stayed about Pachperwa for two or three weeks had traveled very far on the road toward spiritual realization. I first met him with Haweli Singh. A full moon was making black shadow prints under the trees. The sadhu's bare arms projected from what looked like a gray bag, tied at the waist, and he had a white cloth tied over his head and under his chin, like a hood. His wooden sandals were carved into lotus petals where his toes rested. Heavy eyebrows and a mouth darkly stained with pan juice gave his face a masklike appearance in the white moonlight.

The next day I learned that he had breakfasted with the Tashildar. They had a religious talk, but the sadhu used such difficult words the Tahsildar could scarcely understand him. "He knows about *pranayama*, that method of saving breath I was telling you about the other day," the Tahsildar added. I remembered his assertion that a man's life consists of so many breaths—to be exact, 20,600 on a daily average. If one could learn control of breathing through pranayama, an exercise in Rajayoga, doubtless all the breaths saved might be tacked on to prolong life at the other end. The Tahsildar was impressed by the sadhu's statement that his own "big guru," through practising pranayama, had lived to be five hundred. "I don't know if it is true or not," he added cautiously, "but that is what he says."

I suggested that the sadhu might be willing to give us a demonstration, to which he obligingly agreed. We retired to the Tahsildar's room, where the sadhu seated himself cross-legged on the bed. First he took off an apricot colored undershirt, and then he drew himself up very straight,

pressing his fingers against his eyes, nostrils, and lips.
After a few quick breaths, he took one deep one and held it
for perhaps a minute. This was the first exercise. If you
practised it every day for a year, you would be able to hold
your breath for an hour, he said. No real sadhu, of course,
would have given any such exhibition. My impression that
he was an impostor was later confirmed by Dukhi. It seemed
he belonged to a company of nine sadhus who ordinarily
lived in the forest near Gonda. They bore a very poor reputation. Twice, according to Dukhi, the band had been investigated by the police in connection with certain robberies,
though nothing had actually been proved against them.

The villagers welcomed this man as well as all the others.
Often I saw little groups squatting on the ground under a
tree around some holy one. No matter how illiterate he
might be, he could always retell the stories and legends and
religious parables he had picked up in Benares, Allahabad,
Hardwar, Ayodya, or other pilgrim centers. I preferred the
sadhus who accompanied themselves as they sang with castanets to those with wheezing little harmoniums, transplanted
into India, I dare say, by evangelical missionaries. But
such trivial matters did not bother the villagers.

The feeling of respect for the man of religion was so
strong that in Pachperwa it made little difference whether
he was a Mussulman or a Hindu. The Peshkar made a
special journey to the Mohammedan baba, Yasin Khan's
guru, who paid us a three-day visit on one occasion. "I don't
know if he is good or not," he remarked, "but if he is good,
then I may get some profit, and if he is not, I lose nothing."
One day I was astonished to see our Mohammedan Station
Master coming along in the wake of a matted haired sadhu.
The train inspector had caught him riding without a ticket
—in these commercial days even sadhus are supposed to pay
their way—and accordingly he was put off the train at the
next station, which chanced to be Pachperwa. Instead of
turning him over to the thana, as he was expected to do,
the Station Master had permitted him to go through the

village and try to raise the price of his ticket. Two rupees had been collected, but one was still lacking. The Station Master himself had brought him to me, suggesting that I might wish to contribute the last rupee and so save him the painful obligation of having a holy man arrested.

One old sadhu, who lived under a bit of thatch near the bazar, made his daily begging rounds of the village. He had been a Bania, but sons and wife were dead, and twelve years ago he had turned sadhu. He had made pilgrimages to many places, he told me proudly—among them, Brindaban, the birthplace of Krishna, and Ayodya, Rama's birthplace. Not yet to Rameswaram nor to Kailash! One evening, not long before I left Pachperwa, the Pujari was explaining his puja duties in the village. The old sadhu came along and sat down with us. A small round ball in the corner of the cloth over his shoulder indicated the handful of grain he had succeeded in begging that day. Presently a well dressed stranger came up the hill, and he, too, sat down in the circle.

"I have been told that in spite of their poverty the village people of India are happy. Do you think so?" I asked my strange assortment of guests.

"No," they answered. "How can they be happy when they are hungry? They are very poor."

"Are you three happy?"

There was silence for a moment. Then the Pujari spoke: "How can I be happy with this affliction?" He placed his hand on his bandaged leg. No, with leprosy one could scarcely burst into song.

"And you?" I asked the stranger, who did not look as if he knew what hunger was.

"No, I am not happy," he replied. "Though I have sixteen acres and two plows, I cannot make the rain fall. Last harvest was very poor. And a month ago my son died."

And the sadhu, was he happy? Having renounced the world, he could no longer be oppressed by its cares. He did not reply directly. He merely indicated by a gesture that his wrinkled stomach was not often filled. Ascetic or beggar, he

still had to eat. He might have quoted from the *Upanishads*
—if not the text, the idea—to show the thought behind this
quiet acceptance on the part of India of life's ills. India
neither seeks nor expects to find enduring happiness in the
ever changing environment. "Only when men shall roll up
the sky like a hide will there be an end of misery, unless
God has first been known."

GOING AWAY

W HEN the table which had served as a desk for what the Ayah called my "paper work" was starkly bare, I had a feeling as if autumn leaves were falling. I stood in the door and through the mango trees watched the deep red fire of a last sunset, while big spiny fruit bats darted and swooped over my little maidan.

The Happy House had taken only two days to dismantle. There was nothing to do but pack a few personal belongings. The estate was taking over the house; the tables, rugs, and chairs were all to remain in place. Everything else had found a new owner.

Bottles, superfluous cakes of soap, a tea set, empty biscuit boxes, pots and pans were seized upon by the immediate members of my "family." All the articles were first piled on the kitchen table. Then, beginning with the Ayah, who had been with me the longest, each one pulled out something in turn in the game of jackstraws, until Jumai drew the last of the booty, a perfectly useless can opener. The Ayah had already borne off the cotton stuffing of my green leather floor cushion, a Japanese hat scarf, and a pair of cast-off shoes. She would use the cotton to make padded jackets for herself. The heels of my shoes she would have cut off so she herself could wear them. The scarf could be made into a stomach band or neckties for her son-in-law.

The chicken house, the Wyandotte cock, and one small chick—sole survivors of the poultry farm I had optimistically launched—went to the Station Master with my compliments. The Pixie phonograph was chosen as a memento by the Peshkar, and the Tahsildar was pleased to accept my big table lamp. Mrs. Massey asked for any left-over medical supplies. Since she had once taken a training course at the Balrampur Hospital, I gave her everything, though with some misgiving. An hour later she sent back the cholera mixture by a small boy, begging me to tell her again just what the bottle contained. She was sorry she had forgotten so soon.

That night there was a farewell celebration at the tahsil. The Peshkar had kept me informed of the plans for days. At one stage the budget had included an item of twenty rupees for printing invitations at Lucknow. Perhaps my urgent remonstrance had some effect. The original idea of inviting all the bigwigs of the estate and borrowing the Maharaja's band and ordering foreign refreshments from Balrampur happily fell through. Instead, we had a feast such as the village could produce, served in the tahsil grounds, and the guests were neighbors—about a hundred in all.

The feast was to begin at seven. I joined the official group entitled to occupy the half-dozen chairs, but the Tahsildar requested me to take a special seat in front of his table, facing the general assembly, now seated around the edge of a great cloth spread on the ground. Since my chair was actually on the dining cloth, I wished to remove my shoes, but I was emphatically begged to keep them on. As soon as I was seated in the place of honor the Tahsildar rose and made a pleasant little speech, explaining how I had come to study Indian village life and that I was not a spy, as some had thought in the beginning—probably including himself. He wound up with an account of my medical services to the community, tactfully mentioning that I had always insisted I was not a doctor—the Doctor himself was present—but that I had desired to help where I could. And of course he ended by saying no one in the village would ever forget me. Then he came forward and presented me with the "Order of Pachperwa," a ceremonial necklace of tinsel and embroidered plaques of green satin. Later, Asgar expressed a great curiosity to examine the necklace. He had heard it was of real gold and silver, he said, and that it had cost two hundred rupees.

I felt proud that I could understand the whole of the Tahsildar's speech. I myself could make only a very short one in reply. The main point I wanted to make clear was that though I had originally come to Pachperwa to study village life, this year had meant more to me than I could ever say. If they were going to remember me, I, too, was going to remember them and all their kindnesses for the rest of my life. Everybody clapped loudly—even in a village so much of Western ways had crept in—and then emotion was suppressed in favor of food, my chair first being carefully removed from the lantern-lighted cloth.

The Peshkar oversaw the locking, strapping, and tying of my boxes and bags the next morning and had everything put on two bullock carts, which had been waiting for hours under the trees of Devi's shrine. It was raining hard, and the world looked polished and very wet. I had intended to write letters of appreciation to all my friends, including notes to the thekedars who had lent me their elephants during the year, but they had been crowded into the last minutes. I sat down and began typing, unaware that gradually the Happy House was filling with people. When I drew the last letter out of the machine and looked around, I was surprised to find at least thirty visitors who had come to say good-bye.

At this moment Din Mohammed rushed in excitedly. A Kori had picked up my water bottle to carry to the station. He was dumfounded when I assured him that it would make no difference to me if a Chamar or a Dom carried my water bottle. The Peshkar distributed the little pile of silver rupees, and our procession of three elephants started for the station. A great crowd came along, including the lame Brahmin beggar on his crutch, calling down Sanskrit blessings on my head. Mrs. Massey prayed *Issa* to take care of me, and

Dukhi solicited the same favor from Allah. All the Marwaris were at the station, and two thirds of the village. Suddenly there was a deafening bombardment. The Station Master had ingeniously placed fog signals under the wheels of the incoming train to provide a farewell salvo.

Fortunately I did not have to wait long. "You look very happy," Dukhi called out, as I did my best to smile at all the friendly faces on the platform. "Are you glad to leave us?" The train pulled out with more popping of fog signals. The faces vanished, and I saw the last of Pachperwa across rice fields in a driving rain. My tears fell, but who would notice a few tears more or less in this wet world? The clicking wheels were repeating monotonously, "Over, over, over."

THE END

GLOSSARY

achchha good, yes.

admi man.

Ahir milkman, herdsman—a caste.

ankus elephant goad.

anna one sixteenth of a rupee, approximately two cents.

arhar pulse, Indian peas.

ashrama retreat.

Atman the Eternal Self.

ayah woman servant.

baba father, a holy man.

babu educated Hindu.

bagh garden, grove.

bahut very.

bakshish gratuity.

bangla bungalow.

Bania trader, shopkeeper—a caste.

Banjara cartman—a caste.

bankas a kind of fine grass.

Barai dealer in *pan*, or betel-leaf—a caste.

barat wedding procession.

basanta spring.

begar forced labor.

bel a kind of fruit.

bela a species of jasmine.

bhairav musical mode expressing asceticism and reverence.

bhajan devotional song.

Bhand jester—a caste.

bhang an intoxicant made from hemp.

Bharbhuj grain parcher—a caste.

bhusa husk.

bhut evil spirit.

bigha five eighths of an acre in standard measurement, one fifth of an acre in Oudh.

bin the gourd flute used by snake charmers.

bira prepared *pan*.

biroh a tune expressing sense of separation.

biswa a measure of twenty paces.

Brahmin member of the highest Hindu caste.

Chain collector of jungle produce—a caste.

chaita a tune to express summer.

Chamar leather worker—a caste.

chapati unleavened bread.

chaprasi messenger.

charpai string-bed.

chaudhari a headman.

chauk square.

chaukidar village watchman.

chillum wood or clay pipe.

chital spotted deer.

chula small stove.

dai midwife.

dal lentils.

dari cotton rug.

dasuyu enemy, slave.

desi local, of the country.

devi goddess.

dharma religion, religious duty.

dharmasala free rest-house.

Dhobi washerman—a caste.

dhol drum.

dhoti piece of cloth worn as lower garment by men.

Dhuniya carder of cotton—a Mohammedan occupational caste.

dhup pine tree.

doli palanquin.

Dom scavenger—a caste.

dupatta a scarf.

durbar regal assembly.

ekka small two-wheeled cart, drawn by a pony.

esraj stringed instrument.

fakir Mohammedan religious mendicant, a name also used for Hindu mendicants.

Gadariya goatherd—a caste.

gali abusive language.

ganja an intoxicating drug made from unfertilized flowers of female hemp-plant.

garib poor.

ghat bathing steps.

ghi clarified butter.

gorait village servant.

Goshain a member of a Brahmin subcaste.

guru spiritual teacher.

hai is, yes.

Haj Mecca pilgrimage.

Hajjam Mohammedan barber.

Hajji a Mussulman who has made the Mecca pilgrimage.

haldi turmeric.

Halwai confectioner—a caste.

hansiya sickle.

hookah water pipe, narghile.

huzur term of respect.

Issa Jesus.

jamadar chief of a group of persons.

jamun kind of tree or its fruit.

Jat member of a cultivating caste of the Punjab.

jhil artificial pond, or tank.

Jogi corruption of *Yogi*.

Julaha Mohammedan weaver.

kajli a tune of the rainy season.

Kalwar liquor vendor — a caste.

Kanphata "split-ear," follower of Gorakhnath.

kanungo land-revenue official.

katha story, legend.

Kayasth member of writing or clerical caste.

kazi registrar of Mohammedan marriages and other functions.

kebob meat roasted on a skewer.

khaddar homespun.

Khair collector of catechu—a caste.

khar coarse grass used for thatching.

kharif autumn harvest crop.

Khatri member of a mercantile caste.

Kori Hindu weaver—a caste.

kos a measure of two miles.

Kshatriya member of the second highest, the ruling, caste, a warrior; same as *Rajput*.

Kurmi member of a cultivating caste.

kurta, *kurti* shirt, waist.

kutcha raw, undesirable, poor.

lakh one hundred thousand.

langha a skirt.

lathi staff, cudgel.

lila play.

linga phallic symbol.

litchi a kind of fruit.

loharin a species of poisonous snake.

lota a brass jar.

machan tree-platform used for shooting.

mahout elephant driver.

Mahabharata a Sanskrit epic.

maidan an open park.

Mali gardener—a caste.

mantra sacred mystic word, or text.

Manu an ancient Hindu law-giver.

Maratha a race of Hindus inhabiting southwestern and central India.

Marwari Hindu or Jain, originally from Marwar, member of commercial or banking group.

maulvi Mohammedan religious teacher.

maund a weight equivalent to 82 lbs.

megh cloud.

Mehtar sweeper—an "untouchable."

mela fair, religious gathering.

mir a Mohammedan title.

mistri master carpenter.

Mochi shoemaker—a Mohammedan occupational caste.

mora bridegroom's headdress.

munshi clerk.

must said of a mad elephant.

nai no

naib assistant.

nala ravine.

Nau Hindu barber—a caste.

nautch dance.

nazarana customary gift preceding an interview.

Nirvana extinction, "blowing out" of illusion.

nilkant roller, species of jay.

nim a kind of tree.

ojha exorciser.

Om symbolic Sanskrit word for Supreme Being.

padri, *padrin* Christian missionary, man and woman.

pailagan form of greeting used to superiors, "I touch your feet."

pakar a kind of fig tree.

pakki food cooked in oil or *ghi* and without salt.

palki palanquin.

pan an astringent leaf of pepper used for chewing.

panch member of panchayat, councillor.

panchama tune expressing mood of clear night.

panchayat group of elected councillors, traditionally five persons, caste council.

pani water.

panseri measure of five handfuls.

papaya a fruit.

popiya cuckoo.

Pasi member of former criminal caste.

Pathan Indian-Afghan.

patwari   village accountant.

peon   messenger.

peshkar   one who submits papers, etc., personal clerk.

pice   one fourth of an *anna*, a half-cent.

pie   one third of a *pice*.

pranayama   control of vital force, usually through breathing.

puja   worship.

pujari   priest.

pundit   Brahmin teacher, a learned man.

punka   fan.

Puranas   Hindu books of mythology.

purdah   "screen," seclusion of women.

puri   cake fried in oil or *ghi*.

purohit   family priest.

rabi   spring harvest crop.

raga   Indian equivalent for musical scale.

raja   Hindu prince.

rajas   dynamic principle of the essence of nature.

Rajput   member of warrior caste; same as *Kshatriya*.

Ramayana   a Sanskrit epic.

rani   wife of a *raja*.

razai   quilt.

rishi   seer.

rudraksha   stones of a berry, used by Hindus for rosary.

rupee   standard silver coin of India, about one third of a dollar.

ryot   cultivator who owns his own land.

sadhu   holy man.

sahib   gentleman, master.

sal   hard-wood tree.

salami   present made on being introduced to a superior.

samaj   society.

sambur   rusine deer.

samiti   group, association.

sarai   free rest-house for Mussulmans.

sarangi   musical instrument, prototype of violin.

saras   crane.

sari   dress, draped garment worn by Indian women.

sarpanch   headman of a panchayat.

sati   woman who burns herself on her husband's pyre, self-immolation.

sattva   harmonizing principle which forms the essence of nature.

sawak   money advanced to hired plowman by employer.

seer   measure of weight, a little more than two pounds.

shadi   marriage.

shaitan   devil, Satan.

Shastras   authoritative Hindu scriptures.

Sheikh   in India a member of important group of Mussulmans.

Shia   Islamic sect, of which the Persians are the chief representatives.

sipahi   soldier, sepoy.

sir   rent-free land.

sirkar   government, also representative of government.

sitar   stringed instrument.

siwala, shivalaya   temple of Shiva.

sowkar   money-lender.

stri-dhan   woman's property.

Sudra lowest of four Vedic classes or castes.

Sunni Islamic sect.

swaraj self-government, self-control.

tahsil revenue district, headquarters of a *tahsil*.

tahsildar sub-collector of revenue, in charge of a *tahsil*.

taluqdar title of a powerful landlord in Oudh.

tamas inertia principle of the essence of nature.

tamasha celebration.

Tamboli dealer in *pan*—a caste.

tarai low-lying land.

tazia decorated representation of shrine of Hassan and Hossein, carried by Mussulmans during Moharram.

Teli dealer in oil—a caste.

thana police station.

thanadar officer in charge of police station.

thangdar professional receiver of stolen cattle.

thakurdwara temple.

theka contract.

thekedar rent contractor.

tiddi locust.

tika ceremonial mark on forehead.

tol Sanskrit school.

upanayama ceremony of sacred-thread investiture for boys of "twice-born" castes.

Upanishads philosophical portions of the *Vedas*.

Vaisya member of Hindu commercial group.

Vedanta concluding portion of the *Vedas*.

Vedas earliest and most authoritative Hindu scriptures.

vina stringed instrument.

Yogi follower of *yoga* practices, an ascetic.

zamin land.

zemindar landlord.

zenana women's quarter, harem.

zilidar tax collector.

INDEX

DATE DUE